Star Wars and the Hero's Journey

ALSO BY VALERIE ESTELLE FRANKEL
AND FROM MCFARLAND

*The Villain's Journey: Descent and
Return in Science Fiction and Fantasy (2021)*

*Wonder Women and Bad Girls: Superheroine and
Supervillainess Archetypes in Popular Media (2020)*

Women in Doctor Who: *Damsels, Feminists and Monsters (2018)*

The Women of Orphan Black: Faces of the Feminist Spectrum (2018)

*Superheroines and the Epic Journey: Mythic Themes in
Comics, Film and Television (2017)*

The Symbolism and Sources of Outlander: *The Scottish Fairies,
Folklore, Ballads, Magic and Meanings That Inspired the Series (2015)*

Women in Game of Thrones: *Power, Conformity and Resistance (2014)*

*Buffy and the Heroine's Journey:
Vampire Slayer as Feminine Chosen One (2012)*

*From Girl to Goddess: The Heroine's Journey
through Myth and Legend (2010)*

EDITED BY VALERIE ESTELLE FRANKEL
AND FROM MCFARLAND

*Fourth Wave Feminism in Science Fiction and Fantasy:
Volume 2. Essays on Television Representations, 2013–2019 (2020)*

*Fourth Wave Feminism in Science Fiction and Fantasy:
Volume 1. Essays on Film Representations, 2012–2019 (2019)*

Outlander's *Sassenachs: Essays on Gender, Race, Orientation and
the Other in the Novels and Television Series (2016)*

Adoring Outlander: *Essays on Fandom,
Genre and the Female Audience (2016)*

The Comics of Joss Whedon: Critical Essays (2015)

*Teaching with Harry Potter: Essays on Classroom Wizardry
from Elementary School to College (2013)*

Star Wars and the Hero's Journey

Mythic Character Arcs Through the 12-Film Epic

VALERIE ESTELLE FRANKEL

McFarland & Company, Inc., Publishers
Jefferson, North Carolina

ISBN (print) 978-1-4766-8429-1
ISBN (ebook) 978-1-4766-4379-3

Library of Congress and British Library
cataloguing data are available

Library of Congress Control Number 2021008924

© 2021 Valerie Estelle Frankel. All rights reserved

No part of this book may be reproduced or transmitted in any form or by any means, electronic or mechanical, including photocopying or recording, or by any information storage and retrieval system, without permission in writing from the publisher.

Front cover image © 2021 diversepixel/Shutterstock

Printed in the United States of America

*McFarland & Company, Inc., Publishers
Box 611, Jefferson, North Carolina 28640
www.mcfarlandpub.com*

Table of Contents

Introduction	1
The Phantom Menace	5
Young Anakin's Traditional Hero Quest 5 • Padmé and the Power of Disguise 8 • Qui-Gon and Obi-Wan: Warrior Monks 11 • The Droids as Ordinary Heroes 16 • Darth Maul's Failures 18	
The Clone Wars and the Fall of the Republic	23
Anakin's Descent 23 • Padmé's Romance and Fall 41 • Obi-Wan: Failed Father to Sage 48 • The Jedi vs. the Sith 50 • Yoda Battles the Emperor 54	
The Original Trilogy	59
Luke's Classic Journey: Youth to Champion 59 • Leia: Rebel Princess 85 C3PO: Servant to War Hero 96 • Han Solo: Beyond the Antihero 100 • Chewie: Perpetual Sidekick 108 • Lando: Collaborator-Ruler to General 111 • Darth Vader: The Failed Tyrant 114 • Obi-Wan and Yoda: Ascension to Spirit Guides 122	
The Sequel Era	127
Rogue One and the Heroine's Sacrifice 127 • The Mandalorian Finds His Clan 138 • The Mentors Fade 150 • Finn and Poe 167 • Kylo Ren: Nihilism to Redemption 177 • Rey's Heroine's Journey 192	
Conclusion	219
Works Cited	221
Index	229

Introduction

George Lucas explains of his most beloved epic, "I knew from the beginning that I was not doing science fiction. I was doing a space opera, a fantasy film, a mythological piece, a fairy tale" (Bouzereau 5–6). He had always been interested in fairy tales but was struck by the lack of modern mythology. Some forms, like fantasy and the western, had adapted epic tropes, but there had been little since. As he adds, "I wanted to take all the old myths and put them into a new format that young people could relate to" (Bouzereau 27). Accordingly, he created a new hero quest for a modern age and set it in space, like the beloved *Flash Gordon*.

The film caught on more than anyone would have believed and remains one of the biggest American franchises. Its power comes from this visceral origin, a dream-pattern related to ancient initiation ceremonies. "What *Star Wars* has accomplished is really not possible," says Harrison Ford. "Nobody rational would have believed that there is still a place for fairytales. There is no place in our culture for this kind of stuff. But the need was there; the human need to have the human condition expressed in mythic terms" (Rinzler, *Making of Empire* 2). Seventies' films were largely dystopian and depressing. *Star Wars*, by contrast, indeed featured a "new hope," as the young hero grew from obscurity to success and won the day for the Rebellion. It came along when people needed to see good overcome evil. Instead of the moral confusion of the Cold War and Vietnam, they needed to be reminded of idealism and a worthy cause. After tying in the excitement of the space race and new marketing to younger fans, everyone was hooked.

More to the point, this new myth perfectly followed the hero's journey pattern, so well it has often been used to teach it. Scholar Joseph Campbell in his seminal book observed that myths and fairytales worldwide followed a similar structure, with a symbolic journey into the underworld and emergence as an adult. Lucas concludes, "It was *The Hero with a Thousand Faces* that just took what was about 500 pages and said, 'Here is the story. Here's the end; here's the focus; here's the way it's all laid out.' It was all right there and had been there for thousands and thousands of years, as Dr. Campbell pointed out.... It's possible that if I had not run across him I would still be writing *Star Wars* today" (*Hero's Journey* 180). Lucas notes that *The Hero with a Thousand Faces* distilled the epic plot down to the essentials and thus helped him solidify his vision. "[Campbell] is a wonderful man, and he has become my Yoda," Lucas concludes (180).

There are traditional elements to look for, exemplified perfectly in Luke Skywalker's story—the hero, from King Arthur to Harry Potter, is raised in obscurity by unsympathetic foster parents. At last, a mysterious wizard comes to his door. The youth has a great destiny and must take up his father's sword and go on a quest. The hero initially refuses this frightening call, but eventually gives in. From here, he crosses into the otherworld, a place of different rules. Frequently, a threshold guardian blocks the way, giving the hero an initial challenge to overcome. The hero's companions, meanwhile, represent the myriad of conflicting voices from within. One is the anima, the feminine guide who introduces the hero to his unexplored spiritual side and offers lessons from the unconscious realm. In the otherworld, the hero descends into the belly of the beast, an inner cave representing one's unexamined darkness. For this ultimate ordeal, the hero may literally face death or symbolically attain it, falling unconscious or being frozen in a temporary sleep (or carbonite!). There, the hero faces the shadow, all he has rejected in his life. Having accepted this dark force, a symbolic or literal father-tyrant, he has achieved adulthood and wisdom. He thus returns to his community to share all he's learned. Campbell's steps are as follows:

Part I: Departure
The call to adventure
Refusal of the call
Supernatural aid
Crossing the threshold
Belly of the whale

Part II: Initiation
The road of trials
The meeting with the goddess
Woman as temptress
Atonement with the father

Apotheosis
The ultimate boon

Part III: Return
Refusal of the return
The magic flight
Rescue from without
The crossing of the return
    threshold
Master of two worlds
Freedom to live

The heroine's journey is similar to the hero's, sometimes identical but sometimes reversed. Part one follows the pattern, but the heroine quests, not to defeat the dark lord, but to protect her loved ones and thus become the archetypal mother. Instead of a sword, she generally receives a talisman of perception or one that represents the lifecycle she defends. She partners with the animus, who teaches her masculine skills like logic and warfare. Her romance is with a frightening beast who often conceals a prince underneath. Sometimes, however, he is a complete beast—a Bluebeard figure who can tear her asunder. By contrast, when she meets the archetypal father, she discovers she's much stronger than he has ever been. The heroine's shadow is the wicked witch, destroyer of innocents, representing the wicked mother. By confronting her, receiving her strength but rejecting her path, the heroine triumphs. In the more masculine franchise of *Star Wars*, the heroines rarely meet the witch but instead battle male world-destroyers like Tarkin, Vader, Krennic, and Snoke. All of these personally threaten the heroine and her cause, the service of life. True, some women undergo the male hero's journey—Rey's lightsaber and Jyn's war story fall into this pattern. At the same time, female mentorship and a sensitivity to their place in the universe mark their journeys as something deeper.

The shadow, a Jungian concept, is the disturbingly compelling nightmare figure. This is someone eerily similar but who made opposite choices and thus channels all the hero has rejected in himself. Vader as Luke's shadow is the perfect example. At the same time, the shadow has useful qualities—Vader has maturity, purpose, and knowledge of the Force, as well as command over the galaxy. Each time he faces Vader, Luke learns valuable lessons and finally comes to accept and love this damaged, raging shadow. When he does, he embraces the neglected part of himself. All this is a metaphor for the journey from childhood to maturity.

At the same time, *Star Wars* offers journeys other than Luke's. The most common fictional journey is the innocent child's discovering heroism and growing to maturity through facing his dark father as tyrant. However, this is a limited segment of the complete cycle. After achieving this adulthood, the young hero must beware becoming the very tyrant he has overthrown. Han tangles with Boba Fett, the amoral gangster he himself was on the path to becoming, and Lando, trying to be a good leader, faces Vader, the bad one. The prequels, meanwhile, offer a rare depiction of a full lifecycle—sweet young Anakin achieving heroism in *Phantom Menace* and then falling into villainy as a world-destroying tyrant in *Revenge of the Sith*. As the saga continues, the adult warriors at the height of their power must finally relinquish leadership, as Obi-Wan and Yoda do, to fade into obscurity as mentors. The other option is to fight, to cling to power long past the age of retirement as the Emperor does. After the mentor has taught his lessons, another test appears, to surrender one's grasp of life and fade away, continuing on as a spiritual advisor. Once more *Star Wars* perfectly epitomizes this stage of the journey: Those who die are not gone forever but influence the hero's life as Force ghosts. Their legacy continues eternally. As older heroes die and young heroes like Ben Solo are born and named for them, the cycle goes on and on.

These stages of life, explored through the hero's journey, are child, hero, ruler, sage, and spirit guardian, or Young Anakin, Luke, Vader, Yoda, and the Force ghosts. Passage from each stage to the one beyond is marked by a trial—one faces one's shadow, like Obi-Wan's dueling Vader or Yoda's dueling the Emperor, and chooses dominance or surrender, resistance or understanding. In this tradition, the sequel era features Han, Luke, and Leia refusing duels and choosing a quieter path of love and redemption but passing on, nonetheless. Meanwhile, Rey, Jyn, Kylo Ren, and the others must accept the darkness within in order to choose the light. All the characters of the saga incorporate elements of the classic hero quest, but by offering such different archetypes and age ranges, *Star Wars* offers something special—a unique understanding of our place in the universe as we grow toward enlightenment.

The Phantom Menace

Young Anakin's Traditional Hero Quest

"Anakin represents the motif of the 'seed of evil' where his innocence and childish nature are underscored by fear and aggression. These are the seeds that live in him, that will grow in him and flourish as he matures," explain Michael J. Hanson and Max S. Kay in their hero's journey exploration, *Star Wars: The New Myth* (129). Anakin Skywalker's destiny awaits before his birth. "Who was his father?" asks the visiting Jedi Qui-Gon Jinn after sensing Anakin's incredible Force-potential. His mother, Shmi, replies, "There was no father. I gave birth to him, I raised him.... I can't explain how it happened." In fact, the expanded universe novels reveal that the Emperor and his own master created him to balance the Force.

Virgin births indicate a power of self-sufficiency and self-creation as well as a divine ancestry. "Such images are associated mythologically with the mystery of incarnation and psychologically with the ongoing integration of archetypal energies through their engagement by human consciousness," explains Stephen A. Galipeau in *The Journey of Luke Skywalker: An Analysis of Modern Myth and Symbol* (263). On hearing this revelation, Qui-Gon becomes certain that Anakin is the Chosen One of Jedi prophecy. He also shows his magical giftedness through his skill with machines. Further, he's the only human capable of podracing. This is a traditional mythic story pattern—a child with unusual powers grows up in austerity and then wins his freedom with his skills. These tales of overcoming one's lowly birth status appear in our oldest traditions, inspiring listeners that they too can overcome their destinies.

In an ironic twist for viewers, Anakin is generous, sweet, and helpful—the antithesis of what he will become. Anakin naively sees the world as good and evil, and he's driven to be kind. When he first meets the travelers, he greets Padmé with adoration, and, on seeing that they're unused to the desert, invites them home with him. "You'll never reach the outskirts in time ... sandstorms are very, very dangerous. Come on!" he bursts. Richard H. Dees notes in his essay on moral ambiguity:

As a child, Anakin is clearly on the side of good. He reaches out to Padmé and Qui-Gon on Tatooine, offering them shelter from a sandstorm. Hearing their troubles, he immediately seeks to help them, risking his own life in the Boonta Eve Podrace to win the prize money that Qui-Gon needs to buy the spare parts for their damaged starship. In *The Phantom Menace*, Anakin is nothing but innocence and goodness. No moral ambiguities here [59].

Building on this, the film novelization describes Anakin saving a wounded Tusken Raider, simply from benevolence. Of course, this reverses his actions of *Attack of the Clones*, emphasizing how much he will transform between the films. Further, in a chilling moment of foreshadowing, he thinks, "He might not ever be afraid for himself, but he was sometimes very afraid for his mother. What if something were to happen to her? What if something awful were to happen to her, something he could do nothing to prevent?" (Brooks 77). At the thought, his courage crumbles. This moment emphasizes that she is his weak point, one that will aid in his downfall.

Young Anakin, spunky and appealing, gives the two Jedi a quest—not only to rescue this potential Jedi but to end the cruelty of slavery. With this, he represents childish idealism and purpose. Of course, the Council reject his pleas. Even as the Jedi Council at its height is introduced, they are revealed as followers of rules rather than saviors of those in peril. Sadly, no one in the galaxy cares about Anakin and his mother—only Anakin's potential talents. Still, young Anakin aspires to be a Jedi to save those he loves—he sees the Jedi as just those saviors, even as they deny it:

ANAKIN: No one can kill a Jedi.
QUI-GON: I wish that were so…
ANAKIN: I had a dream I was a Jedi. I came back here to free all the slaves … have you come to free us?
QUI-GON: No, I'm afraid not…
ANAKIN: I think you have … why else would you be here? (*The Phantom Menace*)

Young Anakin is completely idealistic, even in the face of contrary evidence. In fact, he doesn't just mirror the Jedi's lost innocence but arguably Lucas's own. "His first ambition was to be a race-car driver, and it was only after he was nearly killed in a terrible accident, when he was eighteen—he lived because his seat belt unaccountably broke and he was hurled free of the car—that his interest shifted to film" (Seabrook). Echoing this youthful faith as well as a racecar enthusiast's drive, Anakin offers the Jedi the pod he's built and adds that he'll risk his life for them. His mother protests, but he replies, "Mom … you said the biggest problem in the universe is nobody helps each other…" and she's convinced. As the classic threshold guardian, she blocks him from heroism at the start, but also has clearly trained him in altruism. Both believe in helping others, which makes them stand out from all the film's other characters. Following this, Anakin triumphantly wins the day with skills that are more than mortal, establishing himself as chosen one in truth.

After the pod race comes his reward, another classic step for the hero. Qui-Gon reveals that they've freed Anakin, who can now become a Jedi. Here, Qui-Gon offers him a choice:

> **QUI-GON:** Anakin, training to become a Jedi is not an easy challenge. And if you succeed, it's a hard life.
> **ANAKIN:** But I want to go. It's what I've always dreamed of doing. Can I go, Mom?!
> **SHMI:** Anakin, this path has been placed for you; the choice is yours alone.
> **ANAKIN:** I want to do it.
> **QUI-GON:** Then, pack your things. We haven't much time.
> **ANAKIN:** Yippee!!
> Anakin hugs his mom and starts for the other room, then stops. Anakin has realized something.
> **ANAKIN:** (Cont'd) What about Mom? Is she free too?

His tie to her is the true threshold guardian here, even more so than Watto. After Qui-Gon explains that he couldn't manage it, Shmi, sacrificingly, tells Anakin that her future is on Tatooine while his will be greater. They say a tearful goodbye. Destiny whisks him off, giving him few moments to make choices and leaving him with unfinished business. His love for his mother links him permanently to the past, giving him a purpose beyond the Jedi agenda. "leaving him with worry and guilt over his desertion of her. It is obvious that these are emotions that can be manipulated for malevolent ends," note Hanson and Kay even before Episode II comes out (363).

Eventually, Padmé, the magical princess who instantly captivates his heart, carries Anakin to Naboo. Her home is a wonder of endless water and greenery—enchanting to the desert-born slave. Gleaming ships soar through the blue skies, while lakes and cascading waterfalls abound. Extravagant palaces tower over all, and Anakin indeed feels that he's crossed into a magical realm. Of course, the planet is in terrible danger.

Droids are the anti–Jedi with no place in the Force. They are the enemy of life, the counter to the naturalistic Gungans. In modern fantasy, the heroes often take nature's side and this time is no exception. The Gungans hurl energy balls—charged organic matrixes containing unstable energy—both natural and mystical. They are also mostly passive, meeting gunfire with shields. The contrasting force are lifeless, compassionless, soulless. Their foot soldiers "are nameless and reside in giant racks in which they are folded. Each one is without character and named only by number" (Hanson and Kay 115). They march to militaristic music. Of course, their weakness is a giant central "brain" aboard the command ship.

In the showy climax on Naboo, Anakin, who is one with the Force, helps destroy the droid command center. Making the fatal shot, Anakin thinks in the novelization, "He was back in the Podraces, locked in battle with Subulba, and he could see what no one else could, what was hidden from all others. He reacted without thinking, responding to a voice that spoke to him alone, that whispered always of the future while warding him in the present" (309). Clearly, the Force gives him an extraordinary gift.

To defeat this enemy, Anakin makes the traditional descent, entering the enemy's stronghold. This technological great dragon can only be defeated from within. Symbolically, evil may dominate superficially, but it has no heart or inner defenses. By shooting it, he saves all his friends and emerges triumphant, as a war hero. He then confronts death, not his own but his master's. "As in any bildungsroman, a significant step in the young hero's journey is the separation from his mentor. Qui-Gon Jinn perished in the Battle of Naboo at the hands of the Sith lord Darth Maul," Julia Lam explains in her own monomyth exploration. Only youthful, overly strict Obi-Wan, days out of studenthood himself, is available, so he takes on the training.

After the hero's separation from the community, he returns in his new identity. At the celebratory parade that concludes the film, Anakin dresses as a young Padawan, with hair cut short save for the customary braid. His tan Jedi robes mark him as a disciple. Having fought the beast and returned, he has been initiated. However, in the novelization, he pictures not only lost Qui-Gon, but also Padmé, who's barely spoken to him, and to his mother, whom he's left behind (322). His sadness and uncertainty set up his fall in the second film.

Of course, the Jedi reliance on total selflessness, to the point of forbidding romantic love and marriage, helps start Anakin down his dark path. This is the series warning: that complete denial of human nature will lead to evil. The goal for humankind is not total goodness but balance. It will be a hard lesson.

Padmé and the Power of Disguise

While the world of the original trilogy is worn down and utilitarian, the prequels represent the Old Republic at its cultural summit—luxuriant and wealthy. The Planet of Naboo is "the idolized zenith of cultural sophistication. Every act carried out by the Naboo people, whether a lowly laborer or a royal courtier, is steeped in tradition and adorned with symbols. Theirs is a culture that takes pains to protect their traditions and keep impersonal modernity out of their daily lives" (Hidalgo, *Propaganda* 21). Amidala's capitol is Theed, with a domed palace of teal roofs and many waterfalls. It's a fairytale setting—Sleeping Beauty's palace or Shangri-La. Now the princess is preparing to awaken.

Padmé observes in the novel *Queen's Shadow* that "The office of Queen of Naboo requires a certain suspension of self" (Johnston 226). Indeed, from the first, Padmé's superpower comes from costuming and concealment. As *Star Wars Meets the Eras of Feminism* explains:

> Womanliness is a mask which can be worn or removed as the woman deliberately uses her own body as a disguise. In Amidala's costume, hair, and face paint, gender looks quite unnatural, emphasizing how much being a queen of Naboo is an artificial role. At the same time, it underscores the artificiality of femininity—to be the new damsel of *Star Wars*, Padmé's actress is playing a role that's just as false [Frankel, *Star Wars* 47].

Her many costumes—eight, as well as four for Padmé the handmaiden—dominate her, offering a royal persona she can hide behind for increased authority. Magic cloaks and gowns are a way of remaking the self, to reveal people's natures or disguise them. Most of her looks take the latter approach. Her first costume, the crimson dress, is the color of royal authority and power. Red symbolizes life as well as blood, fire, passion, and war. The sweet, youthful princess has none of these characteristics, so she borrows them from her clothes. She hides in this costume, letting her decoy take her place in it and relying on the costume's strength to mask her. The stark white facepaint as well as the lack of eye makeup help de-emphasize her features. The film guide explains that Amidala's stylized white makeup draws upon Naboo's ancient royal customs (Reynolds and Fry 41). This makeup and likely the costume have been passed down from generation to generation, uniforming all the replacement queens into a single type. As Amidala, she's the opposite of yearning, individualized Padmé. She is the Queen of Naboo.

When hiding as a handmaiden in sunset colors, Padmé fades away even more. Costume designer Trisha Biggar explains, "For episode I, George [Lucas] wanted the Queen's handmaidens to have a mysterious quality, their faces obscured when they are seen in public. This is accomplished with soft hoods, constructed to extend out and create deep shadows over their faces" (Biggar 41). Long-sleeved draping robes minimize the handmaidens' presence beside their queen.

Indeed, Queen Amidala and Padmé the handmaiden are arguably inversions—all that one has rejected, the other embodies. One represents total power, attracting all possible attention with dominating costumes. The other serves, hiding in obscurity and anonymity. Sometimes they are the same person, though in *Phantom Menace*, they are most often separate actresses. By silently observing her decoy Sabé or stepping into her role, Padmé can take on her double's power, then discard it to fade away.

Her test is a classic one for the heroine—silent endurance, even as she battles the natural pity that tempts her to her limit. From her safe position, Padmé must watch her people suffer at the Neimoidians' hands, even while unable to fight. "Can I watch my people starve, and maybe die, and not give in," she wonders in the children's novelization, offering a conflict young fans can understand (Wrede 36).

The greedy Trade Federation and their unnatural droids are the enemy to all this ancient beauty and decadence. Thus endangered, the young queen resolves to leave her homeland and quest to the hierarchical Coruscant to plead her case. This is a traditional path for the heroine—not to the Innermost Cave like Luke in *Empire* but to the patriarch's stronghold where she is at his mercy: "In many fairytales from Andersen's 'The Little Mermaid' to 'The Six Swans,' the heroine's most dire struggle takes place high in the prince's castle, far from the mysterious protection of the forest or ocean. This, like the wicked witch's castle or the Death Star, is the world of order and tyranny, where the young heroine is truly helpless" (Frankel, *Chosen One*).

Of course, before they arrive, Padmé's ship takes a massive diversion, On Tatooine, they search for parts to repair their ship, and Padmé ventures out into the desert on an adventure. Growing from girl to woman, "a transformation more radical than from boy to man," is all about changing bodies and changing desires (Gould 108). To fulfill this quest, girls become shapeshifters, reflecting this with the powers of the clothing they sew to conceal themselves. As an ordinary girl in a homespun gray tunic and simple braids, Padmé doesn't hide under a deep hood or the queen's massive regalia. For likely the first time since becoming queen, she can explore the universe and make friends as just herself. This is a classic fairytale twist—the ruler or god exploring the realm as an ordinary subject and discovering how people truly live. Beside the Jedi and droids, Padmé also functions as the audience stand-in, giving them a relatable hero to follow.

Tatooine is the wilderness, an empty desert with no expectations or demands. This lifeless, stark place is that part of the psyche with no impact from human civilization though it reflects the vast unconscious realm underneath. To enter there, a woman withdraws from the world's expectations—gender roles, society's judgment, and even others' eyes. Here, Padmé can explore and simply be.

After Anakin's podrace and a Jedi battle—all male heroism on behalf of the young queen that lends itself to traditional gendering—she reaches Coruscant. This is a planet with endlessly stacked city layers, the science fiction equivalent of an immense tower. Reaching towards the heavens is a symbol of male power, trying to emulate God and reach higher levels of civilization. It's the ultimate home of the patriarchy.

Pleading for her people before the galactic Senate, the queen appears in an extraordinary gown: red black and gold of imperial authority. The imposing headdress binds her hair severely in golden bands, emphasizing how bound she is by duty. Golden fringe around her painted face disguises her further, while the Royal Sovereign of Naboo medal rests directly on her head—another reminder of her authority and duty. "The regal attire also hides Amidala's feelings and helps her stay courageous and aloof" (Reynolds and Fry 41). Her plea, unfortunately, fails as the scheming Neimoidians use the system against her. Next, Palpatine manipulates her into calling for a vote of no confidence in Supreme Chancellor Valorum, allowing Palpatine's election in his place. By falling for his ploy, she launches his galactic dominion. Clearly, this planet is a treacherous minefield for the young queen.

Amidala leaves Coruscant, where she is buried under the bureaucracy, to return to her place of power. There, she changes from warrior to leader. As her decoy addresses the Gungans. Padmé suddenly steps forward and reveals herself to Boss Nass. With this, Padmé dramatically drops to her knees and begs for his help. Here, she has shed her protective mask, revealed as completely vulnerable. In contrast with the decoy queen's strength, Padmé in her handmaiden guise has mastered humility and wields it as a tool. Stepping into her shadow's role wins her the day here.

Infiltrating her own palace and fighting with fast reflexes and the use of her decoy once more, Padmé defeats the enemy. When her double, so authoritative and better dressed, arrives, the Neimoidians immediately assume she's the queen. Near-invisible Padmé, however, snatches two weapons from a hidden throne compartment and disarms her enemies, using all the skills she's perfected. Holding them at blasterpoint, she wins the day and demands a new treaty. Padmé ends the film presiding over the reward ceremony and honoring the men for their accomplishments, much like Leia in the original film. Both moments stress traditional gendering, with queen and princess cast as the warriors' reward. Still, Padmé's fighting on the frontlines establishes her as action heroine, one who will risk her life to win the day.

Qui-Gon and Obi-Wan: Warrior Monks

Obi-Wan and Qui-Gon are not action heroes or knights but diplomats and sages. The danger for such characters is that they may block progress instead of guiding it. In their heyday, there are over 10,000 Jedi, working in a system that has existed for 24,000 years (Wallace *Jedi Path* 12, 150). They are noble, but overly bound by tradition.

The master-apprentice relationship is central. As the novels reveal,

Obi-Wan and Qui-Gon begin their partnership with a rocky start, mostly because they are so different. Obi-Wan's devotion to the rules leads him to clash with his mentor (and even report him) as he will later struggle with rebellious Anakin. As such, they are shadows of a sort, committed to opposing paths. In the *Phantom Menace* novelization, Obi-Wan thinks about how frustrated he is that "his mentor was too eager to involve himself when it was not necessary. He was too quick to adopt causes that were not his own. It had cost him time and time again with the Jedi Council. One day it would be his undoing" (Brooks 51).

As *Phantom Menace* begins, the two Jedis' contrast is clear. Obi-Wan is cautioned by the older, wiser Qui-Gon to concentrate on the present, even as Obi-Wan protests that he's been trained to mind the future. This reminds viewers that Obi-Wan is still less than an adult warrior. "Strongly influenced by other leading Jedi as well as by Qui-Gon, Obi-Wan is more brooding and cautious than his teacher. He is careful to weigh the consequences of his actions and is reluctant to entangle himself unnecessarily in transgressions against the will of the Jedi High Council," the film's visual guide explains (Reynolds and Fry 22). Obi-Wan is so devoted to rules and traditions that he finds Qui-Gon's more intuitive approach incredibly frustrating. Qui-Gon is compassionate, more intuitive with people, while Obi-Wan is distant and "sometimes it took him longer to see when someone was hurting, or what they might truly need" (Gray, *Master* 87). By contrast, Qui-Gon obeys morality above the law, calling his student more devoted to ideals than reality.

The hero's journey, like listening to the Force, involves letting go and accepting esoteric wisdom from the unconscious world. This is Qui-Gon's particular strength. He is a true believer and discerns that Anakin will bring balance to the Force. His faith in prophecy actually makes him the most mystical of the Jedi. Critic Jason Fry notes:

> He's something never encountered in the movies before or since—a maverick Jedi. We first see him on a secret mission for the Chancellor, one that winds up causing all sorts of problems, we last see him passing on his defiance of the Jedi Council to his Padawan, ensuring he'll tick off Yoda posthumously. Along the way he teases Queen Amidala, never quite letting on that he sees through her disguise: uses the Force to try to cheat shopkeepers; and vexes the Council by hauling a child from Tatooine for testing, making it clear to them and us that Anakin will be trained whether the Council likes it or not. He doesn't care about anything except the will of the Force as he hears it whispering in his cells, which is pretty admirable on the one hand and pretty obviously dangerous on the other. Qui-Gon's not an instantly recognizable archetype like Luke Skywalker or Han Solo, but he might just be the most nuanced and interesting character in the whole saga ["50 Greatest Reasons" 145].

Claudia Gray's novel *Master and Apprentice*, released in 2019 and featuring Obi-Wan's apprenticeship with Qui-Gon, shows his own growth as a character. Once, Qui-Gon was Dooku's padawan, intrigued by the ancient prophecies that the Council had long dismissed as worthless or worse, a path to the dark side. In their partnership, Qui-Gon and Dooku find several commonalities: "self-reliance, skepticism, and a reluctance to take the Council's word as sacred" (19). To their startlement, one prophecy comes true: "When the kyber that is not kyber shines forth, the time of prophecy will be at hand" (117). This suggests that the Jedi have reached the point when all the prophecies will find fulfillment, such as "the one who will bring balance to the Force." Now as an adult and master, Qui-Gon soon receives more of these and dreams of a disaster at the novel's climax. Yoda supports him. However, the rest of the Council are dismissive, and Qui-Gon realizes, "They were no longer the sort of Jedi who could trust in a pure vision" (217). He is shocked to find that he believes in the deep teachings of the Force in a way the Council no longer can.

Ultimately, he accepts this change in himself, telling his padawan, "Now that I stand where the prophets have stood, I must listen to them in humility, not in judgement. When I was younger, I was capable of that. I only hope I can find the strength to believe again" (229). By the end of the novel, he's a true disciple, eager for the time of prophecy when slaves will be freed and peace achieved. This is an internal journey but follows the traditional pattern all the same. With this, he becomes a new kind of sage. As the fictional guidebook *The Jedi Path* explains, "The so-called gray Jedi have been with us since the beginning. Although they do not break with the Jedi orthodoxy concerning the dark side, they bristle when asked to take orders from the Council. Gray Jedi make compromises, cut corners, and hide their actions from scrutiny, all under the assumption that their experience makes them authorities on policy." Obi-Wan notes that many call Qui-Gon this (Wallace 151).

Beyond this difference in philosophy, the pair work as a polished team, with Qui-Gon's experience balancing Obi-Wan's youth. In *Phantom Menace,* their first enemy is political as the Neimoidians blockade the planet Naboo and attack the Jedi with their droids. The rolling, uncoiling droidekas are inhuman in appearance, "made only for combat and specialized for the single purpose of destruction" (Reynolds and Fry 37). Rolling, squat creatures, their arms are replaced with blasters. As the threshold guardians, blocking the way to Naboo, the Viceroy and his Neimoidians are also anti–Jedi as destroyers of the rule of law.

On Naboo, the heroes descend into a magical world—not the forest but the numinous water. The Gungan village resembles a palace of lit bubbles—more jewels than buildings. It's a fantasy realm far removed from the politics of the surface-dwellers. Their swamps are likewise a primitive base, full of life. "The Gungans have *adapted* to their surroundings, using nature and letting nature use them to their benefit. They do not seem to be out of place, or even to be destroying their environment in the upkeep of their city. Instead they are a natural part of the seas, their presence adding to the cycles of ecological life" (Hanson and Kay 67). There, the Jedi learn a different kind of wisdom, one of blending in and listening to others. Journeying beneath the waves symbolizes a trip to the magical world, a fairyland of different customs and rules. The water is the feminine realm, cradle of life and nature instead of technology and space battles. Making this descent is like returning to the womb or perhaps to the wellspring of the Force.

There, they pick up a guide, who helps the wise Jedi connect with their inner child. "Jar Jar Binks captures the vulnerability, awkwardness and naiveté that children and adolescents feel and try to hide for fear of being shamed, ridiculed, and ostracized" (Galipeau 266). Together with Queen Amidala and her handmaidens, they escape Naboo, but repairs force them to land on Tatooine. There, Qui-Gon discovers, to his irritation, that the Jedi mind trick won't work on the junk seller, Watto. To outwit him, the Jedi must welcome a new set of skills.

More interestingly, their being stranded on Tatooine puts them in contact with Anakin. The sandstorm, a rather coincidentally timed natural phenomenon, gives the Jedi a reason to shelter in Anakin's home and thus solve all their problems. Some fans believe the Force is manifesting here, giving destiny some help. It's also possible that Qui-Gon responds so eagerly because Anakin reflects the idealism he seeks within himself. Either way, Qui-Gon's dreams are realized when he discovers young Anakin is the Chosen One of prophecy. He willingly places all their fates in his hands (and the Force) when Anakin podraces for the part they need. Obi-Wan, however, is far more skeptical, learning from his mentor's teachings, but not committing fully. The pair present a contrasting partnership, each voicing the doubt submerged inside the other.

Eventually, they return to Naboo where the two Jedi battle this film's nemesis—dark Jedi Darth Maul. He personifies the Sith—primal rage at the entire Jedi way and all who follow it. The *Phantom Menace* novelization adds that Maul "was driven by his messianic hatred for and disdain of the Jedi Knights, the enemies of the Sith for millennia" (284). All his life has been focused on defeating his people's enemy. As such, he's all shadow—the emotions civilized society has rejected and refuses to allow into its daily activity.

Maul's dual blade means twice the destruction. As a force of entropy and murder, he's far different from the opportunistic Neimoidians, who quest for power and profit. They, indeed, are easier to outwit. He also contrasts with the scheming Sidious whose wise plots last for decades. Instead, Maul is physicality and combat force. "He is an attack dog, owned by Sidious. He doesn't think, he doesn't speak (anything of importance), he has no 'personality'; he is simply a combat machine, an animal. This is starkly evident in his fight scenes with the Jedi," notes Chris Foxwell in his essay on the character. During their standoff, parted by energy fields, he doesn't bother matching wits with the Jedi. Physical might is his only drive. Further, as the impersonal force of evil, he has no relationship with the Jedi (in contrast with Obi-Wan and Vader or Luke and Vader). Thus, there is nothing to say.

> The elegance of the silence is what makes the fight scene. No words, no taunts, no banter. Sheer, silent ferocity and intent. The Jedi and the Sith, fighting once more after an entire millennium. The impact is entirely visual and dialogue would have been out of place. Recall Maul's facial expressions during the duel. They are bestial, savage, fierce, befitting his entirely physical role; his face and his body movements communicate all that needs be said.... He is like a caged animal. As the fields ignite, he glances up and around, searching, his only intent to find a way to continue the battle. He tests the field's integrity with his saber, and after determining that it is impenetrable, he starts to pace, glaring down at the kneeling Qui-Gon. Again, words are out of place here; Jinn and Maul know that this is a fight to the death, and that nothing need be said. Maul gloats almost, like a predator who knows that the kill is near, and that glare and his pacing say it all [Foxwell].

Facing him requires channeling the heroes' top Jedi skills and finally changes their status as mentor and apprentice forever. "This battle illustrates the cycles of life because though Qui-Gon is renowned as a great warrior, his time is drawing to an end. His age will not allow him, no matter how well he fights, to defeat Darth Maul. It is time for the younger heroes to step into the spotlight" (Hanson and Kay 97). Qui-Gon falls. One moment of violence and the mentor is lost, leaving Obi-Wan the new senior Jedi. There, in the innermost chamber, he faces his own adulthood test. "Obi-Wan and Darth Maul duel within the heart of Theed Palace's immense generator complex, their anger and intensity an echo of the roiling, energized plasma coursing through the generator's innards" (Reynolds and Fry 25). Of course, this is a moment where the immature hero reveals whether he is prepared for the challenges of adulthood.

Defeating Maul requires Obi-Wan to give himself over to the Force completely, master his rage and loss to find his center. It's a true Jedi test. "In the end, Obi-Wan regains his focus and uses the Force, not his rage, to defeat Maul with the blade of his master's saber, the hero is reforging his father figure's sword and uses the power of the psyche, not of strength to best his foe" (Hanson and Kay 127). He nearly dies himself, defeating Maul in a final desperate strike. Here, he succumbs to his grief and rage, if only for a moment. Of course, in the lore of the light side and dark, he teeters close to destruction in the internal war as vital as the physical one. Slicing a person in half "is rightly considered barbaric and evidence of the furious emotions of the dark side," according to the Jedi handbook (Wallace 77). He does more than face Maul but for a moment steps into his place and uses his own brutality, accepting its presence within himself. Afterwards, Obi-Wan accepts this lesson—he pulls back and regains his self-mastery, refusing to succumb in future.

After winning the battle, Obi-Wan is advanced to Jedi Knight, much like Luke after facing Vader in Episode V. As the Jedi handbook specifies, he has faced evil incarnate, suffered pain and great loss, and matured through the struggle. This ties in symbolically to his losing his father figure and having to step up, defeat the great evil, and then take Qui-Gon's place—he has clearly claimed the adult role. After comes his mentor's funeral, in which they burn his body. As is established here and in larger canon, Jedi have lost the art of fading into Force ghosts. "In *Revenge of the Sith*, we learn that this isn't a standard Jedi feat. It is something that Qui-Gon Jinn picked up from a Shaman of the Whills, and it can only be accomplished through compassion, not greed" ("Secrets of the Force" 22). Only Qui-Gon's descent into mysticism lets him eventually make this transition, and then tutor Obi-Wan and Yoda, who in turn teach Luke and Leia. While passing from mentorship into the spirit realm is a standard step of the hero's lifecycle, few stories address it as clearly as this one.

The Droids as Ordinary Heroes

The original film casts R2-D2 and C-3PO as several among many identical droids—ones who only stand out after Leia gives Artoo a secret mission he's determined to fulfill. The prequels cast a new spin as they retcon the droids into far more significant characters. This time, Anakin built C-3PO (leading to many hilarious memes), Padmé owned R2-D2, and both droids witnessed their wedding and then guarded the secret of their doomed love. All this makes the droids much larger characters, firmly entangled in Old Republic history.

The first appearance of R2-D2, chronologically, occurs when the astromech droids of the queen's ship are called into service. All are killed but Artoo who courageously stays at his post, makes the needed repairs, and saves the day. The queen publicly thanks him and sends Padmé to scrub him (a puzzling command, suggesting that the real queen has nothing better to do than manual labor, unless Padmé is using this as cover for an errand). At the film's climax, Artoo partners with Anakin, helping him in his mission to destroy the Trade Federation's shield and stop an entire droid army. Side by side, the pair risk death against this overwhelming foe and finally triumph. With this, Artoo accomplishes a death-descent and return alongside Anakin. However, his lack of suffering or growth as a character leaves him somewhat removed from the hero's journey plot.

C-3PO's origin is a bit more puzzling. A protocol droid on Leia's diplomatic ship makes sense, but one assisting a slave woman deep in the desert is less logical. One assumes that Anakin had to scavenge whatever droid he could find, however unsuitable. As the visual guide admits, "A protocol droid offers no obvious benefit to a household of Mos Espa slaves, but Anakin figures C-3PO can help Shmi and run errands. Doesn't even a wrecked droid deserve a chance?" (Reynolds and Fry 78). In the novelization, young Anakin sweetly names Threepio "choosing three because the droid made the third member of his little family after his mother and himself" (Brooks 68). If the two humans are the parents, Threepio is the innocent child who makes them whole.

Anakin is desperate to free his mother and end slavery, but this compassion does not extend to droids. In fact, Threepio is treated as an object in episode one. Anakin shows off his creation to Padmé, ending his demonstration with a promise to show off his racer next. On leaving the planet, Anakin switches him on to bid him farewell, like a toy. Without consulting Threepio's feelings, Anakin decides to leave him behind with his mother forever, once again, like a toy he's outgrown. Shmi must finish building him on her own, finishing the project as a legacy to her vanished son.

In this trilogy, most droids are voiceless soldiers forced to endlessly kill. Threepio and Artoo contrast these societal shadows while emphasizing the many droids' helpless plight. Lucasfilm Story Group head Pablo Hidalgo writes, "The Republic was branded as inhumane for weaponizing cloning technology to make *organic* soldiers, while the Confederacy of Independent Systems preserved life by relying on lifeless droids. In either scenario, the droid ended up as the voiceless part—whether casting droids as weapons of protection or offense, no side ever stopped to wonder what the droids wanted" (*Propaganda* 38).

The second film carries both droids into battle. This time, Artoo rescues Padmé by stopping the conveyer belt she's trapped on. In the novelization, this is more panicked as "R2-D2 coolly continued his work, trying to put aside his understanding that Padmé was about to become encased in molten metal" (305). To rescue her, he defeats a tyrannical machine much larger than himself, one committed to mindless destruction unless the clever and caring Artoo can outwit it. Facing such a droid means confronting this potential in himself and defeating it. Once again, there's at least a glimpse of a hero's journey here.

In a more direct shadow battle, Threepio is remade as his inverse, a soldier and killer instead of the polite indoor diplomatic droid. In battle,

C-3PO samples his dark side. Of course, this is played for humor, as he frantically apologizes to those his soldier body shoots. "There's been some terrible mistake! I'm programmed for etiquette not destruction," he sobs. At least superficially, he experiences true combat as a destroyer of innocents and returns to himself having learned the costs of war.

The novelization of *Revenge of the Sith* reveals that Anakin has no possessions to offer his new bride, so instead he gives her C-3PO. At this point, he's matured, and so he specifies that Threepio is not a slave but is free now: "What I'm really doing is asking you to look after him for me" (Stover 107). Padmé turns the line back on him when Anakin is made a Jedi knight—she gives him R2-D2 to fight beside him. Anakin then continues his passion for tinkering to rebuild Artoo to some extent, once more impacting history. "Anakin has tweaked the droid's processor and memory matrices and improved his interchangeable component design by upgrading his tool kit" (Luceno, *Revenge Visual Dictionary* 18).

Revenge of the Sith once more takes the droids to the front lines. In the first scene, Obi-Wan's astro-droid R4-P17 is killed by a swarm of black and yellow buzz droids—like wasp-droid hybrids that swarm the outer shell of the starfighter, emphasizing Artoo's possible fate if he doesn't defend himself. In the first twenty-minute sequence as the two Jedi rescue the kidnapped chancellor, Artoo kills a fighter destroyer and then incinerates two killer droids. As he's attacked and nearly hurled into space, he's not the deux-ex-machina, but a vulnerable character in deadly danger. Threepio, meanwhile, suffers along with Padmé, longing to help her but unable to do so in a worsening galactic takeover.

Later, C3PO and R2-D2 heroically rescue the injured Padmé and get her onto their ship. As they most often do, they enact the role of tiny helpers who aid the hero when he or she is too injured to act, like little supportive voices from within. However, they end the epic trilogy being ordered to silence, with a memory wipe in Threepio's case. This death and rebirth sequence reverses the traditions of the hero's journey by resetting Threepio to his original innocent origins, depriving him of all the wisdom and affection he has gained.

Darth Maul's Failures

Darth Maul is a demonically menacing figure, especially in his silence. As the script describes him, "Darth wears black boots, a black cloak, a black shirt, has a red lightsaber, wears red and black face paint, and has horns. He is EVIL." In the first film, he has no arc or narrative conflict. Critic Tom Bissell notes that this makes him a flat character:

> Darth Maul is irretrievably evil and therefore uninteresting from a dramatic point of view.... What makes Maul so compelling on film—coolness, impenetrability, calm, makes him ludicrous on the page. There is no struggle in an evil character. One can be tormented and do evil things—Raskolnikov is the supreme example forever—and retain dramatic interest, but one's evil nature cannot be a foregone conclusion [14].

He has only five lines and fulfills the Sith's mission with no emotional struggle or personal agenda present.

In the larger picture, he represents a "phantom menace" indeed: the return of Sith to the Jedis' awareness. The Council spend the first film sending Obi-Wan and Qui-Gon to investigate and destroy this first scout, though they remain unaware of the larger manipulator behind him.

As his master's antithesis, Maul lacks a secret identity, instead bluntly attacking his enemies. "With his yellow eyes and horned head a black-and-red mask of arcane sigils, it was all he could do to prowl the fringes of The Works in the dead of night without instilling fear in nearly every being whose gaze he caught," his origin novel *Darth Plagueis* explains (Luceno 302). He is established as the brute force of the story, an apprentice skilled in combat but not subtlety.

Despite his lack of nuance in episode one, the expanded universe gives Maul more struggle. As the visual dictionary explains, "Maul has bided his time as Sidious's instrument, limited to secret missions against rebellious servants. He burns to reveal himself to the Jedi, simultaneously punishing the Sith's ancient foes and proving himself to his Master. He's delighted to be sent after Naboo's missing Queen and her Jedi protectors. At last the Sith will have their revenge" (Reynolds and Fry 9). Through all his youth he has trained as the perfect warrior, indoctrinated but never allowed to wield his power. Indeed, the comics expand on his endless waiting. Sidious, his master, warns him against impatience, adding, "Your anger, your thirst for vengeance makes you fearsome. But if you endanger my preparations and maneuvers again, it will not be a Jedi who casts you down" (Bunn). Sidious not only struggles with his long-term plans, dependent on concealment, but on maintaining their hierarchy with himself firmly in charge. Of course, this somewhat mirrors the Master-Padawan relationship seen with Qui-Gon, Obi-Wan, and Anakin on the other side, emphasizing how much the teams mirror each other.

"I have endured great suffering as part of my training. All so I might be an instrument of revenge. So I can kill Jedi," Maul thinks in his origin comic (Bunn). He captures a Padawan and bitterly tells her how her people slaughtered his. Now he seeks to prove himself against her but also longs for revenge. She needles him, like a shadow, observing how he's concealing himself and how his slinking in the shadows indicates cowardice. Maul tells himself, "She is not my equal. She is—like all Jedi—inferior. But I need this fight to prove it to myself. That is why she must die." After he wins, he realizes that his rage and ambition have only intensified. He longs to kill more and more. He succumbs to this untampered fury, as he has rejected the Jedi path of discipline and calm.

Maul has an extensive arc in the *Clone Wars* cartoon, setting up his appearance at the end of *Solo*. The show introduces him and his brother Savage Oppress as Nightbrothers, slaves to the Nightsisters on Dathomir. Long ago, Palpatine adopted this Zabrack baby from his desperate mother—she marked him with the traditional red and black tattoos and handed him over since she perceived Palpatine's power and wanted to free her child from his potential fate. However, Palpatine trained him more as a tool than a true apprentice. As Palpatine explains in *Darth Plagueis:*

> I stranded him on Hypori for a month without food and with only a horde of assassin droids for company. Then I returned to goad and challenge him. All things considered, he fought well, even after I deprived him of his lightsaber. He wanted to kill me, but was prepared to die at my hand.... He was already humbled. I chose to leave his honor intact. I proclaimed him my myrmidon; the embodiment of the violent half of our partnership [Luceno, *Darth Plagueis* 267].

After several adventures, Oppress finds his bisected brother. The clan leader, Mother Talzin, restores Maul's sanity and gives him cybernetic legs. This death and return set him on the path to new adventures, as he sets himself up as the master, with his brother as apprentice. Notably, Maul and Vader are both cut to pieces and yet survive: This stresses the physicality of the dark side—the quest to avoid death, like Voldemort's in *Harry Potter,* leaves them monsters who cling to a corporeal existence by unnatural means. "For a Sith, there is no transcendent quality to their existence, at least that they can conceive of. There's nothing beyond what they have right now … if you die, you can't get any more stuff" Sam Witwer, voice of Darth Maul, explains ("Revival" Video Commentary).

After this, Maul becomes craftier, forming a criminal empire called the Shadow Collective through various alliances which included the Pyke Syndicate, the Black Sun, and the Death Watch. This indicates his development, expanding from brute force to strategy. "I'm going to make myself known in this conflict and I want my own power base," showrunner Dave Filoni says of him in the episode commentary. Moreover, Maul is reborn into a different universe, one in which the Sith are gaining ascendancy. Using this alliance, he conquers Mandalore, slaying Duchess Satine whom Obi-Wan once loved. With this, he frames himself as the Jedi's nemesis but also Obi-Wan's personal one.

In "The Lawless" (516), Sidious addresses Maul's quest for domination—taunting his former student for his arrogance, he kills Oppress and demotes Maul. As he contemptuously concludes, "Remember, the first and only reality of the Sith, there can only be two. And you are no longer my apprentice. You have been replaced." At this point in the cartoon, each of the Sith, including the new apprentice Dooku and maddened Jedi-killer General Grievous, is cultivating apprentices and plotting the overthrow of the other branches. "With these Sith, there's a lot of machinations going on. They're always scheming," Filoni says.

Next, in the comic *Darth Maul: Son of Dathomir* (incorporating storylines intended to wrap up his path on *Clone Wars*), Maul captures Grievous and Dooku, taunting Sidious with his might. In some ways, he's still a follower, not only obsessing over his former Master's hierarchy, but taking revenge on behalf of his sacrificed mother, whom Sidious has slain. Maul also suggests Dooku serve him and that their combined strength can defeat Sidious. This too is the power of the Dark Side, alliances and betrayals. When Obi-Wan arrives, Dooku accepts Maul's offer and fights beside him, insisting to Obi-Wan, "Only our shared hatred of you could be strong enough to unite us" (Barlowe). The Sith do not form friendships, but they ally through expediency. Of course, the alliance falls apart, and faced with Sidious's wrath, Maul flees. Sidious smiles that he has maneuvered everyone deliberately into just this position.

The *Clone Wars* episode "Phantom Apprentice" (710), taking place concurrently with *Revenge of the Sith*, shows Maul grown to crude leader and philosopher. He stews over Sidious's abandonment, realizing that the great plan is taking place, but without him. His perpetual anger emphasizes how much he still lets rage rule him. Decisively, he orders his syndicate leaders into hiding, adding, "Soon, the galaxy will be remade, and in the chaos, we must seize what power we can." In the midst of Sidious's epic plan, he launches his lesser scheme, one designed to give him what opportunities he can snatch. With no place in the hierarchy now, clinging to scraps of power is his only option. First, he tries to lure Anakin close to kill him and deprive Sidious of his chosen apprentice. While Obi-Wan and Anakin ignore his trap, Ahsoka, their cast-out student, arrives instead. Maul sees in her shades of himself, expertly trained and then abandoned—as he insists, "We were both tools for greater powers." Ahsoka, a momentary voice for the lost goodness in him, pleads with Maul to share his information and aid the Republic, to choose goodness instead of evil. However, he dismisses this as a pointless act. "There is no justice, no law, no order, except for the one that will replace it!" Though he has little faith in Sidious's reign, he knows it is inevitable. In the traditional dark side pattern, he offers Ahsoka an alliance so that together they can take Sidious's place at the top of the hierarchy. However, she defeats him and has the Stormtroopers carry him off, unaware as she is of the upcoming fall of the Republic. As he rages in his cell, he enacts the voice of the collective shadow, bottled up but returning whenever there's a chance. Ahsoka finally frees him, not out of sympathy but so he can cause chaos at the moment she most needs. This is Maul's only worth—a force of unrestrained violence that can only be redirected at a different target.

After his work with the syndicates, including in *Solo,* the *Rebels* episode "Twin Suns" has Maul quest into the desert to find Obi-Wan. As showrunner Dave Filoni explains, the Jedi Master has matured a great deal from the prequel era character: "I felt strongly Obi-Wan, if he could help it, would really rather not kill Darth Maul. Obi-Wan is at a point, in my mind, where he's become rather enlightened. He's been in the desert discovering who he is, really evolving as a character." However, Maul clings to the moment at which his life went wrong and tracks Obi-Wan obsessively. Obi-Wan, reluctantly bowing to the inevitable, kills his adversary quickly and cleanly, comforting him as he dies. His reluctance that shows how much he's moved beyond the need for revenge. This emphasizes their differences—Maul himself has never found wisdom or advanced beyond petty schemes for domination. His rage carries him on his futile desert quest only to find a quick death at the hands of his former nemesis, who has long moved beyond him. At the apex of his wisdom, Obi-Wan need only banish the primitive predator and he vanishes. Filoni adds:

> It really is to express the difference between the Jedi and the Sith. Which is the Jedi become selfless and the Sith remain selfish. When pressed, because Obi-Wan is protecting someone else in the end, he does fight. But because he is so true and knows who he is in that moment, you can't defeat that. So Obi-Wan is going to strike down Maul because Maul is such a broken and lost person, which I think is why in the end you see Maul being cradled by Obi-Wan. This idea is that Obi-Wan is willing to forgive this person who is so cruel and terrible because he feels pity for him. To his dying breath Maul is hoping there will be some revenge exacted upon his enemies. And in my mind, Obi-Wan expresses sadness there because that means that Maul has never grown and will never be released from his suffering [Lussier].

The Clone Wars and the Fall of the Republic

Anakin's Descent

> Palpatine smiled inwardly. Guide you to me, young Skywalker.
> Dooku had talent and could be a powerful placeholder. But this seemingly guileless pleasant-faced boy, this Forceful boy, was the one he would take as his apprentice, and use to execute the final stage of the Grand Plan. Let Obi-Wan instruct him in the ways of the Force, and let Skywalker grow embittered over the next decade as his mother aged in slavery, the galaxy deteriorated around him, and his fellow Jedi fell to inextricable conflicts. He was too young to be trained in the ways of the Sith, in any case, but he was the perfect age to bond with a father figure who would listen to all his troubles and coax him inexorably over to the dark side [Luceno, *Darth Plagueis* 368].

In the first film, Anakin is ten; in the second he's twenty. He begins the latter acting like a rebellious teen, pushing the limits his foster-father and the Jedi Council have set. As Chosen One, Anakin is set apart. Further, he grew up outside the Jedi world, furnishing him with a more complex view than automatic obedience to the Temple. This leaves him with family connections particularly difficult to shake off. Anakin poignantly asks in the fictitious Jedi handbook, "I miss people outside the temple and would do anything to protect them. Does that make me a bad person?" (Wallace, *Jedi Path* 25).

Beyond this, his entire ascetic path is a difficult one for him, arguably one that asks too much. To become such a monk, one must abandon all worldly desire and ambition as well as human ties. Anakin, of course, is badly suited to these expectations. The *Clone Wars* novelization reveals, "He was already full of attachment and emotion, too set in his ways of being a messy, ordinary human to adopt the aloof serenity—the unloving detachment, the arm's length and measured compassion—a Jedi needed" (Traviss 78).

All this comes to a head when he's confronted with his childhood crush. Lucas says, "Anakin has been in love with Padmé ever since he was ten years old. He worshipped her when he was young. And now they're finally getting back together" ("Love Featurette": *Attack of the Clones*). She arrives at a particularly unsettling time for him as he has nearly finished growing up, but not entirely. He stands at a threshold, as he hasn't yet given all he is to the Jedi. Palpatine suggests Obi-Wan protect Padmé and thus throws Anakin together with his greatest enticement to stray from the Jedi path. By fulfilling his duty, Anakin stands vulnerable to temptation, as he slides down the slippery slope.

To Anakin, Padmé is the perfect woman, the princess he will serve as devoted warrior. Jung called such a figure the anima, the woman who evokes all the spirituality and feminine grace the male hero lacks. "The anima is a personification of all feminine psychological tendencies in a man's psyche, such as vague feelings and moods, prophetic hunches, receptiveness to the irrational, capacity for personal love, feeling for nature and—last but not least—his relation to the unconscious" (Von Franz, "Individuation" 177). Of course, by loving her as a projection, Anakin fails to see the real woman or consider her ideas. To him, she is perfect, and he falls hard. Upon seeing her, he's disappointed that she still thinks of him as a child, and immediately begins fighting with his father-figure in front of her, posturing and strutting. Within minutes he goes from nervous fidgets to playing her knight-errant.

> **PADMÉ:** I don't need more security, I need answers. I want to know who's trying to kill me.
> **OBI-WAN:** We're here to protect you, Senator, not to start an investigation.
> **ANAKIN:** We will find out who's trying to kill you, Padmé. I promise you.
> **OBI-WAN:** We will not exceed our mandate, my young Padawan learner.
> **ANAKIN:** I meant that in the interest of protecting her, Master, of course.
> **OBI-WAN:** We will not go through this exercise again, Anakin, and you will pay attention to my lead.
> **ANAKIN:** Why?
> **OBI-WAN (APPALLED):** What?
> **ANAKIN (BACKING DOWN):** Why else do you think we were assigned to her if not to find the killer? Protection is a job for local security, not Jedi. It's overkill, Master; investigation is implied in our mandate.
> **OBI-WAN:** We will do exactly as the Council has instructed ... and you will learn your place, young one.

As Anakin directly defies Obi-Wan, asking why he must obey, and then withdrawing the comment, he's testing their boundaries. "He's rude, arrogant, and ungrateful. While he talks about the respect he has for Obi-Wan's wisdom, he never acts as if he believes that Obi-Wan has anything to teach him. He ignores Obi-Wan's explicit instructions at every opportunity, he picks a fight with Obi-Wan in front of Padmé to prove his loyalty to her over his teacher, he refuses to listen to Obi-Wan while chasing

Zam Wesell, and he abandons his mission to Naboo to look after his own personal affairs" (Dees 59). Arguably, *Attack of the Clones* is an antihero's journey, as the rebellious young man travels towards adulthood but in the process falls into darkness.

It must also be noted that Obi-Wan is not only hidebound for such a young instructor but unpracticed. Anakin is his first student, accepted moments after his own ascendency not because he was qualified but because no one else would take the boy. Further, Anakin's fully aware of all this. "Sometimes he felt Kenobi was stability and safety; sometimes he thought he was an overbearing older brother who held him back and even competed with him," explains the *Clone Wars* novelization (Traviss 44). Obi-Wan embodies Jedi ideals like selflessness and obedience, which frustrates Anakin further. Looking for love and support, he's angry that the other man originally took him on out of duty. Obi-Wan, meanwhile, must always compare himself to his more flexible, dream-driven master: "How might Anakin have fared under Qui-Gon's guidance? he wonders in *Labyrinth of Evil*, as he's desperate to live up to his mentor's memory" (Luceno 80–81).

Everything about the teacher and student contrast. Obi-Wan gave up his love for the order, as *Clone Wars* show later explores. Obi-Wan is calm and reflective, obedient to the point of his own detriment. He was raised by the Jedi and accepts all their dictates. At this point, Obi-Wan carries a green lightsaber like Qui-Gon did, linking him with the wisdom of the lifecycle. Green is carried by Consulars, more reflective, cautious senior Jedi, like Yoda. Anakin's lightsaber is blue like Obi-Wan the Padawan had in the first film, emphasizing their switching roles. He builds it in one of the junior novels that explores his training, but this scene also foreshadows his future. "Anakin Skywalker had visions of the dark side while in his trance-like state in the sacred caverns of Ilum, where he meditated on the construction of the lightsaber. The weapon is in contrast to the delicate saber design of his master, Obi-Wan Kenobi. Anakin built his saber instead for maximum power" (Hidalgo, *Lightsabers* 32). Indeed, Anakin prefers fighting directly to evasion as his introduction in the second film reveals.

Similarly, Lucas describes Anakin as having "a James Dean sullen edge to him" ("Love Featurette"). He's the bad boy, one who shows off his cool as he banters, steals a speeder, and finally jumps from it while pursuing Padmé's assassin. Clearly, Anakin is stuck in the rebellious phase—more anti–Jedi than wise master. Whatever Anakin does, he feels that guarded Obi-Wan is judging him and slapping him down for carelessness. Further, Obi-Wan is quick to judge and criticize, so Anakin rebels and breaks away, and the vicious cycle continues.

Of course, Anakin spends a few minutes of screen time with the evil mentor—Palpatine, who encourages his worst impulses. The emperor-to-be cultivates his pride and arrogance, which convince him he should defy Obi-Wan and the Council when his judgment conflicts with theirs. Palpatine tells him, "You don't need guidance, Anakin. In time, you will learn to trust your feelings. Then you will be invincible. I have said it many times: you are the most gifted Jedi I have ever met." Of course, this is teaching the wrong lessons, as Yoda relies on humility and consensus, listening to the Force and to his fellows rather than making unilateral decisions.

Further, the color, shape, and materials of Anakin's episode two clothing allude to his future—Anakin's black suit or crimson tunic and brown leather surcoat are a break from Jedi traditional clothing. Costume designer Trisha Biggar says, "His costume is the darkest of all the Jedi, with rich, deep, dark browns that read almost black in low light" (3). His cloak gives him a Vader silhouette. Among knights, "black is associated with sin, penitence, the withdrawal of the recluse, the hidden, rebirth in seclusion, and sorrow"—all aspects he will bring the Jedi (Cirlot 171).

Anakin's next challenge comes when he finds himself falling more deeply for Padmé, though he also values being a Jedi. "It's that confusion that causes him all that anxiety," his actor Hayden Christiansen explains ("Story Featurette"). The Jedi life is one of emotionless restriction and denial, while Anakin longs to break out through heedless passion. Lucas explains, "The movie is essentially a story about Anakin and Anakin's dealing with his emotions and the difficulty of his being torn between his duty and his emotional needs, which relate to Padmé" ("Story Featurette").

He accompanies her to Naboo, her beautiful homeland of stretching meadows and gorgeous waterfalls. The lake country is described as "almost mystically bewitching" (Beecroft 14). For the desert-raised Anakin, Naboo is still a paradise of lakes and waterfalls—the nurturing water of the feminine sphere. "All waters are symbolic of the Great Mother and associated with birth, the feminine principle, the universal womb, the *prima material,* the waters of fertility and refreshment and the fountain of life" (Cooper 188). In the novelization, he even describes daydreaming of beautiful Naboo when he's sad and wants to lift his spirits (Salvatore 146).

His tour guide, Padmé, embodies this place. Padmé means lotus, a flower that represents the primordial mother goddess, source of creation and enlightenment. It is "all renaissance, creation, fecundity, renewal and immortality. It is also perfection of beauty" (Cooper 100). In keeping with this image, she's all he's ever sought in a mate—beauty, passion, and innocent idealism. Padmé comments in the novelization that she was elected queen partly for her scores "But for the most part, my ascent was because of my conviction that reform was possible. The people of Naboo embraced that dream wholeheartedly" (Salvatore 147). They wanted an idealist, a spiritual voice for hope. Anakin too is swept away by her vision and optimism.

Their time together resembles Frodo's visiting Galadriel in her forest or Arthur meeting the Lady of the Lake—a journey into natural beauty that offers lessons from the hero's submerged feminine presence. This enriches his spiritual side and helps it grow.

> It is the presence of the anima that causes a man to fall suddenly in love when he sees a woman for the first time and knows at once that this is "she." In this situation, the man feels as if he has known this woman intimately for all time; he falls for her so helplessly that it looks to outsiders like complete madness. Women who are of "fairy-like character" especially attract such anima projections, because men can attribute almost anything to a creature who is so fascinatingly vague and can thus proceed to weave fantasies around her [Von Franz, "Individuation" 180].

Padmé's gold gown in the meadow reflects her role as the storybook princess in their romance, while Anakin, dashing in black, rides the animals and shows off. In alchemy, gold is a spiritual pinnacle of achievement, echoed in the alchemical wedding of perfect balance between male and female. "The lady to whose service the knight pledged himself and for whom he performed his heroic deeds was naturally a personification of the anima" (Von Franz, "Individuation" 187). The risk is that if she is an ideal woman, he won't see the human one there. Indeed, Anakin fails to learn from Padmé's beliefs, dismissing them as well as her skills and duty. While he and Padmé flirt in the meadow, Anakin foreshadows his belief in dictatorship—arguing that a good government should appoint someone to make all the politicians agree. When Padmé is disturbed, he suddenly insists he was joking. As with Obi-Wan, he makes this an adolescent test, and when Padmé is appalled, he withdraws his assertion. Of course, the audience thus learns how he really feels.

When they eat a secluded dinner together, he uses the Force to feed her a piece of fruit—a reversal on Eve's temptation of Adam as he pleads with her to sin and give in to her feelings. Of course, this could destroy both their lifelong callings. Here, she is dressed in her most seductive gown of the show, black and low-cut, mirroring his colors as she approaches Anakin's point of view. More rational and cautious than he is, Padmé points out that her constituents and all their allies depend on them—they've committed to be senator and Jedi, each sworn to defend the helpless. She adds that if they subvert their oaths, they will no longer be heroes but selfish liars and hypocrites.

He finally lets her morality guide her: he concedes that he couldn't live a lie forever, as "It would destroy us." His final comment is quite prescient, as choosing selfishness and hypocrisy, even for love, carries them towards destruction. This all-too-human side, the one Padmé and Obi-Wan urge him to ignore, is his weakness. Lucas adds, "Anakin's flaws, like all classic mythological heroes, are the flaws everyone carries with them. The issue that he's confronting is that a good Jedi overcomes those flaws and kind of goes above the normal human tragedy that most people have to experience" ("Story Featurette"). As the Jedi demand he be an emotionless paragon just out of teenagehood, forced to bodyguard the only woman he's ever adored, he's ready to snap.

Adding Anakin's lost mother into the mix raises his emotional state to the breaking point. She becomes his new quest, as he switches from guarding his lady love to saving his mother. In the novelization, he dreams that his mother has turned to glass and shattered (Salvatore 2). This emphasizes her fragility and how easily she could be lost. It also idealizes her, emphasizing how Anakin, who lost her at a young age, never saw the full personality (nor did the audience). Driven by dreams that she's dying, Anakin visits Tatooine and discovers a new family with a stepbrother foil—his inverse in every way. He too is methodical, unemotional, and duty-bound, fully prepared to inherit the family legacy rather than rebelling. As Shmi thinks in the novelization, which gives their family more development:

> In truth, the two boys were very different in temperament. Owen was solid and staid, the rock who would gladly take over the farm from Cliegg when the time came, as this moisture farm had been passed down in the Lars family from generation to generation. Owen was ready, and even thrilled, to be the logical and rightful heir to the place, more than able to accept the often-difficult lifestyle in exchange for the pride and sense of honest accomplishment that came with running the place correctly.
> But Annie…
> Shmi nearly laughed aloud as she considered her impetuous and wanderlust-filled son put in a similar situation. She had no doubts that Anakin would give Cliegg the same fits he had always given Watto. Anakin's adventurous spirit would not be tamed by any sense of generational responsibility, Shmi knew. His need to leap out for adventure, to race the Pods, to fly among the stars, would not have been diminished, and it surely would have driven Cliegg crazy [Salvatore 16–17].

Of course, Anakin's stepbrother is not the problem but his lost mother—when the Sandpeople kidnap her, he gives in to the darkest of emotions. To Anakin, his mother is the original anima, a source of perfect love and protection. Page one of the novelization shows him dreaming of her in a sweet fantasy: "But most of all there was the smile of his beloved mother, so happy now, no more a slave. When she looked at him, he saw all of that and more, saw how proud she was of him, how joyful her life had become. She moved before him, her face beaming, her hand reaching out for him to gently stroke his face. Her smile brightened, then widened some more." This is who she is to him, salvation and validation. When she is killed, these vanish from his inner being, replaced by rage. Dying, she takes a few moments to express her love and then leaves him.

Once again, Anakin doesn't learn from the other person's kindness and ideals, but only from the loss he feels. Natalie Portman calls the film "an extended portrayal for how evil evolves" ("Story Featurette": *Attack of the Clones*). All fans consider his savage slaughter of the Sand People, including the innocents and children among them, a defining moment, in which he surrenders to rage and revenge. Their outward mutation reflects Anakin's inward one, showing how far he's fallen.

Afterwards, Anakin is distraught. He tells Padmé: "I'm good at fixing things ... always was. But I couldn't...." Tears erupt as he asks, "Why did she have to die? Why couldn't I save her? I know I could have!" When she tells him that some things are inevitable and that he's not all-powerful, he memorably responds, "I should be!" Irrationally, he blames Obi-Wan for holding him back and hurls a wrench. At last, he breaks through his blame and anger to face his guilt as he tells Padmé what he's done: "I slaughtered them like animals.... I hate them!" He breaks down sobbing and a stunned Padmé nonetheless comforts him without judgment.

Padmé doesn't reprimand or correct him as Obi-Wan would have but comforts him and thus supports him as he steps down the wrong path. Further, when he expresses his frustration at being unable to save his mother from the Sand People, he vows to become "the most powerful Jedi ever" and to "learn to stop people from dying." Creepily, a hint of Darth Vader's theme music plays, reminding viewers where he is headed. This is a choice—an emotional one but one he makes over and over. As Anakin confesses to Padmé, "I'm a Jedi. I know I'm better than this." Still, he chooses evil. In his next adventure, the *Clone Wars* film novelization emphasizes how twenty-year-old Anakin keeps flashing back to his guilt over not saving his mother and his conflict as he cannot let go of love. "It's not darkness. I'm not dark. This isn't anger" he thinks, though he worries the opposite is true (Traviss 25).

After this comes another test—a distress call arrives and Padmé pushes him to abandon his orders to guard her on Naboo and take her to rescue Obi-Wan on Geonosis. Reluctantly, he agrees. In contrast with the Sandpeople's slaughter, this is a generous, selfless action, though another rash one. The pair travel into a warren of droid factories on a world inhabited by insects—a monster world where they have no power against the forces of technology or the creatures who command it. This is the Belly of the Beast.

> Geonosis' gigantic factories mass-produce droids, vehicles, weapons, and military parts for a select range of shadowy clients. The underground factories are grimy, noisy, foul-smelling places cut from the rock of the planet and maintained by a slavish workforce of flightless Geonosian drones.... It is in this inhospitable environment that Anakin and Padmé find themselves battling for their lives against the machines' inhuman might [Beecroft 28].

Anakin's fight here is fully physical, against unreasoning machines. He survives, but his lightsaber is crushed, foreshadowing the hand he will lose here. Clearly, he's not as invincible as he believes, though he ignores this lesson as he has so many others.

The symbolism of coming here is reflected through the film. Visually, there's a great deal of descending and falling—many ship landings, Obi-Wan and Anakin's drops from their ships pursuing the assassin. On Tatooine, Anakin leaps down onto the raiders, and on Geonosis, he and Padmé fall together onto the droids' conveyor belt. As Anakin quests after his mother on Tatooine, he speeds under a red sky, filled with clouds. As Yoda observes, "Begun the Clone Wars has," the clones march onto their ships under a menacing red sky. Red can mean "blood; blood-lust; blood-guiltiness; anger; vengeance; martyrdom" (Cooper 40). All of these are coming. Further, the struggle within is mirrored by the one without.

After escaping the factory and its deadly conveyor belt, they're thrust into the deepest, most violent place of all. Still, there's a moment of light in the darkness as—with all hope and illusion gone, Padmé finally confesses her love. The Execution Area is a cave in truth, as it's carved from a natural cavern. Fierce monsters fill it, preparing to consume the heroes, while the Geonosians cheer. They sit above the heroes, who battle in a stark petri dish. Anakin saves himself and his friends through the usual daring, a scene that fills him with the usual overconfidence. He manages trick riding, kills a monster, saves Obi-Wan, and finally rides off with his lady clinging to him. This success leaves him ill-prepared to face the film's great villain.

On being freed by the Jedi cavalry, Anakin goes after the apparent mastermind Count Dooku, but easily gets distracted from this mission, demanding to turn back when Padmé falls from their gunship. Further, he rushes into combat with Count Dooku so carelessly that he gets himself and Obi-Wan severely injured. In Dooku's underground hanger, the belly within the belly, they face their adversary. He is the mature father figure of *Attack of the Clones,* one whose dueling outmatches both Anakin and Obi-Wan. A true shadow, he reflects the Jedi as his presence subtly reminds viewers that both sides are equally the Sith Lord's puppets. Chillingly, Dooku is the real truth-teller of the film, revealing that the Republic is under the control of the Sith and that the Council are blinded by the dark side—this last something the prideful Council has kept secret.

His actor Christopher Lee comments, "What not many people realize is that Dooku is apparently Japanese for 'poison.' Very appropriate, really, because he's lethal. And he's a fascinating character in many respects because he is one of the very few Jedi [to quit the Order], one of the Lost Twenty" (Biggar 36). He represents disillusionment with the Republic and the traditional way of life—a suggestion that the Jedi way is not for everyone. In this, he mirrors the churning resentment within Anakin, who's discovering the same conflict in himself.

The novel *Dooku: Jedi Lost* further positions Anakin and Dooku as shadows. In this story of his leaving the order, Dooku abandons the Jedi to side with his sister Jenza and his birth world. Like Anakin, he cannot cut the ties of love. The book also functions as foreshadowing, as it ends with his ordering the murder of this sister for whom he reshaped his destiny—love may make one fall to the dark side, but then the dark side will corrupt this love, turning it to cruelty. Anakin will follow just this pattern.

Of course, Anakin's barb during their fight, "I am a slow learner," rings true as it reflects his obliviousness through the film. It hampers him particularly here, as cautious Dooku is the superior fighter. Lucas says, "I needed a Jedi that was an older Jedi, that had left the world, who was very good. I decided to go with a more elegant, sophisticated kind of person, reminiscent of Obi-Wan Kenobi as an older man" ("Story Featurette"). Against such a disciplined, wise warrior, Anakin is outmatched. He and his master are both incapacitated—cut down by Dooku's lightsaber with Anakin's arm sliced off. As they lie unconscious in their death and rebirth, the force of discipline and mastery takes their place in battle. Yoda saves both Jedi, defeating Dooku, but this is not a victory—the Clone Wars have begun.

The final scene offers a traditional ending to the hero's journey as he gains his reward, the princess. With her comes marriage and adulthood, a celebration by the community of this new status. On a deeper level, a wedding symbolizes spiritual balance: "A connection has often been made between marriage, psychological unity, and the nature of the cosmos" (Pearson 47). However, Anakin and Padmé's wedding subverts all this. It is not a triumphant celebration but a clandestine, illegal, reckless act. Further, instead of either fixing themselves, they look to the other to fix them. "Blinded by fear, pain, doubt, and anger, Anakin turned once more to Padmé.... Marriage should have been a joyous event in Anakin's life, but it was only another step to his eventual fall and destruction. In the cycle of the hero's journey, Anakin's period of initiation, darkness, and suffering far overshadowed the preceding and succeeding events" (Lam). Behind them, the sun is setting, heralding an ending. The time of peace, innocence, and adolescence is over, replaced by something darker. Anakin's artificial hand likewise foreshadows his descent into Vader. "As a result of his impetuous actions, Anakin has begun to lose his humanity" (Reynolds, *Clones Visual Dictionary* 17). More inhumanity soon will follow.

The Clone Wars

The Clone Wars themselves launch, with Anakin a general commanding the 501st legion of Stormtroopers and continuing clandestine missions as a daredevil pilot. "Anakin was named a Jedi Knight after his actions on the planet Praesitlyn, where he almost singlehandedly saved a Republic communications facility" (Luceno, *Revenge Visual Dictionary* 9). No longer an apprentice, he has a padawan of his own, sweet teenage Ahsoka. David Filoni, the director of the computer-generated movie and following television series, explains:

> We see more of Anakin as a good person and a hero, not as dark and tormented. Our Anakin is a cross between Luke Skywalker and Han Solo. He is cocky like Han, but a bit naive like Luke. And we see him interact with many more characters—like his Padawan [Ahsoka]—and we see more of what really makes Anakin a great Jedi and leader. And we'll learn all kinds of new information about the "galaxy far, far away." We'll go to new planets, meet new Jedi, encounter fierce enemies [Minkel].

During the Clone Wars, Anakin is known as "the Hero with no Fear" (Luceno, *Labyrinth of Evil* 17). He saves the day in many episodes, reminding viewers that he's a celebrated general. As the central protagonist with his rebellion and cleverness wielded in the cause of heroism, he draws viewers' support. They also watch his brotherhood with Obi-Wan, who becomes a best friend and partner now that the pair fight as equals. Having a padawan of his own and a beloved legion to command elevates him from rebellious team to patriarch. By the last few episodes, his hair is longer and he's displaying show-offy, even rude attitude, though he's still fighting unreservedly for the Jedi cause.

Some episodes offer clear shadow descents, like the arc where Anakin confronts three beings called Father, Daughter, and Son. As part of this storyline, in "Altar of Mortis," a vision of himself beguiles him to join the dark side. Further, tie-in novels from this era introduce him to rogue Jedi who have married, offering him tempting alternatives to the Jedi path. All these foreshadow his fate in Episode III even as they challenge and entice him.

Of course, the wars are fully orchestrated by Palpatine. In the novelization of Episode III, Palpatine tells Anakin the truth when he says the Clone Wars were just the distraction—but he blames the Jedi for attacking him in what he calls their grab for power, insisting they wish to take over the Republic, while deflecting from the fact that he has done so himself (Stover, *Revenge of the Sith* 273). Of course, the Jedi mandate appointed them the galaxy's peacemakers and scholars—their using their abilities to lead the war is a hypocritical failure in itself. Their shadow, the Sith, tempted them into war, and they too-eagerly accepted. "The Clone Wars have always been, in and of themselves, from their very inception, the revenge of the Sith. They were irresistible bait…. And they were constructed as a win-win situation. The Clone Wars were the perfect Jedi trap. By fighting at all, the Jedi lost" (Stover, *Revenge of the Sith* 349).

Through the series, wise Jedi like Yoda and Mace Windu are framed as understanding the dark side, dipping into it as needed and then rejecting it.

Anakin, however, is certain of his own rightness and never questions. This leaves him particularly vulnerable. Combining this with his terrible vulnerability in Padmé, his forbidden love, and he's primed to be toppled.

Revenge of the Sith

Anakin dresses darker and more dramatically in the third film. "Red is the color of hellfire and damnation and also of unbridled passion and lust" while black suggests "death, mourning, and the underworld" (Bruce-Mitford 106). It's implied that Anakin wears the striking colors to look cool, but they foreshadow his decent into evil and death.

He begins Episode III by battling Dooku, triumphing over his enemy, though becoming more compromised as a result. As Anakin confronts him to rescue the kidnapped Chancellor, Dooku continues his role as shadow and truth-teller, voicing the doubts and worries Anakin tries to keep buried. He tells Anakin, "I sense great fear in you, Skywalker. You have hate, you have anger, but you don't use them." Anakin finally slices off both his enemy's hands, ending the physical threat, though not the psychological one.

The Chancellor, held hostage through all this, is bound in a chair that suggests his throne. As Palpatine urges Anakin to kill Dooku, the battle echoes *Jedi*, in which he will goad Luke to kill Vader in turn. He represents the evil impulse, the whispering voice from within. These two enemies, the public one and the secret one, are too much for Anakin to withstand. In the novelization, Anakin finally taps the fear and anger within to defeat Dooku. "Palpatine's words 'rage is your weapon' have given Anakin permission to unseal the shielding around his furnace heart, and all his fears and all his doubts shrivel in its flame" (Stover, *Revenge of the Sith* 79). With this, Anakin succumbs to his feelings and executes Dooku, helpless as he is. "The symbolism of beheading revolves around the psychological imperative of gaining control over destructive impulses that are acted out in the body" (Galipeau 126). However, Anakin's destruction is just beginning. Palpatine smiles, "It is only natural. He cut off your arm, and you wanted revenge. It wasn't the first time, Anakin. Remember what you told me about your mother and the Sand People." With each word, he urges Anakin down the slippery slope.

Anakin has constructed a new lightsaber after losing his on Geonosis. However, he lacks the wisdom that should accompany it. "On the metaphysical level, the sword is symbolic of discrimination; the penetrating power of the intellect; spiritual decision; the inviolability of the sacred" (Cooper 167). Anakin is meant to use his weapon to destroy evil and preserve good—such is the calling of a Jedi. Their lightsaber building is a specific rite of initiation, only undertaken when they're spiritually ready. Here, however, Anakin fails the test of discernment. Anakin kills Dooku, but as the Sith apprentice dies, it's as if Anakin absorbs his power and replaces him.

Next, Palpatine urges Anakin to abandon the unconscious Obi-Wan, but if this is a test, Anakin defies him. He picks up his friend and carries him along, willing to sacrifice an enemy but not his beloved comrade-in-arms. He then returns home a hero. Clearly, Anakin has reached his zenith—he's famous and admired, he has the girl, and as he soon discovers, she's pregnant. He reacts with joy and confidence—to Anakin, this pregnancy is a beacon of hope. "Padmé can be seen as a redeeming love, for she brings the autonomy and ability for Anakin to be himself and especially the promise of children, which are the links to his past, that can redeem him and save Anakin from himself" (Hanson and Kay 364).

However, Anakin is growing frustrated with having it all, and prepares to throw a bomb into their equilibrium. He tells Padmé he wants to kiss her in public, adding, "I'm tired of all this deception. I don't care if they know we're married." Their secret relationship fills him with guilt as he's endangering her and betraying the Jedi. It also creates endless tension. It's unclear whether the Council are overlooking it through self-delusion or whether they're so distant from human emptions that they can't recognize them. For Anakin, every moment is filled with the fear of discovery—and also terror as he feels losing Padmé would truly destroy him. In his prophetic nightmares, she dies in childbirth. As the film's true conflict, this fear gives him a new quest, one that will take him into total darkness.

Lucas asks, "It's a matter of how does a person who *is* good turn to become an evil person?" ("The Chosen One Featurette"). It's a step-by-step process. Christensen says, "Where we left him in episode two, he was consumed by conflicting emotions: his love for Padmé, a resentment of his Jedi obligations, the restrictions that that placed on his life, a feeling that he was being held back, a lust for power, which was really magnified by his mother's death. And a fear, which is important—a fear that this occurrence could happen again…. 'Fear is the path to the dark side. Fear leads to anger. Anger leads to hate. Hate leads to suffering.' When we find him in episode three, he's still very much enveloped by these same tormenting feelings, the feelings that the Council aren't affording him enough respect." All this leads to "a rising disillusionment" and then "culminates into an anger" as he questions Obi-Wan ("The Chosen One Featurette").

Indeed, after his vengeful slaying of Dooku, Anakin gives in to rage when he's denied master status. The novelization has Anakin desperate to be a Master because only they can access the holocrons of all the Jedi's accumulated wisdom. With it, he hopes to discover how to defeat his visions of Padmé's death and block them from occurring. Of course, this path is denied to him. In the film, Anakin seeks advice from Yoda who is kind but withdrawn, telling him that death is a natural part of life he shouldn't battle. The chamber is all shuttered, keeping out the light, so they sit in shadows. These foreshadow what must follow. Further, Yoda insists Anakin must train "to let go of everything." The advice is reasonable for a group of monks who have abandoned worldly cares. However, for terrified, loving Anakin, it's worthless. It only confirms that the Jedi will never help him. George Lucas explains: "The problem that Anakin has in this whole thing is he has a hard time letting go of things. As he sought more and more power to try to change people's fate so that they're the way he wants them, that greed goes from trying to save the one you love to realizing you can control the universe" (*Return of Darth Vader*).

He has other supports but remains unable to see them. Over and over, Padmé pleads, "Don't shut me out. Let me help you." Padmé's dressing in water imagery, evoking purification and baptism, suggests she offers redemption for Anakin should he choose to take it; however, he ignores the message and her advice through the film. "Worship of the anima … brings the serious disadvantage that she loses her individual aspects. [This] can create endless trouble because man becomes either the victim of his erotic fantasies or compulsively dependent on one actual woman" (Von Franz, "Individuation" 188). Even as Anakin idealizes Padmé and ignores her words, he has become so dependent that he cannot risk letting her die. With this, she becomes his weakness rather than his partner.

Next, the Jedi ask Anakin to spy on Palpatine. This not only insults and disgusts Anakin but reveals to him that the Jedi have strayed from their high-minded ideals. "You're asking me to do something against the Jedi Code. Against the Republic. Against a mentor and a friend," he protests. If they have become corrupt, perhaps their warnings about Palpatine and even the Dark Side are less than righteous.

At the opera, shrouded in black, Palpatine uses this unworthy request to drive the wedge in further: The Jedi, as he insists, are afraid to lose their power. As he adds, the Jedi and Sith are not so different. In turn, Palpatine knows Anakin's weakness and offers him the one thing he wants most— Padmé's safety. Once again, the shadow voices the dark thoughts from within, a person's selfish longings he's never let himself experience. Beaten down by worry, fear, and exhaustion, Anakin is very susceptible to anything that can save his beloved. Palpatine tells the story of his own mentor, Darth Plagueis "the wise," a forbidden story he insists the Jedi keep secret. "It's a Sith legend. Darth Plagueis was a Dark Lord of the Sith, so powerful and so wise he could use the Force to influence the midi-chlorians to create life." In fact, this is the story of Anakin's birth. As Palpatine concludes, this Sith learned how to save his loved ones from death. When Anakin is hooked, his mentor adds that the power is teachable, but not by the Jedi. Lucas says, "The emperor starts to work on him and make him doubt things, make him doubt his relationship to the Jedi, make him doubt what is good in the universe. He throws out the possibility that he could keep his wife and save her from death. These are all seduction things which cause a great deal of turmoil in Anakin." This, he adds, is the moment at which Anakin "succumbs to the devil" ("The Chosen One Featurette").

At this point, Anakin is only involved in an abstract conversation. This is the descent through the slippery slope, self-assurance that he has not given himself to the dark side or done anything that terrible. Palpatine understands this (having followed this slow path to corruption himself in the *Darth Plagueis* novel). Therefore, he's cautious and supportive while preying on the other's flaws. While the Jedi say pride is unworthy of their order, Palpatine flatters Anakin and acknowledges how special he is. Christensen adds, "He pulls each string with such charming yet evil precision" ("The Chosen One Featurette"). During this sequence, they sit watching hologram planets like lords of the universe. In black side by side, they already appear partners.

Christensen says that the prophecy has particularly made Anakin vulnerable. "I mean, he believes he is the chosen one. He's not doing wrong things knowing that it's having a negative impact. So there's that naiveté to him now that wasn't there before. It makes him more human in a lot of ways" ("The Chosen One Featurette"). Of course, one could argue that Anakin's fate is predestined—thanks to the midichlorians, to prophecy, to his unstoppable, unsought love for Padmé. One could also blame the Emperor, who has helped these along. In the storytelling sense, the Emperor is the embodiment of pure evil. Thus, his temptation of Anakin and later temptation of Luke (accompanied by Vader's rejecting him at last) symbolizes their relationship with evil incarnate.

"If Obi-Wan was, as Anakin sometimes said, the father he never had, then Palpatine was his wise uncle, advisor, mentor in all the ways of life outside the Temple" (Luceno, *Labyrinth of Evil* 28). Anakin is willingly tutored by this force of evil and so, only somewhat wittingly, succumbs to evil himself. The Chancellor also emphasizes his friendship and trustworthiness: he tells Anakin that the younger man need not conceal secrets—his marriage to Padmé, his raging slaughter of the Sand People, his angry killing of Dooku—as he conceals them from the Jedi. "Do you understand that you need never hide *anything* from me? That I accept you exactly as you are?" (Stover, *Revenge of the Sith* 273). For the choked-off, frustrated young man, this is a great gift. Palpatine points out that the Jedi train everyone to be selfless, but that Anakin, raised as a normal child with a loving family, cannot embrace this as the temple-raised children can. "You're different, Anakin. You had a real life, outside the Jedi Temple. You can break through the fog of lies the Jedi have pumped into your brain" (Stover, *Revenge of the Sith* 278). He urges Anakin to take what he wants—a loving family, ambition, power. This is a human path, giving in to emotion and desire, not self-denial. After over a decade of repression, Anakin is desperate to embrace all this.

As he drops these seductive words, Palpatine finally reveals himself as the Sith Lord. Anakin pulls his lightsaber, but the emperor fights a different way, coiling Anakin in his tempting voice. "I know what has been troubling you.... Don't continue to be a pawn of the Jedi Council!" He promises Anakin a life of greatness beyond ordinary Jedi and that he can save Padmé from death. They circle each other as if dueling. Anakin insists he'll turn Palpatine over to the Council, but he's still uncertain. When he finally reports his discovery to Mace Windu, he fumes when Mace insists he remain behind. As he waits, he hears Palpatine's whisper: "You do know, don't you, if the Jedi destroy me, any chance of saving her will be lost."

Anakin arrives just as Mace Windu holds Palpatine helpless. However, the Sith lord hurls lightning and Mace sends it back at him. With his face deformed by force lightning, his inner self finally reflects the outer. The visual dictionary adds, "'Always two there are'—not only master and apprentice, but persona and true face. Unmasked by deflected lightning during his duel with Mace Windu, the Sith Lord's true face is revealed to the world" (Luceno 60). In the novels, Mace has the gift of seeing which people and moments can completely change the course of the galaxy. This is such a moment—focused on Anakin. Here, he will destroy the galaxy or save it. This mirrors the struggle within, in which he will choose light or darkness.

However, from his point of view, Mace is the betrayer. With Padmé's life at stake, Anakin insists, "He must live. I need him," even as Mace prepares to kill his helpless foe, in what appears a betrayal of Jedi principles. Desperate, Anakin slices Mace's arm off and Palpatine kills him.

After choosing this side in a moment of panic, Anakin mourns, "What have I done?" However, he realizes there is no going back. Having gone too far down this slope to return, Anakin kneels and pledges loyalty, becoming Vader from this moment on. As Anakin stands, stooped a little, his old self is gone. He is now pure Vader, visually paying constant homage to his new master.

Sidious names Anakin "Darth Vader"—since the latter word means father, this symbolically ties into his role as expectant father to Padmé's twins that has prompted his transformation. *The Book of the Sith* suggests Darth means "triumph over death" or "emperor" in ancient galactic languages (Wallace 72). The new Vader quickly falls into his mentor's patterns. Both Darths have their faces turn a sickly yellow white "in anger" (Luceno, *Revenge Visual Dictionary* 61). Vader also begins walking with his hood up, suggesting his desire to disguise himself.

On the spot, Palpatine sends Anakin on a mission that proves his loyalty and means crossing another line—he must go to the temple and kill all the Jedi there. The temple is a place for man to commune with God and ascend spiritually. However, Anakin in his hubris sets himself as the new god-king of Coruscant. He murders everyone there, rejecting its symbolism. The temple is "a spiritual world center; the earthly counterpart of the heavenly archetype; the dwelling place of divinity on earth; the sheltering power of the Great Mother" (Cooper 169). All this he tears apart in himself and for the galaxy.

After this slaughter, the Sith Lord sends him to Mustafar, a planet of flowing lava and sulfurous skies. "On hellish Mustafar the final acts of the Sith plot will be played out, resulting in the deaths of enemies, the deaths of friends—and, ultimately, the death of love" (Luceno, *Revenge Visual Dictionary* 7). There, Vader kills the leaders of the Trade Federation and reaches the film's climax. When Padmé arrives, frantic with worry, it's to find Darth Vader in Anakin's place—in the novelization, he wears his old self like a disguise: "He spent a moment reassembling his Anakin Skywalker face: he let Anakin Skywalker's love flow through him, let Anakin Skywalker's glad smile come to his lips" (387).

She still acts as his anima, urging him to listen to the love and gentleness within. "You are a good person. Don't do this," she insists. "Come away with me. Help me raise our child. Leave everything else behind while we still can." Her pregnancy, more evident than ever, silently urges him to accept fatherhood, normalcy, and goodness.

He could give in to this temptation, retire from the Sith and go with her to Naboo. However, he's filled with power-lust now. Having stepped on the dark path, he now revels in what it offers, insisting, "I am more powerful than the Chancellor. I can overthrow him, and together you and I can rule the galaxy. Make things the way we want them to be." She's shocked at his tyrannical desires even as he scoffs at her morality. More than ever, he's dismissing her actual wishes. Further, when Anakin sees Obi-Wan, his paranoia takes over. "You're with him. You brought him here to kill me!" He chokes his beloved Padmé and she falls. Symbolically, he has killed the voice of gentleness and goodness within himself.

Obi-Wan comes down, and they circle, each in short Jedi tunics, Obi-Wan's white, Anakin's black. Hero and shadow finally face off in their epic duel. Further, Obi-Wan confronts him with the truths Anakin doesn't want to hear: "You have allowed this Dark Lord to twist your mind until now ... until now you have become the very thing you swore to destroy." He draws a blue lightsaber, mirroring Anakin's, and they fight. In their spectacular duel over the lava, they are equally matched. Symbolically, the light-dark battle for the galaxy could go either way, superimposed as it is against Yoda and the Emperor's. At last, the young Sith is defeated—not so much by Obi-Wan as by his own arrogance. Obi-Wan leaps from the lava river to safety on the bank. He yells, "It's over, Anakin. I have the high ground."

"You underestimate my power!"

"Don't try it."

The young Sith, who has won so many battles and bragged throughout the film of a power greater than the Jedis,' flips over to Obi-Wan's position, but Obi-Wan cuts his young apprentice at the knees, then instantly slices off his left arm. Vader's dismembered body, helpless, rolls down toward the lava. His metal arm gropes at the crumbling soil but isn't strong enough to save him. This moment, grotesque as it is, follows the traditional steps. Dismemberment is "the death and rebirth symbolism of initiation; the necessity of the death of the self before reintegration and rebirth" (Cooper 52).

His sword rolls away, and Obi-Wan takes it. The sword is a hero symbol, divinely endowed as a sacred trust. In his case, the Jedi took Anakin on the quest to find its crystal and fashion it, but Anakin the Jedi is dead. Like King Arthur, now that he is no longer worthy, he must return the sword to the larger universe for the next hero to take up. "Often the breaking or loss of the sword signaled the loss of royal authority or of heroic mana, and the hero's consequent death" (Walker 31).

Baptism by fire burns away that which is not needed (in this case Anakin's handsome face and the limbs through which he interacts with the world). Without them, he is only a mind and a knot of emotion—love, fury, frustration, and ambition. His impulsiveness and desire for the physical vanish with his skin and his limbs. Certainly, this is a spiritual death for Anakin. It's implied their medical technology is so sophisticated that losing one hand needn't be an overwhelming loss. However, losing both hands (and legs as well!) suggests losing one's connection to one's fellows. Vader can only be reborn as a cybernetic monster. In his analysis, Campbell compares Vader to Faust—the machine gives him great power, but he loses too much including "what the human spirit wants and needs" (*Hero's Journey* 182).

Visually, he dies as Anakin as the Emperor encloses his remains in the black suit. Horrific black medical droids covered in sharp appendages transform the newly cyborg villain. Here, black means "evil; the darkness of death; shame; despair; destruction; corruption; grief" (Cooper 39). In Christian tradition, it represents the Prince of Darkness, spiritual emptiness, and corruption. When he rises from death, he has become a monster, fully in service to evil.

Still, he asks for Padmé. This moment undercuts his darkness, emphasizing that he still loves. However, Palpatine lies that Anakin has killed her to destroy that love and cement his rage. As the room crumples in his fury, Anakin's transformation is complete. Now Anakin realizes that at the crucial moment when Padmé tried to take him away with her he was only thinking of himself. In return, he will be alone with only himself forever (Stover, *Revenge of the Sith* 417).

A recent series of comics explores the newly established Vader's path to complete his descent with new lightsaber and fortress, as he takes command of the Inquisitors from the *Rebels* show and exterminates surviving Jedi. In the first collection, the Emperor sends Vader questing to kill one of the last Jedi and take his lightsaber. Vader is defeated and only wins when he attacks civilians, forcing the Jedi to split his energy saving them. Here, Vader learns that the power of darkness comes from endangering the helpless. After this, the Emperor directs Vader to Mustafar, where he is to harness the well of dark energy and use it to corrupt the Jedi's kyber crystal and make it bleed. There, the green crystal smashes his eyepiece and a human eye peeps through. On the spot, Vader has a vision of coming to his senses, taking the light-filled green saber and challenging the Emperor. The pull of the light is his new weakness, the new shadow whispering from within. However, he refuses this path, insisting, "This is all there is." With this, he chooses darkness. He pours all his pain, fear, and loss into the crystal and turns it.

Not only is Vader tested by the Emperor, but also by Imperial officers who feel that he has no place in their hierarchy. Thus defied, he demonstrates his brutality to gain their respect. In fact, the Dark Lord of the Sith disposes of many human obstacles to claim his place at the Emperor's side. He also turns on allies because his power derives from pure hate and rage. Observing these patterns, the Emperor tells the newly changed Vader, "My friend, at times I think you might kill every being in the galaxy. With the Jedi gone, very few opponents remain who are worthy of our skill and power. It can be ... deadening, I know" (Soule, *Legacy's End*). Evoking the Empire's racism, Palpatine urges him to see "lesser beings" as a target for his dark emotions. The Emperor also observes later that if Vader does his job, people will always hate him and plot against him. "And so you will never lack for people to destroy."

In collection 3, *Fortress Vader*, he chooses Mustafar to be his own world. Vader admits only that he has found a well of dark power so deep that anything seems possible there. The Emperor is amused: "Perhaps your Padmé does await you on Mustafar. Perhaps the dark side will bring her to you. Go. I think one way or another, you will learn a great deal. That is good." Indeed, at the Emperor's urging, Vader studies the memories of an ancient Sith lord who sought to freeze time and pierce the veil of death. However, the Sith lord warns him that they serve the dark side, not the reverse. "If we do not serve … if we fight the will of the dark side, try to control it … then … well … just look at you." Dismissing this advice, Vader continues trying to force the dark side to bring him his goal, Padmé, but he fails. Deep in meditation, descending through the images of all his victims, he finds Padmé and begs her to come with him. However, he still doesn't understand her desires. "Anakin Skywalker is dead," she tells him and falls from her balcony, surrounded by red lightning. Ultimately, he can see through the door to the other side but not pass through. Thus, he learns the limitations of his power.

Vader's castle came from the old MacQuarrie designs, described in the script as "a towering, monolithic obsidian fortress of stark, brutalist design" (Kushins 175). It is empty, comfortless, and stark, like himself. "The foreboding setting is a place of refuge for Vader—the violence and turmoil of the roiling purgatory outside the castle walls providing scenery appropriate for a Dark Lord, while also illustrating the evil of his own twisted soul" (Kushins 175). This nods to Vader's image as a dark knight or king, straight out of the medieval or fairytale tradition. It also gives him a stronghold of personal power—set among ancient lava and Sith ruins rather than technological spacecraft.

Beyond this, it's interesting that he has chosen the planet with nothing but ruins—the one where his former friend defeated him and he lost his limbs. More, it's the place where he believes he killed Padmé. Story writer Gary Whitta said, "You realize that he's this crippled, broken, tragic figure—and that what he's looking at through his window is the location where his duel with Obi-Wan took place. The fact that he'd chosen to build his living mausoleum here is a nod to the conflict in him—that he would go back to this place to reflect on what happened to the man he once was" (Kushins 176). He has achieved near-total power, but the price is eternal regret.

Padmé's Romance and Fall

"The lotus depicts spiritual unfolding as it starts with its roots in the slime and, growing upwards through the opaque waters, it flowers in the sun and the light of heaven. Its root signifies indissolubility, the stem the umbilical cord attaching man to his origins; the flower is in the form of the sun's rays; the seed pod is the fecundity of creation" (Cooper 100). Following this imagery, Padmé, whose name means lotus, grows into queen and woman, choosing a path for herself at last.

In fact, Episode II gives her a personal conflict. Portman says, "She really struggles with the career versus romance issue" ("Story Featurette"). At the film's beginning, her safe world is shattered with an attack, one that kills her decoy. Padmé begins the story not just facing her friend's loss but the loss of a part of her—one sharing a resemblance even. Symbolically, she must now carve out a new self.

The true enemies, who plan her assassination and then create a civil war, are the hidden Sith, since Count Dooku works for Palpatine. As with many heroines, her quest is to fight through the layers of paternalism and condescension and find the truth. However, just as Anakin fails his adulthood test, she arguably does too. She remains duped by Palpatine and ends the second film succumbing to selfishness over duty.

The novel *Queen's Shadow* follows her coming to a crossroads as queen and then struggling with life afterwards as a senator. She begins with a mission to free the slaves of Tatooine, acting on Anakin's quest rather than her own. However, duty soon sends her on a new path, even as she relies on Palpatine the patriarch to end slavery (which of course he doesn't). Through it all, she uses her power of disguise and switching with her handmaids to spy and subvert opposition. She also joins committees to befriend Mon Mothma and Bail Organa, gaining sympathy for their slowly growing cause. When she resolves to stay a senator and bring justice to the larger universe, Sabé notes, "You'll be Amidala…. And you'll be Padmé too" (Johnston 333). At last, she's linking her identities and finding wholeness.

After the heroes of the second film flush out the assassin, Padmé disguises herself again, this time as a refugee. Once again, she casts off a life of duty to discover her true desires … this time including Anakin. As the novelization explains: "Senator Padmé Amidala, formerly Queen Amidala of Naboo, certainly wasn't used to travelling in this manner…. She knew that she should be back on Coruscant, fighting the efforts to create a Republic army, but somehow, she felt relaxed here, felt free. Free of responsibility. Free to just be Padmé for a while, instead of Senator Amidala" (Salvatore 140).

Leaving the capitol takes her to the magical world, but this is her home, where she enjoys the self beneath the senator's costumes. On Naboo, she flirts with Anakin in dazzling gowns, but ones that are sensual and sometimes skin-baring rather than statuesque and heavy with authority. "I found that with Iain [McCaig, the concept artist] on Episode I, it came easy for him to make Padmé look like an innocent girl who was not aware how beautiful she was, whereas when I drew her in Episode II, she was much more aware of her beauty and sexuality," comments Dermot Power, co-concept artist (Biggar 166). This emphasizes a new, more mature Padmé, no longer child but maiden in love. Though she's falling for Anakin, she holds back from commitment. Portman describes Padmé's struggle as "can I be selfish and fall in love myself when I have all these aspirations and all these things I need to accomplish" ("Love Featurette"). There's also her worry for impetuous Anakin, who stands to lose his Jedi standing. She needs to make the right decision for him as well as for herself. Lucas calls Padmé, "the more mature one, the more rational one, the one that's not letting her emotions run away with her" ("Love Featurette").

A cut scene available on the DVD and on Disney+ gives her more of a personality: Visiting her family, Padmé chats about their lives and shows off photos from her childhood. She wears a white velvet cloak with a dragonfly pattern. Dragonflies symbolize evanescence, fragile beauty that will shortly be lost. As this foreshadows, Padmé's world of family and politics will soon fade away, like her very life. The dragonfly also symbolizes free will, as the glistening creatures fly wherever they wish in all six directions. This mobility comes from maturity and experience, allowing transformation through self-understanding. Thus dressed, Padmé teeters between love and duty, using her wisdom to choose. "As the color of the sky and water, blue symbolizes calm, reflection, and the intellect. It is also the infinite and the void from which all life develops" (Bruce-Mitford 107). Once again, Padmé is developing her power of discernment.

"Men are tested by having to endure pain, hunger, and thirst to prove their forbearance—the strength of self all heroes need to overcome their initiation. Heroines, however, must resist pity, withstanding the claim of what is nearby for the sake of a distant abstract goal," explains the heroine's journey guide *From Girl to Goddess* (Frankel 124–125). In their most intimate scene by the fire, Anakin begs for her love: He tempts her to leave her well-behaved path and give in to the sensuality and selfishness she's always forbidden herself. This too is a shadow confrontation. Here, Anakin's completely straightforward and vulnerable—something that presumably attracts the politician who spends her life in diplomatic maneuvering. As she generally must in fairytales, the heroine confronts the question of giving in to pity or holding herself aloof. Eventually, she gives into love, though the Jedi would have been better served by her remaining resolute. By letting Anakin lead her, she advances to the next lifestage, growing to wife and mother, but this decision is a selfish one. Watching, viewers must suspect how dangerous this relationship will be—if they marry, they will never spend a life together or bring up their children.

In fact, she gives in to pity over and over, supporting Anakin's needs as they fly to save his mother and then Obi-Wan. This too is a traditional goal for the heroine, emphasizing that Padmé is following this traditional arc, however simplistically.

> The true goal of the heroine is to become this archetypal, all-powerful mother. Thus, many heroines set out on rescue missions in order to restore their shattered families: a shy princess knits coats of nettles to save her six brothers from a lifetime as swans, Psyche quests for her vanished lover. Demeter forces herself into the realm of the dead to reclaim her daughter, while Isis scours the world for her husband's broken body. Little Gerda in Hans Christian Andersen's tale quests all the way to Finland to rescue her playmate from the unfeeling Snow Queen. This goal does not indicate by any means that the girls are trying to "stay at home" or "play house." Though they redeem beloved family members or potential husbands, these heroines work as hard as any fairytale hero. And they do it without swords [Frankel, *Girl to Goddess* 4].

As she leads Anakin to save his mother and then Obi-Wan, she embarks on this form of the heroine's journey. It's framed as benevolent of Padmé to attempt to rescue their friends and family to build a larger circle under her queenly protection. Both times, however, they fail in their mission and their arrival worsens the situation, emphasizing the wrongness of their choices. She's putting his impulses before her better judgment, passively supporting her lover as he commits a terrible mass murder on Tatooine. Portman describes Padmé's struggle as "If evil can love, then what is evil? If y'know, love is what makes you human. And then, is someone who is evil human still? I mean, it just makes all the questions involved in the film a lot more complex" ("Love Featurette").

Still, these adventures don't test her spiritually, only physically, and she's soon having Anakin rescue her again. In the quest to save Obi-Wan, she and Anakin venture to Geonosis, another patriarchal, even alien planet where she lacks all power. This is a stronghold of insectoid Geonosians, where she and Anakin find themselves being crushed in a droid factory—the belly of the beast and anti-life stronghold indeed. After this, all three are sentenced to death in the arena with their enemies lording over them. However, at the edge of death, Padmé has a revelation—is she is to die, she wants to choose love. She kisses Anakin and declares her feelings. This moment has given her the revelation that will change her forever. Still, it's not much of an arc.

On Geonosis, she could have confronted her political counterpart and the film's shadow figure, Count Dooku, and wrangled with him using her diplomatic training. In a cut scene, Dooku tells Padmé, while asking her to join the Separatists, "Aren't you fed up with the corruption, the bureaucrats, the hypocrisy of it all? … Aren't you? Be honest, Senator." Of course, this functions as the hero's temptation, the suggestion that she act on her buried impulses and release her anger. In addition, Dooku's offer is most insidious because of its truthfulness. He insists the "cult of greed" and the bureaucrats will overwhelm the Senate and corrupt it past the ability to function. Padmé retorts that she doesn't believe him, but in fact that's just what happens within three years. Though a pawn of Palpatine as she is, Dooku is ironically correct.

The Trade Federation Viceroys, humiliated and defeated in the first film, spend the second one trying to assassinate Padmé for personal reasons. In the cut scene of her trial on Geonosis, Nute Gunray says, "Get on with it. Carry out the sentence. I want to see her suffer." As he plots her murder repeatedly, he makes a viscerally personal enemy for the heroine. However, this confrontation too is cut. In the third film, her gallant knight-turned-villain Anakin kills them on her behalf, though mostly because Darth Sidious has ordered it. With all these scenes gone, Padmé loses the confrontation with her political shadows and the chance to destroy her enemies. The only remaining plot is the thinly suggested heroine's journey within her romance arc.

Revenge of the Sith

With her marriage and pregnancy in the third film, Padmé has abandoned her fierce defense of her people and Galactic freedom to focus inward. She's isolated and has dismissed her decoys, perhaps so she and Anakin can better sneak around. Each day, she gives up more for him. In fact, she spends the movie wanting to withdraw from politics, retreat to Naboo, and raise her family there.

> Focusing on his role as dashing hero, Anakin spends the film treating Padmé as housebound and hysterical—a victim of dark forces he's driven to save from death. The prophetic dream she will die in childbirth—another gothic staple—drives him. Comforting him after his premonition, she wears a vulnerably bare-shouldered pale nightgown, hair loose and curly. The blue-grey silk is trimmed with pearls and a spiral brooch, nodding to luxury and the trim of her wedding gown, but mostly suggesting sorrow as her eyes fill with tears. In the eighteenth century, light blue was associated with the romantics and melancholy—the young lady wasting away from being spurned in love [Frankel, *Star Wars* 95].

Padmé spends the film housebound in nightgowns, suggesting her vulnerability as her hero betrays her. Her "other self," the senator, wears dark, full dresses that conceal her pregnancy, leaving her as masked as Anakin, in her own way. This pregnancy is isolating too, making her keep secrets from her trusted allies.

However, Anakin's increasing rage is the unseen threat in her life. "When the youthful spirit marries the predator, she is captured or restrained during a time in her life that was meant to be an unfoldment," warns Clarissa Pinkola Estés in her groundbreaking *Women Who Run with the Wolves* (50). Padmé's arc, unfortunately mostly cut from the film, is in the deleted scenes and novelization.

Only a glimpse remains onscreen as her eyes slowly open to her predicament. She asks Anakin whether it's possible that the Republic is corrupt and suggests he persuade the Chancellor to back down. When he refuses her, she uses her own political power. Uniting with her fellow senators, she conspires to try preserving the Republic. This select group vow to one another to tell no one about their struggle, setting Padmé at odds with Anakin even as they begin the earliest form of the Rebellion. Finally, she presents "The Petition of the Two Thousand" to persuade Palpatine to set aside some of his war powers. She faces him down in his office. However, Anakin's standing behind him is a source of frustration for her—she is doing the right thing, but this pits her against her beloved. After she leaves, Palpatine drives a further wedge into their relationship, hinting to Anakin that she's clearly hiding something. This shining moment, cut as it detracted from the main plot, is her only act of assertion in a morass of depressed dependency.

> Their relationship deteriorates through the film as he dismisses her political opinions and refuses to confide in her. When he rejects her arguments, she doesn't keep persuading but simply asks to be held. Already she's softening, giving up on keeping Anakin on the side of light. As she describes how much she loved being held by the lake when they had no war to contend with, she's clinging to the past, not who Anakin is becoming. Neither one sees the other honestly—only through a romanticized lens [Frankel, *Star Wars* 97].

Pregnancy is a time of transition for the heroine as she quests for a mother's strength. Padmé still believes that politics can work. However, as she sits in the Senate and sees Palpatine scapegoat the Jedi, he declares their Republic replaced by "the first galactic Empire." To her horror, everyone applauds. The veneer of democracy has been swept away at last, revealing the truth.

Another, more devastating revelation follows. The Padmé that crouches in her home in a soft robe (with silver bars confining her hair like a suggestive cage), insisting over and over that her Anakin could never slaughter younglings is not yet strong enough for the responsibilities of motherhood. First, she must confront the horrors of her life and discover the truth ... even if it kills her.

She follows Anakin to the fire planet of Mustafar in brown pants and tunic a little reminiscent of Leia's *Empire* clothes. At last, she is taking charge and setting out on the quest. Of course, this choice too dooms the galaxy as Obi-Wan stows away onboard. Still, the audience can relate to this desperate emotional choice. Her love theme plays softly, like a dying hope, as she lands.

She confronts Anakin there and discovers the truth. He has slaughtered children and torn down the Senate she believed in—her heroic husband in fact is gone. The most common romantic partner in the hero's or heroine's journey is the shapeshifter, sometimes a monster like Bluebeard under a handsome face. At this point, Anakin has become Vader, wearing his old self like a clumsy mask. With yellow eyes under a drawn-up hood, Vader is all that remains.

Bluebeard is the dark animus who takes over the entire psyche, devourer of the self. The assertive heroine must fight back, protecting those emotional parts of herself, such as intuition and autonomy, that the creature most wants to control. "Today, it is generally understood that the romantic and spiritual man-god—the male ideal worthy of a woman's self-sacrifice and worship, for whom she is expected to set aside herself and her life—simply does not exist" (Pearson and Pope 35). However, Padmé has imperiled her job as senator, given up her female friends, and chosen Anakin over Obi-Wan and her own sense of morality. She has given up all she is to let her beloved take over every aspect of her personality. "Anakin, all I want is your love," she insists.

The questing mother must be a force of independence and strength so she can teach and protect the next generation. Therefore, Padmé must draw back the persona, or layer of good behavior and discover what Anakin is hiding. She confronts him and discovers he's a murderer seeking galactic conquest. "Now the naive self has knowledge about a killing force loose within the psyche," Estés explains (55). Anakin is tearing her world apart and she's finally aware of this. "You're breaking my heart.... You're going down a path I can't follow," she sobs.

So confronted, some fairytale heroines flee, and others kill the evil lover or try. Early sketches had Padmé attempt to stab Vader in this scene—this would have been a good choice as she would have struck to defend the galaxy as well as herself and her babies. This too is cut, leaving Anakin to choke her until she falls. This represents a death-and-rebirth sequence on the edge of her new life stage, though it also gives the men the chance to fight over her. Obi-Wan defends the helplessly collapsed heroine in an epic lightsaber battle, depriving her of agency once more. The droids, tiny helpers like fairytale animal sidekicks, get her to her ship.

When she awakens, her husband is dead, or so they all assume, and she is dying. Further, her babies are coming. Padmé and Anakin lie screaming in parallel scenes, as she gives birth and he is enclosed in the metal suit. This becomes a rebirth sequence for each, but one that she does not survive. The medical droid's assertion that "she has lost the will to live" is highly problematic, since women in childbirth don't die for no reason. "Smart, colorful fan theories have tried to account for the mystery, suggesting the Emperor saps Padmé's life to raise Vader, for instance, or that Padmé's throat injuries really are fatal but she forces herself to live long enough to save her twins. The droid's making an error (or an edit cutting the ridiculous line) would solve matters, but the film doesn't solve the mystery" (Frankel, *Star Wars* 103).

Padmé's children are born and she dies, while Vader rises. With this, technology and the galactic empire triumph as the heroine passes from queen and leader to spirit, though she fails to become a living mother or sage. She dies, living on only in her children and in the rebellion she helped begin. Meanwhile, several novels mention Leia's visions of her mother, a guiding force as she becomes a hero herself.

Padmé's funeral gown is the dark blue of motherhood and sorrow with strings of sequins like sunlight on the waves. A cascade of tiny white flowers in her hair makes her appear floating. Portman notes, "Someone said to me that it was very 'Ophelia.' With the flowers and the hair, it does look like I'm drowning" (Biggar 200). Producer Rick McCallum notes that as costume designer Trisha Biggar envisioned it, "The color—this beautiful azure blue—and the rippled fabric matched the ethereal and melancholy landscape of the Naboo lake retreat at Lake Como, where Padmé and Anakin fell in love. This is where Padmé had wanted to escape with Anakin, and the funeral gown symbolizes her spiritual return to that lake" (Biggar 200). Visually, she has not only passed on but become one with her beloved nature.

Obi-Wan: Failed Father to Sage

In the third film, Obi-Wan joins Anakin in rescuing the Chancellor. He duels Dooku and is knocked unconscious ... and then awakens to a changed world. Dooku, head of the Separatists, is dead. In fact, he's hanging upside down, emphasizing the topsy-turvy shifting loyalties he will find. Fighting their way free involves nearly crashing a ship into Coruscant, but they triumph at last. His optimism, expressed in phrases like "we still have half a ship," will be tested to the utmost as the central stabilities of his life—his friendship with Anakin, the Jedi Council, and the Republic—will all soon be torn apart. When Mace suggests they turn on Palpatine, Obi-Wan is stunned. In the novelization, he thinks, "It was as though the darkness in the Force was so much thicker here on Coruscant that it had breathed poison into Mace's spirit—and was even breeding suspicion and dissension among the members of the Jedi Council" (Stover, *Revenge of the Sith* 154). As the Council are increasingly replaced by holograms each scene, they're divided but also becoming ghostly. All the stable parts of the Jedi establishment are crumbling.

On Utapau, Obi-Wan tracks the last Separatist leader, General Grievous. His companion on this adventure is not a droid but a friendly riding animal. Green and feathered, it links him to the natural world, emphasizing the instincts and emotion he will need to survive. By contrast, the enemy is a cyborg, mostly technology housing a living brain augmented by the Emperor with terrible rage … foreshadowing who Anakin will become. They share an epic lightsaber battle, with the general wielding lightsabers he has taken from murdered Jedi—in this battle, Obi-Wan fights as the Jedi representative and avenger. He finally shoots Grievous in the vulnerable heart, even as his own is about to crumple.

Commander Cody, who'd fought by his side moments before, and had years of partnership with him in the *Clone Wars* show, shoots him. His mount perishes saving him, and Obi-Wan hurtles down the mountainside. His plunge into the lake is a death and rebirth sequence. As he falls, around the galaxy, all the Jedi are shot down, amid rain and tragic music.

The humble helper and friend, in this case, Bail Organa, rescues Obi-Wan and Yoda. In the novel, Obi-Wan sobs for his friends, for Anakin—whom he thinks has died—for the children whom the Jedi vowed to keep safe, for twenty-five thousand years of history, destroyed in a moment (Stover, *Revenge of the Sith* 362). Yoda must remind him to control himself—they are Jedi, and even if they are the last two in the galaxy, they still have a duty to shut down the trap at the Jedi Temple and defeat the Sith. Revitalized, Obi-Wan reconnects with the Force. "Empty, he found clarity. Scrubbed clean, the Force shone through him" (Stover, *Revenge of the Sith* 363).

In the Jedi Temple, Yoda and Obi-Wan discover the nature of their enemy. Acting as Obi-Wan's mentor, Yoda gives him a mission, to his horror: he must kill Anakin, whom he loves like a brother. The film's climax, the fight between Anakin and Obi-Wan, takes place on Mustafar. "Anakin and Obi-Wan have become enemies," explains Rob Coleman, animation director. "The mentor is hunting the apprentice. It's the end of hope and friendship. It's the bowels of hell" (Robertson). Fire is "passion; immolation; change or passage from one state to another" (Cooper 66). Thus, this becomes a crucible as well as a place of transformation.

While the traditional enemy of the questing hero is the father-tyrant, the young villain rebels against the good father. Obi-Wan and Vader are completely equally matched—rival knights fighting for good versus evil. This is cut against Yoda versus the Emperor, which is a different level of fight. The former is personal, the latter political., but both will reshape the galaxy.

Obi-Wan wins, but at a vicious cost to himself and Anakin, as he slices up the other man. The fictitious Jedi handbook describes cutting off several limbs at once as "a forbidden variant" thanks to its savagery. "You should never need to use [it] against a living being given the many alternatives"

(Wallace, *Jedi Path* 76). Humorously, Obi-Wan adds in the book that he can't imagine himself using such a method. This savage act of fury and despair also symbolizes taking apart the self and reassembling. The Jedi are nearly destroyed now and none of the old ways of surviving in the universe will work any longer. At the same time, Obi-Wan has stepped very close to darkness to defeat Vader.

Seeing his friend defeated and helpless, Obi-Wan releases his misery: Anakin was supposed to balance to the Force and destroy the Sith. He has lost his faith in the prophecy. All his illusions, like Anakin's raging, dismembered body, have been burned away. This suggests purification—reducing the self to its essence.

"I hate you," Anakin howls. He lies as a visual image of the rage and pain Obi-Wan has rejected in his life, cut to pieces and impotently howling. The lava takes him over. Fire often represents "truth and knowledge as consumers of lies, ignorance, illusion and death and as scorchers of the impure" (Cooper 67). With this young rebellious side of himself singed away, an older, wiser Obi-Wan can emerge.

Watching him burn, Obi-Wan realizes he still loves his best friend, but, achieving a moment of enlightenment, lets Anakin go. "In the end, he was still Obi-Wan Kenobi, and he was still a Jedi, and he would not murder a helpless man. He would leave it to the will of the Force. He turned, and walked away" (Stover, *Revenge of the Sith* 407).

At film's end, Yoda's final mission to Obi-Wan—not only to watch over Luke but to train at communication with lost mentor Qui-Gon—gives him a new path. Here, Yoda emphasizes Obi-Wan's next stage: no longer patriarch on the Council but grandfather-mentor to Luke with one foot in the spirit world. The film ends with baby Leia's adoption, then Luke's complete with his music. Though the heroes have fallen, a new one rises.

The Jedi vs. the Sith

The original Jedi concept was, of course, that of an order of monks. "Jedi robes are virtually indistinguishable from the simple robes worn by many species throughout the galaxy. This signifies the Jedi pledge to the service and protection of even the most humble galactic citizen" (Reynolds and Fry 23). Brown monklike robes suggest leaving the material concerns of the world. They emphasize the wearer's degradation and sometimes penetrance as he embarks on a spiritual path. Liam Neeson comments, "The look of these costumes taps into concepts that we all subliminally recognize. They tap into a void we have as human beings. We have lost something; we have lost an oral tradition of storytelling, of myths and legends.

I sense that my character, this Jedi, is a kind of Samurai, a very special and spiritual breed of people with great powers, great humility, and great learning" (Biggar 11).

Their enemy, the Sith, have more distinctive looks from Darth Vader's helmet to Maul's startling tattoos. Jedi travel throughout the galaxy, fulfilling missions on behalf of the Council and acting largely interchangeably. By contrast, Sith act for themselves, creating frightening names with lordly titles. "The Jedi conceal themselves in their hoods, not for the purpose of deception, but only for anonymity and humility. For it is their affiliation, not their personal names, that earn the esteem of others" (Hanson and Kay 59). The Sith, on the other hand, hide their identities in order to manipulate. Their names are chosen to invoke fear of their power.

In each of the prequel films, the Jedi exist at their height, with thousands of them training in the Temple and embarking on missions for the Council. All three films show the Council uniting (or fragmenting at times) in their struggle to battle the Sith ... a struggle they finally lose.

The return of the Sith worries the Jedi Council, who end *The Phantom Menace* wondering who remains—the apprentice or the master—and whether they face more violence in the near future. Darth Maul affects them little more than this and makes an adversary just for Qui-Gon and Obi-Wan. He is a violent warrior but not a cautious planner. However, the next two films see the Council itself face the growing enemy threat as they confront their collective shadow.

> The current war had been the result of a thousand years of careful planning by the Sith—generations of bequeathing knowledge of the dark side from mentor to apprentice. Rarely more than two in each generation, from Darth Bane forward, Master and apprentice would devote themselves to harnessing the strength that flowed from the dark side, and to making the most of every opportunity to allow darkness to wax. Facilitating war, murder, corruption, injustice, and avarice when—and wherever possible. Analogous to introducing a covert malignancy to the body politic of the Republic, then monitoring its spread from one organ to another until the mass reached such size that it began to disrupt vital systems... [Luceno, *Labyrinth of Evil* 135].

Palpatine cultivates his appearance as "an enlightened leader, capable of saving the lesser masses from being ruled by their unruly passions, jealousies, and desires. In the face of a common enemy, real or manufactured, they would set aside all their differences and embrace the leadership of anyone who promised a brighter future," as the novel *Darth Plagueis* explains (Luceno 123). This book, commencing with Sidious's own mentor Plagueis killing his teacher, details Palpatine's rise to power from a spoiled aristocrat on Naboo. After killing his family so he can wield his ambition unchecked, he moves to Coruscant and becomes a politician, with his mentor Plagueis as the power behind his throne. He learns to court admiration but also to hide and sneak about, consorting with the criminals of the lower levels.

His mentor has told him, "To we who dwell in the Force, normal life is little more than pretense. Our only actions of significance are those we undertake in service to the dark side" (Luceno 38). From the first, all Senator Palpatine does is empty gestures—only his life as Darth Sidious matters. This foreshadows his arc in the prequel trilogy—his political moves are hypocritical and shallow, as he moves the galaxy's real players with brilliant strategy. The pair also discuss their contempt for the Jedi hypocrisy and naïve insistence on morality. Thus, they make it their duty to tear them down, beginning by clouding their vision.

Palpatine is the one to propose young Padmé for queen—a malleable, naïve girl who's the daughter of unworldly mountain folk. With his aid, she wins the election (Luceno 298). He also builds up the Trade Federation, even as he aids them as Darth Sidious. Further, he and his master channel the dark side to its utmost and actually compel it to conceive Anakin. As time goes on, he adopts Maul and discusses the Jedi's flaws with Dooku, recruiting new followers for himself. He considers all subordinates to use as he pleases, of course, rather than friends or beloved students. With this, the power of the Dark Side grows.

His greatest weapon is the Jedi self-assurance—that the Sith are gone, that even a clouding of their senses is nothing to worry about. They ignore prophecy and dismiss human weaknesses, while Sidious glories in learning about them and twisting them to his own ends. "Two hundred years before the coming of Darth Sidious the power of the dark side had been gaining strength, and yet the Jedi had made only minimal efforts to thwart it. The Sith were pleased by the fact that the Jedi, too, had been allowed to grow so powerful, because, in the end, their sense of entitlement would blind them to what was occurring in their midst" (Luceno, *Labyrinth of Evil* 135).

Even as he appears an avuncular councilor, Palpatine tempts Padmé into appointing him to power—preying on her trust. This she does and the galaxy is doomed. Of course, his kindly manipulation is the source of his power. "His disguise is literal and figurative, in that his identity is hidden to us, and he is manipulating events from behind the scenes, never in the forefront. This is an archetypal manifestation of the 'shadow' side of one's personality" (Hanson and Kay 61).

Count Dooku is the enemy of the second film. At this point, two hundred systems have joined him and the separatists. He is a rebel; moreover, he is a Sith. To this point, only Obi-Wan has battled a Sith lord and survived—it's suggested the others have not seen one in living memory. As the traitor who abandoned them, Dooku is a shadow figure for all the Jedi in *Attack of the Clones*. When Master Windu confronts him at the arena,

Dooku smirks, telling him the disturbing truths the shadow always reveals, which the hero always fears is true: "Brave, but stupid, my old Jedi friend. You're impossibly outnumbered." A hundred Jedi against countless Geonosians and a thousand battle droids may indeed be doomed. In fact, Mace and his Jedi fight bravely, but are defeated. When Mace refuses to let his people be hostages, Dooku looks regretful. "Then, I'm sorry, old friend. You will have to be destroyed."

Matthew Stover's novel *Shatterpoint* follows Mace Windu through an adventure as he wrestles with his guilt from the events of the second film. If he had killed Dooku, an entire war would have been prevented. Mace once considered Dooku a friend and was personally hurt in the film's novelization at his betrayal of the Order (Salvatore 60). At the time, he felt the connections Dooku had forged with the Separatists. "I could feel that without him to maintain its weave, to repair its flaws and double its thinning strands, the web would rot" (4). Dooku was the war's shatterpoint.

Mace discovers through the course of the novel that Jedi fighting as soldiers, killing others and choosing who will live and die, takes a hideous toll. Becoming soldiers means they are losing themselves as Jedi. He realizes their true enemies are not Separatists or even Sith but "power mistaken for justice. Our enemy is the desperation that justifies atrocity" (406). He decides Anakin must be their true shatterpoint, the one prophesized to end the darkness and restore them to the light. "If he is—if Anakin is the being born to win that war—it does not matter if every other Jedi in the galaxy died," he decides, prophetically (406).

When Anakin and Obi-Wan pursue him in the second film, Dooku proves more than they can handle. Impulsive Anakin rushes him, and he knocks Anakin out with Force lightning—something they haven't seen before. Dooku then engages Obi-Wan. "I have spent the last ten years learning to use the power of the Dark Side. It gives me infinitely greater power," he smirks. He has also spent more decades dueling and is a far superior swordsman. His actor calls him "A man of immense power—mental power and physical power" ("Story Featurette"). Defeating him will require true maturity and wisdom from a greater master than himself ... his old teacher Yoda.

Meanwhile, Dooku is defending his territory, while all the Jedi become compromised, not just Anakin. Their new clone army of unnatural slaves has little morality, while creating them is a further immoral act. Further, the Jedi are the aggressors on Geonosis. Mace has insisted that the Jedi are "keepers of the peace, not soldiers," but he brings a small Jedi army into battle. "He has turned to both aggression and technology and in so doing has taken further steps away from the light side" (Bodden 68). Mace mourns in *Revenge of the Sith*, "How have we come to this? Arresting a Chancellor.

Taking over the Senate—! Dooku was right—to save the Republic, we'll have to destroy it" (267).

Yoda, ignoring this imperative to a greater extent, leads an entire army and arguably begins the Clone Wars in that moment. Of course, on Geonosis, Yoda's parrying of Dooku's Sith lightning, according to the novel *Labyrinth of Evil*, suggests Yoda has faced the Sith and studied their methods (Luceno 169). Yoda is the smallest, humblest Jedi, leaning on his walking stick and appearing quite dismissable. He is the perfect Jedi, embodying all of their humility and wisdom. In an antithesis to Dooku, he cares nothing for superiority: "Count Dooku. No interest in contests, do I have," he insists. Thus, his becoming compromised in this film is quite symbolic. Still, he defeats Dooku, and when the count flees, Yoda protects the two fallen Jedi from hurtling equipment rather than stopping the traitor. To Yoda, life is always the calling. With this, Dooku escapes to continue the civil war. Lucas says, "It's the beginning of the end of democracy in the republic" ("Story Featurette"). Shadow and hero have faced off, but the shadow has won.

Dooku continues as an adversary through the Clone Wars. He recruits and trains his own apprentice, Asajj Ventress, and teams up with villains like a resurrected Maul. The *Revenge of the Sith* novelization reveals that Sidious has promised Dooku capture and a safe cell as the war concludes. With Palpatine's new powers he can then rule the galaxy and appoint Dooku to a position of power. "Blinded by pride, Dooku has failed to grasp that, like Darth Maul before him, he is little more than a placeholder for the apprentice Sidious has sought from the beginning: Skywalker himself" (Luceno, *Revenge Visual Dictionary* 13). Anakin kills Dooku and swiftly takes his place as the new Sith apprentice. The universe's fall to the Dark Side is complete.

Yoda Battles the Emperor

In the first film, Yoda acts as Council member, ruling on Anakin's training and on the Force. Yoda has his own fears, which lead him to reject Anakin from the Jedi. With this, he ignores the will of the Force, an act with many future repercussions. In the second film, he becomes more active, investigating the clone army and bringing them to save the day when the Jedi battle is nearly lost. With this, he shows cleverness in knowing when to seek help rather than rush into battle—he contrasts with the other Jedi, especially impetuous Anakin and Obi-Wan. In fact, he saves the latter two after his stunning lightsaber battle with Dooku, his former student.

Of course, Yoda remains unaware of his nemesis the dark lord of the Sith. Still, for the audience, the pair mirror. "Like the Dark Side itself, the

Emperor is hard to see and an obvious foil to Yoda. Both Yoda and the Emperor are ascetic devotees of the Force. Both wear simple robes. Neither is tempted by bodily pleasures. Both appear to live monkish lives of religious devotion," William O. Stephens explains in his essay on stoicism in the series (24). Like Yoda, the Emperor has a serious mind and the deepest commitment.

Unlike in many hero's journeys, Yoda remains unaware who his nemesis is. Through most of the three films, as well as the *Clone Wars* show, he faces off with the Sith lord's apprentices

> He had an image of himself drawing aside a veil only to find another, and another beyond that. The dark side frustrated his every effort to see clearly. The experience was still something new to him. Even though he'd had centuries to grow accustomed to foreboding, he had lived far longer without it. The dark side never completely disappeared—it scratched at the surface like an insect crawling across a transparisteel panel—and he had been able to sense its incremental increases in strength when the Jedi erred, or when the Republic erred, and soon the two were hand in hand [Luceno, *Labyrinth of Evil* 252–253].

In the third film, he begins as advisor, but once again must leave for battle. At last, the veil is cleared from his eyes. On Kashyyyk, he feels it as his Jedi allies are slaughtered, and he only escapes through his friendship with the Wookies in their tree world. Next, he and Obi-Wan reach the Jedi temple and discover Anakin's murders. Yoda insists, "Destroy the Sith, we must." With their identities revealed, the path is clear.

Facing down Palpatine is his great moment of arrogance. Yoda enters Palpatine's holding office beneath the Senate Rotunda and flattens the red guards with a single Force push. "Nine hundred years of study and training, of teaching and of meditation, all now focused, and refined, and resolved into this single moment; the sole purpose of his vast span of existence had been to prepare him to enter the heart of night and bring his light against the darkness," the novelization relates (Stover, *Revenge of the Sith* 386).

They battle in the empty Senate chamber, an amphitheater with an absent audience that shows that this duel is confined yet will decide the fate of the galaxy, did the people in it but realize. The Sanskrit chanting adds gravitas to their encounter. This is the Emperor's place of strength, like the Death Star where Jedi lack power. They represent the incarnation of two philosophies, light and dark. Yoda insists, "Faith in your new apprentice, misplaced may be, as is your faith in the dark side of the Force."

As they duel, the Emperor blasts him with Force lightning and then gloats and cackles as he lies prone. Yoda fights the Lord of the Sith but soon finds himself crawling away, through the crawlspaces of the Senate chamber, defeated by the might of the pure tyrant. The Emperor is in his prime, climbing to total ascendency, while Yoda is aging and transitioning to sage.

He lacks the pure raw might to topple such a force. Still, the pair are tied through the reflection of the shadow. "Yoda realizes he is overmatched and deserts the fight, perhaps because his spirit has been broken by so many Jedi deaths" (Luceno, *Revenge Visual Dictionary* 35). "Into exile I must go. Failed, I have," he decides sadly.

The novelization gives his story a twist: In the midst of battle Yoda realizes that new techniques are needed to defeat the Sith. "He knew, at that instant, that his insight held the hope of the galaxy. But if he fell here, that hope would die with him" (Stover, *Revenge of the Sith* 397). After, he indeed regroups and much more humbly plans with Obi-Wan. He will no longer be a Jedi master but a recluse hiding on Dagobah. Further, he has realized all he still must learn and becomes a student again as Qui-Gon returns from death to advise him.

The final *Clone Wars* episodes take him on a hero's journey arc as he investigates a strange pull from the Force. In a sensory deprivation chamber, he hears Qui-Gon call him to a distant planet. While the Jedi Council fear he's going mad, he escapes them with Anakin's help. In a glowing nebula, he shuts off his instruments and lets the Force guide him. Giving himself over to pure faith is only one test of many. It carries him to the planet where life is created and where the midi-chlorians are made, the planet where the Living Force and the Unifying Force are one. When he lands, he leaves behind his ship, lightsaber, and R2-D2. Traveling on, Yoda meets five priestesses, who each signify an emotion: Confusion, Anger, Sadness, Joy, and Serenity. They agree to train him because they know someday he will train someone of great significance to the universe. They add, "At death, in order for you to preserve your identity, you must know yourself, your true self, and then let go. On that island dwells all that remains unconquered, what, in your existence, some call evil, otherwise known as fear, all which must be finally overcome before the journey can be taken. Free yourself, you must" ("Destiny," 612).

Yoda confidently replies, "A Jedi Master I am. Know all that dwells within I do. Mastered my weaknesses and conquered my fears I have." Of course, he finds that it's not so simple. He battles a shadow of himself, monstrous and laughing. However, rejecting the shadow makes it stronger. It chortles, "You spend your days in the decadence of war, and with that, I grow inside you. Know your true self. Face me now or I will devour you." It needles him for turning to war as all the Jedi have. Only admitting it's part of him makes it fade.

For his next trial, in the Valley of Extinction, Yoda is challenged by temptation. He enters the Jedi Temple and sees a possible future: the dead bodies of his friends lie there. Dying, his student Ahsoka Tano blames him for misjudging her and blindly banishing her from the Jedi Order. A second scenario shows the Jedi at peace and the Clone War never beginning. Adi Gallia, Tiplar, and Qui-Gon all live, joking with Dooku, who's still one of them. However, Yoda rejects this vision, as he accepts the guilt from the other. His regrets come from the students he failed, those he feels he mentored imperfectly or never trusted.

Next, he travels to the original Sith homeworld of Moraband, He faces ancient illusions, from Darth Bane to Syfo-Dias. However, the real Darth Sidious attacks him there, reaching him through his old student Dooku's blood. Yoda duels Sidious, determined to see under his hood. Meanwhile, Sidious attacks an illusion of Anakin, taunting Yoda that he cannot save his friends and battle evil. "Why not let him go? Let him die, and you can stop all that I will do" ("Sacrifice," 613). This taking of hostages threatens the mature teacher, whose students are his vulnerabilities. Yoda keeps Anakin alive, even as he fights, which slows him. Even as he pulls back his enemy's hood, Sidious vanishes. Still, Yoda has passed the test and won the right to train with Qui-Gon. He's also learned a valuable lesson. As he concludes, "No longer certain that one ever does win a war I am. For in fighting the battles, the bloodshed already lost we have. Yet, open to us, a path remains that unknown to the Sith is. Through this path, victory we may yet find. Not victory in the Clone Wars but victory for all time."

In the novelization and a cut scene in the film, Qui-Gon advises him in a trance on how to become eternally conscious and exist forever as part of the Force. This requires the wisdom of sacrifice: "You will learn to let go of everything. No attachment, no thought of self. No physical self." Overcome by this wisdom, offered in a time of such despair to bring a new salvation, Yoda replies, "A great Jedi Master, you have become, Qui-Gon Jinn. Your apprentice I gratefully become." At the end of *Revenge of the Sith,* he tells Obi-Wan that while they wait for Luke and Leia to grow, they can learn from Qui-Gon and come to understand how to ascend to a higher spiritual plane. He thus inducts his old student into this new enlightened state, which both will study as they await the growth of the young hero twins.

Episode IX emphasizes that the Emperor has taken the opposite journey. While the Jedi learn to completely release the self, Palpatine fills a secret planet with ghastly experiments—mutated, suffering clones. All this, he hopes, will produce a single stunted body he can inhabit. As the novelization reveals:

> Plagueis had not acted fast enough in his own moment of death. But Sidious, sensing the flickering light in his apprentice, had been ready for years. So the falling, dying Emperor called on all the dark power of the Force to thrust his consciousness far, far away, to a secret place he had been preparing. His body was dead, an empty vessel, long before it found the bottom of the shaft, and his mind jolted to a new awareness in a new body—a painful one, a temporary one [Carson 220].

There, his minions care for him and continue the experiments. His plan in the final film, to take over the body of his heir, emphasizes his grasping nature. Beyond all the misshapen lives he has created, he's determined to usurp others in order to prolong his existence. This is the ultimate selfishness.

The Original Trilogy

Luke's Classic Journey: Youth to Champion

Despite the starships and blasters, the original epic trilogy has a clear fantasy structure. Lucas comments, "I put this little thing on it: 'A long time ago, in a galaxy far, far away, an incredible adventure took place.' Basically, it's a fairy tale now. *Star Wars* is built on top of many things that came before. This film is a compilation of all those dreams, using them as history to create a new dream" (Rinzler, *The Making of Star Wars* 106).

After the stormtroopers and Leia face off, after the droids leave her ship to wander in the desert, the film introduces Luke. His world is a barren desert, which he and his family scour for moisture. It's an ugly, modern world, not one of magic and enchantment. "Tatooine is both a desert and an alien land and with a clear absence of material from a conscious world using directed thinking. It is the ideal homeland for the hero Luke because it symbolizes his own cognizance: without direction and focus and with reliance instead on his subconscious for decision and function. This is his state before he is called" (Hanson and Kay 138).

Lucas describes casting Hamill because he was "a little younger, more idealistic, naïve and hopeful, a little more Disney-esque" than the competition (Rinzler, *The Making of Star Wars* 124). While the story's earliest version wrote him as a combination of young Force master and tough smuggler, the film version is as innocent and pure as Percival, growing up in the forest with no knowledge of knighthood. Continuing the fairytale pattern, Lucas "saw Luke as an ugly duckling, sort of like Cinderella; he is made fun of and wants to become a star pilot, but when he is confronted with reality, he still thinks like a farm boy. He is simple, honest, and good-hearted" (Bouzereau 22). All adolescents go through this stage, trying to become someone other than who their parents raised them to be.

The original film's costumes are very basic and iconic, instantly recognizable for viewers. Luke wears pale Japanese-cut tunic and britches, foreshadowing the warrior he will become. Desert puttees around his legs link him with his environment. Lucas added a Sergio-Leone Western-style poncho for this space–Western with plenty of samurai heroism, in a combination recognizable across these genres. "Luke was inspired, really, by a Saxon sort of costume. He was a very simple, homespun country boy, and we wanted something which was comfortable and very simple" added John Mollo, costume designer from episodes IV and V (Alinger 37).

A little time in the hero's ordinary world helps set the scene before he's catapulted away on a fantastic adventure. Typically, as these stories begin, the hero has been getting by, coping with an imperfect life. However, a force invades from outside that makes it impossible to continue the status quo. As is traditional, the hero grows up obscurity like King Arthur or Harry Potter, raised by foster parents. Even when they are not cruel, they lack understanding, leaving the hero feeling as if he's living the wrong life. Indeed, Brown says of his character, "Uncle Owen was a straightforward curmudgeon—which I am anyway" (Rinzler, *Making of Star Wars* 141). The novelization of *Attack of the Clones* adds of Luke's foster parents, "The Lars family had only the simple things, mostly the company of each other, to keep them amused and content. For Chegg, this had been the only way of life he had ever known, a lifestyle that went back several generations in the Lars family. Same thing for Owen. And while Beru had grown up in Mos Eisley, she seemed to fit right in" (Salvatore 12).

As the music crescendos, and Luke gazes at the horizon dreaming of better things, he stands before two suns, echoing his solar symbolism. The solar hero is the young questor, son of the sky god and battler of the underworld. This scene also suggests the child and mature hero or father and son duality. Of course, even before he faces Vader, Luke is torn between two ideologies—while on the planet, the droids, Obi-Wan, and his own yearning spirit urge him to leave, even as his uncle insists he stay. After he goes, he continues to be split, as Leia urges him to join the Rebellion while Han stresses independence and caution. The second and third films will add the temptation of the dark side and Yoda's insistence on a spiritual existence removed from the cares of mankind.

"Heralds have the important psychological function of announcing the need for change. Something inside us knows when we are ready to change and sends us a messenger" (Vogler 56). The droids take this role as they bring Luke his mission. They serve as the reminders of a bigger world with a galactic rebellion underway. "Well, if there's a bright center to the universe, you're on the planet that it's farthest from," Luke tells them. Being at the center of everything means knowing the self and being comfortable with it. Luke, however, is stuck on the periphery of his own potential and self-knowledge. Being at the center of everything means knowing the self and being comfortable with it. The adolescent still doesn't fit into his world.

"Our hero feels poised on a new world of experience and understanding, echoing the changes inside as she or he grows into adolescence. Somewhere past the familiar threshold is a world of adventure and new opportunities. The child needs only to step over" (Frankel, *Chosen One*). Luke's friends have already left, and only his irascible uncle's orders keep him around. However, the teenager is growing into his own man.

R2-D2 shows him only a glimpse of a world of tyrants and princesses, intergalactic struggle and desperate need, in the snippet of Princess Leia's message that he plays. Gazing at her, Luke is entranced—she is the damsel needing rescue, the lovely princess who represents a potential love interest (as he thinks). Heroes often project an anima onto someone—their image of an idealized woman. Leia appears to Luke in a quite literal projection—the image of the beautiful princess offering adventure and knowledge of a deeper world. Instantly he's transformed, not just by the literal princess but by what she represents.

Seeking answers, Luke removes Artoo's restraining bolt, suggesting freeing his own curiosity and opportunities. "By removing the restraining bolt from the droid, Luke has unwittingly set the stage for removing the restraint on his own life" (Galipeau 24). Of course, Artoo echoes Luke's restless spirit and enacts his secret longings: he rushes off to find Obi-Wan, dragging Luke on an adventure when the duty-minded teen chases after him. In the desert, they are attacked by Sand People—the savages in the wilderness. They are the threshold guardians on the classic journey—a warning that plunging into adventure will mean threats and monsters to overcome. Battling the creatures is too much for the untried teen and civilization-bound Threepio—Luke faints and Threepio's arm is torn off (the first of many times for him). All the literal dis-arming suggests dismantling the old way of life and finding another path.

Even Artoo, the most adventurous of them, tries to slip into the shadows, until a rescuer arrives, frightening the monsters away with terrible cries. Obi-Wan is the little old man of the forest who appears in fairytales to send the hero on the right path. Like Luke, he wears earth colors—brown, tan, cream. In fact, Obi-Wan's monk's robe appears patched and mended from years of wear. All this emphasizes his humility but also his connection to the land. In his cave, he's a hermit devoted to meditation and higher thought. Mentors, the heroes who have gone on the descent and return journey many times, now are experienced enough to teach others. For Luke, Obi-Wan represents the adult self, "an embodied symbol of what Luke's personality can become, now that it has been awakened by the anima archetype and nudged into life by the droid and the message he carries. Kenobi is a man who has fulfilled his life in a way that reflects Luke's potential, which makes him an excellent carrier for a projection of the Self" (Galipeau 30). Obi-Wan can fearlessly defeat Sand People and understands the wider world he's experienced—all what Luke yearns for in himself.

Obi-Wan wakens Luke and they all set off for his home, where Luke reassembles Threepio and Obi-Wan sorts out Artoo's message. As the mentor, Obi-Wan guides their story to the next stage—understanding the quest. The first mission he describes is not Alderaan but the issue of Luke's father. Obi-Wan presents Luke with Anakin's lightsaber, adding, "Your father wanted you to have this when you were old enough, but your uncle wouldn't allow it. He feared you might follow old Obi-Wan on some damned-fool idealistic crusade like your father did." This is what the lightsaber represents—exotic danger and space battles far from Uncle Owen's farm. Campbell explains, "He gives him not only a physical instrument but a psychological commitment and a psychological center" (Campbell and Moyers 180).

In Tarot, the Suite of Swords represents knowledge and the intellect, with the Ace of Swords in particular depicted as a blade of truth cutting through layers of deception and confusion. "The Bodhisattva carries a flaming sword and this is the struggle for the attainment of knowledge and liberation from desire ... similarly, Vishnu's sword, which was a flaming sword, was the symbol of pure knowledge and of the destruction of ignorance" (*Dictionary of Symbols* 959). In *Star Wars*, swords can bring harm or help, and thus both sides wield them, separated only by their color. The sword is the traditional gift on the hero's journey, a symbol of birthright as well as power.

> Early in his tale, the traditional young hero draws the sword from the stone. This magical sword (wand, lightsaber...) is often a gift from his mentor, left to him by his father, the sword of destiny that only one of true birth may carry. Kit of Duane's *Young Wizards* series makes a car antenna into a wand. Lyra's friend Will has the Subtle Knife, powerful enough to cut anything. In Lloyd Alexander's *Chronicles of Prydain* Prince Gwydion wields the sword Dyrnwyn. Luke has his father's lightsaber, Arthur, Excalibur. Harry Potter finds that "the wand chooses the wizard" and he resonates with the wand that is twin to his nemesis Voldemort's [Frankel, *Chosen One*].

Within the franchise, it's the symbol of a Jedi Knight, judges and sages who have carried these elegant energy blades for a thousand years in their mission to defend peace and righteousness. These Jedi are chosen ones, set apart from the ordinary through their mystic connection with the Force as well as their training. "Their weapons, their way of thinking, what they did, had to be different from everybody else," said Lucas. "So I came up with the lasersword and a lot of different powers." ("Secrets of the Force" 18). Lucas invented this weapon as one that needed willpower more than physical strength. Though Luke hasn't yet heard the larger history (nor had the audience in 1977), this moment shows him claiming the Jedi legacy as one of very few summoned and trained since the Order has fallen.

To Luke, this is a link with the Jedi, and more immediately, the legacy of his father. Of course, word of his father is one of the things Luke has always sought most. "Many times, the orphan's life is dictated by the quest to find his father and with it, his destiny. Upon the discovery of his father, the orphan realizes his place in the family pattern and is allowed to fulfill his role in the nuclear struggle" (Hanson and Kay 142). Luke is desperate for any lore of his missing father, even as he follows his example. The image of Anakin, space adventurer, has always been more compelling than his prosaic uncle's ordinary life. In the novelization, Obi-Wan says, "You see, Luke, that's where your father and your uncle Owen disagreed. Lars is not a man to let idealism interfere with business, whereas your father didn't think the question ever worth discussing. His decision on such matters came like his piloting—instinctively" (Lucas 68). This is the ultimate model for frustrated Luke.

With the lightsaber comes a story that motivates Luke through the film, as well as offering him knowledge of a deeper reality. As Obi-Wan tells it, his evil pupil Darth Vader "betrayed and murdered" Anakin as well as slaughtering the Jedi (clearly steering Luke to destroy Vader rather than becoming his disciple). This highly-edited story falls in with the traditional lore of the mentor: the hero most often quests to defeat the tyrannical dark lord. He represents the wicked all powerful-patriarch—the father figure the young hero must supplant in order to reach adulthood.

Obi-Wan also introduces the film's spiritual component. The Force is like what Jung called the collective unconscious, a level of psychic reality from which religious experience, myth, symbol, and art emerge. Tapping it represents finding one's power of dreams and insight and using it to achieve individuation—to understand and tap the hidden parts of the self. The hero has not yet discovered the wealth of magic and understanding to be found in the unconscious—the realm of dreams and imagination. One guide that can help him reach it is the mentor, who has already undertaken such a journey. No longer an adventuring hero, the mentor is content to train the young hero to face the journey he's already encountered. An even better guide to the unconscious is the feminine presence or anima.

Moments after Obi-Wan reveals the power of the Force, he calls up Leia's message. Luke stops his work as the lovely girl's image flickers before his eyes. Moments later, then watch the message together and receive their specific quest: taking the Death Star plans to Alderaan. Luke hears her voice like a call from his innermost spirit and is driven to help. However, this type of quest is too gigantic, too terrifying as the hero must leave the ordinary world he knows to go adventuring in space. Luke insists he can't get involved. "There's nothing I can do about it right now. It's such a long way from here."

Obi-Wan protests, "That's your uncle talking."—Uncle Owen is the voice of rules and propriety in contrast with the calls to heroism. Still, Luke refuses and heads for home. He insists on refusing his destiny and clinging to ordinariness. All his years of farming and family are hard to set aside. "Despite his misgivings toward his uncle, Luke will refuse the initial call from Obi-Wan because of Owen's words. Owen represents the protective and safe images of a father. At this stage, he is the only patriarch Luke has to follow" (Hanson and Kay 142).

The young hero often loses his or her parents. This forces him to go forward without the protection of mom and dad. Making them unsympathetic or more biologically removed makes the separation less traumatic for the audience. The death can also motivate the hero's revenge. Luke returns home but discovers the Stormtroopers have beaten him there. With his adoptive parents killed by the Empire, Luke makes up his mind. He commits to traveling with Ben and becoming a Jedi.

They head into town, and Obi-Wan demonstrates that he is more wizard than man—using the Force, he can not only understand the world but manipulate it. His ability with the Force obviously emphasizes its power for evil from someone like Vader. "In the hands of a creative personality, relationship with the collective unconscious can have a positive effect as it has through great religious figures like Moses, Christ, and Buddha. It can also have a destructive effect when a person (like Hitler for example) connects to the darker dimensions of collective psychology and has the ability to influence people accordingly" (Galipeau 36). Obi-Wan uses it on the Stormtroopers, murderous villains who are "weak minded" enough to obey evil. With this, he models for Luke a deeper universe of power and potential for adults with the discernment and mental discipline to wield it.

Of course, his example of a Jedi Master is the film's metaphor for a wise and complete adult. Obi-Wan demonstrates a Jedi's chivalry for Luke as he subtly distracts the Stormtroopers rather than killing them. Likewise, he avoids fights in the bar, but attacks swiftly when he cannot pacify the aliens. A hero may defeat a threshold guardian by learning to outwit it through absorbing its lessons. "Ideally, Threshold Guardians are not to be defeated but incorporated (literally taken into the body). Heroes learn the Guardians' tricks, absorb them, and go on. Ultimately, fully evolved heroes feel compassion for their apparent enemies and transcend rather than destroy them" (Vogler 51). Obi-Wan tries sympathizing with the attacker in the cantina—trying to buy the man a drink and talk him out of the conflict. Of course, when the man persists, Obi-Wan simply, elegantly disarms him. Watching wide-eyed, Luke sees the model of a perfect Jedi. When he invades Jabba's palace two films later Luke has fully incorporated Obi-Wan's controlled, suave manner—he's become his mentor at last.

In the bar, Luke meets more monsters of a sort in the spectrum of aliens. Among the untrustworthy are Han and Chewie. Still, wise Obi-Wan discerns that they are rough though altruistic and capable smugglers with the power to aid them. (It should be noted that Han insists on a hefty payment but does in fact fulfill his contract to the letter and beyond without betraying his passengers). "The Ally in dreams and fiction might represent the unexpressed or unused parts of the personality that must be brought into action to do their jobs. In stories, allies remind us of these under-utilized parts and bring to mind actual friends or relationships that may be helpful to us in the journey of our lives" (Vogler 75). The hero's friends traditionally bring skills the hero does not already have—while Luke is a boy and Obi-Wan a monk, Han is incredibly worldly. He's also creative, with his modified ship and talent for avoiding scrapes. "Chewbacca, who mostly growls to express himself, well exemplifies the wild man archetype. With Chewie present, a basic, instinctive dimension is added to the unfolding drama" (Galipeau 38).

Luke learns from the contrasting advice of Han and Obi-Wan as they fly together on the Millennium Falcon. While Obi-Wan teaches faith and obedience, Han is the rebel and skeptic. Artoo is a force of courage and creativity, unwaveringly performing his duty with a tool for every job. Threepio is a pacifist apologist while Chewie takes the direct approach—their holographic game emphasizes this when Threepio lectures on the rules, Chewie threatens to rip arms off, and Threepio instantly capitulates. All these contrasting personalities model potential choices for the hero and guide him to develop all these qualities in himself.

At last they find themselves in the remains of Alderaan, where the Death Star ensnares them and sucks them aboard. "It is a symbol, a black planet of destruction and terror ... technology used at its worst" (Hanson and Kay 333). Destroying an entire planet of noncombatants to terrorize a single girl emphasizes the cruel, whim-driven power of the Empire. Its representative, Vader, kills entire families, his own men, whoever he wishes, as a representative of the equally-brutal Empire.

It is also embodied by the Stormtroopers. "No humanity shines through any crack in the combat gear of these modern soldiers, for to show flesh is to show weakness in the face of a mechanized enemy" (Hidalgo, *Propaganda* 45). Indeed, the Empire is also a place of faceless homogeneity. On board the Death Star, everyone is encased in armor, featureless and uniform. This armor emphasizes an invincibility to being reached or reasoned with—these masked soldiers cannot be deprogrammed. All obey the military hierarchy and its bureaucracy. Tarkin gloats, "The Empire sweeps aside false social constructs in favor of a rule that is clear and absolute. The burdens of unnecessary freedoms have been shed, and centralized power is made plain. No one doubts their place in the new order" (Wallace, *Imperial Handbook* 135). This is represented in the army.

The Death Star is a modern labyrinth of twisting corridors and soulless armies. Vader holds Leia captive in its center. "Its mythic implications are many, representing the mechanical dragon that the hero must slay, the labyrinth that the hero must negotiate, and the insurmountable evil force that only one of incredible valor and strength may overcome" (Hanson and Kay 333). This ultimate machine is built as a tool of galactic terror and also a deterrent, meant to enforce the Empire's domination. Of course, it is painfully flawed. Like the Titanic, the Death Star is built to represent the pinnacle of human engineering, but its prompt destruction instead demonstrates its creators' hubris and incompetence. The heroes defeat the Death Star in many ways through the film: first the heroes hide in Han's smuggling hold to sneak onboard. Next, Obi-Wan infiltrates the ship to switch off the tractor beam, using his powers of sense and misdirection to outwit the mechanical sensors and weak-minded crew in its service. Artoo controls the ship's workings, and Han and Luke masquerade as faceless Stormtroopers. They hide in the garbage chute and escape pursuit. Afterwards, they successfully fly away and finally destroy the entire edifice. Each time, the protocols meant to perfect military might and discipline offer gaps for the ragtag rebels to exploit.

Luke unwillingly waits behind on the Falcon so Obi-Wan can disable the tractor beam, apparently passing the heroics of the story on to his mentor. Still, when Artoo reveals the princess is onboard, Luke finds himself with a new mission, and enlists Han's help. With Obi-Wan absent, Luke takes charge, seizing the leader role as well as the hero one. The novelization observes, "He had grown used to old Ben and Solo giving directions. Now, the next move was up to him" (Lucas 120). Constructing a plan worthy of Obi-Wan for its disguise and misdirection yet using ordinary human power without a trace of the Force, Luke leads his friends to the center of the maze and frees the princess.

"Having survived death, beaten the dragon, or slain the Minotaur, hero and audience have cause to celebrate. The hero now takes possession of the treasure she has come seeking, her Reward" (Vogler 16). Luke escapes with both the Death Star plans and Leia, who can read them and find the Rebel base. All of these are keys to defeating Vader—his true quest. In traditional stories, the hero also saves the princess, marries her, and inherits the kingdom. She represents more than marriage but the anima, the hero's spirituality, grounding, and soul.

> She (the Hero's lover) is the maiden of innumerable dragon slayings, the bride abducted from the jealous father, the virgin rescued from the unholy lover. She is the "other portion" of the hero himself—for "each is both": if his stature is that of world monarch, she is the world, and if he is a warrior, she is fame. She is the image of his destiny which he is to release from the prison of enveloping circumstance [Campbell 342].

Through this film, Luke and Han squabble over Leia more than with her and see her as simply "the princess"—the high-status prize. The audience is encouraged to see her likewise, as she has little growth or change—at this point, she is more icon than character.

Saving the princess also symbolizes the hero's deepening sensitivity. When Arthur meets the Lady of the Lake or Frodo meets Galadriel, the goddess trains him in the mysticism and spirituality he lacks. It's also notable that Luke has parted ways with Obi-Wan and never gets him back as a mentor, except on the spiritual plane. Leia becomes his replacement mentor, tutoring him not just in sensitivity but also duty and loyalty to the Rebellion. She is the voice of caring about larger values, while Han channels selfishness. These represent the warring values within Luke as he creates his future self.

On the Death Star, she also takes over the leadership role, with an experience as a soldier and planner the others lack. When they're cornered, she shoots the wall and orders them all to escape into the garbage dump. As a tentacle snags Luke, he vanishes temporarily under the water in a small death-journey or truly disgusting baptism. "Led to a place by a feminine figure, Luke is trapped by the world of primitive instinct and primal ooze most often associated symbolically with the mother. In a sense, this is the first of many experiences of rebirth for Luke, as he is eventually released from his underwater entrapment" (Galipeau 63). Dropping into this underworld, in this case a watery womb, ensnared by a primordial tentacle from an unseen creature, suggests being overwhelmed by primitive instincts. Only through conscious thought can the hero persevere.

Of course, for the desert-born hero, journeying to the magical world and plunging into its waters represents the opposite of his entire life experience. "Immersion in water not only symbolizes the return to the primordial state of purity, death to the old life and rebirth into the new, but also the immersion of the soul in the manifest world" (Cooper 188). Further, Leia, the first feminine presence in his life who's young, lovely, and lit with motivation, is the one to lead the entire team there, sharing her insight with them all. Under her guidance, the team dive into the waters, symbolically seeking "the secret of life, the ultimate mystery" (Cooper 188).

Nnedi Okorafor's clever short story "The Baptist" builds on this imagery through a surprising new character. It casts the tentacled creature as a force-sensitive who feels the same power coming from Luke and is compelled to grab him. "A shade of him sloughed off, the flesh of this shade pale and delicate looking, naked. It shook off him, the face of this dim version of him wide-eyed, the mouth open, shocked. Then the shade dissolved in the water. Omi's mission was complete" (330). She anticipates her death during the destruction of the Death Star but trusts in an eventual rebirth through the power of the Force. More importantly, it is the Force that has chosen her to anoint Luke in this way. As she thinks after the heroes' escape, "She'd been chosen to baptize him through a sort of death. To her people, water was where life was given. Water was the Great Cleanser When It Was Time to Be Cleansed" (331).

This is known as the Supreme Ordeal—the crucible that tests the hero to the breaking point, the moment at which he might die and lose everything. "First the audience and the witnesses at hand (Han Solo, Princess Leia, the Wookie) see a few bubbles come up, a sign that Luke is still struggling, alive and breathing. So far so good. But then the bubbles stop coming. The witnesses begin reacting as if he were dead" (Vogler 162). He may in fact be dead—and if so, who will the viewers use as their character with whom to identify? When the robots react with horror on hearing Luke and his friends screaming in apparent suffering, the droids stand in for the audience and act out their fears. However, the hero survives. "Luke Skywalker explodes to the surface, slimy but alive. He has died to our eyes, but now he lives again, rebirthed by the companions who help him to his feet. At once the audience feels elated. The emotions ride higher for having been brought down so far" (Vogler 162).

Of course, another danger arrives as the room itself turns on them. As the heroes scream in terror, the trash compactor threatens to crush them all. With help from the rational observers—the droids—Luke and his friends make their way to safety and run for the Falcon, their bird that can carry them away. However, Luke is stunned to see Obi-Wan battling Vader. His two fathers, two potential futures, battle externally even as they fight within him. Lucas adds, "I wanted the father to be Darth Vader, but I also wanted a father figure. So I created Ben as the other half. You have one who is the light half and one who is the dark half.... This sort of gave a twist to the whole story" (Bouzereau 34).

For the same reason as losing one's parents, the hero cannot keep his mentor with him forever. Most stories kill off Gandalf, Dumbledore, or Aslan—leaving the hero to fight his great battle alone. Of course, Obi-Wan has done the team a last service by releasing the tractor beam. Symbolically, they were ensnared in the force of the father's personality, as Luke struggles to become a rebel even when confronted by the patriarchy's overwhelming power. If the Millennium Falcon is caught in the Empire's (or the patriarchy's or the force of evil's) complex, Obi-Wan has released them. As with the droids opening the garbage collection unit, it is the force of rationality and experience (Obi-Wan) who can free the naïve hero from this trap. The key to fighting off the unconscious grip of emotions is Obi-Wan's cosmic self-awareness.

The heroes hope they are free of the morally bankrupt maze, yet the Empire still tracks them. "Psychologically, this is quite significant, representing the fact that we may get out of the grasp of a powerful complex, but it will seek to regain its hold and can, at any opportune moment (not opportune for the conscious ego), try to regain control of us again" (Galipeau 71). A space battle follows, and they fight their way free of all entanglements (or so they naively hope) and journey towards the next stage.

The rebel base on Yavin is built on the ruins of ancient temples, suggesting a hidden spirituality. All this connects Luke to the natural world and the ancient lore of the past—all that the mechanized Imperials have rejected. The scenes were actually filmed at Guatemalan temples. Here, the mystic feel contrasts with the modern, mechanized Death Star. One represents the power of life while the other, their shattering. The evil Empire resolves to destroy all who oppose it—freedom, democracy and choice as well as the ragtag rebels. As the climax approaches, it prepares to destroy the green, vivacious planet and all who dwell there, especially the princess. The fighter pilots are thus defending their way of life and their own families and friends, not just battling evil.

"Heroes may find that surviving death now grants new powers or better perceptions" (Vogler 180). After witnessing Obi-Wan's death (complete with his promise that this will only increase his power) Luke begins to hear his mentor through the Force. This is his first unguided step into a wider world. after all, that is the purpose of initiation—to become an adult who no longer needs guidance. With Obi-Wan only a whisper in his ear, Luke is now the decision maker. At the same time, Obi-Wan's transformation emphasizes the realms of possibility awaiting Luke someday. Director Irvin Kershner notes, "Having Ben come back is almost like Zen, a Buddhist notion that you don't die, that you come back and have to suffer again until you do enough good and decide that you don't want to come back.... Ben in the story is still alive but not corporeal" (Bouzereau 137).

Guided by his mentor and the Force, Luke speeds down the Death Star's trench to destroy it. In this metaphor for his entire journey, past and future, he must fly speedily and expertly, using his insight to save the universe.

Reaching the end of the trench, he makes a leap of faith, shutting off his navigation computer to channel the spiritual. Lucas says, "You'll notice Luke uses [this trust] quite a bit through the film—not to rely on pure logic, not to rely on the computers, but to rely on faith. That is what that 'Use the

Force' is, a leap of faith. There are mysteries and powers larger than we are, and you have to trust your feelings in order to access them" (*The Mythology of Star Wars*). This he does in each film, and this time the Force itself aids him. In fact, his mission is one on behalf of freedom and all the beings of the galaxy. As raging Anakin failed to learn but Obi-Wan always knew, one must act in harmony with the universe and the universe will respond in turn. Luke comments in one of his handwritten notes in *The Book of the Sith*, "I may have been the one who fired the shot, but the Force itself wanted to purge the galaxy of the Death Star. It was the embodiment of everything that's wrong with the Dark Side" (Wallace 151). He destroys the evil machine, freeing the galaxy from its tyranny. With this, everyone is saved.

The film ends with a presentation ceremony. For it, Luke dresses closer to Han, with military striped pants, a black shirt, boots, and an open gold jacket. This demonstrates his grown-up heroism, journey complete as he molds himself after the adult rogue. Of course, Han is not a model of a wise sage like Obi-Wan, only a man a bit more mature than Luke himself. Leia presents the medals. "The subtle subtext that each of these figures is honored with an award for selflessly serving the feminine principle—which, in turn, can help a man become more deeply connected to his true self. For Luke, this means his new connection with the Force and his ability to attune to it; for Han, it means working in relationship with others" (Galipeau 82).

Leia shines in a more elaborate white dress with silver jewelry. To the Buddhists, white means "the highest spiritual transformation through womanhood, 'she who leads out beyond the darkness of bondage,' the Mother of all Buddhas" (Cooper 42). Silver is likewise a sign of spiritual ascendency and purity. Thus, the reward ceremony of being blessed by the princess in white signals spiritual ascension through the goddess. Leia gives them medals but also her smiles, suggesting her love and protection.

Though it's only revealed later, Luke's journey parallels his birth father's. As shown in the prequels, Anakin too grew up on Tatooine until a different bearded Jedi told him he was strong in the Force and had a great destiny. With his companions, young Anakin accompanied Qui-Gon on his mission, only to find himself defending a lovely princess from greedy aggressors. Here, young Anakin saved the day with his fighter pilot skills, only to be rewarded with the young queen's ceremony, followed by Jedi training. The divergence comes from Anakin's eventual selfishness and rage, while Luke passes this test to commit to a more spiritual path. With this, the larger saga shows Luke walking his father's path but repairing it, setting it right even before he restores the galaxy itself.

Certainly, Luke has much further to go. In the 2015 comic book series that follows *A New Hope*, Luke battles Vader and is easily defeated. Vader calls him an "untrained child" and taunts him that he's no Jedi. After, Luke doubts himself, telling Ben's ghost he's just "some stupid *farm boy* from Tatooine." However, when he spies Imperial guns and speeders, he summons his training with flying and shooting womp rats, and charges back into the fight (Aaron, *Skywalker Strikes*). The goal here is not to abandon all the old lessons, but to realize how many can be applied to new situations.

Desperate for training, Luke visits Obi-Wan's home and finds his diary, then seeks out the Jedi temple on Coruscant. He continues to explore the galaxy, seeking sources of Jedi lore as he realizes he isn't prepared for his ultimate destiny. Luke and Han also receive battlefield promotions to salute their increasing skill and commitment. *Last Flight of the Harbinger* has Luke face off with Vader again, fighter to fighter. "Next time I'll be ready," Luke vows. Vader, meanwhile, has discovered who Luke is and seeks to teach him himself. With this, both prepare for their inevitable direct confrontation.

The Empire Strikes Back

As the long-awaited sequel begins, Luke appears tiny on the landscape of a vast, frozen world. He's finally taking his place on a larger universal stage. His dressing in grey instead of beige (as Rey will later) suggests he's becoming morally more complex. He heads deeper into the snow on his tauntaun steed, seeking a fallen meteor. This suggests a questing personality and curiosity—he's literally going off to catch a falling star instead of sticking to his routine. Of course, such heedless creativity is often punished. Luke soon falls afoul of a monster. The eleven-foot wampa is another threshold guardian, a small antagonist for the hero to defeat.

> In psychological terms we would say that Luke's encounter with the Wampa has opened up the unconscious, foul contents and all. He has escaped being swallowed by primitive emotions and is, in fact, receiving protective assistance from the sacrifice of instinctive life (the tauntaun) that must take place in order for the transformation that comes with conscious integration to happen. Now other layers of the psyche speak to him through the vision of his former teacher, Ben Kenobi, so that he can receive further guidance [Galipeau 95].

This small battle brings him unexpected gifts in the form of insights. It also represents a small death-descent as he plunges into the hidden underworld and returns with new understanding. A cave, hidden from the outside world, echoes the hero's inward passage seeking enlightenment through introspection. In the cave, Luke discovers he can use the Force to free himself. He reaches for his lightsaber, brings it to his hand, and slices himself free (the first time Luke accomplishes such a feat onscreen). With this, he reaches a more powerful spiritual plane.

He earns an additional reward even as he passes out from the cold. Obi-Wan returns and offers him guidance in the former of a new Jedi master, Yoda. It's implied that he arrives now because Luke is at last ready. "Perhaps the reason for Kenobi's appearance at this precise moment was the effort used by Luke in the cave and his return from within. For as much as Kenobi and Yoda can aid their young apprentice, Luke must begin to act independently. The discovery Luke makes about himself has to be made alone, for the sake of his own confidence" (Hanson and Kay 182). The hero frequently has trouble returning from the spiritual realm, where he is quickly growing in power unheard of in normal reality. Thus, his friend must come to drag him out. This Han does, telling Luke to stop babbling of his visions and plunging him into the dead Tauntaun's belly. Onscreen, Luke thus undergoes a visual death and rebirth sequence, born from the disgusting body cavity as a new baby—he is no longer a farm boy but an initiate, off to seek training with the guru of the forest. His rebirth is followed by more of this imagery as Luke must heal in a womblike bacta tank.

Likewise, Luke's friends might never leave the planet, save for the attack from the Empire. The Walkers are instruments of terror, emphasized by the ominous music as they suddenly block out the sky on Hoth. "Each footfall echoes with a tremor that is felt long before the walker itself looms into view" the *Imperial Handbook* gloats (Wallace 77). Aghast, rebel leader Mon Mothma writes in the margin, "The Alliance can't use these vehicles. We stand for hope, not fear" (Wallace 76). These mechanized creatures are terror embodied, something more for the heroes to battle.

Risen from his near-death, Luke sets a new course literally and figuratively, and heads to the Dagobah system to find the mentor Obi-Wan has promised him. When he arrives, thick clouds fog his scopes, forcing him to move beyond technology and rely on his instincts. Having the ship sink into the swamp has a similar effect.

Soon after, the tiny creature Yoda arrives and begins unraveling all of Luke's preconceptions. He riffles through Luke's belongings and steals a lantern (representing enlightenment on many levels) with which he taunts the hero. He criticizes Luke's food, his guardedness, and also his perceptions as he dismisses Luke's quest for a "great warrior" with "Pshaw. Wars not make one great." He defends the "slimy mudhole" as his home. Ironically, "yoda" is Sanskrit for "warrior." Here, Lucas enforces that the ultimate warrior is the tiny, deceptively frail master, who nonetheless is indomitable in battle (as Yoda proves in *Attack of the Clones*).

Of course, his goofiness is also a test of patience and perception, one that Luke mostly fails. His dismissal of the strange alien leads viewers to overlook him as well.

> Yoda then acts like a silly beggar. He finds, nibbles on, and discards an untasty snack bar in Luke's supplies. When he fights over a tiny power lamp with Artoo, Yoda looks even sillier. Luke is impatient to find the Jedi master, but the goofy goblin wants to eat first. So our first impression of Yoda is of a solitary, harmless, vulnerable, shabby, hungry geezer with a quirky sense of humor and an odd manner of speech. Yoda's appearance inspires no awe at all [Stephens 30].

With all this, before training even starts, Yoda emphasizes that Luke needs to stop valuing weapons, but instead rely on a cleverer path. "A strange unknown creature lights the way for him. Luke will have to learn how to expand his conscious awareness in order to know how to shed light on the dark and sinister situations he encounters" (Galipeau 108). Yoda invites him to share a meal, to willingly enter Yoda's world, to eat primitive swamp food and see how good wholesome ingredients can be. The entire place is a descent into primitivism and a new way of thinking. Before Luke knows it, he's lurching into the fog after the strange creature. Soon enough, he's sitting down to dinner in a doll-sized house, having abandoned his ship, droid, and equipment, all to try unraveling the odd little man's sentences.

Lucas notes, "I wanted Yoda to be the traditional kind of character you find in fairytales and mythology.... The hero is going down the road and meets this poor and insignificant person. The goal or lesson for the hero is to learn respect for everybody and to pay attention to the poorest person because that is where they key to his success will be" (Bouzereau 167). Of course, Yoda is the woodsman living deep in the forest, the little old man guiding the hero. The conversation between Obi-Wan and Yoda suggests the baggage of the previous generation, as does their continuing presence in Luke's life.

Yoda is revealed gradually, as he's one with the swamp and emerging from it. Indeed, Dagobah is the enchanted forest, a place of magic where the rules no longer apply. It is here that Luke learns to use the Force deeper and more spiritually. This symbolizes the intuition an adolescent must develop to become an adult, through training and experience.

Yoda is framed as perfectly enlightened, living as part of nature like the Ewoks and Wookies: "Yoda's house expresses his oneness with nature, using no technological appliances or fittings. All the furnishings in the house of clay, sticks, and stones were handcrafted by Yoda himself" (Reynolds, *Star Wars Visual Dictionary* 25). His speech patterns suggest riddling as well as unorthodox wisdom. Lawrence Kasdan comments, "I remember that George had a feeling about the kind of speech he wanted Yoda to have. It had to do with inversion and with a kind of medieval feeling with religious overtones" (Bouzereau 176). Soon they were inverting all his words. Director Irvin Kershner says that he adapted Yoda from Zen concepts (Bouzereau 176). He's a mystery for more than Luke but also for the audience. "When Bantam wanted to do the backstory on Yoda," Bantam *Star Wars* novel editor Tom Dupree notes, "George said that was off limits, because he wanted him to remain a mysterious character" (Seabrook).

While Obi-Wan modeled the adult Jedi, Yoda is the pinnacle of wisdom and selflessness, a higher model yet. "The Stoic wise man, just like Yoda, lacks the vices of fear, anger, hate, and aggression" (Stephens 19). He's willing to fight (most notably in *Attack of the Clones* but also in the advice he offers Luke in *Empire*), but never through anger. His placid philosophy lets him be content even in such isolation and simplicity. He lives humbly, in obscurity, in a small mud hut with a simple pot of swamp stew. His patience seems even vaster contrasted with Luke's haste and personal connections. Historically, the Stoics, upon whom Yoda seems modeled, believed this sort of commitment to goodness and abstinence was quite rare. Stoics emphasized interconnectedness and harmony with their environment—all of Yoda's principles.

Under this wise tutor, Luke begins formal training. Critic Judith Barad notes that the exercises are symbolic:

> The first step in the Jedi training Yoda imposes on Luke is intensely physical. Its point is not only to increase his endurance but to provide a crash course in Jedi virtues of discipline and persistence. By developing endurance, a Jedi padawan has the capacity to work his way through difficulties despite the frustration inherent in the task. One will learn to continue striving in the face of seemingly insurmountable obstacles and defeat. Endurance, requiring self-control, provides a padawan with the ability to struggle over an extended time to achieve their goals. On Dagobah, the Jedi Master pushes his young student to the limit. Racing in and out of the heavy ground fog with Yoda on his back, Luke is winded as he climbs, flips through the air, and leaps over roots. Yet, he endures and continues striving [59].

Next comes balance, ascertaining that he can control himself and his surroundings. As he levitates more and more objects, he learns to divide his attention, listen to different problems outside the self even while maintaining perspective. This is a knight's discipline, finding an equilibrium between control and abandon. Lucas's notes for *Empire* focus on what Luke must learn include the following: "control your dream—stop the world"; "erase personal history—give up self-importance"; "use death as an adventure"; "perform each as if it were your last battle on earth" (Rinzler, *Making of Empire* 9).

To teach all this, Yoda is presented as the true embodiment of wisdom. While Obi-Wan lies and confesses to failing Anakin, Yoda is presented as more enlightened. He's also found the balance of a true Jedi, or an earth philosopher. He dismisses adventure and excitement as things a Jedi chooses not to crave. Likewise, he advises Luke to accept and dismiss things beyond his control.

Of course, Yoda also urges Luke to face evil. Its appearance here, without Vader, emphasizes that the dark side itself is the true threat, a constant temptation for the young hero that exists irrespective of the Empire. Offering this lesson is the cave, enforcing how easily Luke could turn. There, he discovers that he contains the dark side within as much as his enemies do. The Emperor and Vader can tempt him to give in to it. Still, this dark side inherently lies within Luke so he is the one who must choose each time.

To achieve Yoda's balance one must understand one's fears and vulnerabilities, facing them to conquer them. Luke enters the cave innocently, assured he's entirely a good person. Of course, this lack of self-knowledge means that he's been constructing his life on a shaky platform. This cave will show him the truth. He brings his saber with him, unwilling to be vulnerable. Yoda does not countermand Luke's decision, but it's possible that by ignoring Yoda's advice to leave it behind, Luke fails a small but vital test.

Within the cave, he must confront his own inclinations for evil and capacity for destruction. His own face reveals that he has a Vader side, much as he hasn't experienced it before this point. Luke even draws his weapon first here—another Vader-like quality. In the novel, he thinks, "He wondered if he were really fighting himself, or if he had fallen prey to the temptations of the dark side of the Force" (Glut 296). At last, he defeats the dark side of himself and beheads it (in contrast to his wiser interaction with Vader in the next film). Still, this beheading suggests controlling his dark side and ending its power. As he frets that he may become Vader, it takes him quite a long time to leave the cave.

His next lessons are cut short. On Dagobah, Luke is mastering wisdom, and he knows it. "Luke truly felt ready to unlearn all his old ways and willing to free himself to learn all this Jedi Master had to teach," the novelization observes (Glut 280). However, sensing that his friends are being tortured makes him lose control. Psychologically, this amount of emotion is too much for the untried hero and overwhelms him. He must either stoically accept suffering in the world or leave Dagobah to act against it and try to save his friends. It's arguable that he fails a great test by choosing the latter.

He arrives as Han is tortured by Vader and finally left near death. The carbonite chamber is horrific, with dark nozzles jutting steam. The red and black room evokes hell. Objects fly at Luke, suggesting that, overwhelmingly, the entire world is against him. As he falls into the freezing chamber but emerges, he's channeling Han, who also descended into this near-death.

Luke, the spiritual side of their joined character, emerges to battle evil incarnate, in the form of Vader.

Luke charges in with his lightsaber … just as he did in the cave. Of course, Luke was shocked at the power of the dark side and its presence within himself … this time he will fare even worse. They follow each other through a maze of opening and closing doors. "During the fight, Vader is often hidden and Luke is seeking him out. This staging depicts Luke searching for the truth about Vader, as well as his subconscious search into his own evil" (Hanson and Kay 212). At last, Luke and Vader battle on a sensor balcony suspended over a vast reactor shaft.

George Lucas and Leigh Brackett decided during story meetings that "The challenge with the confrontation between Luke and Vader was to play it like a seduction, a temptation; the audience knows that Luke is not going to die, so the ultimate hook is the fear that Luke might turn to the dark side" (Bouzereau 210). In fact, Luke duels Darth in what was modeled after a diving or pressure suit (Alinger 114). This subtly emphasizes the increasing pressure Vader is inflicting.

Luke is sucked out of the shaft through gas exhaust pipes and dangles from a weathervane from the underbelly of Cloud City. Luke is not yet a Jedi and not prepared to battle such an overwhelming force. Literally and symbolically, Vader disarms him, depriving him of his ability to act. Away flies the one weapon he had relied on to save him. Worse, losing his hand is a sacrifice of a small part of his humanity—a step towards becoming Vader. Horrified, Luke inches away from his aggressor to the end of the walkway. There he dangles from his one remaining hand, with nowhere to retreat from the force of evil itself. Worse, this evil is telling him he exists within Luke as well. *The Book of the Sith* suggests taunting an opponent to weaken him. "It takes only a few words to expose your opponent's lack of confidence and to lay it out to manipulate" (Wallace 83). Of course, even as Luke insists he knows Vader is his family's enemy, Vader exemplifies this strategy perfectly.

> Vader responds by saying "No Luke, I am your father." With those words the saga has changed on a dime and the dynamic of the Skywalker saga comes full circle. The paternal mentor Obi-Wan is destroyed by the sword of his true father, the villain of the saga. Again, the Oedipal aspect of the saga come through as Luke was attempting to kill his father the entire time, without realizing that Vader was his father [Koch].

With his weapon, his agency destroyed, Luke has nothing remaining but willpower. With Vader's revelation, that too is taken from him: "His body was battered, was exhausted; his spirit was prepared to succumb to his fate. There was no reason to fight any more—there was nothing left to believe in" (Glut 342). His courage failing, he allows himself to crumple, though not to take Vader's outstretched hand when it's offered. This is the true test.

The Original Trilogy

Lucas notes, "It's all through mythology. The gods are constantly tempting. Everybody and everything. So the idea of temptation is one of the things we struggle against, and the temptation obviously is the temptation to go to the dark side" (*The Mythology of Star Wars*). This sort of test represents fighting the evil within oneself. Feeling himself weakening, Luke chooses self-sacrifice over any notion of destiny and hurls himself away from his father. He takes a leap of faith and lets go, plunging into the abyss. Ben and Yoda have taught him a way to break the cycle, a path other than following his father's example. An initiation ritual (which often involves symbolic or literal scarring or dismemberment) divides the boy from his dependency on his parents. Campbell explains, "One of the functions of the rituals again is to kill that infantile ego. Then you have a death-rebirth motif. So the individual falls into the ground of his own being and comes out an adult, a responsible adult, who's undergone certain transformations" (*Hero's Journey* 132). This sort of initiation ceremony, mostly vanished from modern American life, still appears in other cultures. Such a moment is Luke's personal climax—he gives up but does not embrace evil. Further, he returns from this suffering an adult and a Jedi.

The fictitious Jedi handbook describes specific trials required to achieve mastery. The Trial of Skill involves self-discipline in the face of distraction and describes floating pebbles while balancing upside down, much as Luke does with Yoda. The Trial of Insight involves seeing through illusion and deception and finding a solution that avoids violence. The Trial of the Spirit involves a "mirror test" in which one faces temptations. This is Luke's moment in the cave, repeated more horrifically in his duel with Vader. The Trial of Courage could involve facing a Sith lord or doing another great deed. A war injury would get one an automatic pass on the Trial of the Flesh. "Padawans who had defeated a Sith Lord sometimes passed the Trials of the Flesh, Skill, and Courage simultaneously" (Wallace, *Jedi Path* 100). Battlefield promotions are possible, but one way or another, the young learner must pass the trials. This handbook makes it clearer why, after Luke has battled Darth Vader with his training incomplete, and even lost the encounter, Yoda pronounces him a Jedi—this moment, in which Vader not only battles and wounds Luke but also offers him the truth and tempts him to the dark side, could be said to cover all five areas of testing.

Without a hand, Luke cannot fight, but he exercises his free will while succeeding at the Trial of Insight. "We can determine that the fall is a significant archetypal act. This descent is symbolic of his failure with his father and his lack of understanding of the dark side" (Hanson and Kay 214). The moment shows that Luke is imperfect, that he is at risk for temptation after all. However, he is fighting the dark side, so he does not tumble straight to hell. He hurtles upside down through a tube, another rebirth journey portrayed quite literally. There he clings to a weathervane, blown about in the exposed wind with no protection. He hangs on the brink of death—suspended on the edge and unable to save himself without aid.

It's Leia, the nurturing feminine presence, who senses his distress and comes to save him. She hears him through the Force (foreshadowing her parentage) and gets him medical care. The medical devices of his world expertly replace his hand. This is common in fairytales, in which losing the original means a loss of agency while its restoration is a magical gift that allows a new type of ability. With his hand restored in a sense, Luke is gaining a new capacity to interact with his world. Still, Boba Fett escapes with a frozen Han against a pain-filled red sky. The dark side is triumphing over the heroes.

They end the story standing together, a new foursome. In their simple white clothes from the previous film, Leia and Luke are taking a moment to connect with who they were before—young heroes bereft of mentorship (Obi-Wan, Yoda) and friendship (Han, Lando, Chewie). With their companions gone, they will need to seize heroism on their own. He smiles at the princess in her shining gown and puts an arm around her, buoyed by her own faith and hope in her love.

The interim novel *Shadows of the Empire* has Luke working with the Bothan spynet as they discover the plans for a second Death Star (leaked by the Emperor as part of his trap). Luke leads Bothan fighter pilots to capture a secured computer with the plans, and, indeed, many Bothans die in the process. Luke begins second-guessing his abilities as he worries, "He was a lousy commander. Every time he went out, he lost people. And there was no one else to blame for this.... He was too cocky, too self-confident, too certain the Force would show him the right path. Wrong" (Perry 174). As with the interim comics, he realizes his flaws and seeks training to improve.

Through the book, he also constructs a new lightsaber for himself, using the plans he finds at Ben's house. This return to his childhood planet shows him how much he has grown as he trains, meditating and coming to understand what will be required of him. During his battles, he tries repeatedly to summon the Force. While rescuing Leia and thinking beyond himself, however, the Force suddenly fills Luke. "It felt as natural as breathing. That's what the Force was, he realized. A natural phenomenon. He had struggled so hard to attain it, and all that it required was that he relax and *allow* it, instead of trying to create it. Simple" (Perry 297). With a new confidence, he begins giving orders and his friends follow them without question, accepting him as leader. He contacts Leia telepathically, and she's struck by how "now he felt strong, in control, potent" (304).

Finally, a smuggler friend gives him "a coarsely woven, dark gray hooded cape and cowl, a plain shirt and a simple vest, pants and jacket, knee boots, all in black, without any insignia. Maybe it was not quite the uniform of a Jedi Knight, but it was close enough" (303). In his new uniform, he attains a new role—not just apprentice but true Jedi. This gives him a striking new look for the third film. Hooding him in an Obi-Wan style cloak adds mystery and maturity. "Luke's costume is very dark, and actually very fitted. It's almost tailored. He was becoming a man; he was more and more stoic," says costume designer Nilo Rodis-Jamero. "The whole saga is about Luke growing up. George wanted Luke to look as old as absolutely possible" (Alinger 131). The outfit suggests a comfort with the dark side—acceptance over fear, along with the tantalizing hint that Luke might succumb to it.

Return of the Jedi

In the third film, Luke is far more collected. He radiates maturity and control—the gawky kid is gone. The loss of his friends, of soldiers under his command, of his mentors, and finally of his hand and his illusions have all carried him to adulthood. Emerging from the underworld has brought with it powers to rival Obi-Wan's like his mind trick. His every utterance brims with confidence. He also willingly risks his life to save his romantic rival, emphasizing a mature fairness. This gesture suggests he's moved beyond personal desire for a wider worldliness—loving everyone in Jedi fashion rather than the single woman of Anakin's more selfish path.

Moreover, Luke's creating his own weapon suggests a separation from the father. Lucas says, "The new lightsaber that Luke built himself in *Jedi* symbolizes that he has detached himself completely from his father and now is on his own. The central issue is that Luke confronts his demons, and his demons basically revolve around whether he will follow in his father's footsteps, whether he will succumb to the dark side" (Bouzereau 275). It seems he's learned his lessons at Dagobah, since this time he steps away from the Rebellion, first to return to Yoda and then to save Vader. He's accepted that commitment, family, and restoring good on a small level—single souls—is his goal, not winning wars. "By becoming a Jedi, Luke essentially leaves the Rebel Army—the modern resistance—for the Jedi cult—an ancient code of warrior. One can think of this as a transformation from a military officer of a modern army to a knight of medieval times: he has left the Rebellion, but he is still fighting for the same cause, on a more individual basis" (Hanson and Kay 392).

Luke appears in the black of maturity ... also the color of Vader and the Emperor, suggesting he's slid a little closer to understanding them after his brush with death and loss of his hand. Hamill notes, "In *Return of the Jedi*, I told George that my costume was very Vader-ish, but he said, 'It's supposed to be" (Biggar 9). He is Vader's equal and opposite—a worthy rival for the dark lord. Returned from the underworld, Luke is an adult now, brimming with the power of the Jedi, though Jabba is skeptical.

Luke has intended to leave Tatooine behind and find adventure in the stars, but he clearly has unresolved issues here. These appear in the form of the greedy, vicious, monstrous Jabba. He represents lust, selfishness, corruption, and all the now-spiritual Jedi holds himself beyond. Visiting Jabba's palace is like Luke's visiting his immature self, fully acknowledging all he has to offer, and rejecting him for the life of higher contemplation he's chosen.

Jabba's palace is a haven to corruption—smuggling, bribery and theft have made him rich and encouraged his lust and gluttony. "Once bold and daring, he has settled back in his old age to a life of debauchery in his palace on Tatooine. Jabba enjoys violent entertainment almost as much as he enjoys profits, and he arranges deadly gladiatorial games and creative executions on a regular basis" (Reynolds, *Star Wars Visual Dictionary* 44). Inside the palace are music and exotic dancing, but also dancers hurled to their deaths in the rancor pit and droids worked to death. Further, extended universe materials reveal that he has taken over the temple of the ascetic B'omarr monks and corrupted it to fit his disgusting self-indulgence. It's a place of sacrilege as well.

In the throne room, Luke beholds the captive princess—no longer a hazy hologram but now his beloved friend. This emphasizes his growing connectedness. (Her gold bikini also signifies a greater level of maturity and even lustful temptation for the emerging hero. Of course, Luke doesn't give in.) Still, he delays in saving her as he's learned to focus on the bigger picture. Meanwhile, Han, insisting Luke has "delusions of grandeur," enacts the role of shadow figure, questioning Luke's new power. His selfishness counterbalances Luke's habitual selflessness.

Jabba hurls him down into the underground—or at least the underground pit—so he can fight the rancor beast. Rancor of course means bitter resentment. "The rancor, as Jabba's pet, represents Jabba's disowned resentment, embitterment, and overall emotional monstrosity" (Galipeau 190). Luke must battle these feelings and learn to overcome them in Jabba—representing the unexplored monstrosity, greed, and corpulence within himself. Luke comments in one of his handwritten notes in *The Book of the Sith*, "It was half-starved. Though I didn't have a choice, I'm still sorry I had to kill it" (Wallace 77). This shows his compassion—rather than rage or primitive emotions. Through it all, he maintains a Jedi's detachment and suave coolness.

Since Luke defeats everyone nearly singlehandedly, he emphasizes his startling new level of ability. As he faces them, the fiercest monsters of his childhood home crumple and are destroyed. At last, he swings himself and Leia off the remaining barge, saving all the good guys including the droids. There isn't a single injury or flaw in his plan—all goes seamlessly, as it did for Obi-Wan in the first film. Luke appears to have succeeded his old mentor perfectly.

After this, Luke returns to Yoda only to hear that his training is complete or will be when he confronts Vader. His mentors speak with him one last time and both offer important truths: Yoda confirms that Vader is his father and adds, "Unfortunate that you rushed to face him … that incomplete was your training. Not ready for the burden were you." He warns, "Remember, a Jedi's strength flows from the Force. But beware. Anger, fear, aggression. The dark side are they. Once you start down the dark path, forever will it dominate your destiny." With this, he cautions Luke against the tyrant's descent, so common in one who has grown powerful. As he concludes, he encourages Luke to continue the lifecycle by becoming a teacher as he has: "Pass on what you have learned, Luke … There is … another … Sky … Sky … walker."

Yoda dies. The novelization adds, "Luke had known the passing of old mentors before. It was helplessly sad; and inexorably a part of his own growing. Is this what coming of age was, then? Watching beloved friends grow old and die? Gaining a new measure of strength or maturity from their powerful passages?" (Kahn 400). As he learns these hard lessons, he must also undergo his greatest challenge alone.

After this, Obi-Wan comes to him and confirms that the other Skywalker is Leia. He also accepts Luke's anger at his lie about his father, accurate "from a certain point of view." As Obi-Wan explains, Luke must learn that life isn't black and white. When Ben tells him he must face Vader, another ambiguous pronouncement, Luke assumes Ben means to kill him. He's still too caught in the hierarchical pattern of competition. Meanwhile, Ben's insistence on "a certain point of view" encourages Luke to see the galaxy's conflicting perspectives and understand that there are many versions of truth to different people. Flexibility and discernment will be needed.

On Endor, Luke finds a different kind of education. The rebels already use old, broken, outdated technology cobbled together as they can manage. They progress (or perhaps regress) from this to fully embrace nature in *Jedi*. Endor represents the mysterious forest, a place for the growing hero to learn mysticism and ascend spiritually. The Ewoks there share a mystical bond with the forests, with village shamans serving as intermediaries. At the birth of each new tribal member, a life tree seedling is planted, and the guardian tree and Ewok mature together: On death, the Ewok's spirit takes up residence in his or her tree (Luceno, *Inside the Worlds* 41). They listen to their tree partners and have much to teach the heroes about using nature and the Force to persevere. There, Luke searches for Leia, once again representing the buried sensitivity within himself.

The Ewoks take the team prisoner. However, Luke saves them with his controlled, spiritual powers rather than a physical fight. He understands how they think and manages to connect. After Luke has passed this test of intuition, he and his friends find Leia and are all welcomed into the tribe. Campbell notes of initiation ceremonies, "It becomes apparent that the purpose and actual effect of these was to conduct people across those difficult thresholds of transformation that demands changes not only in the patterns of conscious but also of unconscious life" (10).

One more plot point remains for Luke on Endor—telling Leia her heritage. In this forest sanctuary, Leia appears in flowing hair and an Ewok dress. "Her no-nonsense disposition has ebbed into a warm and loving persona. She is now the embodiment of woman in classic mythology—a vessel of nature and the giver of life" (Hanson and Kay 259). She embodies the anima qualities Luke hasn't yet demonstrated, coaxing him toward deeper development. Discovering Leia as his twin means fully accepting a platonic feminine spirituality as a part of his life—equal in every way to his ego. As Luke asks about his lost mother, he opens himself to the first, most critical lost feminine. Having experienced her through Leia's description, he carries this spiritual connection as protection when he goes to battle his father.

With this, Luke finally accepts the destiny he's fled since the second film and surrenders to the Imperials, willingly. He's taken into the Belly of the Beast once more. Walking side by side with Vader, both in black, Luke is stepping into Vader's world, becoming like him. In the novelization, for the first time, Luke has "a brief murky image of himself standing on his father's body, holding his father's blazing power and sitting at the Emperor's right hand" (Kahn 458).

Still, Luke understands that just as he contains the potential for evil, Vader contains the potential for goodness. He's determined to redeem the villain, not just to save his father, but to balance the warring light and dark he feels within himself and settle his internal struggle. "Search your feelings, father. You can't do this. I feel the conflict within you. Let go of your hate," he urges. This hate, of course, has taken over all aspects of Vader. "Vader has used fear and hatred to achieve his ends for so long that now his superior hatred and aggression of the Emperor use him. That is how Vader's mastery of the Dark Side is at the same time servitude to it" (Stephens 27).

Of course, no one comes with him on this journey, not even Artoo. Luke is taken to the control room, where the Emperor dictates the fate of the galaxy. "The throne room is Emperor Palpatine's command center and seat of power aboard the second Death Star. With its gleaming decks, exposed superstructure, and shadowy recesses, it is both intimidating and menacing" (Luceno, *Inside the Worlds* 45). Rising from the Death Star II's north pole, the Emperor's hundred-story isolation tower is anchored to the station. Towers symbolize patriarchal power, soaring toward the sky away from the earth that is the feminine realm. In fact, the Emperor makes Luke gaze out onto the space battle like a god of Olympus overseeing mortal squabbles. This is the true moment of temptation as the Emperor invites Luke to claim the power he already wields and become a god in truth.

As the ancient sage, the Emperor is controlled, with gravity and devotion to his cause. "The Emperor's hatred follows a cool logic of its own. His cruelty is calmly calculated, not haphazard. The Emperor shows an icy rationality and self-possession that is a shallow reflection of the Stoic's passionlessness. His is an arrogant rationality which seeks to dominate, exploit, and enslave people through careful planning and use of the Dark Side" (Stephens 27–28). In service to his cruel cause, he is a murderer of innocents—not only the Rebel ship but the inhabitants of Endor, of course. This world is no threat, a sanctuary moon protected as a nature reserve, but he sets his trap there nonetheless. This is the goal of evil: Darth Plagueis, Sidious's mentor, explains in his novel, "Every death I oversee nourishes and empowers me, for I am a true Sith" (Luceno 322).

As a symbolic spirit of evil and temptation, something like Dementors and Ringwraiths, the Emperor wears a simple black robe. "It literally hung from the Emperor's frame, forcing him to move slowly and deliberately. The waffle cotton cloak was cut with kimono-style sleeves, which were gathered and stitched on top, causing them to bunch at the wrists and hang low from the arms" (Alinger 162). These robes shroud the character so the audience sees only glimpses of the frail body beneath. The cloak shadows but also draws the eye. Such a simple, iconic costume telegraphs the character's sinister qualities for the audience. As the novel of Palpatine's rise details, "The Jedi Order's homespun cloaks announced: I want for nothing, because I am clothed in the Force; the cloaks of the Sith: I am the light in the dark, the convergence of opposing energies" (Luceno, *Darth Plagueis* 294).

Of course, the Emperor brings Luke to his throne room to watch his friends die and let the hatred take him over.

> **EMPEROR:** From here you will witness the final destruction of the Alliance, and the end of your insignificant Rebellion. (caressing lightsaber) You want this, don't you? The hate is swelling in you now. Take your Jedi weapon. Use it. I am unarmed. Strike me down with it. Give in to your anger. With each passing moment, you make yourself more my servant.
> **LUKE:** No!
> **EMPEROR:** It is unavoidable. It is your destiny. You, like your father, are now mine!

Before Luke's horrified eyes, the Emperor blows up a ship. "In the numbing grip of despair, with the hollowest of voids devouring his heart, Luke's eyes, alone, glinted—for he saw again, his lightsaber, lying unattended on the throne. And in this bleak and livid moment, the dark side was much with him" (Kahn 470). When Vader eggs him on and finally threatens Leia, Luke gives in to rage. She is the last hope for the galaxy, after all, his personal symbol of goodness. He knocks Vader to his knees, filled with the dark power of rage. For a moment he prepares to give in. "Luke didn't bury the thought, this time; he gloried in it. He engorged himself with its juices, felt its power tingle his cheeks.... He had the power; the choice was his" (Kahn 477).

However, he regains control. Seeing his father's severed mechanical hand, he realizes how closely they are linked—that hating Vader is like hating himself. Luke realizes in this moment that everyone bears darkness—the key is defeating and mastering it. He has a choice and he accepts and controls the evil within. Luke throws away his lightsaber and declares, "You've failed, your highness. I am a Jedi, like my father before me."

Showing his maturity, Luke chooses death over evil, and calmly tells the Emperor he cannot succeed. The Emperor gloats that Luke's compassion for his father and faith in his friends are his undoing. Clearly, the Emperor is the voice of fear and uncertainty from within. Luke realizes he is the evil impulse but only a whisper, one that he can ignore. "External Shadows must be vanquished or destroyed by the hero. Shadows of the internal kind may be disempowered like vampires, simply by bringing them into the Shadows and into the light of consciousness" (Vogler 68). As Luke rejects the Emperor, connecting himself with the larger universe, Han and his friends destroy the bunker—the Emperor's defenses crumble in the face of Luke's defiance and understanding. With this, the Emperor's appearance of invulnerability is gone.

However, he unleashes uncontrolled rage on Luke, insisting, "If you will not be turned, you will be destroyed." The lightning casts the Emperor as a sky god, the supreme patriarch of the galaxy but also one completely removed from humanity. Like Vader, he is tinged with artificiality and the capacity for destruction. However, while Vader is imprisoned in a machine, the Emperor's electric power (previously only seen in artificial characters like R2-D2) casts him as the machine itself. *The Book of the Sith* describes abilities like Force lightning and fists that glow hot to the touch ... which tear up the host's body as well as their intended victim's. Luke comments in one of his handwritten notes, "Sith tactics do as much harm to the user as to the victim. The dark side corrupts everything it touches" (Wallace 92). It cannot even bring true success, only harm to both sides.

Dying at the Emperor's hands, Luke pleads for help, and the buried goodness in Vader finally awakens. Vader picks up the Emperor and hurls him down the hundred stories into the engine's depth. The Emperor is pure cruelty—the only solution is to purge him from the galaxy with fire, as Frodo does with the ring or Indiana Jones does with the Nazis (Galipeau 245). "Literally and symbolically Darth Vader has now become Luke's personal father. He has mediated powerful psychic energy that threatened to overwhelm his son so that his son could survive and come back to himself" (Galipeau 244).

Restored, Anakin insists Luke remove his mask and let his human side breathe in the world, if only for moments. He looks at Luke with love and finally dies. Luke drags him to a shuttle, flies them down to Endor, and gives him a Jedi funeral. After, at the celebration, Luke sees that Anakin has joined Obi-Wan and Yoda's spirits, and they all watch over Luke's triumph. Symbolically, they are still watching over him (and indeed, these Force ghosts appear a few times in the novels, even as Yoda returns in *The Last Jedi*). Vader has thus turned from the villain of the trilogy to Luke's guardian and advisor like the others. Luke comments in one of his handwritten notes in *The Book of the Sith*, "Palpatine failed. My father overcame his master's evil. I witnessed the return of the Jedi who had fought in the Clone Wars, and I know that he found solace in the light side of the Force" (Wallace 77). Luke, meanwhile, can step into the patriarch's shoes as a man in his prime, wielder of the Force and a leader of the galaxy, no longer child but hero.

Leia: Rebel Princess

As the script describes her, "A beautiful young girl (about sixteen years old) stands in front of Artoo. Surreal and out of place, dreamlike and half hidden in the smoke, she finishes adjusting something on Artoo's computer face, then watches as the little robot joins his companion." In Hawaiian, the meaning of the name Leia is "child of heaven" or "heavenly flowers." This mystic, mystical princess is the viewpoint character as she defiantly mouths off at Grand Moff Tarkin for invading her ship. Lucas says, "Carrie is a very warm person; she's a fun-loving, goofy kid who can also play a very hard, sophisticated tough leader" (Rinzler, *The Making of Star Wars* 125). Lucas found he preferred these qualities to a sweet, traditional princess. In the first film, Leia enlists the droids and summons the male heroes to the quest. Of course, she also has her own arc to follow.

A secret Skywalker like Luke, she is not only heir to the Force, but also a chosen one. However, much of her arc goes unseen. When the film opens, she has already ascended to the rank of princess but also senator—the latter one requiring skill and effort. In fact, the novel *Leia, Princess of Alderaan* shows that the throne of Alderaan requires similar tests of skill. In it, she earns her status by completing a three-part challenge: Representing her world in the apprentice legislature, doing charity missions, and climbing Appenza Peak—the mission her mother succeeded at for her own challenge, though she was so severely injured that she could never have children. The other two missions present unexpected challenges. In the first, while making friends like Amilyn Holdo, Leia falls into diplomatic traps set by Palpatine and Tarkin. Here, as well as on her humanitarian mission, she stumbles across the Rebellion's activities. Fulfilling her missions while safeguarding her family and people and also staying under the Empire's radar becomes a true rite of passage worthy of the princess. Still, all this takes place outside the film's canon, in a novel that only arrived in 2017.

In the original film, she begins not only as a teenager but an unformed hero, still playing at legitimate senator while keeping her rebel side well hidden. White is suitable for the virgin princess, symbolizing "innocence; chastity; holiness; sacredness; redemption; spiritual authority" (Cooper 41). Carrie Fisher comments, "I spent the first film in a white turtlenecked dress meant to emphasize my purity—pure only by the color of the costume" (Biggar 113). She also famously was asked to tape her breasts down to appear more modest and girlish.

Nonetheless, Leia's armed with a laser pistol and fires at the invading Stormtroopers until they manage to subdue her. The image of a single teenage girl fighting a raiding party suggests that though young, she's still formidable. Further, Leya is Spanish or Hindi: for "the law" or "lion." Certainly, she is the embodiment of decency and right in the galaxy—the naïve, dispossessed senator battling for rule of law. She is also a lion, savage and physically powerful. When Vader arrives, Leia resists him "both as a characterization of Leia as a strong, determined, and heroic young woman and as the attitude of the deeper unconscious to a conscious attitude driven by power: it will not give up its profoundest mysteries and secrets" (Galipeau 33).

"The Revolutionary commits to a value she believes will humanize the world, then acts to embody that value. This requires taking a firm stand and struggling for that right, if necessary" (Leonard 237). However, Leia is still naïve, unaware of the cost that will follow. Facing off with Vader, Leia appears a childish figure indeed, short and dressed in white. "Revolutionary action requires action that is honest, spiritually centered, and totally focused. It requires dedication to a cause and a willingness to give up one's egotistic desires, to make the necessary sacrifices, to die away from one kind of life and pursuit and into another kind of life and identity" (Leonard 238). Leia faces her own death in Grand Moff Tarkin's threatened execution but is far more horrified at the man's plans for her entire world. This threat to millions of her loved ones breaks her, or at least, so it appears: When he decrees that her homeworld will be destroyed, she capitulates and confesses the Rebel base's location, only revealed later as a false one.

Of course, Tarkin memorably destroys her homeworld all the same as she screams in horror. This represents the death of her childhood—parents, friends, pets, bedroom, school, palace—her entire life to that point is disintegrated. Symbolically, this leaves her prepared to commit fully to the Rebel Alliance, with no conflicting ties to hold her back. It's also a horrific, incalculable loss, devastating her to the point of death. After this, the men lock her in a blank cell and plan her execution. However, the princess has already lost all she has been fighting for—the friends and family she loves and the citizens she's sworn to protect.

Onscreen, this moment establishes the villains' evil and the heroine's victimization but does not actually provide the princess with character growth. The film does not follow her mourning for this incredible loss, though the novels and comics do. In a comic that takes place directly after the award ceremony of *A New Hope*, Leia meets an Alderaanian soldier called Evaan Verlaine, who bows with exaggerated, near-mocking deference. As a student of Leia's mother, she resents Leia for not showing more grief and tells her Leia should not dispense with the formalities, as the monarchy is a central part of their culture. Inspired by this shadow figure, so blonde and aggressive in her orange flight suit, envying all Leia is and yet embodying all she wishes to be, Leia is moved. She declares she has a new mission—to gather and protect the survivors of Alderaan. Through the arc, she grieves her family, even as she becomes a true protector to her people, relying on the diplomatic ties she's already forged. After they succeed, with Imperials coming for them, Leia gives an inspiring speech, claiming her role as princess and rebel together. She sends Evaan, the woman who values their culture and people so much, to be their new leader and find them a homeland, while Leia returns to the rebellion (Waid, *Princess Leia*).

For a large part of the original film, Leia vanishes, bravely resisting torture and interrogation that nonetheless go unseen. The radio play adaptation expands this, showing the torture scenes with visceral cruelty. Similarly, in Alan Dean Foster's *Splinter of the Mind's Eye* (a book that's only semi-canon as it was released before *Empire*), Leia has time to process her feelings. Alderaan is too raw for her to dwell on, but the possibility of a second session with Imperial interrogators sends her cringing to the back of a jail cell, breathing unevenly and sweating. She recalls "the remorseless black machine, illegal, constructed by twisted Imperial scientists in defiance of every code, legal and moral. It drifted over to her, moved down, metal limbs preparing to perform efficiently, emotionlessly, in response to inhuman programming" (124). Even as she struggles to discuss her trauma with Luke, she's offered a chance to work through her rage in a moment of heroism. Vader appears, and Leia actually duels him with Anakin's lightsaber. "The fear did not leave her, but she forced it to the back alleys of her mind through sheer will" (278). In this, she gains some closure.

While film Leia logically finds heroism defying torture and later overcoming the trauma, her plot does not resume until the men arrive to rescue her. Upon escaping, she takes charge of their ragtag team and helps devise their escape. She's tough. However, she doesn't exhibit much growth or learning. A pillar of strength for the others, she gives orders, offers quips, makes the plans, and helps get them off the Death Star in one piece.

At the film's climax, Leia's life hangs in jeopardy while she directs the attacks on the Death Star from the Rebel base, even as the Death Star prepares to destroy her haven as it did her childhood home. Besides killing her, this would demolish the Rebellion, leaving the Empire to destroy any final strongholds and sympathetic planets. She manages bravely, directing the battle even in the face of certain doom. However, once again, she changes little from her arc. Leia's survival results in hugs and happiness, but no more growth than this.

In earlier drafts, Leia becomes the new queen (Bouzereau 120). Onscreen, however, she continues in her usual position as mistress of ceremonies. In this final scene, she functions as prize and anima alike for the heroes, rewarding them for their own heroism.

PRINCESS IN LOVE

The second film gives her far more growth, though specifically as part of the romantic plot. As the film starts, Leia appears tougher—no longer a princess with elaborate hair but a rebel in a white snowsuit, braids tight to her head. She's fully committed to her cause, but in a way that leaves little room for womanly growth. "Leia is a woman in the grip of the animus: a fine leader, devoted to her principles, but unaware of her humanity as a person and as a woman" (Galipeau 92).

When Han Solo insists on leaving them, she unbends enough to ask him to stay, but she cannot tell him of her feelings. When he pushes the issue, insisting, "You want me to stay because of the way you feel about me," she denies it, insisting she values him only as a leader for the Rebellion. Acting as her animus and evoking the romantic side she's never developed, he encourages her to grow emotionally, telling her as a goad, "You could use a good kiss!" The comment is chauvinistic, even brutish, but he's provoking her to branch out. Of course, she refuses and insists she'd rather kiss a Wookie. Disgusted by her lack of relationship courage, he walks away.

One test the heroine often faces on her journey is the test of pity. This comes early with Luke lost in the snowy wilderness and Han out rescuing him. Leia does not embark on the showy rescue, but the quieter leadership role of endurance and waiting. Tougher than Padmé, who succumbed to Anakin over and over against her better judgment, Leia reluctantly closes the shield on their base to protect all those inside, though her beloved Han and Luke remain outside it.

Afterwards, she coordinates the evacuation, so devoted to duty that she fails to escape herself. Han must drag her away and then save her life. When a cave-in blocks her from leaving on a Rebel ship, he guides her on an alternate path—coming with him. Just as he's been immersed in her heroic world, she soon gets a taste of smuggling. Together they dodge through an asteroid field, make a suicidal run at an Imperial ship and even hide on it, floating away with the garbage. This all shows Leia an alternate lifestyle, one of adrenaline and even fun. This is the role of the animus, teaching her skills she's never discovered.

Though the ship breaks down, leading them deeper into smugglers' shenanigans, Han and Leia find time for romance. First, she literally falls into his arms (suggesting her emotional body is making choices outside of her duty-bound mind). Then when she can't attach a part (a similar moment of symbolism), he goes to help her. Both their hands are dirty—they're no longer being clean and proper. For Han is, as she calls him repeatedly, scruffy-looking, a scoundrel, and a no-good smuggler. Being around him is tarnishing her perfect princess persona as she tumbles off her pedestal. Of course, Han stands ready to catch her. "Oh, you make it so difficult sometimes," she complains.

He's forced to agree, though provocatively: "I do, I really do. You could be a little nicer, though. Come on, admit it. Sometimes you think I'm all right." She does, and they kiss. He understands that his allure comes from being outside her previous experience and offering her surprising adventures. The reality is that Han is a scoundrel and a nice man at once. "Leia needs to realize that her 'ideal' of a man is too one-dimensional and that her feelings are leading her to a more balanced experience with a man who is genuinely human and alive, not an abstraction" (Galipeau 111). Her judgmental comments from *A New Hope* are being displaced.

Of course, rational thought and responsibility, in the person of Threepio, spoils the moment. He interrupts and the confused young couple scatter. On the asteroid, they must deal with mynocks and pace slugs—the ugliness of the universe that suggests people's ugly little flaws.

They reach Bespin, where Leia finds herself in a flirtation triangle with the suave, dashing Lando Calrissian. A diplomatic and charming leader rather than a scoundrel, he's more like the men she's used to … though she much prefers Han. On Bespin, she wears a brick-colored Indian tunic and harem pants, with a floor length cream silk robe. Red can signify danger or a subconscious rebellion against the all-white world of Cloud City (as well as against the black of Vader when he suddenly appears). Over it goes the white cloak, suggesting she's still the pure heroine on the outside, but deepening and strengthening within. The sun pattern on the robe represents enlightenment and the pinnacle of achievement.

As soon as Lando reveals himself as a traitor and Vader captures Han, Leia returns to her white snowsuit, prepared for action. She's once more a beacon of hope as she comforts Han, gives him a reason to survive, and finally proclaims her love. The death-descent is not hers, but watching Han lowered into the carbonite represents the destruction of the old self and proper husband's reemergence. After this, she senses Luke, possibly in her first use of the Force, and rescues him. Here, she offers a blend of action heroine and protective feminine icon, just as the white snowsuit blends purity and ability. She ends the film in her white dress, like a pre–Han Leia, though still hoping to reclaim him. At last, she's found her mission, a selfish personal one separate from the Rebellion.

Maturity

Leia spends the interim novel *Shadows of the Empire* fretting over Han's goodbye—why couldn't he have said he loved her? Seeking intelligence, she goes to the crime syndicate of Black Sun. There, the alluring Prince Xizor uses his reptilian pheromones to seduce her. Chewie's intervention and her memories of Han pull her out, but this moment provokes her emotional response, breaking down her sexual barriers. The plotline also sets up the events of *Jedi*: Prince Xizor's assistant gives Leia a suit that once belonged to the Ubese bounty hunter Boushh, while Lando and Luke give her the thermal detonator, equipping her with all the tools for her descent into Jabba's palace.

A different, more recent novel also bridges the gap. Leia begins the young adult novel *Moving Target* insisting to her mentor Mon Mothma that she would never use their resources for the personal mission of saving Han. Mon Mothma startles Leia by saying she had been planning to propose such a mission. To Leia's further surprise, the other woman asks what she owes herself and emphasizes that everyone needs a personal life—the Empire, which has stolen so much innocence from the galaxy, should not take Leia's chance at happiness (Castellucci and Fry 66). Next, Leia leads a solo mission and loses several of her crew. At novel's end, she's developed emotionally in the same way Han, Lando, and Luke have. She decides, "We fight for a cause but what we're really fighting for is each other. That's why our pilots fly into fire instead of abandoning a wingman and our commandos stand their ground rather than leave a flank unguarded. It's because they care for each other. We fight for duty, yes. But we also fight because we love each other. And that's something even more powerful" (Castellucci and Fry 222). With this, she resolves to go save Han and seize her chance for love.

The plan to rescue Han involves masks and disguises, emphasizing the heroes' growing power as tricksters who challenge the mighty force. Leia's disguise is tough and faceless like their enemies Boba Fett and even Vader. It projects the outer toughness she wants to channel. With this, she is remaking herself as an amoral killer—the strength and independence she will need to truly lead the Rebellion. She is Boushh the fearsome bounty hunter, displaying Chewbacca as a prize and engaging in a deadly showdown with Jabba, thermal detonator armed, to prove her might. She passes this test and he accepts her as "fearless and inventive" like himself.

Leia's bomb of course offers a moment of staring into the abyss—a brief death journey and return. As she presses the button, she prepares to be an instrument of her own destruction. Since she is battling what she has brought with her, this echoes Luke's cave battle. "This is an archetypal event that gives insight into the inward journey. For truly the fight is within oneself and not against an opponent" (Hanson and Kay 229).

Having dueled the monster—the greed and selfishness that represent the evil the young princess has barely tapped—she wins entry to the palace, her true goal. Under cover of darkness, she reveals her true agenda and frees Han. At last, she's embarking on a personal mission instead of only one of duty. She also cares for Han after he's freed from carbonite. "Thus, the Princess is able to repay her rescue by rescue of the heroes themselves. The most important aspect of her action is not always a physical rescue, but the rescue of the spirit that the motherly caregiver is able to perform" (Hanson and Kay 388). When Han awakens, in a twist on her first film's adventures, she removes the disguise, revealing herself to him and the audience. With this, she directly proclaims her love, reveling in her emotions instead of suppressing them. In this moment, she owns her true self, finding the vulnerable woman within.

Of course, her moment of triumph and power is instantly undercut. Jabba's mocking laughter intrudes, and he reveals he's been condescendingly watching her entire rescue. Like the voice of the shadow, he emphasizes that Leia is no conquering hero, just a puppet dancing for his amusement. Driving his point home, he enslaves her and has her dressed in the demeaning gold bikini. This male stronghold at first glance resembles the Death Star—an evil fortress where the heroine has no power. As shown by the slave girl chained to the throne, "the feminine principle is not allowed to live freely; it is enslaved to the lusts of others and treated with disrespect" (Galipeau 181).

Looking deeper, more is going on here. "The scene at Jabba's palace seems to imply a gangster cult that is heavily male-dominated. However, the images of Jabba, the rancor, and now the Sarlacc suggest that it is really a primitive society in service of the dark feminine" (Galipeau 191). Jabba is a force of lust and greed; the rancor is a monster of anger. Meanwhile, the gaping pit of the Sarlacc suggests the feminine force, endlessly devouring all the universe allows. It is a primordial monster from the dawn of time—a leviathan often slain by the solar hero. All these threats emphasize that Leia has entered a dark realm that's surprisingly feminine in its monstrosity.

The wicked witch of Snow White poisons her, but also dresses her in a strangling corset and stabs poisoned combs into her hair. She's forcing the young heroine to grow up, to dress as a sexual woman not a girl. Ursula the Sea Witch offers Ariel similar lessons on how to flirt with "body language" before sending her to seduce the prince. On the one side, Jabba is the patriarch tormenting Leia. On the other, he is the lustful monster forcing her to face her unexplored sexuality. Leia's gold bikini thus becomes a metaphorical step on her road to adulthood.

To this point, Leia has flirted with Han, but only commits to him as he is taken from her and frozen in carbonite. Now, nothing is stopping them from moving forward, but the virginal princess is uncertain how. This training in the realm of the dark side teaches her sensuality. It's a beauty and the beast moment, albeit with a truly disgusting beast, which prepares her for all the sides of a relationship. After, she runs off with her handsome daylight prince and decisively strangles the beast in his own drool. In one of the sequel novels, an admiring crime boss names her Huttslayer, "a far greater title than either senator or princess could ever be. The Niktos know you for the warrior you are" (Gray, *Bloodline* 65).

Now a rebel leader among others, Leia volunteers for Han's command team (though he is cast as the leader, despite her experience). Another significant character introduced is the Rebellion's leader Mon Mothma. "Her presence and name (Mon Moth[er]ma) symbolically reflect the connection to the feminine principle that permeated the rebel cause during the battle against the original Death Star" (Galipeau 204). Such a variety of life forms, aliens big and small, emphasize the power of life against the Emperor's forces. Mothma, taking in all those who have lost their homes, is the all-wise mother. Of course, the film does not show her comforting and advising Leia or particularly interacting with her. In the novels, by contrast, she takes more of a mentor's role.

Leia's journey isn't as strong, dramatic, or deathly as the men's, but she travels the steps in *Jedi*. Chasing the Stormtroopers, she's knocked off her bike and falls unconscious. This bike, light and speedy as it is, suggests a feminine conveyance in itself. When she wakes, it's to a new type of consciousness. In the novelization, she admires the forest. She feels "her own smallness next to these trees. They were ten thousand years old, some of them, and tall beyond sight. They were temples to the lifeforce she championed; they reached out to the rest of the universe. She felt herself part of their greatness, but also dwarfed by it" (Kahn 428). Gazing at them, she feels connected with the larger universe. This ties her to the lifecycle as a whole.

Wicket the Ewok appears and approaches her warily. She charms him, and then he warns her of danger, helps her fight a pair of stormtroopers, and guides her to his village. This scene, much like Luke and Yoda's on Dagobah, represents her releasing control, listening to the little helpers speaking from deep within. Leia is less dismissive than Luke was, suggesting how she's closer to instinctive natural powers.

In the Battle of Endor, she unites the primitive Ewoks with the ego-driven rebels to destroy the Imperials and thus the Death Star. As the rebels fight beside the Ewoks, they emphasize the goodness of nature and evils of technology. This can also be a metaphor for the spiritual, natural feminine side being denigrated by the powerful patriarchy.

In the novel, the heroes make speeches to convince the Ewoks to join their cause. Han emphasizes the lessons he's learned about fighting for his friends. Luke describes the beauty of the entire galaxy and how they're connected to all the stars above. Intuitive Leia understands his argument but knows it's too distant. She thinks back to her moment of epiphany among the forest life and tells them "Do it because of the trees" (Kahn 443). At this, Wicket gives his people his own speech that they know of the Force and must fight to protect the interlocked world of life and all that lies beyond it (Kahn 443). With this moment, Leia shows she understands the Ewoks better than the men because, while they have learned about interconnectedness, she *is* the natural world embodied.

That night, Luke tells her the truth of her heritage and she opens herself to the Force. Here she too receives the call of having great power and a special destiny. In this scene, she gains an enormous family legacy as Luke reveals she carries the Force—and that she has a hero brother and villain father. In fact, her status as "another" Skywalker emphasizes that she might be Luke's equal if she wields the power within her. In Gary D. Schmidt's short story "There Is Another," Yoda tells Obi-Wan that he hopes to train *Leia* not Luke. She has the discipline and training through a life of statecraft. As Yoda thinks, "There was the other Skywalker to watch over—impetuous, headstrong, unruly, inattentive. He needed Obi-Wan's eye on him. Unlike the other, whose strength of will and clarity showed all the markings of a great Jedi" (353). Yoda actually considers how Leia would do as chosen one and how fiercely she might fight to redeem Vader. Of course, these remain tantalizing hints, as she receives no Jedi training in the three-film arc and almost none in the sequels.

The brown dress the Ewoks give her suggests she's able to live in both sides of herself—nature woman and fierce warrior. From here on, she avoids white, suggesting her innocence has given way to maturity. Further, she has fully embraced nature, now an Ewok tribe member, but also a forest woman who can fight among the trees on behalf of the people there. While she lost a planet in the first film, she has gained the agency to defend one, and does in the forest's green camouflage. Brown, like Luke's black, suggests maturity, but also a certain muddiness, poised between dark and light in a complex world as both accept the Sith side of their heritage.

As she tells Luke of his mother and thus mothers him, she connects to her nurturing side. Though asking Han to hold her can suggest weakness, it also shows the mature princess taking a moment in their quiet haven to embrace love. While Luke tangles with Vader up in the heavens, Leia and Han face death together down on the planet. Nonetheless, they rise from certain death as Leia blasts the Stormtroopers and Chewie, another embodiment of nature, comes to save them. They quickly defeat the enemy and blow the shield, providing the essential act to transform the galaxy.

When she tells Han that Luke has succeeded and adds "I can feel it," Leia claims power as a fellow Jedi. In the novel, she reaches back for the first time, not just passively listening. "Her brother's living presence touched her through the Force. She reached out to answer the touch, to reassure Luke she was all right. Everything was all right" (Kahn 498).

Having claimed her power, Leia has accepted all her hidden strengths and embraced them. Now as a fully actualized person, she can commit to love and chooses Han. She knows her place as princess, rebel, leader, and heir to the power of the Force.

AFTER *RETURN OF THE JEDI*

Onscreen, she never deals with the repercussions of being Vader's daughter, nor goes through Luke's torment and acceptance of her own dark side. In the novel *Bloodline*, she reveals more of the pain she underwent:

> He made me watch my planet die. He froze Han in carbonite and sold him to Jabba the Hutt. He cut off my brother's hand and nearly took his life. And he tortured me…. He tortured me until I screamed and shook and thought I would just die from the pain. Alone. Did you bother to ask yourself how it might feel, to realize the person who'd done all that was your father? Can you imagine how terrible it is to realize all you'll ever know of your birth father is how much he enjoyed making you suffer? That's what I have to live with [Gray 256].

However, this catharsis is left to the Extended Universe.

The novel *The Truce at Bakura*, just after the Battle of Endor, has Leia confront her feelings—in the person of Anakin himself. He appears to her as a Force ghost and tells her, "I am forgiven, but I have much that I wish to atone for." However, his next line is paternalistic and controlling as he adds, "I must clear your heart and you mind of anger" (145). She orders him out, pointing out that he can't restore Alderaan or her people. She decides, "I can almost forgive you torturing me.... And the evils you did to other people—because those drove so many worlds into the Alliance. But cruelty to Han ... no" (146). Forgiveness for destroying millions of her people, but not hurting her boyfriend skews her priorities, making her appear wimpy and lovesick ... not to mention disloyal.

At the climax, she brushes her Vader side more deeply as she thinks, "Wouldn't this be the perfect justice—Vader's daughter, ramming an Imperial ship for the sake of the Alliance? Even if the maneuver failed, she'd achieved a vicious kind of symmetry" (274). However, Luke's intervention saves her and her friends from the suicidal charge. In the midst of battle, facing death and returning triumphant, she finds a level of peace—she will continue opposing the Empire, but doesn't mind if her father observes. Eventually, she forgives him enough to name her youngest child Anakin in his memory.

Timothy Zahn's *Dark Force Rising* (which launched the Legends universe) has Leia face her heritage through diplomacy. The leader of the remnants of the Empire, Admiral Thrawn, enlists Vader's chosen assassins, the Noghri, to capture her. However, when one catches her scent, he names her Lady Vader, her father's heir. Intrigued, Leia visits their world and finds a way to turn their loyalty to the Republic. However, she must channel her imperiousness as she visits—the text describes her as "drawing herself up and bringing the full weight of her Royal Alderaanian Court upbringing to bear on the aliens facing her. Deference to local custom and authority was all well and good, but her was the daughter of their Lord Darth Vader, and there were certain discourtesies that such a person should not put up with" (149). As she even thinks like a queen and conqueror, she blends her courtly upbringing with Vader's legacy. This is a shadow journey, involving wielding the adult strength of rulership and domination she's rarely sampled.

Other stories give her additional arcs. The 2015 comics taking place after *A New Hope* introduce Leia and Han's new teammate, the bounty hunter Sana, who's Han's ex. On meeting Leia, Sana tells her, "My condolences, dear.... Han's great fun, but he's a scoundrel ... he'll break your heart." *Last Flight of the Harbinger* has Sana still functioning as Leia's shadow, voicing all the secrets Leia keeps secret, even from herself. As truth-teller, she notes that under Han and Leia's bickering, they're "two people madly in *love* with each other but can't bring their stupid selves to admit it."

Zahn's trilogy also has Leia give birth to her twins Jaina and Jacen. Through a lengthy series, she fights to protect them with a mother's strength. As the children grow, she watches them become soldiers in a galactic war and struggle with the dark side, giving her additional challenges as she ascends from warrior and leader of the New Republic to grandmother and guardian. New canon has her mothering Ben before he turns dark, and once again, she struggles to keep him safe in a darkening world in which all she has fought for is crumbling.

C3PO: Servant to War Hero

While the original trilogy gives him a more extensive backstory through retroactive continuity change, *A New Hope* suggests that C-3PO is one Republic protocol droid of many, doing his job on Princess Leia's courier ship until she chooses his friend, an equally random R2 unit, to carry her plans. He also begins the story as exposition, telling R2-D2, "Did you hear that? They've shut down the main reactor. We'll be destroyed for sure. This is madness!" His character is thus revealed as a worrywart and bystander, about as far as one can get from heroism. Anthony Daniels notes of the casting that he had some trepidation about playing a robot. However, as he adds, "I realized he was not an ordinary robot and began to forget all my original ideas about playing a robot" (Rinzler, *The Making of Star Wars* 81). He adds:

> Threepio's character is transparent. I think that's why he's liked by so many people. There's no guile, no deviousness, no mystery. He is so obvious, and he always states the obvious. If everyone is cowering back as a meteor hits the window, he is the one who says, "Look, a meteor." In the wrong circumstances, that can be very irritating, but it can be very funny too ["In Their Own Words" 56].

While Threepio predicts that the princess will never escape, he has no plans to save her. He's contrasted with the Republic soldiers moments later, who defend their princess, guns drawn, and are slaughtered one by one. Meanwhile, C-3PO worries about himself and his best friend, fussing, "What are we going to do? We'll be sent to the spice mine of Kessel or smashed into who knows what!" Moments later, R2 calls him a "mindless philosopher," as Threepio translates, suggesting a thinker, not in any way a doer. Of course, this worry makes him terribly vulnerable, and thus, human. In context of the larger canon, this may be a result of his long partnership with Anakin. "Anakin had packed his creation with so many extra circuits and subprograms and heuristic algorithms that the droid was practically human" (Stover, *Revenge of the Sith* 107).

The original trilogy frames him as an ordinary person far out of his depth. "C-3PO is fluent in over six million forms of communication and has a strongly programmed desire to see things run smoothly, but neither of these traits prepared him for the turbulent events he would face. Transported into a world of adventure, this pragmatic character is often overwhelmed by the extraordinary action around him, but he faithfully serves his masters" (Reynolds, *Star Wars Visual Dictionary* 18). He's always given to panic and fussing. Further, he's defeatist or heroically self-sacrificing, depending how one reads his protest after being ripped apart by the Sand People. He insists, "I don't think I can make it. You go on, Master Luke. There's no sense in you risking yourself on my account. I'm done for." A restraining bolt mount is built into his chest, emphasizing that at every moment, he's only one step away from enforced slavery. He's much less than a person in their world, though he accepts servitude and prejudice as the norm, even counseling Artoo to obey and be grateful

Daniels says, "See-Threepio is a kind of English butler, a cross between Laurel and Hardy with his friend…. He loves being around Luke because that's his purpose—to look after people—he wants to make them happy. I think that's one reason why the part works" (Rinzler, *The Making of Star Wars* 151). In every moment, he's contrasted with R2 (named by Lucas for the film term "Reel 2 Dialogue 2"). Lucas notes, "I remember at some point it seemed dramatically more interesting to me to have both droids talk, but it took some of the mystery, charm, and uniqueness out of the characters. The idea was to make them different, have them bounce off each other to identify them easily as separate characters. I tried to make them as opposite as possible" (Bouzereau 11). Artoo is like a five-year-old—brave but naïve. His voice was modeled after baby babble—understandable even without words. Entrusted with the Death Star plans, he speeds off determinedly, letting Threepio trail behind him, calling in confusion. Artoo drags his friend on his "secret mission," even as he protests, and continues to act heroically even as Threepio panics. The two droids bicker, but their contrasting abilities make them an effective team. Of course, Threepio urges caution while Artoo proves basically fearless.

> C-3PO exhibits many more examples of anticipation, fear, anger, joy, as well as put-downs ("you near-sighted scrap-pile" and "overweight glob of grease," directed toward Artoo) and passive aggression ("fine, go that way, you'll be malfunctioning in a day," again directed toward Artoo). Threepio and Artoo share a very human-like, personable relationship wrought with the same kinds of normal, as well as abnormal, communication that any person may have in relationships. This is probably why we find them so appealing as characters—sometimes more so than the actual human characters in the films [Arp 131].

On the Death Star, they work together to free their friends from the garbage chute. Though they stay hidden, they're like the small animal helpers of fairytales who intervene when the hero needs a helping hand. these represent buried perception, skills the hero is developing that appear when needed. They're a cross between chorus and deus ex machina. Two tiny bureaucrats, the everyman and comic relief, hold the nine-film arc, as well as cartoons and other stories, together.

As far as their hero's journey, Artoo has a bit of a shadow in R5-D4, the red malfunctioning astromech that Owen and Luke reject. Of course, if the droid had not malfunctioned at that moment, the story would have been far different. The short story collection *From a Certain Point of View* tells its conflict—its lack of worldliness and desperation to be bought before sand ruins it completely. Artoo reasons with his counterpart, insisting he must save the galaxy. However, R5 rejects his impassioned plea. At the crucial moment, though, R5 recalls his mindwiped past. "Something inside him—an imprint, a phantom memory, something as old and stubborn as the stars—insisted that he help. Because the cause of the Rebellion was his mission, too" (Carson, "The Red One" 66). He burns up his circuits, endangering his own life, so Artoo can be bought and fulfill his destiny. The poignant story has the droid surviving the Jawas' destruction and going off to find sanctuary on a moisture farm "free and full of hope" (68). Artoo in turn is touched by his counterpart's sacrifice and vows never to forget him.

The robots must split up as the action heats up—Artoo flies with Luke to destroy the Death Star. By contrast, Threepio waits helplessly on the planet with Leia, like her, facing the possibility of instant death. However, he manages a moment of sweet, selfless heroism when Artoo is shot in combat and lies close to death: Threepio offers to donate his own parts. It should also be noted that while Threepio aids Leia and Artoo aids Luke through their programming, Threepio's offer here comes only from love. Of course, the droids return, whole, happy, and gleaming for the award ceremony, emphasizing that they have a happy ending as well.

Empire sees them split up once again, Artoo with Luke and Threepio chaperoning the flirting Leia and Han. Artoo falls into the swamp on Dagobah and appears to die for a moment—just as Luke does in the trash compactor—before he is spat out. Dagobah is certainly the magical world for Artoo, a spooky swamp world where Luke trains in invisible forces and ignores his sinking ship. He even lifts Artoo into the air during the ridiculous training. While Artoo is the voice of practicality for Luke, Luke becomes a spiritual guide for the little droid, showing other paths beyond following the rules.

On Bespin, Threepio's dismembered, in a sort of death and rebirth sequence (though one that's highly comedic). Director Irvin Kershner notes, "When Chewbacca is trying to put Threepio back together and he's got his head in his hands, that's like in Shakespeare's *Hamlet*; it's the grave digger staring down at the skull. That was my inspiration for this scene" (Bouzereau 204). His falling to pieces is pathetic and evocative. After this experience, he returns to be a more independent and capable droid.

Though many may not recall, Artoo saves the entire ship at the last moment, preserving the lives of all the heroes. It's the ignored tiny helper who proves himself in this moment. He continues his heroism in the next film, taking the initiative to open the door to the command center on Endor while he, Leia, and Han are under attack by stormtroopers.

Threepio and Artoo descend into the belly of the whale on their trek to Jabba's palace. To Threepio's shock, Luke has betrayed them—sent them as gifts to the monstrous Hutt. Of course, martyr that he is, he blames himself, fussing, "What could possibly have come over Master Luke. Is it something I did? He never expressed any unhappiness with my work." Aside from the audience, he seems the only one uninformed about Luke's rescue plan. Of course, this circumstance makes him seem even more pitiable. Like Luke, he's back on the planet of his youth confronting all he once was—he reverts from rebel to his previous job of protocol droid and slave fitted with a restraining bolt. This gives him the opportunity to see how far he's progressed.

Further, while inside, Threepio sees droids being horrifically tortured, even as he's informed his new job is a likely death sentence. He interprets for Jabba, but is knocked around in the process. He also faces literal death thanks to the threat of the thermal detonator. After this, he stands beside Jabba and, quaking, must witness the death of all his friends in the Sarlacc pit. He also faces dismemberment again as Salacious Crumb, Jabba's pet reptilian monkey, picks out one of the droid's eyes. This appears to comment on Threepio's lack of perception, as he's been blind to the rescue attempt plot. Of course, Artoo not only zaps Salacious but saves Threepio, knocking him into the sand before the barge can explode. At last, their friends rescue him, carrying him off on more adventures.

Following this, he stands in for a god on Endor. With this, Threepio "undergoes a kind of ironic hero's apotheosis for doing nothing more than looking the part" (Hanson and Kay 258). However, he also wins the Ewoks to the team's side and finally participates in battle. It should be noted that neither droid is built for deserts, forests, or any of the rough worlds where they find themselves—far from their places of power, they nonetheless triumph. Continuing this pattern on Endor, Threepio functions as the distraction at a crucial moment and helps the Rebels win the day, proving, like Artoo, that he has the heart of a hero.

Artoo, meanwhile, once more heroically goes into battle and nearly dies from it. Burned while trying to short circuit an Imperial door, he sizzles to a halt. "My goodness! Artoo, why did you have to be so brave?" Threepio cries. Of course, he's restored at film end.

In the seventh film, Artoo is revealed as having been dormant for some time, withdrawing in a near-death state. His hopelessness with Luke's loss adds a melancholy element to the film. At last, he revives when his old friends need his help. His death and return are not shown to enlighten him, but the emotions carry the audience along. He guilts Luke into helping in the eighth film, and continues to fight in the ninth. Of course, his seeming control through all these events lessens some of his apparent growth.

Terrified Threepio, however, has the real arc. Daniels explains: "In Episode VII, J.J. had so many things to recreate that C-3PO's main thing was a red arm—which we didn't like. And we told him on a daily basis, we didn't like it," he says, presumably referring to himself and C-3PO in a Gollum/Smeagol fashion. "Then in *The Last Jedi*, C-3PO, again, was rather like a bit of decoration at the side somewhere So l was kind of ready to be an extra again. For C-3PO as a character that I love—if he were to go to the movies and watch himself in this last movie, I think he'd be very pleased" (Shepherd 58). It's in this one, *Rise of Skywalker,* that Threepio finally finds heroism. He knows where the Emperor is massing his forces but cannot say, thanks to his anti–Sith programming. The team decide to wipe his memory. However, at the climax of this plot arc, Rey stops and asks him what they should do. Showing admiration for his skills at last, Rey adds that he knows the odds better than anyone. "Do we have a choice?" He concedes they don't. For a silent moment, he stares at the team.

"What, uh, what are you doing there, Threepio?" Poe asks.

"Taking one last look, sir, at my friends." It's a small, sweet moment, but it's an important one—the terrified droid, who stumbled through the films as a mostly unwilling bystander—commits to helping the rebel cause, even at the cost of all he is. Eventually, he is restored, but his simple sacrifice emphasizes the tiny hero's part in saving the galaxy.

Han Solo: Beyond the Antihero

At this point, Han Solo has two origin stories. One, a beloved trilogy by A.C. Crispin, introduces his birth family, whom he deals with in the larger saga. The other, the 2018 film *Solo*, rewrites all this canon. Humorously, the two story arcs are very similar. In both, Han is raised by a criminal smuggler, in the novels a man much like he becomes and a monster mother in the film (with Beckett taking on some of this role model part). He has a single friend, the Wookie cook in the novels and Qi'ra onscreen. He is thrown out of the Imperials for sticking to his principles (in the books for saving Chewbacca). After this, while going on heists, he meets Lando and eventually outgambles the professional player for the Falcon. He also brushes up against the early Rebellion but rejects their idealism for his own selfishness and practically. To his horror, his one true love betrays him, leaving him lonely and cynical.

In the first novel of Crispin's trilogy, Han's love interest Bria calls him "the ultimate pragmatist" (236). He replies, "It would be nice if there were some higher power, maybe. I just don't happen to believe there is" (236). She's an idealist but he just wants to stay safe and financially solvent. After she breaks his heart, he thinks, "From now on, it's just me, Han Solo.... Nobody else. I don't care about anybody else. *Nobody* gets close, from now on. I don't care how pretty she is, how smart, or how sweet. No friend, no lover … nobody is worth this kind of pain. From now on, it's just me…. Solo" (286). Qi'ra, his childhood love in the film, has a similar effect.

Onscreen, Beckett represents young Han's idea of the perfect criminal, with a crew and plenty of smarts. Looking at Beckett, "He felt like a kid, wanting to copy all of Beckett's smooth habits and talents" as the novelization explains (Lafferty 92). "Beckett really shapes Han more than anyone," says director Ron Howard of Woody Harrelson's character. "Han comes to realize that in a lawless time he needs to try to come to terms with some kind of moral code" ("Solo: A Star Wars Story"). The other man is commanding, competent and practical. With the immoral Empire in charge, he's struck a deal with the crime syndicates, who have their own codes. Beckett also has his lady love, something Han longs for in his own life. Watching Beckett and Val, "Han was torn between wanting to look away to give them privacy and wanting to look and see what love was like when you were allowed to have it," (Lafferty 91).

Beckett also gives him new opportunities as he introduces him around. With this, Han's ambition drives him as he meets increasingly better classes of smugglers. Looking at Dryden Vos's party, Han thinks, "He wanted this; he wanted to be one of these people, who were the kind that took what they wanted from those too stupid to hold on to it" (Lafferty 118). After growing up under the thumb of those with power, in an environment of only the fleecers and the fleeced, he wants to succeed. Like many characters, he finds his growth is reflected in the setting. "Most people, especially during the reign of the Empire, are under the control of some kind of force or another—no pun intended," Alden Ehrenreich (Han) says. "Having the resources and stability to call your own shots, do what you want, have freedom, isn't something that comes easily" ("Solo: A Star Wars Story").

Betrayed by Lando, Qi'ra and Beckett at the film's end, Han thinks, "Maybe I really can't trust anyone in this life" (Lafferty 270). Chewie, however, stays with him as family. Ultimately what Han comes to realize about the underworld is that no one is entirely reliable, so he resolves not to trust anybody. In both the Crispin novels and in *Solo*, he shoots his mentor in a life-or-death struggle and ascends to be his own mentor, keeping himself out of trouble. Following this, Han also has a problematic relationship with Jabba the Hutt. Arguably, Jabba sends the rather incompetent Greedo to threaten Han as a warning but not a deadly one. In the remastered scene in *A New Hope*, the pair come to an agreement, as Jabba offers a little more time … before raising the price on his head. All these killers treat Han paternally, leaving him in a family dynamic nearly as twisted as Vader and Luke's. Like Luke, Han must choose for himself benevolent and honorable ways to use his skills while battling the wicked mentors who use them to harm others.

The name "solo" emphasizes his loner status (especially in the film, when he deliberately takes it on). He's clearly descended from the gunslinger types in Westerns. "An Anti-hero is not the opposite of a Hero, but a specialized kind of Hero, one who may be an outlaw or a villain from the point of view of society, but with whom the audience is basically in sympathy. We identify with these outsiders because we have all felt like outsiders at one time or another," Vogler explains (34). All this sets up his cynicism and greed in his first appearance, sitting in the Mos Eisley cantina. As the original film reveals, Han is desperate for enough cash to pay off Jabba after he dumped the Hutt's smuggled spice cargo. Beyond this, however, he seems fully uninterested in the Rebellion.

He's also dismissive of the Force, providing a foil for naïve Luke. "Kid, I've flown from one side of this galaxy to the other. I've seen a lot of strange stuff, but I've never seen anything to make me believe there's one all-powerful force controlling everything. There's no mystical energy field that controls my destiny." Harrison Ford notes that this line really defined his character for him (Rinzler, *Making* 105). Lucas adds, "I was looking for a 'foil' for Luke. Luke is the young, idealistic, naïve, clean kid about to be initiated into the rites of manhood. So to make that really work, I needed something to contrast him against" (Bouzereau 47). Thus, he created Solo as "a cynical world-weary pessimist" (47).

In the hero's journey, the character is guided towards his true inner self—all he's buried and denied within but desperately seeks. "For a character seeking to belong, this dynamic supports Han's romantic relationship with Leia, as finding a soulmate moves a character toward the path of creating a family" (Barr, "Han Solo" 11). In a memorable moment of the first film, Han muses, "Still, she's got a lot of spirit. I don't know, what do you think? Do you think a princess and a guy like me…." Luke says no with finality and looks away. The novelization adds, "Solo smiled at the younger man's jealousy, uncertain in his own mind whether he had added the comment to bait his naïve friend—or because it was the truth" (Lucas 151).

"Look, I ain't in this for your revolution, and I'm not in it for you,

Princess. I expect to be well paid. I'm in it for the money!" Han insists. While he hesitates to battle the Empire and only agrees to rescue Princess Leia because she's rich, he does the right thing repeatedly on a subtle level, suggesting his capacity for more. He protects his passengers and keeps them from the Empire even as he grumbles. He even wishes Luke "May the Force be with you," much as he maintains that he doubts. He's not transforming as much as Luke, but he's certainly learning from the idealists and rebels around him. While Han insists he's Luke's inverse and only deals in the practical, he travels on the opposite path. When Han rushes in at the film's end and rescues Luke, it's not a shocking departure for his character but a feel-good natural progression.

> His affection for Chewbacca is obvious from our first encounter with him, and he quickly develops an older brother's affection for Luke. Even more importantly, Han shows a capacity for something more. When Leia rebukes him, "If money is all that you love, then that's what you'll receive" and then turns to Luke to add, "I wonder if he really cares about anything or anyone," Han is clearly hurt. When Luke chides him for refusing to join the Rebel attack on the Death Star, Han looks obviously guilty, and Chewie reproaches him as only he can. So while Han claims that he rescues Luke from Darth Vader in the Death Star trench because "I wasn't going to let you [Luke] get all the credit and take all the reward," we know that he does it for Luke [Dees 41].

At *Empire*'s start, he's an established rebellion member and even a general. Leia tells Han, "You're a natural leader...." while coaxing him to stay. Certainly, Han has presented himself much more like a loose cannon to this point. Still, Leia as the anima can see his potential—who he can become to save their rebellion. Of course, Han believes he wants no part of this.

Despite his growing interest in Leia, Han's true anima is his ship, which he calls "she" and addresses with loving phrases like "Come on, baby, hold together." As the *Solo* novelization describes, "It was the most beautiful thing he had ever seen. No other Corellian freighter had ever looked like this" (Lafferty 149). The prequel trilogy describes his first seeing the ship as falling completely in love. The ship represents freedom, while Leia brings the more off-putting responsibility and duty.

Han starts *Empire* attempting to leave. As a truly reluctant hero, he's packed and halfway out the door, refusing the Rebels' call in decisive fashion. However, responsibility hauls him back once more when he discovers Luke has vanished. Though Han turns off his communicator, refusing Leia's calls to action, Threepio tracks him down and delivers them in person. The herald always finds a way. Han's haste in going to find his friend suggests he only needed an excuse to stay: He has embraced the Rebel cause, even if he hasn't admitted this to himself. Outside, he has his own death-descent (not as dramatic as Luke's) as he vanishes into the snows while his rebel friends gaze helplessly out into the wastelands and Chewie moans in despair.

He returns from the snows with Luke, not in possession of new Force powers, but with a new acceptance of his ties to his friends. Even when the base is evacuated, he delays, rushing to the command center to protect Leia (and incidentally, Threepio). He insists on escorting her to her ship, and when the way is blocked, he takes her with him on the Falcon. He even pauses to rescue the irritating droid.

In the second film, as he pursues Leia, he is ascending spiritually, learning to value another over himself. After all his pronouncements that he'll never succumb to love or others' causes, he hates how much he's falling for her. Still, he finds himself opening up. This is also a path towards the lofty goals of the rebellion. Another death and rebirth soon follows in the asteroid cave, where the team realize their haven is a monstrosity and then make a dramatic escape … foreshadowing and paralleling the events on Bespin.

"Symbolically the space slug is representative of any experience involving hideous fears that suddenly develop out of nowhere and threaten to consume us" (Galipeau 120). To Han, the creature is the smothering monster—the all-powerful mother who will leave him wholly dependent and obedient to all her whims, a mother figure as big as a small world, which keeps him tethered while he longs for independence. (This image goes even deeper after the revelation in *Solo* that he was raised by a similar-looking creature.) It's an exaggeration of how he sees Leia. Of course, Han dreads getting caught up in responsibility just as much as he fears giving in to love. Escaping the creature provides a sort of catharsis even while proving he can flee intact.

The pair share a brief romance on board his ship. Director Irvin Kershner says of *Empire*, "We didn't need to spend too much time of the love story. When Han tried to kiss her, that was enough. In the *Star Wars* series, a kiss is the equivalent of a sex scene" (Bouzereau 172). Han, Luke, and Leia also share aspects of the complete hero, with the pair deepening romantically even as Luke expands spiritual awareness. Likewise, while Luke is learning calm and mastery, Han's attacks, even the suicidal charge at the Imperial ship, emphasize how he's enacting the active part. Leia remains the thinker and planner who obeys her duty.

They set off for repairs on Bespin, where Han encounters another foil. Symbolically, Han visits to reconcile with his disreputable past before moving forward with the Alliance and with Leia. However, he immediately sees all his worst flirtatious, untrustworthy, amoral qualities appearing in his old friend. Lando greets Leia as a "what" not a who, ignores Threepio, and insults Han, as well as laying claim to his precious ship. He's Han at his worst. Of course, he maintains the mask or pretense that he is a responsible leader and willing to serve the Empire.

Another, darker shadow appears as well. By the second film, Jabba has hired unprincipled, deadly Boba Fett to bring Han back to him. Han and Boba tangle in the prequel novels trilogy, during which Han develops respect for this deadly predator. Irvin Kershner, *Empire*'s director, explains: "He's not really a character, however. Boba Fett is a frightening dramatic element to create tension which puts Han Solo in danger. The concept worked dramatically. The idea of a bounty hunter means someone who will never give up" (Snyder 33).

Boba Fett is presented as Han's shadow, not only because the other man is hunting him. Fett reflects Han as a fellow criminal, though one who never saw the light of heroism. Admittedly, Han Solo once smuggled drugs for Jabba the Hutt and even served as a cadet in the Imperial Army. He is not generally a killer, but the part of him that shot Greedo (first!) understands Fett's expedient brutality. "Han Solo, under different circumstances, on a different day, could be Boba Fett, and Fett, given the right tweaks of conscience, could be Solo. This is what drapes both characters in their many fascinations" (Bissell 14).

In fact, the character is presented as a more expedient version of Han himself—not an outlaw with a heart of gold but a true mercenary. In Jeremy Barlow and Daxiong's *Boba Fett and the Ship of Fear*, taking place a few years before *Jedi*, the character explains, "I don't worry about who I am or what I'm supposed to be. I just get the job done." He abandons his victims to burn to death but shrugs off killing them as "there's no money in it." With this, he's presented as truly amoral, neutral in the galactic conflict and also in whether rivals live or die. In many collections including this one and the Han Solo prequels he carefully cultivates his reputation. At the same time, he fiercely follows an honor code in all the expanded universe materials. The visual dictionary explains, "Fett's services are famously expensive, but his honor cannot be bought. He only accepts missions which meet his harsh sense of justice" (Reynolds 50). Fett is cool, calm, self-disciplined. In many ways, this sets him in opposition to Han:

> Not only is Solo a smuggler and a drug runner (hauling glitterstim spice for the gangster Jabba the Hutt), he is unreliable (drops his cargo at the first sign of an Imperial Cruiser), arrogant (sits in a popular cantina when he knows full well there's a price on his head), underhanded (shoots from under the table), a braggart (please don't tell us about that Kessel Run one more time!) and a turn-coat (leaves the Imperial academy, breaks the law by being a smuggler, then joins the Rebel Alliance). From Boba Fett's perspective, Solo must be quite a despicable human being! [Snyder 33]

When Leia speaks with Fett in his short story in *Tales of the Bounty Hunters*, he uses the exact words Han once did, paralleling the characters even further. She offers him "More than *you* can imagine," and he shoots back, "I can imagine quite a lot." She promises, "You'll get it" (D. Moran 296). When she feels like she's negotiating with the unenlightened Han from their first meeting, the readers can see how much Boba and Han echo. He even tells her he doesn't believe the Force exists, and she adds, "You remind me of Han Solo a little" (D. Moran 297). Fett, meanwhile, prides himself on discipline and ethics—disdaining Han for smuggling spice and otherwise breaking ethical rules of the galaxy. Leia must admit he has a point.

While Fett is an adversary, he isn't the central one of the film. On Bespin, Vader, the darkest shadow of all, confronts Han's team, and Han unhesitatingly shoots. In this moment, confronted by pure evil, he fights for goodness. Of course, lacking Luke's training and wisdom, Han fails to kill Vader—pure action is no match for such a villain. Following this, Vader tortures him in order to summon Luke. For Han, however, the physical torture echoes his internal struggle facing his long-buried emotions as he struggles to move past them and begin a new relationship.

Since the fragmented group represents a solo hero, it's clear that each part is struggling toward enlightenment. Threepio's vanishing emphasizes the fragmentation that begins striking the heroes. Their lack of communication as Lando plots to betray them and Han and Leia squabble is the real enemy.

Han and Leia share a moment of love and true understanding as he's frozen in carbonite. This represents transcendence before Han's death and rebirth. Beyond romance, this connection has a deeper significance: In a Sacred Marriage, both sides of the personality come into balance, equally valued and celebrated. By loving Leia, Han loves the idealistic side of himself.

It brings Han not only a temporary death but one of loss and suffering. Director Irvin Kershner notes, "When the cast of Solo in carbon freeze was created for the first time, he was standing straight up, looking normal. That's what the prop department thought I wanted. I said, 'No, he's got to be looking like he is fighting to get out; he has to look like he is in agony'" (Bouzereau 209). Indeed, a total loss of agency, leaving him at the mercy of Fett and Jabba, is the freedom-loving scoundrel's worst nightmare. He who used to immorally smuggle cargo has been transformed into it. In a further twist, this also leaves him more reliant on his loved ones than he's ever been in his life. He is lost to his friends, as Boba flies off with him, the others in pursuit.

When he's awakened in *Jedi,* his blindness emphasizes the difficulty of the road back, as he returns from the underworld and must adjust to his old life now with new insights and understanding. Emerging from death to an equal loving relationship is Han's road of return—which sometimes must be aided by another. This task, Leia performs, mothering him and presiding over his second birth. Now more mature, he and Leia can approach their relationship without denial and squabbling. "Heroes can sometimes experience a profound self-realization after tricking death.... Maybe it doesn't last long, but for a moment heroes see themselves clearly" (Vogler 181).

Just as Han encounters his old self by reconnecting with Lando in Episode V, he now sees his former career in Jabba. After witnessing how Jabba kills slaves, tortures droids, and demeans his slave girls—including Leia, Han is repelled. Now with a taste of being treated as merchandise, Han resolutely rejects the smuggler's life.

The Sarlacc, like the primordial destruction lurking as man's shadow, is the next foe to defeat. As Threepio puts it, "In his belly, you will find a new definition of pain and suffering, as you are slowly digested over a thousand years." Falling into it means a descent into hell and eternal torment.... Lando who betrayed his friend comes the closest. When Han saves him, he emphasizes the power of forgiveness and teamwork. Han's new selflessness becomes clear, and it's Boba Fett, his amoral bounty hunter shadow, who gets devoured instead. In another transformation, Han accepts that the others have risked themselves for him through friendship. "That realization made him feel indebted, a feeling he'd always abhorred; only now the debt was somehow a new kind of bond, a bond of brotherhood. It was even freeing in a strange way" (Kahn 393).

On the film's central mission, Han is put in command, as a general. Clearly, Han has fully given himself to the Rebels and become part of their fight. According to production meeting notes, his camouflage coat represents "the idea is that Han has joined the rebels and been assimilated into the fold while Luke has taken Han's position as the 'individual'" (Alinger 174). Luke of course, goes off on a more selfish quest to redeem his father.

To infiltrate Endor, Han's team plan to disguise themselves as Imperials. This is a shadow moment, tasting the other side's power and masquerading as them long enough to succeed. They fly a small Imperial ship down, entering the Belly of the Beast once again. There, Han lures the troops out by once more pretending to be one of them. Considering that he's a smaller soldier on the side of good—not a gifted Jedi like Luke but an ordinary man, pitting him against ordinary villains emphasizes the many levels on which the war is being fought. He is the baser, more action-oriented part of the hero, as the Stormtroopers are for the villain.

Meanwhile, Han is working with Lando as a friend. Even as he shares his precious ship with the other man, Han is finally letting go of his favorite toy in order to find a more balanced relationship. The novelization adds, "The modifications Solo added had really made the Falcon a part of him—he'd put his love and sweat into it. His spirit. So giving her to Lando now was truly Solo's final transformation—as selfless a gift as he'd ever given" (Kahn 412).

Of course, he and Leia face death together side by side, exchanging a joint "I love you" "I know" before their rescue and triumph. They end the film in love, having earned their happy ending. Han has finally committed, and finally prepares to settle down.

Chewie: Perpetual Sidekick

Chewie is described as intelligent—Han's partner and equal. However, the movies suggest otherwise. He barks, moans, growls, and roars. His irritated companions call him a "flea-bitten furball" and "big furry oaf." He's caught in a trap on Endor because he wants a dead animal swinging from a rope. When Luke tries to handcuff him, he roars in anger, while Han works out the plan and talks Chewie into it. He lashes out violently without thinking things through. In the carbonite scene, only Han's giving him a new mission stops him from his violent rampage. All this makes Chewie appear more loyal dog than person. In fact, "Chewbacca as a copilot was inspired by George Lucas's own dog, Indiana, who used to sit in the passenger seat of his car" (Bray et al. 46). Even Chewie's color scheme was modeled after an Alsatian (Alinger 46). His original actor Peter Mayhew explains, "Chewie's a teddy bear. Everybody has had a teddy bear at some stage in their lives. He's loveable; he's cuddly. I don't know what it is" (Ashworth 40).

In the books, it's clearer that Han converses with him as an equal. In the *Han Solo* trilogy, detailing his youth, Han sympathetically takes Chewie to his home planet repeatedly to see his family. Han also worries about Chewie's judging him. Throughout their adventures, Chewie has a nobility that contrasts Han's expediency. He dreams of saving his people from the Empire. Han thinks, "Freeing an entire world was a noble cause…. He hadn't even thought about the rest of the galaxy" (Lafferty 92). However, Chewie is a quintessential sidekick because of his film plot. He aids Han and encourages him, acting as his copilot and bodyguard in his life-debt, but basically never seeking anything for himself.

Through the original trilogy, Chewie spends his time observing and commenting on the humans' behavior. Peter Mayhew describes ad-libbing about fifty percent of his dialogue, noting, "The way I looked at it, say we're in the cockpit. You've got four people in there. Chewie can't stand there looking like a piece of furniture. He has to react to everybody's attitude. And he can't say verbally what he wants to, so he either has to use his mouth, or eyes, or body language of some sort" (Ashworth 40). A few moments stand out for his laughter, pain or other commentary. These mostly serve to add emotion to the scene like music does—if all the characters make a single hero, Chewie is the wordless sentiment driving important scenes like Han's sacrifices. Director Irvin Kershner says, "When you're in the hangar and the door is closing, I thought, the doors are closing and here is Chewbacca who is like a dog, he is hurt, the one he loves is out there in the snow. So as the doors slam shut, I had him scream in agony. That wasn't in the original script that was a decision I made during filming" (Bouzereau 136).

In earlier drafts, Chewie was introduced on his home planet, where he led his brethren in an uprising (similar to the Ewok plot of *Jedi*). This Wookie revolution would have given them their own goals and thus more of an arc. The novel *Dark Lord: The Rise of Darth Vader* has him bombing Kashyyyk and taking the Wookies as slaves between Episodes III and IV. As with Alderaan, this shows the galaxy the strength and cruelty of the Empire and of Vader himself. It also gives Chewie a reason to hate Vader directly. Thousands die; hundreds of thousands are imprisoned. One of the escapees reports, "Just before we jumped from Kashyyyk, Chewbacca said that he believed he could be of greater help to his people from afar" (Luceno 1083). He travels the galaxy trying to find his captured people and liberate them. Destroying the Death Star with its Emperor is as personal for him as it is for Leia: "Chewbacca will have his revenge on the Empire with the death of the Emperor and the destruction of the second Death Star during the Battle of Endor. Jointly commanded by Chewbacca and General Han Solo, an Alliance task force will restore peace to Kashyyyk" (Luceno, *Revenge Visual Dictionary* 49).

Of course, beyond the loyal dog imagery, Chewie is also a force of nature like the Ewoks and thus the antithesis of the Empire. On Kashyyyk, finally depicted onscreen in *Revenge of the Sith*, wooden catamarans and insectlike fluttercraft emphasize the Wookies' link to nature, as do the forest architecture and beautifully carved wooden weapons. When the larger novel series take the team here, Chewie is in his element and the humans must follow his lead.

Endor presents a similar dynamic, as Chewie has trained to fight Imperials using the natural landscape. Lucas says, "The Wookie planet that I created for *Star Wars* was eventually turned into the Ewok planet in *Jedi*. I basically cut the Wookies in half and called them Ewoks! I didn't make Endor a Wookiee planet because Chewbacca was sophisticated technologically and I wanted the characters involved in the battle to be primitive" (Bouzereau 281).

Chewie's shadow moment comes as he and the Ewoks take over an Imperial Walker. From within it, they see through the eyes of the enemy, feeling the Stormtroopers' typical arrogant power. However, Chewie uses it to beat the troopers at their own game, firing laser blasts at unsuspecting Stormtroopers, and destroying other Imperial walkers. Wielding this weapon, he rescues Han at the crucial moment, blows the base doors, and saves the mission and thus the galaxy.

The rather infamous but somewhat canon Holiday Special introduced Chewie's wife Malla, father Itchy, and son Lumpy. The *Star Wars Encyclopedia* adds that they're short for Attichitcuk, Mallatobuck, and Lumpawarrump. In the Extended Universe, they feature mostly as background characters, understanding that Chewie's debt and friendship with Han mean he will only occasionally visit their world. The new canon novels bridge the gap between *Return of the Jedi* and *The Force Awakens* while dealing with the threat to Chewie's home planet. Upon hearing Kashyyyk will be underguarded for a limited window, Han abandons his Republic mission. He and Chewie gather all their smuggler and bounty hunter allies and set out to free Chewie's home. In a brief scene in *Aftermath: Empire's End*, Chewie rescues his son Lumpawaroo from slavery. It's a wordless emotional scene, punctuated by scent. At last, "Chewbacca lifts his head to the sky and ululates a good song, a true song, a song of family, of lost love found once more" (Wendig 54). After their triumph, in new canon Han convinces Chewie to stay there with his family.

Both series have Chewie accomplish his goal of liberating his world and regaining his family after Episode VI. However, whether on Kashyyyk or sailing among the stars with Han, Chewie doesn't seem to have evolved much. Even after Han's death in *Force Awakens*, Chewie takes the co-pilot seat, leaving Rey as main pilot and planner. After decades of work, he's the sidekick, even to a younger, untrained human.

Joonas Suotamo split the role with Peter Mayhew in *The Force Awakens* but took over the role for the next films after the original actor's death. Suotamo has now played Chewbacca in four movies and enjoys it quite a lot. "It's very much like silent-era film, with Buster Keaton and Charlie Chaplin," he says. "He's a mime character and that's what he does, and I guess in that minimalism comes the beauty of the character" (Grossman, "Tour de Force"). He mixes it up a bit as a younger Chewie (though still about two hundred) in the prequel film *Solo* and comments that this was a different experience:

> You get to play, get to present Chewbacca as some-one who is a free individual, and he has a choice to make whether or not to tag along with this rascal scoundrel called Han. Really, it was interesting to play that decision-making [process] of, "I don't really trust you, but I'm going to hang around for this job with you and see where it goes." It was interesting to play a kind of independent Chewbacca for a second [Spelling 37].

By the sequel films, he's grown into the experienced mentor who advises Rey on what to say to Finn and fights beside the heroes, a bit more of an Obi-Wan figure even as they continue battling evil. At the same time, the conflicts central to Chewie's life are rarely explored. Episode IX ends with his receiving his friend Han's medal, presumably as a nod to the fannish question of why he wasn't rewarded in Episode IV. However, this tiny salute does little to emphasize the character's importance.

Lando: Collaborator-Ruler to General

Lando was imagined as a new Han Solo, a riverboat gambler type, an elegant James Bond, a businessman who thinks he can outsmart the Empire (Bouzereau 196). A bit of all this formed the character.

The Lando Calrissian Adventures, a set of prequel novels, demonstrate several important aspects of his character. A few brief flashbacks reveal his past. "The seventeen-year-old would-be professional gambler writhed inwardly. He'd practically begged for a chance to join the game in the back room of the local saloon. He'd lied to his family, ducked out on school, broken or severely bent several ordinances about minors and environments such as the one he found himself in now" (Smith 253). More interesting is the self-deception. He tells everyone he's an opportunist gambler but actually has a deep moral streak. He discovers an entire population being oppressed by life-orchards that drain the population's intelligence and longevity. This results in a people whom the establishment call "savages" and mercilessly exploit. In response, he travels the galaxy freeing slaves, establishing that he's interconnected, not the solo hero he claims. Lando is rather startled that he's turned humanitarian but accepts it. As he concludes, "Compared to the rest of the universe we're the good guys" (274).

As the trilogy continues, the Sorcerer Rokur Gepta becomes his nemesis. He schemes to control the galaxy, while freewheeling Lando defends the freedoms of those around him. "All Lando wanted was to be left alone. He'd tried explaining via various media, that he didn't care who ran the universe—he'd break whatever rules it suited him to disobey in any case, whoever was in charge" (287). The sorcerer also, as a shadow figure, taunts him about his self-perception. He says, "I suspect that you pretend to be a blasé Core-may-care, live-and-let-live sort of rogue, Captain. But you are a moralist at heart" (251). As he adds, "You're a brave man, Captain Calrissian. You don't like to think of it that way. What do you call it, 'creative cowardice'? You regard yourself a pragmatist, one not given to heroics" (255). Thus challenged, Lando strikes out for the underdogs and saves them … and makes a handsome profit to boot. Off he soars in the Millennium Falcon, still a consummate gambler and lover of fine things with no ties holding him back. Still, these tests have revealed he'll choose morality and heroism when pushed—a strong character point that also appears in *Empire*.

The *Solo* film similarly casts young Lando as a proponent of freedom—especially in his respect for his sassy droid sidekick L-337. As she demands equal rights and insults him, he encourages her, finally mourning her death with great sincerity as he struggles to save her. This devotion foreshadows the friendship he will build with Han. Likewise, his keeping someone who constantly punctures his ego as his copilot emphasizes that he welcomes a reality check. His stylishness with his cape collection and affective speech also pay off in *Empire,* where his self-image as dependable friend, cautious leader, and man innocent of the compromises he's made all confront him.

Of course, all this was filled in long after the events of *Empire.* This very seventies film was matched by the bell-bottomed, flamboyant figure. His capes, very seventies, also mark him as a space-baron or space-adventurer-pirate. "I always liked Errol Flynn, Douglas Fairbanks, Jr., the swashbuckling stars," says Billy Dee Williams (Falcone et al.). Others sensed it too. "Williams' ridiculously suave rogue-trader is given a lavish entrance, striding across the screen in his full swerve-on, 47-degree-angle walk, trailed by a cape and an entourage" (Mitchell 77). Lando's blue cape is lined with golden dragon fabric, stressing his wealthy scoundrel persona. He flirts with everyone, as one critic describes "the heavy-lidded you-belong-to-me stare, the lazy magnetism and liquid seductiveness of Williams's speaking rhythms" (Mitchell 77). Further, his love of crazy schemes and gambling explains his place of Cloud City—a wobbly base literally hanging from the sky.

Even through his friendly flirting, he has a single choice to make—if and when he will defy the Empire. His quandary echoes the Nazi collaborators of a generation before, loathing the occupation but forced to work with it to protect the country's people or under threat of execution.

> Dealing with supply problems, labor difficulties, and the complexities of running a large enterprise, Lando understands, is "the price you pay for being successful." Yet even before we actually meet him, he has been confronted with a nasty moral dilemma: he can either betray his old friend Han and turn him over to Darth Vader, or he can allow Bespin to be overrun by Imperial stormtroopers. We might view Lando's decision as egoistic: he betrays Han to save his own neck. But Lando's decision is not so self-serving. The lives of everyone on Bespin will be made substantially worse if the Empire controls it, so Lando make a fairly straightforward utilitarian decision [Dees 54].

The Empire relies on a patriarchal structure, issuing dictates from the top which those below scramble to obey. Trapped in this system, Lando has made the best bargain he could. Battling it, as must happen on occasion, "The Ruler archetype typically forces a confrontation with power and with the limits of one's power" (Pearson 186). When the conflict comes, Lando fully understands his lack of options. "He's a survivor. It's expediency for him," Williams says. "You know, he was thrown into a situation which he didn't look for and he had to try to figure out how to deal with an entity which is more than just a human." And, he adds, "nobody died!" (Grossman, "Tour de Force").

When Vader arrives and takes Han away for torture, Lando visibly suffers and he pleads for Vader to spare them all. Viewers hope he'll defy the Empire. However, much is at stake for Lando, and not just personally. As a ruler, he lacks the luxury of standing up for his principles—if he disobeys, his people will suffer. Finally, Lando's sudden rescue in the second film echoes Han's in the first—each has a change of heart, choosing morality and friendship over self-interest. This is a great sacrifice, greater than Han makes. "By turning against the Imperial forces of Darth Vader, Lando loses everything he has built as Baron Administrator of Cloud City. Racing through the corridors of the city with Leia and Chewbacca, Lando witnesses Boba Fett lift off with Han Solo, and barely escapes with his life from the city he once ruled" (Reynolds, *Visual Dictionary* 23).

After losing his colony, he is freer to act. Immediately, he teams up with Leia and the others. He risks his life to save Han, emphasizing that his collaboration was for others, not himself. "And, once he has rescued Han, he doesn't hesitate to join the Rebel forces in what looks like a suicide mission to attack the second Death Star. Far from being a narrow egoist, Lando is in fact one of the most morally courageous figures in the *Star Wars* saga" (Dees 46).

In the third film, Lando wears a brown outfit much like the Rebel uniforms, but with a pink cape to give him some swagger. Clearly, he's joined up. Lando not only wants to make amends but seeks glory and revenge in the Rebel Alliance. "The Imperial police had moved in on his action once too often; so this was a grudge match now," adds the novelization (Kahn 364).

Now there is a new group of heroes—including Lando and Wedge—attacking the Death Star as Leia, Han, Chewie, and Luke, the more mature leaders and generals, complete the more personally harrowing tasks. During this mission, Lando gets the hotshot pilot job Luke and Han took in the first film. Lando, like Luke, projects faith in the team. He demands "more time"—in contrast with the Empire's quick and dirty methodologies and the ease of the Dark Side of the Force.

As Luke did, he journeys into the heart of the Death Star. "The hero must find the valor within himself—traveling into the labyrinth of his soul—in order to destroy his foe" (Hanson and Kay 268). There, Lando shoots the main reactor shaft and destroys the reactor—not with the grace of the Force but with hard-earned skill at piloting and a crack team. He bursts from the Death Star just as it explodes in his own near-death and rebirth. "Lando's cry announces a new birth by fire, both for himself and the ship he pilots" (Galipeau 248). He ends the story as a respected teammate and continues his adventures through the novels, from get-rich-quick schemes to trying to win back the Falcon from Han.

The ninth film reveals where he's been in the intervening decades, even as Leia summons him back to the fight. The visual guide fills in more details: "Six years after the tragedy that befell his family," Lando found his way to the planet Pasaana, investigating with Luke. "Lando, however, did find some peace and a sense of community among the humble Aki-Aki; and decided to stay. Once again shielded from an escalating conflict, he felt he had earned his rest after so much sacrifice" (Hidalgo and Terrio 115). Like Obi-Wan, he has faded from general to reclusive monk, and then returned for a final fight, to mentor the young heroes. At 82, Billy Dee Williams returns to the part, welcoming the new heroes in the place of the original trio.

Besides his role as guide, he plays an essential part in the final film, rallying the entire galaxy to fight for the Resistance and vanquish the First Order. His contacts and charm, it's suggested, have brought this about. He ends the film taking off with a young woman who, the *Visual Guide* and novel hint, might be his long-lost daughter. As he protests in the latter work, the forces of evil have made this conflict personal: "The First Order went after us—the leaders from the old wars. They took our kids" (Carson 74). He comments that his daughter, old enough to walk when they took her, is likely a Stormtrooper. Lando adds that they did this "to kill the spirit of the Rebellion for good." If this is the case, he has won his lost child back from them in a personal and spiritual victory, not just a political one. He has also achieved triumphant fatherhood even as he suspected all his life stages had ended. He ends the novel with a new mission: resolving to go find the "thousands, maybe millions of kids" taken by the First Order and free them (Carson 243). With this, he takes an aggressive fatherly role, mentoring the many of the next generation who will need his guidance.

Darth Vader: The Failed Tyrant

Darth Vader, in his first onscreen appearance, strides onto Leia's ship, seven feet of masked, black clad intimidation. He's a mash-up of fright with a motorcycle suit, a medieval cloak, a gas mask, a Nazi helmet, and armored shoulderpiece. John Mollo, costume designer from episodes IV and V, comments, "Darth Vader was mocked up from four separate departments: A World War II German helmet and gas mask from the military department; a monk's cloak from the ecclesiastical division; a leather undersuit from the motorcycle department; and a metal breastplate from the medieval section"

(Biggar 28). Vader's breathing sound, made with scuba gear, emphasizes his artificiality and also his strength of personality—even his breathing intrudes on and dominates his scenes.

Vader is Dutch for Father, emphasizing his role as evil patriarch of the story. One critic writes, "Black robes, helmet, asthma. Brutal, invulnerable, accountable for nothing. His black eyes were opaque, his expression permanently grim, ready to hurt without any thought of consequences or control. It was the lack of remorse that told me everything. Even then, long before the release of *The Empire Strikes Back*, I knew who he was. I knew he was somebody's father" (Krouse 95). His voice is masked, artificial behind all the technology. His helmet conceals his face, offering audiences a compelling mystery. The nearly-destroyed Anakin hides behind all these veils as does the duplicitous dark side, lying in wait for the unwary.

> Endlessly a cipher, endlessly an intrigue, he was the only question *Star Wars* posed to its audience, the only mystery presented. We might imagine behind the mask the face of Hitler, the face of a monster, the face of a machine, a skull with gaping eye sockets, or far, far more, sometime horrifying and primeval, beyond words as well as beyond sight, unspeakable. There was no end to what we could imagine, and for that reason the mask was, needless to say, far more compelling than anything that could be behind it, as is the way with masks [Millet 134].

Surrounded by the fascist white armored suits of the Imperial Stormtroopers, he's pure terrorization. When he first arrives, everyone instinctively backs away and a deathly quiet sweeps through the Rebel troops. Several run. The others he easily destroys.

His tools, from starships to stormtroopers, all emphasize the Empire's massive tyrannous might but also its mechanization. The 1,600-meter Imperial Star Destroyer is the pride of the Imperial Navy, a piercing pale weapon against the emptiness. "Its sharp silhouette has become a symbol of imperial power." In fact, there are "tens of thousands" of these ships 1,600 meters in length, each crewed by 37,000 men (Wallace, *Imperial Handbook* 40). The first shot of the film shows the ship's overwhelming size, a theme that will continue as the Empire dominates the galaxy's tiny individual heroes. Its pure massiveness as it slowly enters the movie frame denotes the Empire's overwhelming power.

All this artificiality and pursuit of total domination over all freedom reflects Vader himself. More than ruling this fleet, Vader has let the machine dominate him instead of the reverse. Campbell explains, "You see, consciousness thinks it's running the shop. But it's a secondary organ of a total human being, and it must not put itself in control. It must submit and serve the humanity of the body. When it does put itself in control, you get a man like Darth Vader in *Star Wars*, the man who goes over to the consciously intentional side" (Campbell and Moyers 181).

The Empire itself is known for restricting individual freedoms and favoring humans over alien races. Visually and symbolically, it takes much from the Nazis and their fascism. Here, too, Vader has allowed this outside force to take him over. He has completely lost touch with his humanity, to the point that he preys on others. Like Voldemort, Sauron, and others, he is the tyrant-king—the evil father and ruler of the series. He rules cruelly, force-choking and even killing his subordinates.

Of course, just as Obi-Wan faces Vader, Vader must face his old nemesis and mentor. He approaches this revelation with caution, though no discernable fear. As the supreme tyrant of the first film (before the Emperor's later arrival), he has achieved the height of power. However, doing so in such a hierarchy means someone always waits to topple him from his position. From the peak, there's nowhere to go but down.

Though Tarkin dismisses Obi-Wan and his ancient "religion," Vader still uses the Force, and moreover, senses the confrontation before him. He goes alone to face his ancient foe, the one who destroyed him physically and trapped him in the life-support suit for decades. This battle reflects the one filmed decades later in *Revenge of the Sith*. As he tells his old mentor, "I've been waiting for you, Obi-Wan. We meet again, at last. The circle is now complete." This time, Obi-Wan takes a classical offensive position and Vader takes a defensive stance. Vader adds, "When I left you, I was but the learner; now I am the master." Obi-Wan has faded to a shadow who's been hiding for decades, while Vader dominates the galaxy. This scene has a further mythic significance: "Their clash embodies many conflicts, Jedi and Sith, Empire and Rebellion, and also a personal distaste for each other" (Hanson and Kay 168).

Cavan Scott's short story "Time of Death" has Obi-Wan observe how carefully they're both fighting, each testing the other's skills after so many decades. "Perhaps we are more alike than I care to think," Obi-Wan concludes, nodding to the hero and shadow connection they share (340). At the same time, he decides his friend is truly dead and refuses to call him Anakin. Obi-Wan is battling the dark side, not his former partner.

The pair battle and Darth taunts Obi-Wan with his age and weakness. However, the saga's sage has a different view thanks to the wisdom he's gathered. He retorts, "You can't win, Darth. If you strike me down, I shall become more powerful than you can possibly imagine." This is a vital point to the series—that mastering the Dark Side does not give one the full range of understanding. There is a deeper, mystical world about which Vader understands nothing. In fact, when Obi-Wan turns pacifist and disengages, he defeats Vader, sacrificing himself to reach a higher lifestage about which Vader understands nothing.

Vader strikes and Obi-Wan vanishes. For the moment, Vader has won the battle. However, Obi-Wan's mysterious death leaves Vader brimming with questions. At the end of the film, he mysteriously fails to kill Luke, who evades him and destroys the Death Star. Once again, the obviously weaker foe finds a place of passive tranquility and, acting through it, defeats his stronger opponent. Another obstacle Vader faces is the power of friendship and loyalty as Han suddenly appears to blast Vader off into space. While Anakin understood love, teamwork, and self-sacrifice, Vader has banished this from his conscious self, and thus it defeats him with its unexpected power. Vader survives, but his nemeses do as well. To defeat them, he must reclaim his understanding of love and attachment, seducing Luke with something as powerful as the bonds he already possesses.

The Darth Vader comics following *A New Hope* offer a significant arc for the dark lord that reveals much about his desires. In the first, he hears that the brash untrained Jedi he keeps tangling with is named Skywalker. At once, he's overcome with flashbacks as he realizes Padmé's child survived. The ship's window splinters as he stands motionless, while his rage escapes his control. The Emperor smirks, "I sense your anger. Great anger. Have you something to say? Some proud, defiant words? Or are you wise enough to *know your place*?" Vader submits, admitting that he only became who he is because of his master's lie. Still, he resolves to find Luke and turn him to the Dark Side.

Darth Vader: End of Games has a dark soul-journey. The Emperor threatens Vader with a possible replacement—the man who constructed his support suit. Vader arrives to kill the man, but he deactivates the suit, leaving Vader trapped in it. This moment emphasizes how easily the technology can twist on Vader and utterly control him. Thus stuck, Vader flashes back to the duel by the lava and his anguish at Obi-Wan's letting him live. He also faces his younger self, who's appalled that he killed his beloved mentor. "Sometimes, although not often, an individual feel impelled to live out the worse side of his nature and to repress his better side. In such cases the shadow appears as a positive figure in his dreams" (Von Franz "Individuation" 173). Thus, evil Vader's shadow is idealistic young Anakin. Vader responds by dueling his younger self and throwing him into the fiery river, dismissing him with "You were a child. I am well accustomed to killing children." Padmé then appears, begging him to stay there with her, but he destroys her too, turning his back on all compassion and harnessing his rage to destroy his rival, even through the deactivated suit. He returns in triumph to his master, having conquered the kind boy within.

As *Empire* and *Jedi*—as well as the comics—reveal, Vader is not as all-powerful a tyrant as he initially appears. In fact, he serves the Emperor as a trusted disciple. If Vader is the tyrant king, the Emperor is more like the evil inclination itself—the embodiment of pure greed and destruction. This is the power with which he turned Anakin. "All-encompassing power has been among the greatest seductors to mankind. Emotion, technology, even life itself are the means toward getting power and using it over others. This is the opposite of Yoda and the Jedi, who use power to preserve the things the Sith would simply use and discard" (Hanson and Kay 407). He is total evil—when he is destroyed, there is no need for more story.

The script for *Empire* specifies, "A twelve-foot hologram of the Galactic Emperor materializes before Vader. The Emperor's dark robes and monk's hood are reminiscent of the cloak worn by Ben Kenobi. His voice is even deeper and more frightening than Vader's." If Ben is the good angel on Vader's shoulder (as he was in *Revenge of the Sith*), the Emperor is the devil. Nonetheless, they echo in their dress and use of the Force. Even as Obi-Wan used to cajole and suggest, the Emperor is a dominator who uses brutality and murder as well as the Force itself: "Yoda says that the Force is his ally. Vader, however, is a servant of the Dark Side. Vader is in its power, because he must obey his Master, the Emperor. So the essence of the Dark Side is mastery over others, or tyranny" (Stephens 37).

Around the Emperor, Vader feels "A feeling of fullness, of power, of dark and demon master—of secret lusts, unrestrained passion, wild submission," as the novel explains (Kahn 395). Even as he welcomes the Emperor, he dreams of killing him, taking all he once held, and ruling the universe. Of course, his son has sparked new feelings of ambition and rebellion—with Luke in his service, Vader can mentor him and take his place as patriarch. This is one of the central metaphors—Vader, while an adult, has lived for decades in the shadow of his symbolic father. Now he longs to destroy him and become the new leader of the galaxy. This is connected with his taking the fatherly role with Luke. For the first time, Vader sees the option of becoming the master to a student—of no longer being the Emperor's disciple. With Luke at his side, he could defeat the Emperor and move upward on the path toward total galactic domination. This is, very subtly, a yearning for love and connection. "Symbolically, we begin to see the 'shadow side' of the dark power-driven figure. Isolated from his own humanity and that of others, he does not wish to remain alone; he desires, even needs, someone to 'join' with him" (Galipeau 161).

The Emperor, force of destruction and paranoia, proposes killing Luke. However, Vader suddenly turns protective:

VADER: He's just a boy. Obi-Wan can no longer help him.
EMPEROR: The Force is strong with him. The son of Skywalker must not become a Jedi.
VADER: If he could be turned, he would become a powerful ally.
EMPEROR: Yes. Yes. He would be a great asset.

Upon persuading his master, Vader vows, "He will join us or die." This sets up a multileveled conflict for him in *Empire*: Vader must overcome Obi-Wan's training and make Luke his disciple, but also keep him alive as the Emperor schemes to kill him. Further, Vader must suspect that, having gained a new apprentice, the Emperor may weary of his own service. Keeping Luke alive may mean forfeiting his own life—it's a difficult tightrope.

Even more complicated are his desires for Luke—a voice long-buried inside Vader craves to love and protect his son, to train and defend him as Obi-Wan did for decades. Now that Vader has killed Obi-Wan, it's as if he has reabsorbed his old master and his teachings—Vader's humanity is beginning to return.

At the same time as this conflict appears, the second film emphasizes his vulnerability. *Empire* shows a glimpse of him without the survival suit, revealing the proverbial crack in the armor. Vader's isolation chamber emphasizes how much Anakin's soul is trapped within the machine—this one only a bit larger than his suit.

Vader harasses Lando and tortures Han before freezing him in carbonite, leaving him at the point of death. Still, for Vader, all these are incidental, a trap to lure Luke into coming to him. While he battles Luke through Cloud City, he also compliments him, noting how strong his son has become and emphasizing that it is Luke's destiny to join him. As the father, he sees Luke as an offshoot of himself, destined to make the same choices and follow his footsteps. At last, Vader makes the offer: "Join me and I will complete your training. With our combined strength, we can end this destructive conflict and bring order to the galaxy." Of course, he does not listen to Luke, but instead insists he already knows the boy's destiny and can dictate it to him. Like many tyrant-fathers, he sees his own path as best and pushes his son to follow it.

Luke tries to defy him, but Vader finally reveals the truth—he is Luke's father. He continues coaxing Luke to his side, adding, "Luke. You can destroy the Emperor. He has foreseen this. It is your destiny. Join me, and together we can rule the galaxy as father and son. Come with me. It is the only way." In this moment, Vader chooses his son over his master, discarding twenty years of partnership. Still, the rebellious son rejects his father's path.

With all this, Luke is presented as Vader's young shadow: "Darth Vader looks at his progeny and thinks, *Why isn't he more like me? And yet he is so much like me.* The two elements together are infuriating. He wants answers. He thinks, *I gave this boy life, and I can take it away too. Who will stop me?*" (Krouse 95). This is a common reaction of the all-powerful father to his child's dissent. They battle again, and this time Vader slices off Luke's hand.

The fictitious Jedi handbook calls slicing off an enemy's hand "a merciful conclusion to battle" as it leaves the enemy unable to continue (Wallace 76). Of course, in their universe, a hand can be replaced by a technological substitute. In *Shadows of the Empire,* the novel bridging the gap between this film and the next, Vader thinks, "Luke had survived with no more damage than an easily repaired amputated hand" (Perry 48). He, who endured so much more and is part machine himself, considers it a simple wound. In fact, through this replacement, Vader's act has made Luke a bit more like himself.

Luke continues to defy him and escapes, but the pair end the story sensing each other and each acknowledging the connection. They are bonded, more deeply than Vader is to the Emperor or Luke was to Obi-Wan—this true father-son connection eclipses all the mentorship bonds. Choosing opposite sides changes nothing.

The novel *Shadows of the Empire* bridges the events of Episodes V and VI, while also giving insights into Vader. In the book, Vader practices healing himself, focusing his rage and resentment at his injuries into power. However, his relief and joy when he succeeds knocks him away from the Dark Side each time and the injuries return. He's still not completely committed to the Dark Side as a small fragment of himself strives for light. Unhappiness is the source of his power, a condition that leaves him perpetually unbalanced.

> Yoda and the other Jedi use discipline, commitment, and training to control themselves, thereby harnessing the power of the Force. Vader and the Emperor, on the other hand, stoke their anger and hatred to empower themselves with the Dark Side of the Force. They feed, rather than overcome, the negative emotions within themselves. They seek to control not themselves, but others, in an ultimately doomed attempt to fill the cold, black void behind the mask or the hood with the false satisfaction that arises from domination and oppression of others [Stephens 39].

Besides the novel's demonstrating his great weakness, it also shows him mulling over his battle with Luke. Slaughtering fighter pilots, Vader thinks, "This was beneath him. Since he had fought Luke on the balcony of the city in the clouds, no other opponent had been any real competition" (Perry 138). Of course, this meeting with someone so much like himself, his one connection to the living world, shakes him up. "The meeting had made Vader *feel,* not a normal occurrence lately. There had been the thrill at meeting a worthy opponent and pride that the one so strongly opposing him was his own son" (Perry 48). He's determined to recruit Luke, not for the Emperor—truly for himself.

In *Jedi,* the Emperor graciously accedes to letting Vader search for his new obsession, Luke, but adds, "In time he will seek you out. And when he does, you must bring him before me. He has grown strong. Only together can we turn him to the dark side of the Force." This gives Vader his goal—to welcome the questing, needy child, like the innocent young Anakin he was so long ago, and corrupt him into darkness, as the Emperor did him. By doing so, Vader can strive for the ultimate position in the galaxy, but also the role of true patriarch and father that's so long been denied to him.

"The Emperor is a propagator of terror, hatred, and cruelty. He gloats and takes pleasure in the distress of others" (Stephens 37). In *Jedi*, he sits gloating on his throne, urging Vader and Luke to duel for supremacy. His embodying the evil inclination limits his ability to act directly: He acts as puppet master but appears quite shocked when Luke definitively defies him, tossing away his lightsaber and insisting he'll never turn. Apparently, his knowledge of the future has not shown him this.

When Vader finally defies the Emperor, he symbolically banishes this inclination in himself and returns to his former goodness.

> When Anakin, as Vader, is watching his son being tortured and slowly killed by the Emperor, it's evident that he's wrestling with a moral choice between devotion to his master and love for his son. John Williams's dramatic score reaches a dark crescendo as it seems all hope for saving the galaxy from tyranny is about to be lost. But then the music suddenly shifts to the triumphal "Force Theme" as Anakin makes his choice and destroys the Emperor—thereby saving his son, restoring freedom to the galaxy, and bringing the Force back into balance—all at the cost of his own life [Eberl 20–21].

Vader sacrifices himself—rebirth as he too goes on a death descent. As the Emperor blasts lethal lightning all around, he hurls the Emperor into the abyss, the heart of the destructive machine he himself created. Lucas says, "The prophecy is that Anakin will bring balance to the force, to destroy the Sith. He becomes Darth Vader. Darth Vader *does* become the hero. Darth Vader does destroy the Sith, meaning himself and the Emperor. He does it because he is redeemed by his son" ("Chosen One Featurette"). This redemption brings him back to his Anakin side. While his original bringing balance to the Force might be interpreted as raising evil to ascendency and destroying the might of the Jedi, Vader ultimately balances it the other way by destroying the Emperor along with himself. This destroys the Empire itself as well as the two-Sith legacy that has existed for centuries. In this moment, he does an act of great heroism, though it cannot make up for decades of mass murder. It's a selfish succumbing, one based on the personal rather than the larger universe. "What goodness remains allows him to resist the absolute evil of the Emperor, but only when his own son is involved. His motivations in killing the Emperor are not that different from his earlier motivations in killing the Sand People: he acts out of love for a member of his family" (Dees 52).

Afterwards, dying, he asks Luke to remove his mask. "The black, armored mask that had been his only means of existing for over twenty years. It had been his voice, and his breath, and his invisibility—his shield against all human contact. But now he would remove it; for he would see his son before he died" (Kahn 493). With the mask removed, Vader is discarding his persona to view his son with his inner, authentic self. The mask has intimidated onlookers for decades, but it also symbolizes weakness and dependency as he needs it to live. Underneath, the face is pallid, scarred, and pathetic. Campbell explains, "When the mask of Darth Vader is removed, you see an unformed man, one who has not developed as a human individual. What you see is a sort of strange and pitiful undifferentiated face" (Campbell and Moyers 177–178). Stuck in the imposed Imperial bureaucracy, he's fallen completely under their control. In this moment, however, he individuates and allows himself to connect with others. He opens himself to true intimacy and vulnerability, and with this, he can pass to the next stage.

This moment offers Vader-turned-Anakin a final revelation: "The boy was good, and the boy had come from him—so there must have been good in him too. He smiled up at his son and for the first time, loved him. And for the first time in many long years, loved himself again, as well" (Kahn 494). He has found his way back to the light. "This tale of a man who began life with such extraordinary potential, only to use his powers for infinite evil, and ultimately redeems himself at the end of his quest, is a poignant, mythical rendering of life as we see it—the marriage of rise and fall, light and dark, good and evil, within a single entity" (Lam). Lucas adds, "In *Jedi*, the film is really about the redemption of the fallen angel. Ben is the fitting good angel, and Vader is the bad angel who started off good. All these years Ben has been waiting for Luke to come of age so that he can become Jedi and redeem his father. That's what Ben has been doing, but you don't know this in the first film" (Bouzereau 271).

Obi-Wan and Yoda easily join the Force when they die. However, "because Anakin Skywalker assumed an identity that was so far from who he truly was, the trappings associated with his one-sided, archetypal identification must be purged" (Galipeau 250). His funeral pyre gives him this pathway to cast off the mechanized body. This moment gives the audience the chance, like Luke, to say goodbye to all Vader was—to see him destroyed and thus allow Anakin to rise from the ashes of thus destruction, reborn in a new form. "All his wickedness is finally forgiven, making him a benign, ghostly figure, watching over his son" (Vogler 68). He joins his old Jedi friends in the spirit realm, ascending, like them, to the mentor's role.

Obi-Wan and Yoda: Ascension to Spirit Guides

"Some Mentors are still on a Hero's Journey of their own. They may be experiencing a crisis of faith in their calling. Perhaps they are dealing with the problems of aging and approaching the threshold of death or have fallen from the hero's road. The hero needs the Mentor to pull himself together one last time, and there's serious doubt that he can do it" (Vogler 44). Obi-Wan's story in the original film begins after decades as a hermit. Of course, the hero frequently goes on a spiritual quest into the desert or wasteland. Such a place offers the freedom to truly hear the unconscious. For Luke, Tatooine is the normal place of his childhood, but Coruscant-raised Obi-Wan requires quite an adjustment. His vanishing here emphasizes his giving up rank and fame, along with everything material—all to ascend spiritually.

The comic *Showdown on the Smuggler's Moon* shows Obi-Wan's life on Tatooine, helping the moisture farmers in small ways. He thinks about how hard it has been to stop being a Jedi, but nonetheless he stays in hiding, only using his power quietly. Owen won't let him train Luke, so Obi-Wan, now simple Ben, has nothing to do. Even as he wonders whether he should have died with the Jedi, he continues protecting his charge. "You never trained me for this, Master Qui-Gon. You never taught me how to *fade away*," he thinks. He's having trouble moving to the next stage of existence—not a warrior, but the grandfather-protector of the next generation.

As the comics arc continues, he watches Luke closely, supplying him with speeder parts to aid his flight training. However, Owen, the anti-Jedi, the good brother who stayed home, confronts him. "I told you, I'm not gonna let you warp the boy like you did his father. You brought him to me to protect, and that's what I'm doing. Protecting him from *you*." When he bellows, "Haven't you murdered *enough* Skywalkers already, Kenobi," he voices Obi-Wan's own guilt. So nineteen years pass.

In a spinoff short story, Obi-Wan, summoned back to the fight by Padmé's daughter Leia, confesses to Qui-Gon that he finds it hard to return. In his exile, he has been retired, more guardian than Jedi knight. Now, comes a return to the life he had left behind. "Every person Obi-Wan had truly loved—Anakin, Satine [his love in the *Clone Wars* cartoon], Padmé, and Qui-Gon himself—came to a terrible end…. The Jedi Order that provided the entire framework for Obi-Wan's life was consumed by betrayal and slaughter" (Gray, "Master and Apprentice" 84). Though consumed by loss, mostly alone, he endures.

These interim stories emphasize how resigned he's become to retirement, a life of quiet and peace. Still, the galaxy's demands invade his solitude and Obi-Wan must take up his lightsaber and fight for the side of goodness one last time.

On the Death Star, Obi-Wan channels these powers he's mastered through decades of fading away. His power of misdirection comes from the Force but also through his self-effacing state. As a humble monk, he chooses stealth over direct conflict and so infiltrates the enemy's stronghold.

At his climax, Obi-Wan recognizes that he cannot destroy Vader, so he bequeaths the task to his pupil. Obi-Wan confesses to Luke early on, "When I first knew him, your father was already a great pilot. But I was amazed how strongly the Force was with him. I took it upon myself to train him as a Jedi. I thought that I could instruct him just as well as Yoda. I was wrong. My pride has had terrible consequences for the galaxy." He failed as Anakin's adoptive father as well as his instructor in goodness and selflessness. Luke, however, offers redemption by repairing Obi-Wan's error and destroying this great force of evil. Obi-Wan gives up his life, certain that Luke will do so. He continues to advise from beyond death, but even more selflessly, acknowledging that his bodily needs have faded away.

On the Death Star, Obi-Wan duels his old apprentice and famously tells him, "If you strike me down, I shall become more powerful than you can possibly imagine." This suggests the power of martyrdom—dead Obi-Wan will be stronger. "Kenobi's sacrifice is an archetypal act, representing selflessness and the understanding of an individual's role in a greater story" (Hanson and Kay 168). Of course, the film emphasizes that Obi-Wan has become skilled enough in the Force to ascend to the spiritual plane—a place Darth Vader cannot comprehend or reach. Cavan Scott's short story "Time of Death" Obi-Wan realizing Luke is in danger, standing frozen and watching the fight. A voice echoes in Obi-Wan's head insisting on helping him. Realizing he won't make it over in time, Obi-Wan lifts his saber and smiles, letting Vader cut him down. He tells Luke to run and adds, "And I am at his side. From this moment, he will never be alone. He will learn, and he will grow, and I will guide him every step of the way. We have all the time we need" (347). Though he couldn't teach Luke in life, he can mentor him in death. "We learn to die well by acquiring ability to accept all of life's losses and disappointments and to recognize the loss inherent in all change. Every change we experience in life is practice for the ultimate transition of death" (Pearson 143). This is a great goal, achieved by those who find balance and wisdom.

The second film has Luke train with a higher level of mentor—the ultimate grandfatherly sage who has given up all worldly cares, even more so than Obi-Wan the reclusive monk.

> Since Yoda doesn't fear, get angry, or hate, he doesn't suffer. Yoda concentrates on what is up to him and what he can do in the present. He thus enjoys impassivity, the lack of disturbing passions the Stoics called apatheia. Yoda is calm and even-tempered. He can tell the difference between the good and bad sides of the Force, and knows what is good, what is bad, and what is neither [Stephens 32].

By the time of *Empire*, Yoda has diminished from a council member into a goofy puppet playing games with Luke. This is a humbling for the great master, a return to basics. In Gary D. Schmidt's short story "There Is

Another," Obi-Wan, newly a Force ghost, comes to Yoda to request he train Luke. Further, he takes the mentoring role between them, forbidding Yoda to die before completing the task. He also promises the realm beyond death will offer many surprises. As Obi-Wan turns Yoda's own words back on him and shows an understanding Yoda lacks, the Force-ghost has truly become an advisor to even his old teacher.

Nearby Yoda's swamp house, of course, is the dark cave. "Yoda it seems lives in a place that contains both the light and dark sides of life, of the Force. To know oneself, one must know the dark side as well as the light" (Galipeau 125). It's easy to picture the wise sage entering the dark place occasionally, wrestling with his doubts and insecurities, and finally accepting them, emerging stronger with clearer answers.

Both characters have the duty to train Luke and send him out to defeat Vader and balance the Force. As *Revenge of the Sith* reveals, both Jedi failed to end the Emperor's tyranny and now must aid the next generation to put the galaxy right. However, Yoda fears Luke will turn to the dark side and hesitates to train him. Knowing Luke's parentage and Obi-Wan's failure with Anakin, these fears make sense. This is one of the mentor's challenges, wondering whether he's fit.

Of course, being a mentor has additional frustration as the sage feels he can do a better job than the young hero, having faced the same challenges, and yet cannot compel the young hero to follow his advice: "While both Yoda and Obi-Wan have put great faith in Luke from the time he was born, even they can only watch Luke's life unfold and help train him as a Jedi. Despite their good intentions, neither has the power to bend Luke's will, as we see in *The Empire Strikes Back* when they plead with him not to leave Dagobah before his training is completed" (Eberl 27).

After the training, both Jedi have a final task—to accept death and peacefully pass on to the spiritual realm. Their transitions emphasize the hero's need to the mentor to fade away gradually and live his own life, as well as the mentors' lack of ability to physically impact the ordinary world. In the spiritual realm, they will lose their selfhood and yet become one with the galaxy. Yoda tells Luke: "Luminous beings are we ... not this crude matter." This is confirmed by the scenes that show the deceased Obi-Wan, Yoda, and Anakin as non-physical, yet luminous, visible disembodied spirits. Campbell writes, "One part of the mythological motif of the hero's journey is acquiescence. For instance, I am moving toward death, as we all are. That's also yielding. And the hero is the one who knows *when* to surrender and what to surrender *to*" (*Hero's Journey* 12).

The prequels clarify that the majority of Jedi cannot do this. In fact, Qui-Gon, the maverick mystic, discovers the path in his studies, and he is the one to return as a Force ghost after death to teach Yoda and Obi-Wan.

The teaching from this first mentor passes on through the generations, and one must assume that this spiritual trio eventually aid their beloved student Anakin. While the film doesn't go into much detail (except in the Episode III novelization), Qui-Gon astounds Yoda and Obi-Wan by returning from death in spiritual form. He spends the intervening decades between this story and *A New Hope* training them both in the lost art. Claudia Gray's short story "Master and Apprentice" details the relationship. Qui-Gon tells Obi-Wan that returning is "A matter of learning to both claim the physical world and detach one's self from it.... A matter of finding center, of calming one's soul and giving one's self over completely to the Force" (86–87). As he adds, "Even after death, we continue to learn" (87).

Qui-Gon exists intermingled with the Force, even the small glimmers of life in the Tatooine desert, and solidifies when Obi-Wan seeks him. His shadowy existence has taught him a new form of higher wisdom, as he has a much wider perspective now: "To Qui-Gon, all human lives now seem impossibly brief. Years are irrelevant. It is journeys through the Force that matter. Some must struggle for that knowledge through many decades; others are very nearly born with it. Most never begin the journey at all, no matter how long they live" (83).

Following his path, Obi-Wan and Yoda know the goal is not to cling to life unnaturally, preserving themselves with dark energy or Vader's technology, but to give Luke the lessons he needs, ascend and release their earthly selves. This they do, and they return to Luke afterwards to offer additional guidance. "For it is not an ending but a regenerative spiral. As one life ends, another begins, and on, and on" (Frankel, *Girl to Goddess* 172).

The Sequel Era

Rogue One and the Heroine's Sacrifice

Rogue One: A Star Wars Story, which takes place 34 years before the sequel era, offers another heroine's journey, as indeed, *Rogue One* follows all the classic steps. "What I love so much about Jyn Erso is that she's an imperfect female warrior—authentic and genuine, truthful and humble, strong and modern without feeling contemporary" said producer Allison Shearmur (Kushins 61). She's rash and unrestrained—unusual traits for a female character.

The story begins with the innocent child losing both her parents as her mother bravely sacrifices herself and her father is captured by the Empire. The family has found a sanctuary on Lah'mu, a simple agrarian planet where people are hiding out from the war (Hidalgo, *Rogue One* 11). There, they dwell in a circular womblike home with circular furniture, from sofa to tables all in brown and grey. This roundness suggests the feminine principle, a place of safety and comfort.

However, the prologue introduces Jyn's great nemesis, her father's shadow. The tyrant. Orson Krennic was once her father's colleague and friend, now his deadly enemy. The spinoff novel *Catalyst* by James Luceno explains that Krennic was Galen's school friend who tricked him into working on an energy project called Project Celestial Power. As it turned out, this was actually the Death Star. Galen is the genius inventor, while his friend is more of a manager. Krennic comments, "I wasn't born brilliant or especially talented, but I'm capable and I'm driven, and that's brought me to where I am. I stumbled onto something I'm good at" (213). The Ersos have felt indebted to him since he saved them from the Separatist planet Vallt. However, they didn't realize he had set this up (Hidalgo, *Rogue One* 16).

Krennic's mission is to destroy the Rebellion, the cause of freedom and life: His actor calls him "an ambitious Imperial leader who intends to use his command of the Death Troopers to take down the rebel uprising" ("Ben Mendelsohn"). Symbolizing his goal, he brings with him not Stormtroopers but Death Troopers in black. These apparently are not zombified reanimated dead soldiers, but "the use of the name gives them a macabre reputation among the Imperial ranks. Their black armor makes their appearance all the more deathly" (Hidalgo, *Rogue One* 28). They emphasize his allegiance to the cause of destruction.

As the film open, he tracks down the small family. He taunts Galen with his knowledge and resolves to find little Jyn to use her as leverage against her father. Jyn is left hiding in the hills, protected only by her parents' teachings and talismans. In classic fashion, her father has left her his love and a nickname, telling her, "Remember, whatever I do, I do it to protect you. Say you understand.... I love you, Stardust." With this, he provides a foundation of goodness and certainty for her through her journey. The father is generally a supportive source in fairytales, endowing his daughter's animus with a moral compass.

Her mother Lyra gives her a crystal pendent—a pale fragment of Kyber crystal, marked with ancient writing. In the *Star Wars* language Aurebesh, it says, "Trust the Force." The crystal follows her parents through their adventures, as her father holds its warmth close. These crystals, as the *Clone Wars* show reveals, are unique and individual, calling out to and bounding with human heroes. Before their extinction, the Jedi regarded Kyber crystals as sacred and kept them from the hands of others. As is told in *Catalyst*, Tarkin and Krennic presented Galen with many crystals, clearly looted from lightsabers and temples, to Lyra's horror. As Galen experimented, he realized the crystals' awesome exponential power. The Jedi had been aware of it but instead controlled the crystals, directing and focusing them, and then using them in their lightsabers to preserve peace. Now, in a symbolic total heresy against Jedi teachings, the Empire is forging the crystals into a superweapon.

The heroine, champion of life, fights to save innocents from such tyranny and death. Giving her mother's crystal to Jyn suggests passing on her father's mind and her mother's heart, along with the tie to the Force and a hope that she'll trust in it. It celebrates life in all its infinite diversity, casting Jyn as the protector of the natural universe. It also brings her a greater spiritual depth beyond her entirely physical experiences. In the prequel novel, Jyn's father insists that her necklace is more than a rock, adding, "That's what makes kyber crystals so special.... They seem like innocent little stones. But they can harness so much more power than you would think. Their history is marred with legend, but the fact remains—they have the potential to change the entire galaxy" (Revis 409). Of course, this works as a metaphor for Jyn herself.

"The actual process of individuation—the conscious coming to terms with one's own inner center (psychic nucleus) or Self—generally begins with a wounding of the personality and the suffering that accompanies it. This initial shock amounts to a sort of 'call'" (Von Franz, "Individuation" 166). In Jyn's case, this is the sudden loss of her parents. Hiding from Krennic, little Jyn climbs down a black gulch into an underground cave in the hills and remains there. In the novelization, she sings one of her mother's songs and lights a lantern through the night. This is a death-and-rebirth sequence—having lost both her parents and her entire way of life, she lies underground, vanished from the earth. In the morning, her parents' trusted ally comes for her. Thus, Jyn is left to be raised by the irascible foster-father Saw Gerrera. His last name, meaning war, offers a clear allusion. "Saw represents that archetype of a rebel fighter who's gone to the very edge," says director Gareth Edwards. "Someone like Che Guevara" ("Sneak Peak").

He becomes a far fiercer father and trainer than the gentle scientist father with whom Jyn grew up—this trade suggests requiring a new kind of training to become a warrior. On the heroine's journey, the young woman is guided by a man who echoes her undeveloped male side. This animus "evokes masculine traits within her: logic, rationality, intellect. Her conscious side, aware of the world around her, grows, and she can rule and comprehend the exterior world" (Frankel, *Girl to Goddess* 22). To begin, the simplest animus, like Krennic, is a force of brute strength who threatens Galen's family and accidentally kills Lyra. As the heroine learns, this figure is replaced by a wiser animus, guiding her through more developed stages: initiative and planning, rule of law, and wisdom. Like Anakin, "Saw has trained with Jedis, but he's lost family members and some of those ideals," says Saw's actor, Forest Whitaker. "He's willing to find whatever means he can to win" ("Forest Whitaker"). These include targeting civilians and using brutal interrogation techniques but also clever plans.

Meanwhile, Jyn has completely rejected her birth father. In the prequel novel, Jyn learns that her father has betrayed them and willingly works for the man who killed her mother. She decides "My father is a coward" and gives up on him from this point forwards (Revis 45). When Saw suggests she's so good at forging Imperial codes because solving puzzles runs in her blood, she quickly denies it, rejecting all of her father's legacy. With this, she cleaves to the planner and strong rebel as her new mentor.

"The Warrior Woman fights with masculine weapons and has a male mentor and a male nemesis. Often she disguises herself as a boy. Her task is still to rescue young women in danger, and she often battles the Patriarchy and absorbs its strength" (Frankel, *Buffy* 9). In this tradition, Jyn has only a bit of a female mentor in the shadowy memory of Saw's sister Steela, seen in *Clone Wars*. He tells her stories of her and adds that the Rebels "need more fighters to die like she did.... The resistance needs a martyr. A tragedy.

Something so horrific that people can't help but stand up and fight too" (Revis 60). Of course, this deed is coming.

Allies

Jyn's prequel novel, *Rebel Rising*, is one of failed hopes. It begins with Saw rescuing her from her hiding place. However, after this, she clutches her crystal and wills her mother to channel the Force and come to her. Nothing happens. Following this come traitors in Saw's small cell, and then the heartbreaking incident when Saw, realizing the Rebels know Jyn's parentage, abandons her with only a knife and blaster to make her own way through the universe. She finds a family but loses them too. At last she rejects the rebels and the Empire, as both cause civilian deaths. As she thinks, "The people of Tamsye Prime had been ants, ants the giants would have ignored. But Saw had made the giant stomp" (Revis 299). Saw is a force of chaos, battling the Empire but not offering to create a stable government afterwards, in contrast with the former senators heading the Rebellion. Further, he doesn't mind taking out a few civilians for the greater good, as he thinks. By this point, Jyn has learned to keep her head down and run from planet to planet, as nothing else can keep her safe. Those who fight, die, and the status quo cannot change.

"It was Gareth's idea to include someone who represents that more militant mentality, almost like an extremist side of the Rebellion," said story writer Gary Whitta. "Every political movement, every resistance movement, has its more militant, more radical tendencies. And Gareth liked the idea of seeing a rebel who was so much more extreme in his approach to fighting the Empire" (Kushins 99). Gerrera, created by George Lucas for the *Clone Wars* series, doesn't mind killing innocents, so much so that the Rebellion rejects his radical approach. Caught between extremes, Jyn must choose her own path.

The paradox between being a terrorist and a good Revolutionary haunts many warriors—can they restore justice without violence? Or at least without harming innocents? Mon Mothma writes in the *Rogue One Rebel Dossier* of Jyn, "I have reviewed her arrest records and find no evidence that she's attacked civilians or tried to swindle them. The targets of her crimes have always been Imperial officials or fellow members of the galactic underworld" (Fry). Though it's barely addressed onscreen and thus left for the expanded universe, she's a moral person. The novelization of the film describes what Jyn's been up to, saying, "Jyn had been at the Empire's mercy before. Sometimes she'd even deserved her troubles—she couldn't blame some petty dictator for ordering her dragged off the street and slammed into holding when she really, truly was planning to blow up his ship and steal his guns" (Freed 30). As the film visits her in adulthood, however, she has no friends to rely on. This lack is significant, since this is exactly what her new adventure brings her.

Of course, her call to adventure is reluctant—when the Rebels rescue her from a prisoner transport, she instantly fights back, determined to escape them as well as the Imperials and manage on her own. Unshackled by Alliance Sargent Ruescott Melshi, Jyn immediately bolts for freedom, to be finally caught by the droid K-2SO. They all drag her to their rebel base and force her to participate. "For Jyn, it's the swapping of one prison cell for another. She cares not for the cause of the Rebel Alliance and being briefed by their command while still in binders does little to sway her. Until, that is, she hears about her father, a man she had decided had died years ago" (Hidalgo, *Rogue One* 34). Rebel intelligence offers her a path to her foster father and a tantalizing message from her birth father—both demand that she reconnect with her lost past.

In the prequel novel, Jyn is shocked to see an organized Rebellion, since she's only encountered Saw's group and other ragtag disorganized rebels. Before this, she had thought all hope was a dream. "But seeing these people, the way they still believed they had a chance—a chance that hinged on *her*—rekindled that spark inside her heart that she had thought died long before" (Revis 410). With this, she agrees to help.

As she undergoes these physical trials, the novelization gives her a spiritual arc as well. It describes a cave in her mind that resembles her childhood hiding place. "The cave wasn't for her protection. Instead it was where she locked away the things she was *done with* but couldn't altogether forget: The Rebellion, Saw Gerrera. People and places buried in the dark for so long that she barely recognized their names as more than cruel, hurtful impulses" (Freed 36). However, after the Rebel Alliance capture her, the hatch is opening, releasing all her buried memories.

The rebels take her to Yavin, a jungle planet dominated by a stone ziggurat—an ancient ruin the rebels have repurposed as their base. There she meets Mon Mothma, a senator and royal figure who's clean and poised in white, committed to the Alliance and their voice of authority—all Jyn is not. She not only helped found the rebellion but publicly denounced the Emperor on the HoloNet (during *Rebels*), becoming the Empire's most wanted traitor.

Mon Mothma gives Jyn her mission—introduce her team to Saw Gerrera so they can investigate the rumors of a superweapon and ally with the extremist rebel. Jyn is not a mystically appointed chosen one (or even blessed by the Force at all) but she is special as the one person Saw might trust. Reluctantly, she accepts the mission though she's not yet committed to the rebel cause.

Traditionally, the classic Warrior Woman—Atlanta, Athena, Mu Lan, Éowyn, Katniss—wields masculine weapons and wears androgynous clothes. On her journey, she has a male mentor and a male nemesis. Jyn clearly follows this pattern, especially in her soldier team who treat her like one of the boys. The leader, Captain Cassian Andor (Diego Luna), is introduced getting vital information on the Death Star ... and then shooting the informant when he's too injured to escape. He's thus expedient and more than a little amoral. He also gives Jyn the inspiring thought that "Rebellions are built on hope." In this scene, he functions as her animus, guiding her to a higher spiritual path as a true believer in his cause. General Draven writes in the *Rogue One Rebel Dossier*, "Capt. Andor has worked with the rebels since he was a child. It is no exaggeration to say that we are his family. He is absolutely loyal to the rebel cause and will do whatever he must to achieve our goals" (Fry). Jyn is much the opposite—the child of a known traitor, adopted by a radical, who claims loyalty to no one.

K-2SO (Alan Tudyk) is also amoral, once an Imperial droid and now reprogrammed to serve the Alliance. This switching of allegiances suggests only a little reprogramming would make him betray them all yet again. Lucasfilm chief creative officer John Knoll describes the new droid "as sort of the anti–C-3PO. C-3PO was bumbling comic relief. Imagine the opposite of that. And he never misses a shot" ("Sneak Peak"). This character evokes Jyn's analytical side, urging caution and a consideration of the odds. He's also brutally rude. As Cassian explains, "He tends to say whatever comes into his circuits. It's a by-product of the reprogram." He is another voice of the subconscious, encouraging her to blurt out doubts and fears instead of bottling them up as the perfect warrior.

"In many ways, the Rebels don't have a leg to stand on," Felicity Jones says. "They're a motley crew, they all have had difficult backgrounds. They're all outsiders in some way, and they're coming together to fight something far bigger than them, more efficient. The Empire is wealthier, and it has everything the Rebels don't, so the odds are definitely stacked against them" (Breznican, "The Empire Will Rise"). In her first challenge of their dynamic, Jyn steals a blaster, and Cassian reluctantly lets her keep it, providing a measure of trust. He clearly respects her as a fellow soldier. Producer Allison Shearmur comments, "Oftentimes, Hollywood wants to see a strong woman apologize for nor appreciating her life or dedicate herself to figuring out why she's a certain way. What I love about Jyn is that hers isn't a story of wishing she'd made other life choices. This isn't an apology. She's equal parts Joan of Arc and Sigourney Weaver's Ripley—a pure hero, independent of gender. Someone who sets out to do something impossible and does it" (Kushins 61).

On the mission, Jyn dreams of her parents. In a flashback-dream in the film, she sees her father telling her, "What's the matter, Jyn? You looked frightened. I'll always protect you. Stardust. Don't ever change." Her mother, like her buried spirituality and hope, begs her to trust her father. This reflects the heroine's turmoil.

Emphasizing this spiritual struggle to climb, Jyn and her team find their way to the planet Jedha. Some believe it to be the origin point of the Jedi Order, while modern believers crowd there. This offers a new perspective besides the Jedi one. "The Force is basically in *Star Wars* like a religion, and they're losing their faith in the period that we start the movie," says Director Gareth Edwards. "We were trying to find a physical location we could go to that would speak to the themes of losing your faith and the choice between letting the Empire win, or evil win, and good prevailing" (Breznican, "Rogue One Director"). Jedha is a wasteland world plundered by the Empire, in contrast to lush Yavin. Broken statues emphasize the former spirituality and beauty, while narrow-streeted bazaars echo the Middle East. Its holy city is sprinkled with golden domes reminiscent of the Dome of the Rock in Jerusalem. In fact, it uses Middle Eastern architecture as a starting point for "the ideals of a Jedi in a film devoid of their presence" (Hidalgo, *Rogue One* 188). It symbolizes a spiritual deepening for Jyn, a connection to her heritage in the crystal she wears and the beliefs of her lost mother.

As the Imperials loot the kyber crystals from the city, they commit sacrilege, all to create their weapon of ultimate destruction. They are the enemy of all that is spiritual as well as life itself. They have turned the place into a wasteland, as Greg Rucka's tie-in novel *Guardians of the Whills* reveals: "All of Jedha was suffering—there was not enough water and never enough food. They were short of blankets, of credits, of power, of medicine" (Rucka 49).

Once there, Jyn encounters a spiritual guide who provides a higher level of animus wisdom:

> **CHIRRUT:** Would you trade that necklace for a glimpse into your future? Yes, I'm speaking to you. I am Chirrut Îmwe.
> **JYN ERSO:** How did you know I was wearing a necklace?
> **CHIRRUT:** For that answer you must pay. What do you know of kyber crystals?
> **JYN ERSO:** My father, he said they powered the Jedi lightsabers.
> **CASSIAN:** Jyn. Come on, let's go.
> **CHIRRUT:** The strongest stars have hearts of kyber.

Cassian calls Chirrut (Donnie Yen) and his friends "The Guardians of the Whills. Protectors of the Kyber Temple." In the book, suspicious Jyn suspects he's a con artist. She also spots his partner machine gunner Baze Malbus (Jiang Wen) and all the weapons he's carrying (Freed 67).

"Within Jedha, even though there's the oppressive foot of the Empire hanging over them, there's a resistance that won't give up and our characters have to go and meet people there to try and secure a person from this group," Edwards says (Breznican, "Rogue One Director"). With heavy armor, repeating blasters, and even a rocket launcher, Baze is the skeptic as Chirrut (with his traditional crystal-tipped staff and light bow) has utter faith in the Force. He's also spiritually attuned to it. Chirrut Îmwe is not a Jedi or Force user. However, he can feel the Force for brief incandescent moments. "The elegant interconnectedness, the ineffable bonds among everyone and everything. Their places in space and in time, their lives, their energy" (Rucka 14–15).

Suddenly, insurgents bomb the marketplace. When Stormtroopers arrest Jyn and her team, Chirrut intervenes. Chanting "The Force is with me and I am with the Force" like a mantra, he strikes out with his staff and knocks out each trooper, dodging their blows with unerring precision. Baze Malbus provides the support. This pair thus model teamwork for Jyn—a useful lesson for this lone hero. "Pairing an ostensible pacifist with a forceful soldier might seem like an unlikely partnership, but their competence and abiding friendship continues a *Star Wars* tradition of 'odd couples' that is at the very heart of the series' appeal" (Kushins 143). *Guardians of the Whills* gives a bit more background, as it follows the hero and his partner working briefly with Saw but being disgusted at his violence.

When backup arrive, Baze shoots the enemy dead. Each has a different lesson to teach—one about faith and one, practical expediency. As Rucka's novel relates: "*No* was the word that seemed to define Baze Malbus these days, all the more since the Imperial occupation had begun. *No*, and in that word Baze Malbus was saying many things; no, he would not accept this, whatever *this* might be, from Imperial rule ... to the suffering the Empire had inflicted upon all those around them. *No*, ultimately—and to Chirrut's profound sadness—to a faith in the Force" (Rucka 6). The opposing pair offer guidance for Jyn, showing her the alternatives she struggles with inside.

This also reflects the people of the galaxy's choices—struggling with faith or faithlessness themselves. "The Jedi are pretty much extinct, so a lot of that spirituality is dying out and people are losing their faith," says Edwards. "This idea that magical beings are going to come and save us is going away, and it's up to normal, everyday people to take a stand to stop evil from dominating the world." (Breznican, "Going Rogue"). Operation Fracture is, fittingly, falling apart—it takes this infusion of faith and willpower to save the team of untrusting skeptics. This new perspective energizes the heroine. When the rebels arrive, it's Jyn who takes charge, dramatically revealing her name as a password.

Saw lives in the catacombs of a monastery, decorated with thousands of skulls. It echoes the destruction he's wrought as well as his own cynicism and upcoming death. As with rebel headquarters, this ancient dwelling is updated with modern power cables, but underneath lies the ancient majesty of what remains. Facing him, Jyn finds an aging rebel, mostly retired from the fight, rebuilt with cybernetic parts, hair white and unkempt. A pressure suit keeps his lungs working. "The armor is integral to my character," Whitaker says of the bulky costume that encases him like a spare-parts Darth Vader. "The costume really helped me play him. You get into what it's like to be Saw. There was a regality to it, like a fallen king. I was trying to play it straight inside the character. I get slightly nervous, but having these lines in this uniform, Saw starts to come alive." ("Forest Whitaker"). Jyn tries to fight with him and address her old grievances, but he's weary to the point of giving up.

Upon hearing she has no interest in the cause, Saw tells her there's something she must see. Hearing her father's smuggled message, "She no longer felt the swaying of her legs. Darkness crept around the edges of her vision, as if the hatch in her mind and the cave where the hatch had been were rising up to engulf her. As if she were descending, falling, to be locked away in her own skull with everything she'd denied" (Freed 102). Her old conflicts and idealism and love—all she's bottled up to become an emotionless solider—all flood through her. Her father not only shares that he loves her but confides in her that he's concealed his true rebel nature and survived. "I learned to lie. I played the part of a beaten man resigned to the sanctuary of his work. I made myself indispensable, and all the while I laid the groundwork of my revenge." This teaches Jyn that there are other paths than war and defeat. Craftiness and subtlety can bring survival.

She loses Saw but picks up another teammate in redemption-seeking former Imperial pilot Bodhi Rook (Riz Ahmed). He's scrawny looking with large eyes—which are wilder after Saw's mental torture. From Jedha as he is, he's struck by the increasing suffering of his people. His Imperial logo is faded as the droid's is scuffed—nodding in both cases to their defection. He brings Jyn a more personal message: "Your father.... He said I could get right by myself. He said I could make it right, if I was brave enough and listened to what was in my heart. Do something about it." Jyn agrees that one person can listen to her inner voice and make a difference ... even if that person is herself.

"A mountainous, secluded world controlled by the Tarkin Initiative, Eadu is the site of high-energy conversion experiments and high-tech construction" (Hidalgo, *Rogue One Ultimate Visual Guide* 11). This is the dark lord's castle, a place where the life-filled heroine has no power. There, she reaches her father but only in time to have him die in her arms. After this, Jyn feels crushed. In the novel, she curls up in the shuttle and dreams of him and Saw and all the people she couldn't save, only to receive a helpful vision: her mother comes to her and tells her to decide for herself (195).

She chooses her path and returns to Yavin to insist that the Rebels follow her father's plan and save the galaxy. As Mon Mothma adds later in the novel, "The woman met then was far different from the one we'd chained. Was she at peace? I don't believe so. But she held herself with a newfound certainty" (Freed 322). Jyn speaks out with confidence against the threat insisting they have no choice: they cannot submit forever, so they must fight. Even at this grim point in the *Star Wars* timeline, when the Empire is at its most powerful, there is unity and courage among the misfits rising against it. The Rebel leaders refuse to take the risk. Still, the ordinary soldiers pledge themselves to Jyn's mission. Jyn observes, "I'm not used to people sticking around when things go bad," and Cassian responds, "Welcome home."

Jyn's team now trust one another and share a single unified goal. This is reflected in the heroine herself. As they reach the planet, Cassian thinks in the novel, "Jyn was changing, it was evident in her fluid movements and her lucid state. She no longer hunched her shoulders, no longer maintained the compact posture of a woman ready to absorb a hit before she hit back. She'd shed none of her intensity, but it came with what Cassian could only interpret as a confidence bordering on invincibility" (Freed 217–218).

Scarif, a tropical paradise, is also "the very heart of the imperial military industrial complex" (Hidalgo, *Rogue One* 11). Concept artist Jon McCoy adds, "You get that feeling of the loss of paradise and the loss of the environment itself to these industrialized canyons of the Empire. You don't want to see that, to see this landscape ruined. It tells you what the Empire is, what they are all about—so it becomes that much more rewarding when the rebels find a way to fight them, when they get the Death Star plans" (Kushins 193). Their battle there echoes many World War II films, down to the palm-studded beaches.

There, Jyn faces her nemesis. "Krennic is a true believer in the Empire. There'd be an argument to say that he believes in it more than Darth Vader does," his actor observes ("Ben Mendelsohn"). If he can successfully deliver the weapon, the Emperor will immortalize his success. Of course, his being so close also means he teeters on the edge of failure. If he loses, Tarkin and Vader will enjoy tearing him down.

Jyn disguises herself as an Imperial deck officer and plunges into the belly of the beast with Cassian. Already within the Imperial base, Jyn must infiltrate the data vault—a multi-storied tower filled with data banks. Surrounded by thousands of cartridges, Jyn faces the test of finding the real treasure—her father has marked it for her, labeling it Stardust. There, in the supervillain's base, she clings to this trace of hope and love and thus triumphs.

Under attack, KSO's final resort is to lock the pair of them in and order them to climb—to manually send the transmission from the tower. They may not escape, but the plans will. As Jyn's thoughts in the novelization relate, the real enemy is the Death Star: "The *thing* that had brought her to Scarif—not her father, not her comrades, not some impulse buried below the cave, but the monstrosity that killed and killed and killed until every little girl and pilgrim and mother in the galaxy was dead—was staring down at her, as real as ever" (Freed 304). It is the ender of life, something the vivacious heroine must conquer.

Jyn's companions begin dying one by one, no longer able to aid her. Bodhi redeems himself by communicating with the fleet and getting them to take down the shield and stand ready to receive the plans. Only after is he killed. With his partner Chirrut dead as well, Baze absorbs the other man's faith. "The Force is with me and I am with the Force," he says. He stands over his dead partner and avenges him with blasters. "He spoke the words and in them he found not comfort but conviction—or the memory of conviction, as if the words were a key to the forgotten faith of his youth" (Freed 293).

Jyn gets a final standoff with her lifelong enemy, passing on her father's triumph: "You know who I am. I'm Jyn Erso. Daughter of Galen and Lyra. You've lost…. My father's revenge. He built a flaw in the Death Star. He put a fuse in the middle of your machine and I've just told the entire galaxy how to light it." Here, the female warrior accepts her father's legacy and defends it, battling a male supervillain on his behalf. This is the androgynous heroine's traditional path.

She and Cassian destroy him but are killed themselves. The death and rebirth sequence is most common for heroes but is not required. Like Yoda and Obi-Wan, heroes sometimes understand that laying down their lives is the greatest triumph. In context of *A New Hope*, these are the tiny heroes, unknown until now, not gifted in the Force, but making the ultimate sacrifice so the Rebellion can succeed. In fact, Jyn's death symbolically imbues Leia, who receives the plans, with her own toughness and certainty, tools she uses powerfully in the first film.

Mon Mothma concludes in the novelization that Jyn did not intend to martyr herself. "I think Jyn fully recognized who she was and sought a way to channel her best and worst impulses, her darkest moments and her brightest, toward a cause worthy of her true incandescence" (322). Mon Mothma ends it with a tribute to Jyn, describing how she grew from a troubled girl failed by so many mentors to a leader who inspired all the rebels to rise. "Jyn I think, never knew the effect she had on others never realized the intensity of her own humanity or the Presence she brought to a room…. In her short life, she had seen relentless hardship and become hard herself. But her fire shone bright" (322).

The Mandalorian Finds His Clan

In 2019, Disney+ launched *The Mandalorian*—an old school Western show in which the taciturn hero wanders the frontier, taking bounty hunting jobs to get by. Dave Filoni of *Clone Wars* and *Rebels* and Jon Favreau of *Iron Man* are the showrunners. While the series is episodic rather than arc-heavy, a distinct hero's journey appears in the hero's quest for family, one that is finally fulfilled through the most unlikely of children.

The Mandalorian's lifestage is that of an adult who resists and finally succumbs to the need for family. While he does not literally settle down, accepting fatherhood is its own part of the cycle, signaling maturity as well as ties to the community.

Episode one begins with the Mandalorian (Pedro Pascal) entering a cantina, winning a fight, and dragging off a nameless Mythrol to turn in to Greef Karga, his Bounty Hunter's Guild liaison. Since such a cantina works as a microcosm of the larger world as well as a testing ground, it's a fitting setting for his introduction: "Bars are natural spots to recuperate, pick up gossip, make friends, and confront enemies. They also allow us to observe people under pressure, when true character is revealed" (Vogler 140).

Strikingly, Mando keeps his T-slit helmet on at all times, permanently concealing his features. Masks suggest facelessness, deliberately presenting a stoic face to the world, or perhaps no face at all, as the Stormtroopers do. Certainly, a mask offers a new personality for the hero—one that's sometimes so overwhelming that it threatens to take over the self. Further, this helmet is shining silver beskar, emphasizing that the seat of cognition and will has been fully upgraded, though the physical skills of the body, encased in mismatched pieces, don't yet match its power.

Mando's scuffed armor is a roadmap of his violent past, even as it establishes his strength and capability. It's also filled with hidden weaponry—Mandalorian vambraces alone may contain flamethrowers, wrist lasers, rocket launchers, retractable blades, blasters, a fibercord whip (which can quickly bind targets' hands), shield emitters, repulsors, Kamino saberdarts, paralyzing darts, nerve gas, projectile buzzsaws, and grappling lines. *The Bounty Hunter's Guide* details more about the individual pieces of armor. Traditionally, over a vacuum-proof combat suit, there's a helmet, shoulder pauldrons, vambraces, breastplate, codpiece, kneepads, thigh and shin guards. An immature warrior, Mando has clearly collected his multicolored, mismatched pieces from different places and lacks the traditional jetpack. Similarly, his ship is ancient and scuffed, displaying his own rough edges. With these tools demonstrating his toughness yet incompleteness, his Call to Adventure appears.

Karga is Mando's mentor and herald, advising him on how to get by in their society and granting him his missions. However, he's notably untrustworthy. Carl Weathers, who plays him, describes him as "a combination of a used car salesman and a puppeteer" (Thorne). This twist is unusual for the hero, who most often fully trusts his grandfatherly guide. Of course, other heroes, notably including young Han, have guides who betray them. The Outer Rim where they exist is clearly treacherous.

When Mando demands the best job, Karga admits there's an unusual one available. "No puck. Face to face. Direct commission. Deep pocket." Off Mando goes to meet the mysterious and unnamed Client (Werner Herzog). He lives in a fortress guarded by Stormtroopers as well as Jabba's robot eyeball. All these tie in with previous villains of the series, emphasizing the Client's unsavory connections. Contrasting with the controlled Client is his assistant, nervous, stammering Dr. Pershing, who appears to have scientific plans for the mysterious bounty. "His enthusiasm outweighs his discretion," the Client manages. The Client also startles Mando by offering a down payment with an ingot of beskar. As the Client concludes, "The beskar belongs back into the hands of a Mandalorian. It is good to restore the natural order of things after a period of such disarray, don't you agree?" This substance, also called Mandalorian iron, is a rare alloy durable enough to withstand a direct blaster shot or lightsaber blow. Mando runs his gloved fingers over the Imperial emblem stamping it: This is a heresy in itself, as the metal belongs only to his people. *The Bounty Hunter's Guide* explains the metal's importance:

> The planets and moons of the Mandalore system are rich in beskar or Mandalorian iron. According to legend, this boon brought the Progenitors to our world. beskar is enormously strong, able to deflect blaster bolts and even lightsaber blades. Yet it is light and flexible, particularly when forged with carbon and ciridium. A skilled naur'alor can shape beskar into almost any form, manipulating its strength, color, and other properties. This knowledge is ours alone—the penalty for sharing it with outsiders is death [Wallace et al. 139].

It replaces the hero sword, as for Mandalorians armor is their true source of power.

Mando brings this metallic treasure to his people's hidden lair. There, the traditions are transmitted and kept by the Armorer (Emily Swallow). Of course, she wears full armor with a concealing gold helm gleaming with horns. Her fur cloak adds to her ancient, even bestial appearance. These mark her as their leader but also (fittingly as an anima figure) Mando's trainer in the natural and mystical world. Accordingly, she uses terms like "whistling birds" and "rising phoenix" for their weaponry, emphasizing the spiritual side of their lore.

When he kneels respectfully before her and lays down the ingot, she tells him, "This was gathered in the Great Purge. It is good it is back with the Tribe." She constructs a pauldron for him, a second piece of the gleaming silver suit he hopes to build. While a piece covering the right shoulder doesn't seem the most crucial, it in fact is the traditional location of the Mandalorian signet, one's coat of arms. Traditionally, Mandalorian warriors decorate their armor with clan colors and insignia, celebrations of their victories, goals or causes, and so on. It's therefore a piece of identity more than practical defense. The Armorer asks Mando, "Has your signet been revealed?" However, Mando's has not. Symbolically, he hasn't yet chosen a path.

At the gleaming forge, the Armorer crafts the piece in a short montage that borrows a bit from both classic Norse mythology and Japanese samurai films. This scene also triggers flashbacks to the loss of Mando's parents in a devastating attack. As the season slowly reveals, this was a foundational moment that included his adoption by Mandalorians. It too was a Call to Adventure with mentors and shadow figures, emphasizing how close the story remains to its mythic roots. "We had a long talk with each other," said Favreau of George Lucas. "One thing he said to me was, 'remember, Jon, the real audience for all stories and all myths is the kids that are coming of age,' because he's really a Joseph Campbell adherent" (Mullally). As Favreau continues:

> We enjoy the stories as adults, but really, storytelling is about imparting the wisdom of the previous generations on to the children who are becoming adults, and giving them a context for how to behave and how to learn the lessons of the past without making the mistakes on their own. That's the hope, that you can teach them how to avoid all the hardship but garner all the wisdom [Mullally].

Embarking on his assignment, Mando follows the tracker to Arvala-7. When he's attacked by two wild beasts of burden called blurrgs, the helpful Ugnaught Kuiil (voiced by Nick Nolte) rescues him. Vogler writes, "The mentor may appear as a wise old wizard (*Star Wars*), a tough drill sergeant (*An Officer and a Gentleman*), or a grizzled old boxing coach (*Rocky*)" (17). In this scene, Kuiil's a bit of all three. Kuiil adds that Mando must learn to ride a blurrg, and the Kuiil will show him to the encampment. This is a traditional fairytale test—the hero who follows the little old man's advice succeeds, and all the others are doomed. This, it seems, has been the fate of many, who failed to take Kuiil's advice and died. Still, Kuiil has faith in him, and Mando accepts. Kuiil trains him to ride a blurrg, in a Western scene but also one that nods to Mandalorian tradition. As he insists, "You are Mandalorian! Your ancestors rode the great Mythosaur. Surely you can ride this young foal." Working with him, Mando learns patience and sensitivity to animals—both a useful prelude for the parenting role that will follow.

On arrival, Mando reluctantly teams up with IG-11, an assassin droid. His overwhelming capability—not only of destroying armies and wielding a gadget for every occasion but also of accomplishing all parts of the mission—reflects Mando in many ways. With this, he functions as a shadow—not only because Mando hates droids, but because of his expedient willingness to murder. Mando, by contrast, still has a heart and conscience.

At last, the pair reach the bounty, and Mando opens the lid on an egg-shaped cradle. In itself, it symbolizes potential. Opening it, Mando discovers their fifty-year-old quarry—still a baby. Since it's devoid of all sentiment, IG-11 goes to kill the child and the camera freezes on Mando's mask, emphasizing his conflict. In a dramatic cutaway, someone fires, and then the droid falls. This leaves Mando alone with the Child. Composer Ludwig Göransson explains that the music expresses the Mandalorian's emotions:

> So, what does The Mandalorian think the first time he sees this little creature? He's not like, "Oh what, is this cute little thing?" He's like, "Oh shit, this is not what I signed up for. I don't even know what this is." So all the music throughout the show is coming from The Mandalorian's perspective and it's what puts his facial expressions on screen because you don't see his facial expression. He's wearing a helmet the whole time. So musically I need to tell the audience what his facial expressions are saying [Chitwood].

Mando hesitantly reaches out to the Child. On this iconic image, the episode ends. Connecting with him symbolizes trying to reclaim Mando's own innocent wonder, everything his closed-off adult self has left behind. "Unless we develop our own inner caregiver, we will always be dependent on others to nurture and care for the child inside us" (Pearson 113). This inner caregiver is the voice that comforts the self, suggests self-care like a nap or a treat when needed. This caregiver often mimics one's parents, whom Mando lost young. With only faceless warriors bringing him up, Mando has spent his life enduring, being outwardly strong and uncomplaining—emotionless and faceless even. Now he's offered a path to deepening within.

When considered as an aspect of Mando, the Divine Child's arrival represents a new level of consciousness, offered from a place of pure creativity. "A child made in the underworld is a magic child who has all the potential associated with the underworld, such as acute hearing and innate sensing" (Estés 431). He offers a path to wholeness, embracing the spiritual, childlike, playful, experimental side of the self Mando generally ignores. Partnering with him will be Mando's guide to a deeper reality. In fact, this child's arrival signals radical ideas inspired by a new, youthful way of seeing. Soon enough, Mando will rebel against the guild and seek his own riskier path. Traditionally, this Divine Child has a supernatural origin. Immediately after birth, the child is threatened by a smothering evil that wishes to deny it consciousness. Forces of obedience like the Client and Karga thus endanger him. Finally, the Divine Child displays supernatural powers, showing the hero's potential when he embraces this new side of the self. Of course, there's much further to go.

Episode two is an exercise in humiliation for Mando when Jawas rob his ship. He attacks them directly and fails. After this, with help from Kuiil, he must negotiate. This is a valuable lesson for the hero, teaching him patience and caution during degrading work. In return for his parts, they send him questing in a small descent and return—to battle a mudhorn in its cave and return with its egg. The egg symbolizes his growing link with fatherhood, of course. Further, as it's a female mudhorn guarding an egg, a feminine symbol, this quest into the unconscious offers Mando skills he's never mastered. In fact, his weapons and conventional fighting nearly get him killed. At the crucial moment, however, the Child uses the Force to stop the beast. This introduces Mando to teamwork (something he dislikes) but more importantly the spiritual reality of the Force. There are things beyond what he can see and touch, qualities he must learn to master. He returns with the egg and repairs his ship, but the mystery of the Child's powers lingers.

Episode three, "The Sin," marks Mando's turning point. First, he delivers the Child to the Client, doing his best to ignore his growing attachment and guilt. In its protective cradle, the Child floats out of the room, still watching Mando. In turn, the Client eagerly pays him the beskar … so eagerly that Mando suspects something. "What are your plans for it?" he blurts. The Client refuses to say.

His reward in hand, Mando brings the beskar to the Armorer and here introduces viewers to more of his people. The crowd of Mandalorians all go helmeted, even the children. Few have survived, as the Empire destroyed them all. Accordingly, Mando's rival, Paz Vizla, is revolted by the treasure as he protests that the Imperials stole this metal after slaughtering their people and consigning them to exile. He is the shadow here, voicing Mando's unspoken worries about the job.

The Armorer breaks it up. "The Empire is no longer. And the beskar has returned. When one chooses to walk the Way of the Mandalore, you are both hunter and prey. How can one be a coward if one chooses this way of life?" She confirms that Mando has never removed his helmet or had others do so. "This is the Way," they all thunder. The group's devotion to a single path, even as they challenge each other for dominance, reflects a traditional structure. "Patriarchies are distinguished by a respect for man-made laws, the favoring of works of art and craft, and obedience to the hierarchy" (Cirlot 218). The Armorer stands at their head. Though she's female, her facelessness, like Phasma's, codes her closer to androgynous. Emily Swallow opened up in an interview about playing such a strong character. "They described her as being an alpha female among alpha males. I love that about her," Swallow noted. "She's not fazed at all by all of the guff that gets thrown her way. But I also really appreciate that she holds her own in a room but she's not pushy about it. She just seems very confident in who she is" (Thompson).

Next, the Armorer offers to craft a full cuirass for Mando with the new beskar steel. He accepts this honor and replaces his battered, mismatched pieces with a gleaming silver set. In heraldry, silver represents sincerity, wisdom, innocence, peace and joy. Its mirror finish suggests impenetrability for the hero but also introspection.

Of course, this gift from his mentor replaces the traditional hero sword. Besides its contrast with all the lightsabers of the films, Mandalorian armor is battle gear, filled with a myriad of weapons and tools that suggest adaptability as well as power. The Armorer offers Mando another honor—a mudhorn signet that will establish his identity. In fact, a coat of arms emblazoned on armor or shield shows "that the knight defends himself by displaying his identity and invoking it in the hour of peril" (Cirlot 294). However, Mando still feels he shouldn't take it. He replies, "I can't accept. It wasn't a noble kill. I was helped by an enemy." With this, more guilt blossoms as he recalls the Child's aid. The Armorer has built him a full suit that makes him appear more impenetrable and emotionless. However, the Child has already gotten inside his defenses.

In his new armor, he returns to Greef Karga, who tries to help him as mentor and drown out his misgivings. "Mando, enjoy your rewards. Buy a camtono of spice. By the time you come out of hyperdrive, you will have forgotten all about it." Mando tries to take a job and fly away. However, he keeps glancing at the knob with which the Child had once played. Even with a concealing helmet, it's clear he's torn.

Abruptly, he returns and breaks into the Client's stronghold. He blasts his way in, flattening all the enemies, and makes his way to the cringing Dr. Pershing. The Child lies there unconscious. On Mando's demanding what has happened, Pershing replies, "I protected him. If it wasn't for me, he would already be dead!" His goal here is unclear, but Mando knows it's unsavory. Mando reclaims the baby and fights his way out.

He has won on a physical level. However, he has neglected the societal repercussions. In fact, in a dramatic scene across town, tracking fobs activate for every member of the Guild, including Karga. A standoff with the other Bounty Hunters follows, as they all confront him. Karga, their leader, orders him to surrender the Child, but Mando refuses. Estés comments, "A culture that requires harm to one's soul in order to follow the culture's proscriptions is a very sick culture indeed" (175). Here, Mando can either obey his guild or his conscience. Though Mando hesitates, he quickly chooses. Hijacking a truck, he roars away, shooting at his former friends and rivals.

He also blasts them with his flamethrower, symbolically burning away his old life. However, he and the Child are outmatched as the entire town turn against them. Mando has betrayed the code he lived by, with an external battle mirroring the internal one.

In western tradition, the cavalry arrives. All the Mandalorians fly in, dramatically blasting the Bounty Hunters. Even Vizla is there, showing that he values his clan above petty rivalries. "Get out of here! We'll hold them off!" he promises. Clearly, this group supports their own, in contrast with the honorless Hunters. "This is the way," Vizla reassures Mando.

"This is the way," the bounty hunter replies, acknowledging this sacrifice with admiration. With this support from his shadow, Mando rallies. Estés writes, "If you have attempted to fit whatever mold and failed to do so, you are probably lucky. You may be an exile of some sort, but you have sheltered your soul" (184).

However, Greef Karga is a more personal shadow, the fellow bounty hunter who ruthlessly enforces the rules Mando is breaking. He blocks the way to Mando's ship as a final threshold guardian, a disturbingly personal one. Like all the others, he symbolizes Mando's own hesitation at leaving. Having learned to place his faith in the Mandalorians' clever gadgets after Kuiil's lessons in avoiding direct battles, Mando blasts steam from his ship and uses its cover to shoot his former friend.

As he escapes with the Child, Vizla flies beside Mando's ship briefly and he watches the jetpack enviously. "I gotta get one of those." Having been upgraded physically, he still seeks more—symbolic of the soul growth he likewise has found but still can improve on. He gives the Child the ship's knob to play with, and they soar upwards into freedom.

This begins the smaller stories that nonetheless tie into the arc. For episode four, Mando and the Child flee to the planet Sorgan. There, they encounter a pair of anima figures. Vogler notes that a western cantina is an excellent place to make allies and enemies. "Countless westerns take the hero to a saloon where his manhood and determination are tested, and where his friends and villains are introduced. Bars are also useful to the hero for obtaining information, for learning the new rules that apply to the special world" (19). While Mando completes and gets jobs at several, this one is located on a rural planet far outside his range of experience, where he indeed learns new rules and makes allies.

In the common house, Cara Dune (MMA fighter Gina Carano) flees from him, convinced that she's his bounty. Since he has similar fears of her, he follows her outside and attacks. They fight to a standoff, emphasizing how perfectly matched they are as equals. Abruptly choosing a different strategy, Mando breaks up their fight with a hilariously deadpan "Want some soup?" As they talk inside, Cara reveals that she betrayed and left the

Rebels as Mando did the Bounty Hunters. Clearly, each can trust the other because they're so similar as perfect partners. Pascal calls Cara "the most dangerous and the most human. And she is also a survivor, a loner, and a reject." He adds that she and Mando significantly "draw together."

Outside, Sorgan is a land of feminine forests and rivers, laughing children and bountiful farms. All this represents domesticity and the feminine sphere. Seeking a hiding place for a time, Mando finds himself staying with a widow, Omera, and her daughter Winta. While the daughter plays with the Child, helping him experience love and friendship, Omera offers Mando something deeper. She's strikingly sensitive to his needs even while pushing him to expand his boundaries—she asks him about his mask, and he tells her he hasn't removed it since he took it on as a child. "This is the Way." Cara pushes at Mando's lifestyle too, but she's more direct, asking whether Mando's people will kill him for removing the helmet. He replies, "No. You just can't ever put it back on again."

In disbelief, she, like Omera, voices Mando's unspoken longings: "That's it? So you can slip off the helmet, and settle down with that beautiful young widow, and raise your kid sitting here, sipping spotchka?" As anima figures, both urge Mando to grow and find love and family. However, Mando echoes the classical knight, "helmeted and closed off in a cubicle of steel, armored against the natural world, featureless behind a helmet" (Frankel, *From Girl to Goddess* 28). Armor is a symbol of isolation, of separating from human closeness. By choosing it, he is rejecting falling in love with the lady, though he does rescue her.

Omera continues her hopeful temptation for him to leave his path and directly invites him and the Child to move in. He turns her down, along with the hand reaching for his mask. It is the Way. Still, he seeks a compromise by leaving the baby with her. Mando the tough warrior cannot settle down, but he hopes that the Child, like the tiny innocent part of himself, can have the chance.

This plan crumbles when a bounty hunter comes for them, so Mando and the Child must keep running. Ostensibly, they take little from the episode. However, subtly, they have gained some grounding as well as certainty that they belong together. As Filoni explains, "*Star Wars* can work in many different ways. It's one of the strengths of the franchise. You can do a one-off and it can be incredibly meaningful, or you can do a broader story arc. And sometimes you're getting the broader arc when you don't know it. So the flexibility of *Star Wars* means an unceasing number of stories that we seem to be able to tell" (Mottram 53).

More episodic stories with deeper lessons follow, in a pair of shadow encounters. Campbell explains the purpose of the path of obstacles, explaining, "The trials are designed to see to it that the intending hero should be really a hero. Is he really a match for this task? Can he overcome the dangers? Does he have the courage, the knowledge, the capacity, to enable him to serve?" (Campbell and Moyers 154). Indeed, the next stories test Mando on a personal level. Episode five has him teaming up with young bounty hunter Toro Calican (Jake Cannavale) on Tatooine. This shadow represents who Mando was just a short time before—willing to sell out a partner for money. While Mando is happy to work with him at first, when the young man turns treacherous, Mando ends things quickly and decisively. By killing the greedy personification of bounty hunters, Mando destroys this voice within himself, choosing friendship in its place.

The next caper teams him up with his old comrades in an even more pointed look at who he used to be and what his new morality will allow. Mando's former associate Ranzar Malk (Mark Boone Junior) sends him on a mission with a team of criminals, who remark repeatedly on his prior reputation. They set out to rescue Qin, whom Mando once betrayed, but the team quickly betray Mando in turn and lock him in a cell. When he escapes, he takes revenge on each in turn, imprisoning the personified brutality and amorality he left behind long ago. He even calls the New Republic on his former allies, emphasizing that he's chosen the law-abiding side.

At last, the two-part finale ties the season together. In a small quest that bookends Mando's break with the Guild, Karga's a small blue hologram summons Mando to Navarro for a quest. The Client has expanded the number of Imperials on their world. Now if Mando can end his reign, Karga will clear his name with the Guild. As Karga offers, with a plan that's a little too convenient, they can set up a meeting with the Child as bait. The hero suspects a trap, but the reward is too tempting—a return to legitimacy. For backup, Mando gathers a crew from the previous episodes: Cara, Kuiil, and a rebuilt IG-11. This last has been reprogrammed as a protocol and nursing droid—an evil shadow now transformed into a sidekick. "I spent day after day reinforcing its development with patience and determination," Kuiil exclaims. Still, Mando is repulsed. He insists an assassin cannot change, a comment that could obliquely apply to himself.

On Navarro, Mando's people and Karga's unite for an old-fashioned blurrg-back ride through the frontier. Savage beasts attack, and the Child heals Karga's injuries. Touched by this kindness, Karga reveals that he had planned to betray Mando and his friends but switches to their side instead.

They infiltrate the Client's lair—the belly of the beast once more. There, the Client reports to his superior, Moff Gideon (Giancarlo Esposito), and thus reveals the supervillain and his own Imperial ties. The Moff arrives, slowly and dramatically in his TIE fighter. As he announces to Mando, he's frantic to reclaim the child for secret reasons of his own. His desperation marks him as the supreme enemy as it pits him against Mando, his new father and nurturer. While they face off, his Stormtroopers kill Kuiil and take the Child.

In Mando's moment of helplessness, pinned down as all this takes place, IG-11 steps up. He is Mando's ruthless killer side, denied and dormant through the show, but finally emerging when a harder warrior is needed. IG-11 defeats the Stormtroopers, rescues the Child, and rides into battle with him to save Cara and Mando. By sharing Mando's devotion to the Child, IG-11 establishes himself as a reflection of Mando, more alike than not. He has cool tough guy lines too, much like Mando's:

> **IG-11:** I am fulfilling my base function.
> **MANDO:** Which is?
> **IG-11:** To nurse and protect.

This final episode has Mando and his entire team battling to save the Child. Their unity emphasizes how much he's assembled all the disparate parts of the self into a single will with a single mission. "A mother with a child who is different must have the endurance of Sisyphus, the fearsomeness of the Cyclops, and the tough hide of Caliban to go against a mean-spirited culture" (Estés 174). In this way, the Child's existence strengthens Mando to fight for his ethics rather than giving in to expediency.

Meanwhile, the enemy, Gideon, has not only pinned them down and holds them prey at the barrel of his cannon, but shows his control by revealing their full identities and backstories. All their secrets are laid bare:

> I am sure that Republican Shock Trooper Carasynthia Dune of Alderaan will advise you that she has witnessed many of her ranks vaporize mid-descent facing the predecessor of this particular model. Or perhaps the decommissioned Mandalorian hunter, Din Djarin, has heard the songs of the Siege of Mandalore, when gunships outfitted with similar ordnance laid waste to fields of Mandalorian recruits in The Night of a Thousand Tears. I advise disgraced Magistrate Greef Karga to search the wisdom of his years and urge you to lay down your arms and come outside.

In a twist, this speech reveals Moff Gideon's own backstory—Mando realizes that this is his family's murderer, since only the local ISB officer knew his name. He has found his true nemesis.

Taking advantage of IG-11's sudden rescue, Mando goes out into the firefight and mows troopers down with their own massive cannon in a moment of teamwork … until Gideon shoots the power generator at his feet. He falls. His friends haul him to shelter, but Mando insists they leave his helmet on, even if it kills him: "I can hold them back long enough for you to escape. Let me have a warrior's death." As he concludes, "This is the Way." However, IG-11, who understands him as no one else does, insists on healing him. Even as Mando protests, "No living thing has seen me without my helmet since I swore the Creed," IG-11 finds a loophole by telling him, "I am not a living thing." It's the shadow's complete understanding that aids Mando through this ordeal.

After eight episodes of suspense, Mando finally removes his helmet and shows his bleeding, vulnerable face. A mask is like a chrysalis, protecting the inner self as it develops. "All transformations are invested with something at once of profound mystery and of the shameful.... Therefor metamorphoses must be hidden from view—and hence the need for the mask" (Cirlot 205). Thanks to this, the removal shows how much Mando has grown through the events of the series. He replaces it, reminding viewers that more growth will follow.

IG-11 heals him and Mando learns that he can trust the droid. This is his revelation, his acceptance of droids as worthy teammates. He lets IG-11 guide him through underground passages, representing a journey through the depths of the soul. However, another tragedy strikes. He discovers his Mandalorian allies have been slaughtered by Imperials or fled. Over a pile of their lost armor, he talks with the Armorer. She's busy following her people's sacred trust and salvaging the pieces. As such, she represents Mando's duty even as she gives him a quest: returning the Child to his people. She tells Mando of the historic battle Mandalore the Great fought with the Jedi but finishes by adding that the Child is not his enemy, but instead a foundling like Mando once was. The Armorer adds that they make a clan of two. With this, Mando accepts the Mudhorn sigil he had rejected earlier. His armor is completed at the same time as his family is. For the hero, having a child often symbolizes fulfillment—not only a new life stage but a copy of the self and link with the future. Together, they have found wholeness.

The Armor continues her mentoring role with a final weapon—the jetpack of their people. As she concludes, "This will make you complete." She has welded his armor for him piece by piece through the season, and now his Mandalorian self is fully assembled. With all his friends surrounding him, and gleaming armor from head to toe, he is indeed a complete warrior at last. Certainly, Mando gets a signet and jetpack. However, like Dorothy, he has been carrying what he seeks for quite some time—a family and clan in the person of the Child. When the mentor reveals this, he has an identity and mission at last.

The Armorer chooses to remain behind, symbolically remaining in the subconscious. As they make their way out, IG-11, the stalwart warrior, offers to sacrifice himself. While Mando shot the droid in the first episode, now he pleads for it to survive: "Wait. You can't self-destruct. Your base command is to watch the child. That supersedes your manufacturer's protocol, right?" With this, he expresses his love and need for the faceless killer side of himself—a side that can fight to save innocents and his loved ones. However, IG-11 tells him, "There is nothing to be sad about. I have never been alive." As it adds, it can discern his sadness in a way no one else can. "I'm a nurse droid. I've analyzed your voice." The shadow perceives all the hero's weaknesses, reflecting the part he's buried. IG-11 detonates with one more epic line: "Manufacturer's protocol dictates I cannot be captured. I must be destroyed." With this, it wades through lava to reach the enemy and explodes itself to kill them, demonstrating the selfless sacrifice of the warrior—Mando's path to protection as the Child's new guardian.

For the final fight, Moff Gideon menaces the team from above in his TIE fighter. Newly a responsible father, Mando must save everyone. He steps up. "I got this." They battle in the air, and Mando, struggling with his new technology and often clinging by one hand, manages to attack a sticky bomb. The fighter crashes. Triumphant, Mando lands solidly on his own two feet.

They stand at a crossroads after, and Greef Karga offers a final temptation to the easy path: Mando can rejoin the guild and have his choice of assignments. However, Mando refuses. He has an honorable mission: to fight in his new child's service as his father-protector. In fact, Mando lifts the child up and flies off with him just as his own savior did so many years before. Having found his new family, he also lets the baby keep his mythosaur necklace. Now they are bound in their clan of two.

In a final scene, Moff Gideon climbs from the wrecked fighter clutching the Darksaber. As the *Clone Wars* and *Rebels* cartoons established, this is the weapon of the rightful leader of Mandalore, passed through combat. The *Rebels* episode "History of the Darksaber" has a Mandalorian explain:

> Legend tells that it was created over a thousand years ago by Tarre Vizsla, the first Mandalorian ever inducted into the Jedi Order. After his passing, the Jedi kept the saber in their temple. That was, until members of House Vizsla snuck in and liberated it. They used the saber to unify the people and strike down those who would oppose them. One time, they ruled all of Mandalore wielding this blade. This saber is an important symbol to that house and respected by the other clans.

In *Rebels,* protagonist Sabine uses it to appoint a more benevolent leader for her people, Bo-Katan Kryze. She appears in season two to summon Mando to a higher cause. Here, Gideon is not only established as the killer of Mando's family, but the usurper of the Mandalorian throne. When Mando battles and defeats him, he may seize a new destiny as the rightful ruler of Mandalore. Like Luke and so many others, he will topple the tyrant and restore his people as their new leader.

The Mentors Fade

HAN'S SACRIFICE

After the events of the original trilogy, old and new canon have Han marrying Leia and having children with her, moving on to a settled, responsible phase of his life. Of course, this domesticity is difficult for him. Leia thinks as they await the birth of their son in *Aftermath: Empire's End*, "It's been hard for Han. He won't say it out loud, but she can see it on his face. Her husband needs something to do. He's *bored*.... Han Solo's got nothing to smuggle, nowhere to gamble, no foolish Rebellion to fight for" (Wendig 29).

Han alternates between home life and missions, especially when his close friends need his help. Of course, this costs him his family, as *Force Awakens* will eventually reveal. When asked in one of the interim novels how Leia and his unborn child will feel about his leaving them to go save Chewie's world, Han replies, "I don't know. They'll hate me, probably. But maybe in time they'll get it. They'll see I had to do this" (Wendig, *Life Debt* 277). This is a noble sentiment, but also foreshadows his divorce and estrangement from his son.

Han begins the seventh film as the smuggler and adventurer he was in the original—lacking ties to the Resistance or greater authority. Once again, a group of idealistic heroes sweep him away. This time, of course, he has memories of the past and the family ties he formed. With this, Han becomes a mentor, using his own mistakes to counsel Finn and Rey on heroism. While Han tries to pass on the mission to his allies, the perpetual mentor Maz Kanata counsels Han to bring BB-8 to Leia himself, adding in the novel, "You were always so good at looking ahead. I think now it's your time to look back. At what—and who—you've left behind" (Foster 168–169). When Coruscant falls and the Resistance (in the form of his ex-wife) summons him back, he answers.

He concocts one of his usual crazy, desperate plans, blasting onto the First Order's base at lightspeed with a bag of munitions to blow it up from the inside. Echoing Obi-Wan's role from the original film, he's the responsible leader directing the idealistic young people. This time around, he's feeling his age: in the novelization, after the Falcon's crash landing on Starkiller Base, Han mutters, "Was a time it wouldn't have been so rough" and shakes off Finn's assurances (216).

His final test, like Obi-Wan's, has him confronting the classic enemy of the aging hero—Mordred, the evil son or protégé, who seeks to tear down all the hero has built. Han does not defeat his son but hazards his life on trying to redeem him. This moment has him stepping up, fulfilling the fatherly mission Leia has appointed him as well as his duty to the Resistance. In the end, he is sacrificed choosing his responsibility to family as well as the side of light.

In facing Ben, Han nearly lets him walk away, but remembers what Leia has asked and confronts him. This, of course, leads to his death. Han reasons with Kylo Ren, insisting that he wants them to be a family. Kylo Ren rejects this: "Your son is gone. He was weak and foolish, like his father. So I destroyed him." Han knows that can't be true and insists that his son is still there. Finally, his son's voice turns vulnerable as he pleads, "I know what I have to do, but I don't know if I have the strength to do it. Will you help me?"

"Yes, anything," Han replies. Of course, he doesn't know what he's promising, but his voice suggests that he truly will offer anything to redeem his son, as Leia does in episode nine. Kylo Ren kills him. "Accepting without quite believing, Han stared back into the face of the creature that had been his son. There was nothing to see there. Only darkness in the shape of a face: alien, unthinking, unfeeling" (Foster 244). This moment echoes real-world fears: of failing at parenting so badly that one's child turns evil and murderous. "All of us bring our own experiences to it," director J.J. Abrams said. "As a father, as a friend to people who have children, I know what it's like to see struggle, to be part of struggle. I know how painful it can be. I know how real it is. And this is, of course, an insane extrapolated version," he added with a laugh. "Patricide is not *ideal*" (Breznican, "J.J. Abrams on Kylo Ren").

It's true that Han's complete surrendering helps Kylo commit the murder meant to turn him completely to the darkness. However, it torments him with guilt and shame, as Luke observes during their duel in episode eight. Because of this, Han's sacrifice in fact does help his son confront what he's become and turn him back to the light. In a final appearance in *The Rise of Skywalker,* Han (or a vision of him) freely forgives Kylo and thus completes his redemption.

Luke Passes On

Luke Skywalker announces in *The Last Jedi*, "It's time for the Jedi to end." This covers one of the movie's themes, about letting go of the past (literally for the characters, but also as a message to the audience). Here, Luke emphasizes to Rey that the Jedi—people who think they have a monopoly on the Force despite the alternate culture of *Rogue One*'s Temple of the Whills—were wrong about many things and shouldn't be resurrected.

In retrospect, this makes sense. The Council's cruelty in refusing to train Anakin, never rescuing his mother, and forbidding him to wed set him on the path to darkness. Jedi are arrogant, judgmental, and privileged. They permanently separate children from their families, all while trying to teach goodness and altruism. Their hubris in *Revenge of the Sith*—concealing that their vision is clouded, and individually attempting to battle Darth Sidious—ended the Jedi Order. They also allowed the greatest darkness in history to grow up beside them for decades, as Palpatine ascends to power. The *Clone Wars* show has another arc about their hidebound lack of vision, as they banished the spunky, loyal heroine Ahsoka from their ranks when she's framed for terrorism. With her name finally cleared, she refused to return, disgusted that no one but Anakin took her side. Continuing this pattern, Luke repeated the Council's snap judgment, when in an instant, he rejected his nephew for exploring the Dark Side. Clearly, Luke has a valid point—training Jedi to be chosen ones and wholly reject evil created despots Sidious and Vader, as well as Kylo Ren.

When Rey finds him, Luke Skywalker in his tattered robes bears a strong resemblance to Obi-Wan's first appearance. In fact, Mark Hamill reprised his role at the age of 64, while Alec Guinness was first cast at 63. He has become his mentor in truth. Meanwhile, his X-wing, dumped underwater and left to rust, emphasizes his disinterest in returning. With all the pressure of rebuilding the Jedi placed on him, he's collapsed.

> While some fans struggle with where Luke starts his Wizard's Journey, his backstory suggests he was less prepared to face the emotional toll of being a Jedi Knight compared to Obi-Wan and Yoda, who received a sophisticated education in the Jedi Temple and were taught from their youngling days of their value in the galactic balance. Similarly, his sister, Leia—who throughout the novel *Leia: Princess of Alderaan* is shown failing but persisting—has learned from a young age to accept failures while continuing to fight on [Barr, "Luke Skywalker" 120].

Of course, Obi-Wan trained Anakin, but failed as he lost him to the dark side. Obi-Wan blames himself and it's suggested that the inexperienced, rather traditionalist and inflexible Jedi did a worse job than Qui-Gon or Yoda would have. As everything cycles around once more, Luke, the last of the Jedi, was given Obi-Wan's namesake Ben to train. Through it all, he feared the same failure, until it came to pass.

The film *The Last Jedi* dwells on his guilt and shame as he refuses to train Rey because he failed so spectacularly with his nephew. Meanwhile, his bionic hand emphasizes his damage. It no longer appears human as it did in *Jedi*, repaired imperfectly but basically indistinguishable from his birth one. Now, he leaves it robotic and artificial: the hand that tried to murder his nephew, that dragged him out of the wreckage of his ruined school, appears to be separate, no longer a part of him. Luke is fragmented, the damaged Fisher King of grail lore seeking grace from above to heal him. He is the elderly ruler seeking forgiveness and salvation. "If Joseph

Campbell's 'hero's journey' is a reflection of humankind's journey beyond the innocence of childhood into the wider world of knowledge and responsibility, then what comes *after* the hero's journey, after the 'happily ever after'? What of the middle-aged hero, who now faces inevitable mortality and loss?" (Szostak 16).

Rey comes to him and dramatically offers him the lightsaber that began his quest as a young man—Anakin Skywalker's lightsaber that he lost when he lost his hand. It's a startling gift from the past, a summoning to resume the adventures of his childhood or at least take up the mentoring role. Unhesitatingly, he tosses it away.

On the one hand, this moment subverts the epic, emphasizing that this won't be the story of Luke's eager training of the new chosen one and return to battle Kylo Ren as Obi-Wan did his old apprentice. On the other, it's a fervent rejection of the classic call—his father's lightsaber and a quest to vanquish the tyranny in the galaxy with a dramatic duel. Luke has decided that heroically saving the universe from evil doesn't work—he ended the reign of the Sith and the Empire, and one generation later, the First Order has taken its place. Surely those who observed the Second World War felt the same—evil wasn't eradicated, only delayed—so what was the point?

Luke pointedly ignores Rey, retreating to his hut and shutting the door against her. However, it's smashed in as Chewbacca charges through it, violently hugging him and demanding he not shut out the outside world. Chewie represents a simple moral code, along with the primitive instinct to choose goodness. While Luke can try to avoid Rey's reasoned calls to duty, he cannot hold back the primal emotions welling up from within.

He learns Han is dead—bringing more guilt and sorrow—as well as the knowledge that his contemporaries are dying. He is the last on many levels. Still, he refuses to train Rey. Rey insists, "We need Luke Skywalker." Clearly, she has bought into his legend and legacy.

Of course, he has fled this reputation, running to the edges of the galaxy. Luke responds sarcastically. "You think, what, I'm gonna walk out with a laser sword and face down the whole First Order?" As she insists that she won't leave without him and follows him around the island, he uses the Force to catch fish and climb cliffs—openly rejecting the path of the warrior and scholar. In his years at this sacred Jedi place of learning, he hasn't even read the sacred texts hidden there. He's been in a holding pattern—rejecting the Jedi legacy but failing to find a new identity for himself.

Further, as he dominates the island as Jedi Master and chosen one, allowing the diminutive caretakers to do his laundry and cook his food, he more than a little resembles the Jedi he's rejecting. The humbler Yoda and Ben did their own cooking and blended into the environments until young Luke overlooked them both. Luke hasn't learned the older masters' lessons of giving up all power to fade away. Since this is his task of the film, a large arc is coming.

Luke enters the Millennium Falcon for the first time in so long. He explores it almost tearfully, recalling his younger adventures. There, he encounters Artoo and gets in a few jokes as he responds to his beeps with "Hey, sacred planet; watch the language!" Artoo, the consummate hero droid who has always pushed Threepio to be brave, now pushes Luke. Luke refuses this call again, saying that he can't help anyone. He insists in a gruff, firm voice, "Nothing can make me change my mind." ...until Artoo shows Luke Leia's recording from the original film. Luke bursts out, "That was a cheap move." Still, Artoo is correct—Leia still matters to him. Further, the recording is a callback to the youthful idealistic boy so enraptured by the princess's image that he flew to her rescue. It triggers a similar feeling this time. Artoo reflects the inner child—the voice of hopes and dreams before reality crushes it. Confronting Artoo, Luke must face that growing voice within himself.

With this, he unbends at least a little. He trains Rey, not in what she has asked—Jedi power and combat—but three lessons (or rather, only two shown) on why the Force can continue without trained Jedi. As he coaxes her to sense the life around them—dark and light, death and life, cold and heat—Luke tells her the Force comes from life itself, irrespective of the Jedi. At the same time as he teaches her this, he must hear it for himself—his own life doesn't matter—just the Force in all its inevitable majesty. The little problems of little people—or even galactic heroes—mean nothing.

Rey also reaches into him, challenging him. As she observes, startled, "I didn't see you. Nothing from you. You've closed yourself off from the Force." To break away from his old role, he's abandoned his perception and understanding. Now, she forces him to face it once again. "This is a movie where a flawed old man with a lifetime of victories and regrets informs the decisions of a new generation of young heroes who need to find a *new* way to hope. Clearly, the old ways didn't work because darkness rises again and there are still tyrannical man-babies trying to be the next Darth Vader. There's a flaw in the system, buried too deep for most to see, and the only solution is to burn it all down," reviewer Jacob Hall explains. Of course, this attitude also springs from the remorse that colors all Luke does. Director Rian Johnson says:

> Ultimately, Luke's exile and his justifications for it are all covering over his guilt over Kylo. The big gloss that he's putting over the whole thing is: "The Force does not belong to the Jedi. This ongoing dynamic between the Jedi and the Sith just keeps renewing itself and just keeps feeding the fire. It's time for this old religion to die so that the truth about God can rise from elsewhere—basically, so that a more worthy god can rise. It's really hard, and it's going to cause a lot of pain, but that's what has to happen. So I'm

going to do the hardest thing I've ever done, what I couldn't do in *Empire*, and not answer the call of my friends so that the Jedi Order dies and something new has to rise and pull the light up" [Szostak 69].

Luke's greatest fear is facing Kylo Ren—not the young wielder of evil but the mistake he made—the beloved family Luke let down by imperfectly training his nephew and then rejecting him. As he teaches her, Rey goes seeking the darkness she senses deep within the island, making pebbles bounce and the ground split. To a horrified Luke, Rey is a second pupil tasting the forces of evil.

Of course, the innocent hero can turn to dark or light, and as Yoda knew, needs to face both. Watching Rey train with her staff then the lightsaber likewise reminds him of his younger self and his quest for heroism. "In looking at this grand plan from ten miles up in the air, Luke is missing this thing right in front of his nose. Here's somebody who needs you, who needs your help. If you think you are throwing away the past, you are fooling yourself. The only way to go forward is to embrace the past, figure out what is good and what is not good about it," Johnson says (Szostak 69).

As Luke tells her after, lesson two is that the Jedi were flawed and overconfident. Once again, this is a soul-baring moment for both. He found his way to this island, as the *Visual Dictionary* reveals, by tracking a path of Uneti trees, Force-sensitive organisms long revered by the Jedi Order. The library is hidden under one, and there are others in the Jedi Temple of Coruscant and fashioning the wood for Chirrut Îmwe's staff. Thus, the tree is a tie to nature and spirituality as well as Jedi history. Beneath it, in the womb of the earth, Luke confides in Rey, facing his guilt at last and telling her how Kylo betrayed him and killed his students. He was too proud and thought he could train his nephew. "By the time I realized I was no match for the darkness rising in him, it was too late." His second lesson to Rey is that the Dark Side corrupts many, especially his own nephew. However, this carries a lesson for Luke, that the Dark Side always waits to tempt its followers—therefore, Kylo Ren is responsible for his own mistakes. Rey promises not to fail him, but Luke cannot trust himself enough to trust another.

Another intruder on the island to shake him out of his complacency is Kylo Ren himself. He does not call out to Luke but, from Luke's point of view, seduces his apprentice Rey, just as Snoke once seduced young Ben Solo. When Luke finds Rey and Ren clasping hands across space, he brutally separates them. At last, goaded by both, he finally confesses. He reveals how, for an instinctual moment, he considered murdering his own nephew in his sleep.

He was frightened by the deep well of darkness he sensed in the boy, far deeper than he'd originally suspected. The knee-jerk reaction of Jedi knights, as shown back in *Phantom Menace* and *Revenge of the Sith,* is to attack and murder the Sith head on, to reject it in all forms without pausing for compassion or discussion. Now Luke regrets that his training made him turn on Ben, in turn intimidating his student into burning down the Jedi temple and murdering those who wouldn't follow him. A horrified Rey asks, "Did you create Kylo Ren?" and he knows that he did.

Luke rejects her and orders Rey off the island, in yet another refusal of the call. They battle, and she urges him to come with them, offering him the lightsaber, but he demurs. He has learned caution, learned to let the universe ebb and flow without him. On his refusal to go with her, she sorrowfully names Kylo, his murderous youthful antagonist, "our last hope"

Alone, Luke lights a torch and heads for the Jedi library within the sacred tree. As he continues on his angry, guilt-riddled arc, he prepares to burn the treasure trove of books. Yoda appears to him, shaking with laughter, and Luke fiercely tells his old master that he is destroying their legacy. Still, Luke hesitates. At this, a gleeful Yoda takes the initiative. The Force ghost conjures a lightning bolt, and burns the library himself, emphasizing to his student that ancient teachings are not the only source of truth. "Time it is," Yoda says. "For you to look past a pile of old books." He actually whacks Luke with his stick, emphasizing his power over the Force to the point of solidifying and showing how Luke still needs sense knocked into him.

> It's important that Johnson lets Yoda burn it all down and not Luke—the passing of the torch is not just the result of the failure of an old man who learned things the hard way, but it comes with the blessing of the wisest character in *Star Wars* canon. Luke knows that the Jedi must end, that they do not monopolize the Force, and that evil has flourished on their watch. But where Luke saw despair, Yoda sees a chance for renewal [Hall].

At the same time, he's sympathetic and forgiving about Luke's rejecting the Jedi wisdom. "Page-turners they were not," the Force ghost says, adding that those scriptures contain no teachings that Rey "already does not possess." (Luke doesn't realize Yoda means this literally—Rey has absconded with the texts and all that's burning is an empty tree.) The goal is to learn from the past, not follow it slavishly (as director Rian Johnson hints to the audience on a metafictional level). Yoda's smirk as he destroys it emphasizes that the next generation has already taken everything of value and left the shell behind. Ending it loses nothing.

Yoda is the mentor, the one who's come to shake up Luke's thinking and get him back on track. At last he, the ultimate teacher and sage, reveals the mentor's true destiny: "Luke, we are what they grow beyond," Yoda tells his former charge. "That is the true burden of all masters." Luke cannot control Rey or Kylo, only advise them as best he can and let them go. It's his lesson of loss that's truly useful here, and one he should teach instead of hiding away. "Luke's failure came not in Ben Solo's fall to the dark side, but in Luke's own reaction to it, both in exiling himself from the galaxy and in rejecting Rey's plea for training and guidance. A Jedi does not fail when his objective is not achieved; a Jedi fails only when he no longer seeks any objective at all" (Hall).

The time has come, as Yoda wordlessly suggests, for Luke to cross over, to grow from mentor to Force ghost and become one with the galaxy. Further, Yoda's lightning burst—an ability never seen onscreen by a ghost—suggests traveling beyond will offer Luke powers he had not anticipated. "In that moment, Luke recognizes a fundamental truth: it may be too late to save Ben Solo's soul, but it is not too late for Luke Skywalker to make a difference once again. Luke completes his Wizard's Journey by accepting this truth about himself and his role as a Jedi Master" (Barr, "Luke Skywalker" 121).

For his epic climax, Luke journeys to the planet Crait, where Kylo Ren is amassing a great army to destroy the last Resistance survivors. There, Luke finally faces Leia and apologizes for not saving her son. She forgives him, insisting, "I'm just glad you're here." This too is a meeting with the anima, one of wisdom and forgiveness as well as wholeness for the sundered twins. "On the verge of military conquest by the First Order, the galaxy needs a spark of hope. Luke bids farewell to his sister, apologizing as much for his own choices as for the fates of Ben and Han. He releases his guilt and regret. And then he does what Rey had asked. He becomes a legend" (Barr, "Luke Skywalker" 121).

Just as the First Order starts to invade the abandoned Rebel base, Luke emerges. He walks through the blazing opening like he's striding into the pit of hell, and indeed this is his testing ground. He appears younger and more vibrant, restored to his appearance of a decade before and clutching his old lightsaber. His black and white robes suggest balance between light and dark. This calls back to his mature black in *Return of the Jedi*, another time when he chose the heroic path of sacrifice and martyrdom to try to save his friends. Fearfully, Kylo orders "every weapon to fire at that man," and they do. Blasting one Jedi with an entire army seems insane overkill, suitable for Kylo's role as immature child desperate to rule the patriarchy. Commander Hux, now cast down to a subordinate position under the angry young man, quips, "Do you think we got him?" However, the debris clears, and there Luke stands, pointedly wiping a speck of dust off his shoulder. Only the unenlightened rely on raw power.

He gets to say, "I failed you, Ben. I'm sorry." As he adds that "the Resistance is reborn," his own hope has reawakened. Out of sight, Rey has accepted the Jedi mantle and is saving her friends. Luke has fulfilled his mission.

Luke and Kylo draw lightsabers and fight, recalling Obi-Wan and Anakin or Luke and Vader. Luke ducks and dodges, once more emphasizing his point about violence. (Of course, he has an additional motive the first-time audience doesn't perceive). Luke recalls Obi-Wan's line from the first film, "If you strike me down, I shall become more powerful than you can possibly imagine." However, Luke's is less about martyrdom and more about Kylo's rage. "If you strike me down in anger, I will always be with you. Just like your father." Here, Luke counsels his nephew about guilt, as he endeavors to pass on the lesson he's learned through his exile. Kylo is his shadow, not just as his surrogate son. Luke, who presumably has carried Kylo all these years after an instant's murderous rage, deeply understands what Kylo Ren feels after actually killing his father. Looking at Kylo, he sees the bundle of his own anger he has carried all this time, and he finally accepts and forgives it. Facing his boogeyman has finally cleansed him of his sin.

Kylo Ren claims that the war is won and that Luke is the last Jedi. "Impressive. Every word in that sentence was wrong," Luke says, emphasizing that Kylo doesn't understand the scope of the ordinary people inspired by the Resistance across the galaxy. Once, Luke too believed that the Jedi Order depended on him. Now he believes Leia, Rey, and the Force can unite to save the galaxy with new teachings. Kylo wants none of this advice and attempts to run his uncle through. However, Luke has never been there.

> In truth, Luke's presence exists only in the Force, a projection through a Fallanassi technique—chronicled by ancient Masters in the sacred texts as Similfuturus. This discipline requires extreme concentration and focus, as Luke essentially pours his living Force presence into the all-encompassing cosmic Force, bridging incredible distances. The transition is so complete that Luke gives his all into the Force, finding serenity in this final mortal moments and becoming one with the great beyond [Hidalgo and Terrio 31].

On second viewing, there are many hints appear that Luke isn't really there. Luke leaves no footprints in the sand. Further, they never clash lightsabers as Luke dodges every blow. "Exactly, by design," editor Bob Ducsay said. "There are many small things that would give you some clues as to what's going on with Luke. He doesn't make a sound. Nothing ever falls on him. Kylo's lightsaber interacts with the salt, and Luke's doesn't" (Breznican, "Last Jedi Spoiler Talk: Mark Hamill").

Kylo, limited in his perception and overcome by fury, misses all this. There is a great deal of foreshadowed irony here, as Luke insisted that the Force is more than just mind tricks and levitation and refused to step out on the battlefield with a laser sword and change everything. Now his great deed is an illusion of just that sort. Further, as Kylo once suggested, such a massive projection kills him.

Luke collapses on his isle at sunset. His theme music plays stirringly, just as it did on Tatooine when he gazed out at the twin suns. With the circle complete, he gazes at another pair of twin suns and fades away. His robe blows off in the wind. His story is done.

In this moment, Rey and Leia both sense him go. As Rey concludes, Luke has passed on but with "peace and purpose." While previously he tried to end the Jedi, now he sacrifices himself so Leia, Rey, and the others can escape and fan the flames for a new Resistance—one not born from the Jedi order, but one that will recruit young Force users across the galaxy.

Leia the Bereft Mother

The classic novels have the New Republic struggle against the remnants of the Empire in a prolonged conflict. In the new timeline, the war likewise lingers, finally concluding after five years at the Battle of Scarif. The Imperial Government at large is dissolved. With this, Leia reclaims her post as senator, bringing all her experience from her struggles and losses. Author Claudia Gray says of Leia in the new timeline novel *Bloodline,* "She has the exact same moral compass that she did when she was nineteen years old and ready for action, but now she has a greater understanding of the complexity of human nature, including her own. So I got to weave that into the story" ("Author to Author" 36).

In *Bloodline,* Leia's a senator among the Populist faction within the New Republic, favoring individual planet rights over the Centrist large central government plan. When they call for a First Senator, she prepares to run, as the strongest Populist candidate, but everyone suddenly learns her father was Darth Vader—dooming her political career. "When her scandalous parentage was revealed, her campaign collapsed and precipitated the succession of Centrist worlds" (Hidalgo, *Propaganda* 100). This revelation is incredibly personal and painful. She tells the Senate, "I was shocked. Horrified. I had never guessed that the truth behind my birth could be so tragic or that my birth father could be a man I had such strong personal reasons to hate. My efforts to accept this lasted a long time. In a very real sense, I still struggle with this knowledge and I expect that always will" (Gray, *Bloodline* 260)

Of course, she is a mother and wife at this point, as well as a political leader. Her warrior days are done and the mystical side barely attempted. Describing why she never became a Jedi, the book character says only, "My duty has always been here, in the work of creating a new and better government" (Gray, *Bloodline* 129). *The Rise of Skywalker* shows her going further in training but abandoning it for fear of her son's fate. Thus, she remains a politician grounded in the practical, eschewing her Jedi heritage and the spiritual growth that might accompany it.

Of course, the First Order begins rising, giving Leia's dream a deadly enemy. *Bloodline* introduces young men who idealize the Empire, collecting its artifacts and dreaming of fighting in its wars. They soon take it too far. "The Amaxine warriors weren't reenacting battles. They were training for them," Leia realizes (Gray, *Bloodline* 173). Here, she realizes that the aftereffects of her rebellion linger and threaten to destroy all she's built.

She begins *Force Awakens* desperately seeking her brother. He is not only a path to redeem her son and save the Republic, but a symbol of spirituality. Like Rey, she longs for the mentor who can offer deeper wisdom of the universe. At this point, Leia has grown from heroine to politician to general—a leader of the Resistance. She is her people's queen in truth, defending the last free planets from the New Order. While the mentor is more of a grandparent figure (whatever the age) having retired from public life, the ruler is actively involved with the day-to-day survival and well-being of her people. Her task is to keep them alive. Leia also embarks on the traditional heroine's quest—saving and reuniting lost family. While she gathers Han and Rey to the fold, even as she struggles to redeem her son, her true quest is to find Luke, for which she sends Poe Dameron as her intermediary. *Force Awakens* establishes that her quests to protect family and community are only beginning.

Like the ancient goddesses, she appoints a hero like Perseus or Heracles to act on her behalf. Thus, Leia can be seen guiding Poe's mission even without being present. Still, she feels the losses of the younger soldiers she sends out in her place. She feels the capitol's destruction as a great disturbance in the Force and thinks in the novelization, "No one, she knew, should have to be witness to the death of an entire world. She had been subjected to two. It must not be allowed to happen again" (Foster 176). She also loses her aide, who has gone to the capitol in her place. "Her character to some degree or another has been defined by loss through this whole saga, starting with the loss of her home planet. She's just taken hit after hit, and she's borne it, and she focuses on moving forward and the task at hand," says Rian Johnson (Szostak 18).

Still, Leia rallies and brings the cavalry to save Han and Rey on Maz Kanata's world. This saves her loved ones, including Han and Chewie. This is often the queen and general's task—to marshal large forces as part of the big picture. Moving on from her time as dignified senator, Leia has gone rough, wearing simple pants and a vest like Han's. After Starkiller Base has destroyed Hosnian Prime, her novelization version demands swift action, in impetuous Han style. She even agrees with him, adding, "We don't have time to wait on analyses and scientific hypotheses. Han's right. We have to act and act *now*" (Foster 204). Clearly, she's learned to adopt his most useful traits. On Maz's world, she faces her ex-husband, but also news of their lost child, now serving the First Order. She insists Han can save him, adding, "Luke is a Jedi … you're his father. There's still light in him. I know it." Once again, she appoints her chosen warrior, though this will end in tragedy. Han, Chewie, and Finn set out on her orders, to destroy the momentous Starkiller Base. Of course, they succeed and find Rey, but Han's son Ben kills him. Once again, Leia loses what matters most.

She ends the film passing the torch to the next generation—not her evil son Ben but the heroic Rey. She sends this young woman off on the film's final mission, to find Luke, once more acting as the distant leader directing her people's salvation.

Last Jedi takes a far different turn, forcing Leia and her friend Admiral Holdo to lead, entering the battle and fighting directly. The film begins with a First Order attack and evacuation. During the battle, Leia senses her beloved son who has murdered her husband and turned to darkness. He aims at her ship, but upon sensing her there and engaging in a brief mental confrontation, Kylo finds he cannot kill her. This is a moment of great significance for Leia, as, presumably, she feels him back down and understands that he still loves her despite his brutal deeds. He is her real, most intimate nemesis, the child she labored and sacrificed for, now a monster set to destroy her.

In the midst of this, her protégé, Poe Dameron, disobeys orders and gets their soldiers killed. Leia vents her general's rage on him but also treats him as a substitute, one she can safely punish in place of her son. After the initial confrontation with Kylo, he and Leia only battle through intermediaries—his army against hers, while Leia squabbles with Poe for dominance. This is a softening of the conflict, shielding viewers from the direct horror of seeing mother and son try to kill each other.

"Poe is in some ways a surrogate son for Leia," Isaac notes. "But also I think she sees in him the potential for a truly great leader of the Resistance and beyond." He adds, "I think Leia knows she won't be around forever, and she, with tough love, wants to push Poe to be more than the badass pilot, to temper his heroic impulses with wisdom and clarity" (Szostak 19). Of course, she has a good adoptive son and evil biological son, mirroring her relationships with adoptive father Bail Organa and biological father Darth Vader. Both these triangles emphasize the heroine being pulled in two directions—with an angel and devil on opposite shoulders.

In the Legends novelizations, when her son Jacen embraces the dark side and commits murder, both Leia and Han sorrowfully condemn him to death. They are not the executioners, but fearfully send their last surviving child, his twin Jaina, to duel him and complete the task. In the novel, Leia fiercely insists, as Obi-Wan once did, that her loved one is dead, and that his new Dark Side personality has murdered him, leaving nothing behind to redeem. This psychological split appears in wicked stepmother fairytales, in which the saintly good mother has died, replaced by the tyrannical monster. In older, more primitive fairytales, these are aspects of the same character, as the loved one becomes a monster, forcing the heroine to confront this tragedy.

> According to Jung, the Mother Goddess as the world and entire source of life comes from pre-birth, during which, for an infant, this is literally true. After birth, this concept is reinforced, as the child depends entirely on her for food, warmth, and safety. As such, the infant is overwhelmed by the mother's importance, and, as she develops into comforter and punisher, the child's split view of the terrible and divine mothers emerges. The heroine's journey is the quest to reintegrate terrible and benevolent mother into a single individual—the self [Frankel, *From Girl to Goddess* 231].

The grown-up Leia's perspective is not so childlike—she courageously faces that her child, like treacherous Mordred, is tearing apart the galaxy and killing all she has so laboriously built. Like King Arthur, she prepares to battle this son who has become a force of destruction, much as she loves him. When the child turns evil, the metaphor is that of Camelot, the new generation destroying the work of the old.

In fact, for the hero-mother, sacrificing her son is a traditional step of the quest. "Aphrodite's beloved Adonis was gored by a boar (her sacred symbol); Horus was critically wounded by Set, the god his mother Isis refused to slay. Gaia fashioned a sickle, symbol of the harvest, and gave it to her son Cronus, so he could slay his father Uranus" (Frankel, *From Girl to Goddess* 251). All of myth is filled with this classic pattern.

> In this phase the goddess is dual: One side is filled with maternal compassion, but the other, darker, side is fierce and terrible, pushing away her son's childish dependence. "For his softness and clinging undermine her, just as her oversolicitude undermines him. His childish need appeals too intimately to her own desire to mother him." The mother has become too identified with the son. His accomplishments are her pride, his needs are hers, to such a point that she cannot separate them into two entities. At the heart, this is egoism—she cannot say no to him because she cannot say no to herself. Her inability to accept that she cannot fix others' lives is the true inability to accept unmendable flaws in herself. While this seems natural, the child must learn limits and learn to separate himself from the mother if he wishes to grow to independence. The mother, too, must surrender the child to move beyond the stage where she sacrifices too much, helplessly mothering all around her [Frankel, *From Girl to Goddess* 251].

Mythically, however, the son does not sacrifice the mother as she represents the eternal goddess, life itself. Primal terror and love for her is ingrained. It is not Kylo Ren who blasts through Leia's ship but his subordinate—another substitute. When the bridge is blown up, Leia is catapulted into space and reveals she has Force powers the audience has never seen. In a stunning scene, she flies through space without a ship, surrounded by a bubble of air. Swelling Disneyesque music plays as she reaches the surviving ship and lets herself onboard, to the stares of her friends. Of course, this is Leia's transcendent moment—rising beyond her human limitations to become not only "one with the Force" but with the entire cosmos. In this moment, she understands how to save herself by using the extraordinary power that's always dwelled within her.

This great moment has weakened her enough that she slips into a coma. With clear symbolism, Rey's homing bracelet falls from her wrist, passed on to Finn, another younger hero who will continue this part of the quest. Leia, however, is incapacitated. This is a common step on the heroine's journey as the (generally) young woman crosses a threshold, manifesting the powers of adulthood, and then is so shocked by original sin (Snow White's apple) or sex (Sleeping Beauty's spindle) that she falls into a magical sleep, awaiting her prince. While this seems a helpless moment, metaphorically Sleeping Beauty parts the protective thorns shielding herself from men when she feels ready—when the time comes for her to awaken and to fall in love and marry. Leia too is caught between lifestages—not adolescence and marriage but wifehood and widowhood. Her fall from leader to advisor is already happening as well. This withdrawal gives her a chance to transition and grieve, to reclaim her new status before returning.

Leia, a grieving widow and diminishing ruler, is not awakened by romance. Subverting this, she awakens herself when the hotshot hero has mutinied and taken over her ship in her absence. Leaning on her cane (a symbol of age and disability but also, like in Yoda's case, a deceptive suggestion of her weakness) and still in her hospital gown (its white a vulnerable color but also a nod to the heroic princess of *A New Hope*), she bursts through the barricaded door of her bridge. With a single shot of her stunner, she retakes it, reclaiming her authority. The prince is knocked unconscious and Sleeping Beauty rules here.

Leia leads her people, not in a flashy battle, but in escaping destruction. To save them, her childhood friend Amilyn Holdo stays behind and sacrifices herself, blowing up Kylo's flagship. As with Kylo's wingman firing on Leia, this is a substitution, a softening of the mother-son battle by proxy. At the same time, Leia loses her second-in-command, a friend from her teen years as detailed in the young adult novel, *Leia, Princess of Alderaan*. In the book, she represents Leia's whimsical creativity, an ability to think outside the box and dream. Onscreen, despite the mauve gown and hair, she's tougher, less willing to give Poe a sympathetic ear. As she dies, Leia suffers, but also symbolically learns about sacrifice and absorbs her friend's toughness to steel herself for the harder losses to come.

Protecting her tribe, safeguarding them with concealment and cleverness, is the queen's role. Further, the planet of Crait is in many ways Leia's place of power. As revealed in *Leia, Princess of Alderaan*, Bail Organa helped found one of the early Rebellion's earliest outposts here. As the Resistance shelter within its mammoth stronghold, the spirit of her father is protecting them all. The planet's white salt over red mineral sand—fitting for a dramatic battle—also suggests the innocent maiden masking the powerful matriarch—the one who chooses who lives and dies.

The story approaches the climax with a few dozen Resistance members facing certain defeat. Their decades-old speeders are crumbling, while the First Order wields AT-M6s and a ramming cannon that can tear down the last shelter, the base's shielded door. In the face of this onslaught, Leia sends her people out to fight and die in a desperate gambit. They are saved by Luke, the lost hero who returns and defends them. This seems less empowering for Leia, but it must be noted that she has summoned him back to the fight. Once more, she enacts the ruling goddess, selecting a warrior to battle in her name. Luke bids her a touching farewell. Just as the male hero has his encounter with the goddess, the heroine encounters the male warrior, and absorbs from him a touch of the duty and wisdom he has to share. As Luke kisses her forehead and they joke for a moment, they connect on this spiritual level.

Leia does not die at the film's end—instead, she feels Luke's sacrifice. Once more, she is facing the loss of her beloved chosen warrior while she must endure and lead her people through her grief. This is the Great Goddess's task. Guided by gleaming crystalline foxes, Leia leads her people on, seeking to stir the galaxy to rise up against oppression. This is how Carrie Fisher finishes the last movie she filmed before her death—as a shining beacon for her people.

The final film had audiences aware that it had been intended to be Leia's story, in which she might battle her evil son, reclaim him from darkness, and train Rey in the Jedi's path as the last survivor of her generation. "She was going to be the big payoff," Carrie Fisher's brother, Todd Fisher explained. "She was going to be the last Jedi, so to speak. That's cool, right? People used to say to me, 'Why is it that Carrie never gets a lightsaber and chops up some bad guys.' Obi-Wan was in his prime when he was Carrie's age!" (Ankers).

Of course, the actress's death derailed these plans. Abrams describes their limited options: "It was impossible. There was no way. What are you gonna do? You can't recast that part, and you're not just going to have her disappear" ("The Legacy of Leia"). A plan was formed to use cut scenes to fill in at least the outline of this plot. What resulted was a vague and ghostly Leia, already somewhat absent, but one who nonetheless had a final arc. Abrams concludes, "Princess Leia lives in this film in a way that is kind of mind-blowing to me" ("The Legacy of Leia").

The novelization explains that Leia has become much frailer: "There was something about growing old that made her connection with the Force even stronger. When the body began to fail, the mind reached out, unencumbered by physical ability." With this comes a stillness and a new gravity. "The truth was, Leia couldn't run through the jungle if she wanted to. Peace and calm came easily because her body craved them" (Carson 7).

As *Rise of Skywalker* begins, Leia and Rey begin on a training course, one where Luke once instructed Leia and helped her build her own lightsaber. It's revealed that she stopped her training before taking on the duties of a Jedi because she sensed that it would not end well. She perceived through the Force that Ben would die if she continued her Jedi training ... a prophecy that, like her father's of Padmé's, fulfilled itself nonetheless. Instead, she left her lightsaber for the one who would redeem her son.

Still, this doesn't mean that she closed herself off from the Force. In the novelization, Leia insists she used her Jedi training every day. "Once you touch the force, it's part of you always." As she adds, "Over the years, I continued to learn, to grow. There were times on the Senate floor when the meditations I'd practiced with Luke were the only thing that kept me from causing a galactic incident" (Carson 7). The new canon book *Galaxy's Edge—Black Spire* offers additional perspective on Leia's walking away as it feeds directly into *Rise of Skywalker*. One admirer explains that avoiding training was the ultimate in discipline and self-restraint:

> "All these years," Ylena mused, her eyes far off. "All these years, she had access to the Force and never used it. She could've swayed the Senate but wasn't willing to use cheap tricks when she believed in diplomacy and freedom. That's a strong woman and a good leader right there. And yet, in her time of greatest hardship, when it benefited not only her own needs but the greater good, she reached deep inside and claimed that connection that had always waited, dormant, for her call" [96–97].

Leia is frequently portrayed in new canon novels as the more disciplined of the twins, and highly suited for the Jedi path. Choosing a life of service without her powers is a clear sacrifice.

As her story ends, she mentors Rey, not only with the obstacle course but with wise advice. Rey also addresses her as "Master," confirming Leia's final status. In the novelization, Leia thinks that she has much of the training to pass along:

> Leia was no Jedi Master, but she had learned from the best. And not just from Luke; over the years she'd occasionally heard the voice of Obi-Wan Kenobi through the Force, and even more rarely, that of Yoda. Some days it had felt as though she'd learned from the Force itself. She was first and foremost a politician and a general, but she had accepted her Jedi legacy and embraced it as best she could [Carson 8].

On learning that the Rebellion's ancient enemy Palpatine has returned, Leia sends the younger heroes Rey, Finn, Poe, Chewbacca, BB-8, and C-3PO to finish Luke's quest for the Sith planet of Exegol. As she departs,

Rey insists on Leia's blessing and Leia grants it. Unfortunately, using the vague dialogue of the cut scenes has her speaking like a fortune teller with answers to others' questions like "Don't tell me what things feel like, tell me what things are" and "Never underestimate a droid." Further, Rey gives her Luke's rebuilt lightsaber, as she feels unworthy, and Leia gives it back only a few minutes later as she sets out on her journey. Nonetheless, Rey and Leia's touching goodbye hug is much more poignant, symbolically bidding all the audience farewell. Rey adds, "There's so much I want to tell you." Leia responds that Rey can tell her when she returns, and viewers realize that will never happen.

A few scenes follow her leading her people, but her time is limited. As she gives her final orders, Luke's spirit calls to her in the novel, telling her it's time to say goodbye (Carson 163). When Kylo Ren lies dying at Rey's hands, Leia intervenes. As Luke did on Ahch-To, she sends her spirit across space to contact her son and heal his soul and draw him back to the light. Luke sacrificed himself to make Kylo look like a fool, impotently blasting and slashing at the desert, and to give the Resistance a chance to flee. Leia's quest is quieter and more personal but parallels her brother's in the power of the feat and what it costs her.

Leia hesitates, clutching Han's medal. It's a sign of happier times—not just her marriage but their first great victory against the Empire. Here, she connects with the young hero-princess who had lost her world yet kept fighting. Now she can strike a final blow to reclaim her son. While she's tempted to stay, she decides in the book, "Letting go wasn't giving up. It was the *ultimate* act of hope—hope for her protégés Rey and Poe, faith in the lessons she'd taught them. The last thing they would learn from her was how to go on without her, thus finally embracing their own destinies as leaders" (Carson 172). She knows it's time to move on.

Leia dies with Artoo in attendance at the foot of her bed. This passing, together with Han and Luke's, emphasizes that the younger generation must fight the war on their own. This gives the story an epic conclusion. Abrams notes, "We also were very much aware this is the end of the trilogy, and it needs to satisfy" ("The Legacy of Leia").

Her white-draped shroud lies there through much of the film, especially as Poe poignantly asks her for advice. As such, it too represents her presence, guiding her friends as they act in her name. Its image allows audiences to mourn together, even as Chewie howls their grief and pounds the ground in catharsis.

Leia's sacrifice and her covered body clearly show the character's influence on the storyline. More than that, as Leia sends Lando to guide them, Maz narrates what Leia must do, Han appears in a vision to forgive Ben, Lando answers when Poe seeks answers at Leia's bedside, Luke counsels Rey in accepting her dark heritage, Rey takes up Leia's lightsaber, Ben accepts redemption, Poe and Finn lead her army, and the galaxy rallies to her cause, all the heroes are acting in Leia's stead, fighting for the light on her behalf. At the film's climax, the Emperor thunders, "The princess of Alderaan has disrupted my plan, but her death will be in vain." Of course, the opposite comes true. Leia's self-sacrifice sends Ben into the fight where he and Rey together defeat the Emperor. Further, when Rey channels the strength of all the Jedi, Leia's voice joins them.

Her body vanishes at the same time as her son's, suggesting that she has waited for him so they can ascend together. A final shot, of Leia and Luke on Tatooine blessing Rey with their legacy, emphasizes how they will continue watching over her.

Finn and Poe

Poe and Finn are linked on their epic adventure. They meet on Kylo Ren's ship—one a hotshot pilot convinced he can handle every situation, and one a complete innocent, raised in a bubble and heavily brainwashed. Each's latest mission has been a vital lesson—Poe is captured, in a blow to his ego. Meanwhile, FN-2187, ordered to murder innocent villagers in his first battle, discovers he can't be a Stormtrooper anymore. The visual dictionary adds that FN-2187 "lacks the combat zeal or submission to authority evident in his squadmates" but "keeps his misgivings well hidden" (Hidalgo 20). On his first mission, he chooses.

Continuing his rebellion, FN-2187 frees Poe so he can pilot them to safety. In turn, Poe mentors him, naming him Finn and giving him the jacket, droid, and mission that launch them on their adventure. Poe reflects in the novelization that "something had ignited some exceptional spark of individualism within him" (Foster 55). He names his new friend Finn to encourage that spark.

Having crashed them on Jakku, Poe vanishes for a time, allowing Finn to self-actualize. Finn is drawn to Rey and, sensing her importance, tries repeatedly to save her from the First Order, though she clearly doesn't need saving. She's his second friend, but as a female intuitive scavenger, strong in the Force, defender of innocents like BB-8, she can teach him the skills he's always craved. He describes himself to her as a "big deal" in the Resistance—a hero, not a villain—crafting a persona like Poe's and one he aspires to.

On Maz Kanata's planet, the perceptive alien offers him a way to refuse the call: people who will take him to the Outer Rim, where he can escape the First Order forever. As she explains, "If you live long enough you see the same eyes in different people. I'm looking at the eyes of a man who wants to run." At this crossroads, Finn goes to Rey and finally tells her the truth of himself: "I'm not Resistance. I'm a Stormtrooper." Rey unconditionally accepts this, and he's emboldened to proclaim his love, at least subtly, telling her, "You looked at me like no one ever had." She refuses to come along, forcing him to choose between affection and safety. He wants Rey, but even more, he wants to escape. "I'm done with the First Order. I'm never going back," he vows. He nearly leaves, but on finding she's been captured by the First Order, feels compelled to rescue this woman who's like the idealistic, heroic side of himself. At last he chooses a side, even if it's for love, not duty.

Maz gives him the lightsaber, but her line, "Take it—find your friend" emphasizes that the sword of Jedi heritage is meant for Rey, not Finn. In the novel, as Finn insists they must save Rey, Maz comments that he's changed. "I see something else now.... I see the eyes of a warrior" (Foster 186). With this, he accepts his mission, embarking fiercely on a quest to save his princess.

Poe and Finn share a joyous reunion, though Poe's disappearance and return have not substantially changed his character. Still, he bridges the way to the Resistance for his new friend. At their base, Finn reveals his true origin and discovers that his familiarity with the First Order base makes him valuable. This acceptance by the larger community ushers him into a larger world. Still, at this point his only priority is Rey, not their cause. This works literally as his commitment to friendship but also symbolically as he seeks out his anima, craving further growth. Desperate to rescue her, he teams up with Han and Chewie and they penetrate the heart of the First Order.

On his mission, Finn gets a brief chance to confront his cruel foster parent, Captain Phasma. A female drill sergeant and mentor is unusual for the hero's journey, especially for a soldier. Still, this gender flip affords the story some nuance. As the wicked mother, rather androgynous and faceless but also a destroyer of innocents, she has raised all the Stormtrooper children to be cruel. In Finn's prequel book, Captain Phasma scolds him for compassion as he aids fellow teammates like the clumsy Slip. She tells him: "You have great potential, 2187. You are officer corps material. Your duty is to the First Order above everything. Nothing else comes before that. FN-2003 must stand or fall on his own. If he stands, the Order is strengthened. If he falls, the Order is spared his weakness. Am I understood?" (Rucka, *Before the Awakening* 55). When he still goes easy on his friend in the combat ring, Phasma sends him on the village raid for a final chance to prove himself.

Now, having betrayed all her lessons, Finn holds her at blasterpoint, hilariously blustering as he demands that she guide them to the shield generator. "My name's Finn. I'm in charge! I'm in charge now, Phasma! I'm in charge!" he insists, as Han cautions, "Bring it down … bring it down.…" They intimidate her into following their orders and then dump her in the trash compactor—not only a callback to A New Hope, but also a symbolic banishment and turning the tables by sending her to the waste disposal where she condemned Finn to work.

At the climax, Finn battles Kylo Ren with a lightsaber, though he's nearly killed in the fight. His courage in doing so when he's clearly outmatched emphasizes his ordinary heroism, defying the massive force of the First Order and also his representative. On sacrificing himself, he leaves Rey to duel in his place. However, when he wakens, he will be more than an ex-Stormtrooper, but a potential hero.

Last Jedi's Reflective Journeys

In the first sequence of Last Jedi, Poe defies orders and sacrifices all the fleet's bombers to destroy the enemy's siege dreadnaught. When he returns, Leia slaps him, though he maintains that he's done the right thing. A massive lesson is coming.

The second film's plot for Poe has him tangling with Laura Dern's Vice Admiral Amilyn Holdo. From his perspective, she's something of a cruel mentor, the bad mother in contrast with Leia, the good one. The film, told through his eyes not Holdo's, subtly begins with this point of view. "Women who look like Holdo—femme fatales, even in their middle age, women who look like women who do *politics* rather than fight, who like frivolous things, jewels and bright hair and makeup even in the darkest moments— we are primed to read women like that as women who will betray. This is an old trope," comments Arkady Martine in "*Star Wars*' Vice-Admiral Holdo and Our Expectations for Female Military Power." All this leaves the audience primed to distrust this frivolous, glamorous "anti–Leia." Still, she's the anima figure who can best inspire growth, finishing the lessons that the good mother has not driven home. "A lot of the friction and conflict for Poe is in that relationship with Admiral Holdo," Poe's actor says. "He's not sure what to make of her" (Breznican, "When Light Falls").

> Here is Vice-Admiral Amilyn Holdo, a tall thin woman in late middle age, wearing a draped floor-length dress that leaves every curve and angle of her body visible; a woman with dyed-purple hair in a style that requires at the very least a great many pins and more likely a curling iron in addition; a woman wearing star-chart bracelets and lipstick and eye makeup. She looks like a slightly-down-on-her-luck noblewoman from the Old Republic. She's not just female, she's *femme*. And she's not just femme, she's *soft*. All her age is visible; there's no architectural framing of that body to disguise how gravity has had its way with it. Holdo, in the middle of the remnants of the Resistance, is a kind of exposed that Leia Organa—who does wear those architectural frames around her body, giving her a grandeur and a solidity—never is [Martine].

He greets her with mansplaining, and she of course dismisses him, insisting she's met many "trigger-happy flyboys" like him. Certainly, her explaining her plan to Poe as he asks would have simplified the film's story. At the same time, audiences assume, as Poe does, that the cocky pilot hero is right and that his superiors should answer to him. The admiral has a different lesson to teach. Laura Dern notes of first hearing of the part that the first thing director Rian Johnson had described was "this quality of someone who is so steadfast that you don't know what side they're on because they don't need the rest of the world to know their plans. The kind of person—the kind of *woman*—who is clear in her voice, and even in the company of men questioning her doesn't need to justify her behavior or her choices" (Yamato).

On their shared ship, the *Raddus*, Finn wakes from his healing sleep to find Rey is questing without him. He attempts to desert—a less-than-heroic moment that emphasizes how much he's determined to escape the First Order and help Rey. She is his mission, not the Resistance. The anima he meets, however, changes it all as she guides him to heroism.

When he encounters Rose Tico, crying over the sister who gave her life for the cause, Rose quickly turns gushing, admiring Finn as a war hero. This shows him his potential as seen through her eyes—a traditional role of the anima. "When Rose first meets Finn, he is 'a big deal,'" her actress, Kelly Marie Tran explains (Bennett 37). Clearly his boast to Han Solo from the previous adventure has come true, as he always dreamed. He wishes her "May the Force be with you," and she gasps, "Wow" through her smiles and tears. He preens a little. Tran notes, "For Rose, when she meets Finn, he's a symbol for everything she's ever worked for. I imagine that Rose has had tough days and thought, 'Think of Finn and Rey who have done amazing things, and that's what we're fighting for'" (Bennett 37). Being reminded of his responsibilities forces Finn to reclaim his heroism. "When he meets her, Finn is trying to escape the whole war," his actor John Boyega says. "He's trying to leave, and she comes in and basically gives him a depiction of himself that wasn't necessarily true" (Breznican "Last Jedi Spoiler Talk: Rey").

However, when she spies Finn's packed bag, she protests in horror, "My sister just died protecting the fleet, and you were running away!" She zaps him unconscious and hauls him off. Here, she functions as the audience stand-in, disgusted by his choice even as she discovers he's a flawed, ordinary person. Still, as they talk, Rose and Finn simultaneously realize how they can disable the First Order's ability to track their ships through hyperspace. Clearly, they're a solid team. Both report to Poe and agree that his impulse to go shoot the First Order ship would be completely pointless. This unravels his classic gendered actions and sends the pair off on a separate journey.

Poe listens to the little people of the fleet, Rose and Finn. He nonetheless launches more hotshot plans—smuggling the pair off to save everyone. This time, Poe's skirting the chain of command kills even more soldiers than his previous one. Kayti Burt explains in "Toxic Masculinity Is the True Villain of *Star Wars: The Last Jedi*": "Poe's rogue heroics—sending Rose and Finn to Canto Bight, for example—not only don't work, they lead to the near-quashing of the entire Resistance force. Hundreds of people die, and it's at least partially because Poe had visions of glory." He believes saving the technology—the big, flashy ships—is the way to go. As he insists when he finally learns Holdo's strategy, "We abandon this cruiser, we're done. We don't stand a chance." Further, her slow retreat in unarmed transport ships is humiliating, a public show of weakness before the might of the First Order. Holdo evacuates nonetheless, putting her emphasis on people. Oscar Isaac explains, "Vice Admiral Holdo is an interesting character that speaks to the nature of leadership. She isn't saying, 'Look at me, I'm the hero.' She does things more quietly" (Hugo 40). Abandoning the great warship, sheltering in the weakest place of all, and slinking away all sit badly with Poe. He's especially antsy because he cannot "jump in an X-wing and blow something up" as he puts it. In fact, the fighters have been destroyed, depriving him of all agency.

As he waits, he has passed the glory to two background players, a sanitation worker and a mechanic, who have set out to save them all. On their mission, Rose is Finn's anima, partner, and teacher. (She does not significantly grow and change through this arc because, like Campbell's traditional anima, she already has all the answers and a full range of perception). Rose takes a traditional woman's role here, awakening Finn to social inequalities and inspiring him to fight. Still, the pair work well together with their contrasting knowledge and skills.

In fourth wave feminist tradition, Finn respects Rose as a partner on their adventures. He listens to her opinion and tries to see through her eyes, as Poe refuses to with Admiral Holdo. While Finn adores the glitz of Canto Bight, Rose opens his eyes to the exploitation there. Out on the balcony, she tells him to look closer at the racing fathers, and he sees the whips and cruelty involved. As Rose explains that the rich people have made their money selling weapons to the First Order, Finn learns to see the history behind the universe's beautiful people. Continuing to push him, in the novel, she advises him to find his own path, not devote himself to Rey's (Fry 142).

Finn explains, "I was raised in an army to fight for a cause … then I met Rey. And for the first time I had someone I cared about to fight for. That's who I wanted to be" (Fry, *Last Jedi* 141). He still has not chosen the Resistance, only defense of a loved one. His description here is not romantic but admiring—he sees her as a model thanks to her commitment and drive. In the next novel, he thinks, "Rey was Finn's friend, yes, but she was also *important*.... If anything happened to Rey, the Resistance didn't stand a chance" (Carson 183). She embodies all his hope of the future.

In prison, they meet the amoral D.J. (Benicio Del Toro), who frees them and assures them he's a codebreaker. D.J., a shadow who voices Finn's worst impulses, insists that moral absolutism is a joke. His motto is "Live free, don't join." Of course, this was Finn's philosophy at the film's start. Confronting D.J. now that Rose has awakened his responsibility, Finn sees that he cares about the Resistance more than he expected.

Rose gains the young faither trainers' help through empathy, invoking their faith in the Resistance and showing Finn how much the galaxy believes in them. This ties in with a major theme of the sequel trilogy—the Resistance as an inspiration that must rouse the ordinary people to its side. At last the Resistance is revealed as trying to create a better world, not merely oppose the First Order's evil. As Rose connects with the child, Finn begins to understand.

Admiral Holdo is also trying to become this beacon of steadfast hope, but Poe can't see it. The pair share a reflective shadow moment when they acknowledge their shared bond—love and lifetime trust of Leia. Together they recall her favorite expression, that hope is like the sun and one must believe even when it's hidden. Still, this connection only lasts a moment.

"Poe is grappling with how to become a leader, which means keeping his emotions in check and thinking things through a bit more," Isaac says (Breznican, "When Light Falls"). Despite this, he mutinies, clearly trying to be the hero with the big gun yet again. Holdo quietly surrenders, giving him his chance. However, the stronger Leia returns and, without letting Poe get a word out, stuns him. Her people drag him onto the evacuation transports, forcing him onto the next phase of the journey. Good mother and bad mother will inflict this lesson if they must, but Poe will learn it. In fact, Poe clearly has never learned the heroine's path, only the hero's: As Joseph Campbell commented in one of his later books:

> In *The Odyssey*, you'll see three journeys. One is that of Telemachus, the son, going in quest of his father. The second is that of the father, Odysseus, becoming reconciled and related to the female principle in the sense of male-female relationship, rather than the male mastery of the female that was at the center of *The Iliad*. And the third is of Penelope herself, whose journey is ... endurance. Out in Nantucket, you see all those cottages with the widow's walk up on the roof: *when my husband comes back from the sea*. Two journeys through space and one through time [*Pathways to Bliss* 145].

The plan involves retreating with stealth, as the First Order isn't "monitoring for little transports." Next, they must hide in a fortified Rebel base on the nearby planet and signal for help—more indignity and pleas instead of fighting. All this uses skills of patience and humility Poe has never learned.

Not so far away, Poe's plan is being enacted. Infiltrating the enemy ship, the Supremacy, Finn and Rose disguise themselves as officers (with BB-8 hidden in a trashcan). They have not only entered the belly of the beast, but to outwit their opponents, they must dress like them, descending fully into their shadow selves. For a moment, Rose and Finn experience what life would have been like had they chosen the other side. While Rose has always firmly opposed the Order, Finn grew up among them as family and still carries the lessons they taught him. As Rose thinks in the novel, "Finn looked like a model officer, striding through the commons like he owned it. He practically radiated aloof confidence" (Fry, *Last Jedi* 209).

D.J. betrays them both, making his point about opportunism even as Finn and Poe both learn what selfishness can cost the larger team. Thanks to Poe's plan, D.J. is in a position to tell the Supremacy's leaders about the Resistance transports, and the First Order begins destroying them one by one. Watching this and facing the loss of all his new community, Finn finally accepts that they're worth fighting for.

Helplessly observing her people dying, Holdo ends this. Understanding impetuous military "flyboys" all too well, she positions their battleship as a flashy target ready for a firefight and then sacrifices it and herself to destroy the First Order's flagship. The film silences. "She was more interested in protecting the light than she was seeming like a hero," Leia concludes. Laura Dern notes, "I do think the idea of willing sacrifice, and someone's silent intent to not need to be a hero but to save everyone is just profound. There's definitely something for me to learn about the idea of perception versus knowing. It's a deep spiritual question, in many religions too, this idea of not needing to prove who you are but knowing it. It's a big question" (Yamato).

Of course, the timing of Holdo's sacrifice saves Finn and Rose. First, it distracts from their planned execution, and then it destroys the carefully constructed facade of power that the ship maintains, revealing it as literally and symbolically full of cracks and holes. At last, Finn duels his evil parent. Phasma draws a baton, and he swings at her with an executioner's axe. Emphasizing how much all the Order's facades are shattering, Phasma's mask breaks, revealing a vulnerable eye. As he battles her, Finn knocks Phasma into one of these pits of vulnerability. She calls Finn scum, and he proudly retorts that he's "Rebel scum," in the perfect zinger. With this, he burns away his past and chooses to fight for the Resistance.

He and Rose make it down to Crait, where they're quickly enlisted into the Resistance's final defense. Poe leads the speeders at the First Order's forces but orders them to veer off rather than committing suicide. He at least has learned Holdo's lesson that retreat is sometimes the best choice. Finn, however, still needs to learn it. As the massive siege cannon prepares to destroy the last of the Resistance, Finn aims his ship at it, following the lone hero model and sacrificing himself. However, Rose slams her own ship into his, canceling his sacrifice and near-fatally injuring herself. As she lies close to death, Finn demands, "Why would you stop me?"

"I saved you, dummy. That's how we're gonna win. Not fighting what we hate—saving what we love." Nearly unconscious, she kisses him and imparts the same lesson Poe has just learned—saving people and protecting them as a team is the path to success. Another anima has instructed her hero. More disturbingly from a story perspective, Holdo and Rose are both willing to sacrifice their lives to impart these lessons.

As Luke arrives, creating a distraction by pretending to engage in a macho battle but actually making Kylo Ren look foolish, Poe understands the lesson. When Finn urges that they help Luke, "Poe wanted to smile—was this the same Finn who'd insisted he wasn't here to join another army? And not so long ago, he would've reacted the same way—looking for anything he could fly and blasting off across the plains. But he'd learned there were other ways to fight—and that those who chose them were no less brave" (Fry 298). He understands that Luke is buying them time to escape.

Back in their base, with his new perception, he seeks a quieter solution. He notices that the crystal foxes have disappeared, and he leads his people in tracking them to the hidden passages out of the base. Now he's leading the retreat, one that's only possible through perception and humility. Leia urges everyone to follow him, proud that he finally understands.

The interim novel *Resistance Reborn* by Rebecca Roanhorse reveals that no one answered Leia's call because their allies were all arrested and imprisoned by the First Order. During a daring mission to free them, Poe has a chance to come to terms with his actions. He confesses to his beloved Black Squadron and is shocked and humbled when they forgive him. Following this, the revered veterans of the Rebellion ask about his choices and he must publicly acknowledge them. In this, "his worst nightmare come true" he's called to account and he asks himself whether he's truly a leader (149). He tells them, "I disobeyed a direct order, I got people killed, I undermined my commander, and led a mutiny. And if you don't think that eats me up, that it haunts me every day, every minute, then you don't know a damn thing" (150). He adds that they all need to learn from their mistakes and finally change the galaxy by following new paths. They can make "a choice to be better" (151). This speech wins the people's hearts and shows Poe what he can become if he moves beyond his mistakes.

For Finn, *Last Jedi* ends with the way paved for a love triangle as he struggles between Rey and Rose. Each still has much to teach him. However, the final film goes a different way. When Poe asks in *Resistance*

Reborn, Finn says that he and Rey are "just friends." As he adds of Rose, "We talked about it, and Crait was … a moment. But that's it. Friends there too" (Roanhorse 183). Certainly, the switching of creators plays a part in this, as does the structure of *Rise of Skywalker* (which pairs Rey with Kylo, sidelines Rose, and introduces Jannah). On a larger scale, this shows Finn struggling with alternate paths, uncertain where to commit his energy. All these anima women, with whom he feels so close in times of crisis, are not meant for romance but to guide him to enlightenment.

Concluding the Epic

Having learned the lesson of teamwork, Finn and Poe eagerly sign up to travel to Exegol with Rey instead of letting her fly into unknown dangers. Any romantic possibilities have solidified into a sincere three-way friendship, with the addition of Chewie and the droids. Together, they all journey into an underground Sith tomb, face Chewie's apparent death, and remain steadfast through it all.

The third film offers a new anima for each hero. For Poe, it's his old smuggler companion Zorii Bliss. She greets him with blaster drawn on the smuggler planet Kijimi. There, she leads the Spice Runners, and, as a traditional shadow, knows all of Poe's unsavory secrets. Instead of coming from the light or the dark, she represents compromise and expediency—lessons Poe has yet to master. Her actress Keri Russell says Zorii exists in a grey area: "She's done some rather sketchy things in her lifetime and she has a tough exterior—she's very much a survivor" (Wilkins 48). In fact, Poe has reversed Kylo Ren's path, beginning as a criminal and then mending his ways to join the Resistance as his parents had done. Poe is drawn to Zorii, partly because of their romantic history and partly because she represents the criminal part of himself he never allowed to grow.

In her concealing mask, only partly removed, she symbolizes the shapeshifter. "In the game of love, the hero and heroine each view their partner as a shapeshifter. This 'other half' they must cleave to like themselves has frightening mood swings and unpredictable desires. Hence, many tales appear about enticing swan maidens from the sea or taming beastly monsters into Prince Charmings" (Frankel, *Girl to Goddess* 76). Now that Poe has learned in the previous film to listen to his feminine side, Zorii offers him a mystery and a challenge. Her refusal of a kiss suggests the playful give and take of flirtation, a demand that he exert himself in understanding her.

However, Zorii does not recruit him into the smuggler life but instead reveals why his heroics are necessary. She shows him the devastation the First Order has wrecked on her world and convinces him to keep fighting.

She even gives him a talisman—a First Order medallion that will let him penetrate their defenses. This is a sacrifice for her, one that demonstrates her faith in him and thus buoys the hero forward. When the First Order destroys her planet, this offers an encounter with death for Poe, who's certain she's lost.

Similarly, Finn faces his dark past and is delighted to find a counterpart who shares this struggle between the dark and light. This is Jannah, likewise raised by the First Order and then defecting. Her Company 77 mutinied at the Battle of Ansett Island after they were ordered to target civilians. "This tale lands heavily in Finn's heart, for he underwent a similar transformation on his very first mission. With such shared histories, Finn and Jannah have an unspoken bond" (Hidalgo and Terrio 158). The pair finish each other's sentences, after finding perfect understanding and sympathy for the first time. Further, Finn never finds his parents, but Lando's interest in Jannah suggests she may have found her own father ... indicating that such a possibility exists for Finn as well.

The introduction of female friends for Poe and Finn doesn't only signify potential romance but a new generation of warriors to inherit *Star Wars'* world. "This trilogy is about this young generation, this new generation, having to deal with all the debt that has come before," Abrams says. "And it's the sins of the father, and it's the wisdom and the accomplishments of those who did great things, but it's also those who committed atrocities, and the idea that this group is up against this unspeakable evil and are they prepared? Are they ready? What have they learned from before? It's less about grandeur. It's less about restoring an old age. It's more about preserving a sense of freedom and not being one of the oppressed" (Grossman, "Tour de Force").

Oscar Isaac reveals that his character is far less confidant than on his previous adventures: "Poe finds himself inheriting a Resistance that is on the brink of collapse. He feels completely lost, and he even begins to wonder if there's really anything to lead at this point. But Poe is reminded about family and friends and not being alone. And he rallies behind those ideas and pushes the others to continue to move forward" (Wilkins 23). As the climax approaches, Poe struggles with command, pleading by Leia's shrouded corpse that he doubts he's good enough for the job. Still, he's learned to trust his team. "There has been a bit of shared history that you haven't seen," Isaac says. "Whereas in the other films, Poe is this kind of lone wolf, now he's really part of a group. They're going out and going on missions and have a much more familiar dynamic now" (Grossman, "Tour de Force"). Black Squadron, who had been absent on a mission in *Last Jedi*, leaving him rudderless, is back, fighting under his command. This signifies his gathering the scattered pieces of himself. Finally, turning his back on arrogance and ambition, he asks Finn to lead beside him, cementing their brotherly bond.

Abrams approached the story like a "living breathing thing," as he puts it. The massive climactic battle up in space is indeed for the fate of the universe. "This has to be the war to end all wars," he says. "This has to be the ultimate battle. Not just externally, but internally, for the characters. In Episode VII these characters are just meeting, and they were almost separate the entire movie. This is the first time you get to see this group of people, this group of friends, together on an adventure—their most challenging yet, against something that is the biggest threat. Can these new, young characters handle it? That, to me, defines the feeling of *Star Wars*" (Shepherd 58).

The final battle is indeed epic. While Rey and Ben fight the Emperor below, Poe and Finn fight them above, Poe in the air and Finn riding beside his new friends. As Finn and Jannah charge, he tells her in the novelization, "Never another kid" (Carson 232). Both are fighting for the childhoods stolen from them. Above them, Poe's fleet is decimated by the Emperor's Star Destroyers. However, when all hope seems lost, Lando brings in a massive Resistance fleet, which nearly blacks out the sky with its masses, including Zorii Bliss, who has survived. Rebel pilot Wedge Antilles (Denis Lawson) from the original trilogy is manning the gunner's seat of the Falcon, and many other familiar faces and ships surround them. Together, they destroy the Sith Lord's armada. This stirring moment emphasizes a unified galaxy all supporting the heroes as they've aligned their goals and their friendship. "It's not a navy, sir. It's just people," one of the First Order officers reports. The systems are rising up.

Once they've won, it's reported that planets all over are rebelling. This has indeed ushered in a new era of peace. As the film ends, Poe has discovered his calling as a true military leader and acting general of the Resistance with Finn by his side (though Zorii is uninterested in romance). Finn, it appears, has found the powers of the Force within. Together, they will create a new era of peace and understanding. With this, the Resistance has triumphed at last.

Kylo Ren: Nihilism to Redemption

The sequel trilogy posed an enormous question: What villain might succeed the one of the other six films? J.J. Abrams explains:

> We needed a villain in the shadow of Darth Vader, one of the greatest movie villains ever. How do you create a bad guy that works in his shadow? Part of the beauty of the answer was in the character acknowledging himself that he was in the shadow of this

character. He was as aware of Vader as we are. We wanted to give his villainy a conflict and not make him necessarily the mustache-twirling, finished villain but rather make him someone who is broken. A villain who's in process, a villain in training [Ashworth 71].

Abrams adds in an *Entertainment Weekly* interview, "Long before we had this title, the idea of *The Force Awakens* was that this would become the evolution of not just a hero, but a villain." Like Anakin of the prequels, Kylo Ren has great plans to change the galaxy to his liking. He too is under the sway of an evil mentor. One difference is that, until halfway through the third film, Anakin is still trying to serve the forces of good. Kylo, in his rebellion against his parents, has deliberately chosen evil.

Adam Driver describes being told that he was basically on a journey opposite to Vader's. "Whereas Vader was very confident when the audience first meets him, over the course of three movies he is chipped away at until he's at his most vulnerable. Kylo's journey is almost the complete opposite. He starts out very vulnerable, very childlike, and then over time he gains experience and becomes hardened and more assured about the choices he makes" (Wilkins 56). He bears a weighty legacy—descended from the heroes who led the Rebellion, but also the evil Vader who killed his wife and Leia's parents. "People always say, 'Why do you think this saga is so popular?'" said Lawrence Kasdan, who not only co-wrote the new film, but also *The Empire Strikes Back* and *Return of the Jedi*. "I really do believe the underlying theme is recognizing your potential and understanding what you're capable of." He said it's a quest everyone is on their entire lives. "It doesn't end. To understand what you've inherited, and what you like about that and what you don't like about that. Have you fulfilled yourself completely—or is it too late?" (Breznican, "JJ Abrams on Kylo Ren").

The shadow of the past is clearly influencing him and his master, Supreme Leader Snoke, pressuring them all to build a bigger, stronger Death Star while continuing Vader's legacy. Even beyond keeping Vader's skull in his quarters as a fetish, Kylo Ren clearly feels the conflict lingering. Abrams notes, "This is a world where the bad guy is going to be cognizant of Darth Vader and when the bad guys have a massive weapon that can destroy a star system, they're going to reference the Death Star because this is their history too" (Grossman, "Reboot" 60).

His lightsaber is "a killer's weapon, and executioner's fetish of choice" (Foster 21). Canon reveals that kyber crystals are powered by the light side of the Force. For a Sith to wield a lightsaber, he or she "bleeds" the lightsaber, usually taken from a murdered Jedi. Overpowering the crystal with dark side energy turns it red. After killing his friends and enemies alike, as the comic *The Rise of Kylo Ren* reveals, the new villain took his own kyber crystal and forced his dark emotions into it. Whether through his inexperience or his raw strength, Kylo Ren cracked his crystal, which now fizzles and spurts. Further, the quillons, which create the crossguards, are actually exhaust vents. The *Visual Dictionary* also explains that Kylo's lightsaber is an ancient design dating back to the Great Scourge of Malachor, during which the Jedi had their greatest victory over the Sith. Perhaps Kylo Ren pictures himself one of these heroes … or perhaps he wants to turn the tables on them. He resembles the twenty-first century Neo-Nazis and net trolls appearing during the film's release, as an unstable young white man who has grown up with privilege yet models himself after his family's ancient enemies and wants to burn down the galaxy.

Of course, young as he is, he's still unskilled in evil. His screaming tantrums as he destroys consoles and equipment with his lightsaber emphasize how much rage is ruling him, rather than the reverse. *The Rise of Kylo Ren* shows his lifelong frustration as he cries, "Whether it's Luke Skywalker or Snoke, neither one sees me as a person. I'm just a … legacy. Just a set of *expectations*." He joined the Knights of Ren in rebellion, but their gang brought him the opposite of individuality or choice and instead had him switch his family pressure for that of his peers (Soule).

Further, he confesses to Vader's skull that he still feels the call of the light, much as he fights against it. In fact, his self-aware determination to pursue evil makes an unusual twist for a central character. Kylo Ren clearly believes the Empire was a source of strength, in contrast with the bickering, fragmented New Republic. He also sees his ideal, Vader, as failing in his quest to destroy the Rebels through a moment's sentimentality. In the novelization, Snoke tells him, "Had Lord Vader not succumbed to emotion at the crucial moment—had the father killed the son—the Empire would have prevailed. And there would be no threat of Skywalker's return today" (Foster 139).

Kylo's mask emphasizes how much this is all a façade. In one scene, while his helmet is off, his rival Hux walks in. Kylo immediately straightens and turns stoic. The great reveal under his mask, of course, is that he's ordinary and human. Abrams explains, "I speculated, maybe his face was not awe-inspiring at all. Maybe it was just a plain face with a flattened nose, a weak chin, and rabbit teeth. Maybe Vader needed the mask because without it he was just a man you passed casually on the street" (Millet 134).

Masks can also externalize demonic tendencies. Speaking to Vader's burned, crumpled skull, Kylo confronts the darkness within himself. "Forgive me. I feel it again. The pull to the light. Supreme Leader senses it. Show me again, the power of the darkness, and I will let nothing stand in our way. Show me, Grandfather, and I will finish what you started." This scene is one of pain and desperation in a world he feels cannot understand him. He has his gang in the Knights of Ren but no true friends or allies.

When Kylo confronts Rey in his torture chamber, he's intrigued by her. Scanning her mind, he feels the Force within her and also a deep connection. He sees that she's been dreaming of Luke Skywalker's hidden waterworld. She's also been adopted by his own parent. He smirks. "And Han Solo. You feel like he's the father you never had. He would've disappointed you." Already, they are symbolic twins, connected through family as well as the Force.

To his surprise, she challenges him. She penetrates his mind in turn and sees, "You … you're afraid … that you will never be as strong as Darth Vader!" She is his anima, sensing all the dark secrets he's bottled up. After, he crouches outside the corridor, panting and shocked. He must show her as well as himself that he can defeat them.

Because Vader failed the test of pure evil by saving Luke, Kylo Ren and his mentor believe this is the ultimate trial for Kylo. Of course, in his case, this means murdering one of his closest loved ones. On a bridge as tenuous as Kylo Ren's self-control, Han lovingly reasons with him to embrace his good side, the side that shared adventures with his father. "Take off that mask. You don't need it," he adds.

Kylo asks him, "What do you think you'll see if I do?" It's a challenge, but also a moment of hesitation, as Kylo fears the weakness that his human face reveals. When Han insists, Kylo doffs the mask, accepting his human vulnerable side and his connection to Han. This is the shadow confrontation—just as heroes like Luke confront their Vader side. Having accepted this link, however, Kylo discards it, insisting, "Your son is gone. He was weak and foolish, like his father. So I destroyed him." Han insists he's still Ben and offers the temptation of seeing Leia. However, Kylo Ren has chosen the Supreme Leader's path.

At last, Kylo lets himself be vulnerable and honest with his shadow side, the good father tempting him back to the light: "I'm being torn apart. I want to be free of this pain. I know what I have to do, but I don't know if I have the strength to do it. Will you help me?" Han promises, and Kylo Ren holds out his lightsaber … and then murders his loving father in front of him. "*Star Wars* had the greatest villain in cinema history. So, how you bring a new villain into that world is a very tricky thing," Abrams explains. "We knew we needed to do something f—king bold. The only reason why Kylo Ren has any hope of being a worthy successor is because we lose one of the most beloved characters" (Breznican, "JJ Abrams on Kylo Ren"). As *Star Wars* always does, it multiplies family conflicts into epic battles of mythic proportions.

However, this act does not solidify Kylo Ren's certainty but fills him with guilt and confusion. As the novel adds, "Stunned by his own action, Kylo Ren fell to his knees. Following through on the act ought to have made him stronger, a part of him believed. Instead, he found himself weakened" (Foster 245).

The final shadow adversary awaits him. "The goddess represents the feminine, the Universal Mother figure, while the father signifies masculine authority; the hero either must defeat or win the approval of the father to continue his or her own journey while the temptress attempts to sway the hero" (Wright 70). In Kylo Ren's flipped, furious ideology, he has destroyed his father, his enemy. Now, he must resist the temptress, Rey. Once again, he feels the pull of the light, though he rejects it, instead inviting her to join him. "You need a teacher. I could show you the ways of the Force," he offers as they're pinned face to face, blue glow against red. This emphasizes each's role as the other's shadow adversary (an unusual gender cross but not unheard of). Of course, she refuses.

Further, Anakin's own lightsaber has come to her. Whatever her birth, she is the Skywalker heir, all he rejected. At last, the knowledge of his own vulnerability is made plain. As she slashes at him over and over, scarring his face, she establishes her superiority and leaves him prone in the snow. She flies off with Chewie and the Falcon, more pieces of his heritage, and leaves him wounded, with nothing at all. To defeat her, he will need a deeper mastery.

THE NEW SUPREME LEADER

In the sequel, Snoke mocks "the mighty Kylo Ren" with his powerful bloodline for losing to her girl who had never held a lightsaber. "Now I fear I was mistaken." Snoke dismisses him as Kylo protests that he has given everything to the dark side. All his training, all his power, is called into question by Rey's triumph as the Force's chosen one with Anakin's lightsaber—though Kylo grew up entitled to this role. Rian Johnson notes of the previous film: "He gets his ass kicked. He has his butt handed to him, absolutely, by someone who should not have been able to hand him his butt. [Laughs] So he's in a very different place than Vader, but I think we hate him maybe even more than we hate Vader coming into this" (Brooks).

Kylo pledges his full allegiance to his dark master, Snoke, but the tyrant snubs him again. "You have too much of your father's heart in you, young Solo," Snoke says, humiliating the privileged young man who cannot leave his father behind, even by killing him. The chamber where they face off is glaringly angry red, with black accents. It's like an artificial crucible of hell where Kylo can be broken down at his master's whim. Red-clad guards stand motionless, observing his mortification as he kneels to be insulted.

There, Snoke orders him to remove his impenetrable mask, revealing the angry vulnerable young man beneath. Underneath, he looks devastated, close to tears. Snoke notices this as well, dismissing his insistence that he chose evil and killed his father. "And look at you, the deed split your spirit to the bone." Their scars reflect, highlighting Kylo's role as imperfect student to a flawed mentor. Adam Driver, alluding it, notes, "I feel like almost everyone is in that rehabilitation state. You know, I don't think that patricide is all that it's cracked up to be. Maybe that's where Kylo Ren is starting from. His external scar is probably as much an internal one" (Kamp).

Snoke continues taunting him that Luke and the Jedi live while Kylo has failed to live up to Vader's legacy and destroy them. "Alas, you're no Vader. You're just a child in a mask." After, Kylo stares at the mask that's meant to make him look imposing and strong. It has failed him. He smashes it against the wall over and over, punishing his outward face.

One's persona is the mask presented to the world—the flawless warrior or beauty queen. Kylo's makes him look impassive, controlled, and frightening—all the qualities he wants to show others and finally make true in himself. However, the prop has failed. This film arc shows Kylo reaching out with his vulnerable side and struggling to fix the damaged child within, seeking someone who won't reject him. Lucasfilm president Kathleen Kennedy notes:

> One of the most interesting things about Kylo Ren is that he's young. So often, villains in stories, are damaged, troubled, older characters. To bring a character into *Star Wars* as a villain who's only 30 years old is interesting. It takes advantage of a troubled teenage life and a back-story that we don't know much about. We recognize this tension between dark and light, which is prevalent in *Star Wars*. We can use it as a metaphor for the path from young adulthood to being an adult. Anybody is capable of having interest in the dark side, and that tension of being drawn into something that is somewhat dangerous is relatable ["Kathleen Kennedy; Bryan Burke" 94].

As he insists on proving his manliness to himself, Kylo flies a bat-winged fighter as Vader once did (a show-offy move in both cases that allows both to experience death at point-blank range). His TIE Silencer is a mashup of a TIE Interceptor and Vader's TIE Advanced X1, emphasizing the legacy he wishes to continue. Further, Kylo's droid, BB-9E, is the evil flat-headed counterpart of BB-8.

As Kylo and General Leia, on opposite sides in the battle, sense each other, both grow still. Leia's gentle theme plays. She stands on her white-lit bridge while Kylo is shrouded in darkness, alone in space. Kylo takes his finger off the button. He may play at being strong, but Snoke was correct—he could barely kill his father and now cannot kill his mother. His wingman fires, allowing Ren to let an intermediary continue the conflict without literally attacking the woman whose presence is so central to his own. On either side of him, his fellow soldiers shoot take the decision from his hands. After, his mother lies near death, and Kylo has won the day for the First Order … or so he thinks.

The next scenes come from Rey's point of view as he bursts in on her thoughts through their strange connection. Just as he's a pitiful call to darkness for Rey, she calls him to the light as she models the heroism of the Resistance. When they talk, she stands on Ahch-To, surrounded by oceans. As such, she's his anima, image of all the nature and goodness he's cast out. He senses in her everything he's denied himself, and he's captivated. Of course, he's as mystified by their connection as she is. Vulnerably, he asks her, "Why is the Force connecting us?"

If the first film had Kylo struggle through his father (and grandfather!) issues, this one has him battling his ties to the anima. As they commune, Kylo notes that he can't see Rey's surroundings, "Just you." This is a vision of the anima and in many ways his shadow—the good student he's long since rejected in himself, now symbolically reaching out. "This is something else," he decides.

Even as he goes about his duties, her personality suddenly inflicts itself upon him, as she demands answers to the hard questions—why did he kill his father? Does he feel remorse? As she interrogates him, he's forced to examine the emotions he hasn't dealt with. Rian Johnson notes: "I thought the dynamic between them was very interesting and the opposing forces, flint striking off each other with the two of them, combined with this power on opposite sides that they both share, was very interesting" (Brooks). Rey balances Ren—light as he is darkness.

Meanwhile, both are questioning the pronouncements of the previous generation and finding them flawed on multiple levels. Both tried to learn from Luke and Han as father figures, and both were let down. In fact, as Luke rejects Rey as he did Ren (though less spectacularly), Kylo sees a strong commonality between them. Both are the new generation, both considering alternatives after a thousand years of Jedi versus Sith. Johnson says, "A big bedrock thing for me was, 'What do you keep from the past and what do you not? What is the value of the myths you grew up with? What is the value of throwing those away and doing something new and fresh? For me, that's prominently illustrated in the movie in the Rey and Kylo relationship: her trying to reconnect with the past and him trying to throw it all away" (Szostak 76). Kylo Ren tells Rey, "Let the past die. Kill it, if you have to. That's the only way to become what you are meant to be." He's taken this to heart in the case of Han and Luke, but his cultivating Vader's memory emphasizes how much he's ignored part of this lesson.

The heroine offers the hero deeper perception. For the spoiled, angry man-child, deeper consideration helps him mature. In turn, he offers Rey disillusionment to balance her naïve hope and trust in mentors. Finally,

Ren reveals the truth in a confession that provides some closure—he did not leave Luke's school but awoke in the middle of the night to find his uncle prepared to murder him. In his abandonment, he destroyed the school, murdering half his classmates in a deeply resonant emotional scene for those Americans who have read about too many school shootings. Kylo was already a nihilistic ticking bomb, but this moment tipped him over the edge. Now, he seeks anyone who will take his side, and Rey finally does, demanding of her mentor, "Did you create Kylo Ren?"

Kylo's relating this moment to her is a catharsis as he works through the buried secrets he's never told another. In this scene, he's shirtless, as he was when Luke tried to kill him. It's a vulnerable moment for him. He is in his private room, and suddenly a girl, his semi-enemy, is intruding. On the armored, helmeted landscape of First Order ships, Ren hasn't had a chance to be vulnerable with anyone in a long time. Interestingly, the other character to appear shirtless in the franchise is Hayden Christensen's Anakin as he tosses in tormented nightmares and dreams of his loved ones suffering and dying. This evokes Anakin's conflict in his descendent, turning to evil to best keep himself and others safe, as the light side has failed him.

Still, he's drawn to Rey. When she holds out a hand to him, he removes his glove and takes it. The Force theme plays. This is a moment of perfect communion, representing the sacred marriage between male and female—an instant of completion and enlightenment. Campbell explains, "A marriage is a commitment to that which you are. That person is literally your other half. And you and the other are one" (Campbell and Moyers 250).

Luke, the force of authoritative morality from his past, pushes them apart. Still, Rey believes in Kylo, as almost no one still does. "I saw his future. As solid as I'm seeing you. If I go to him, Ben Solo will turn." At last, she comes to him. Perceptively, Rey understands that Kylo isn't quite as evil as he wants everyone to think. She tells him, "I saw the conflict in you. It's tearing you apart." As they walk side by side, she bargains to save his soul, much as Luke once did with Vader.

Wanting a partner who's as corrupt as he is, Kylo retorts that she will be the one to turn. "You'll stand with me." In his throne room, Snoke is surrounded by Praetorian guards in red and alien attendants in purple robes. He humiliates Rey, forcing her to her knees. As Snoke mocks her for her humanity, Kylo Ren sees Snoke's shaming of him, and by association, the friend who represents the hopeful kind side of himself. From Kylo's perspective, she's salvation, his one path to not being a monster. He calls his lightsaber to himself and Snoke narrates that Kylo will strike down "his true enemy!"

Suddenly, Rey's neglected lightsaber ignites. Kylo Ren de-powers Snoke by bisecting him, emphasizing his craving for dominance. He committed a similar murder with his own father. However, Snoke's murder propels Kylo even further to the dark side as he perceives himself as Supreme Leader at last. Back to back, he and Rey fight as a perfectly coordinated team and defeat the Praetorian Guard. The audience, like Rey, may believe he has turned to goodness. However, he cannot stop eyeing Snoke's throne.

Johnson comments: "The hero's journey, the myth that Joseph Campbell writes about, that Lucas famously pulled from, it's not about becoming a hero. It's not about becoming Hercules. The hero's journey is really about adolescence. It's about becoming an adult" (Brooks). Kylo is grappling with his parental figures even as he struggles to sit in the big chair, to be the metaphorical adult. After this, he asks Rey to be his subordinate-partner so he can train her. In the Sith pattern and the archetypal one, he is the ultimate master now, and can signal his growth by forming a new household. Close as this is to his revelation that they're not biologically related, he may be hoping for a romantic partner as well.

She refuses him, and calls her lightsaber, but he struggles for it. Despite Kylo's insistence on ending the past, he still craves Anakin's weapon. The ancestral legacy he hates so much will never release him, nor can he give up his obsession. After Rey escapes with its crushed remains, he promptly sets about trying to destroy the remnants of the Resistance, including his mother and the last survivors. In his mind, total power means annihilation of all his enemies, through brute force. He demands Hux's loyalty, ignoring the chain of command and force-choking the other man into obedience. Still a child, he blames Snoke's death on Rey. They then follow the Resistance down to Crait.

The AT-M6 (All-Terrain Megacaliber Six), the First Order's upgraded walkers, are much larger than the AT-AT, armed with a megacaliber six laser cannon. Beyond this, a truly massive battering ram cannon surrounded by red scuffmark like streaks of blood and a host of TIE fighters against men in trenches with single rifles emphasizes the Resistance's lack of firepower. Everything the First Order brings is overkill. With this arsenal, Kylo Ren tries to destroy his mother's rickety forces, and is filled with fury when Rey and Chewie fight back on his father's ship. Having this part of his heritage turn against him is one more cruel reminder. On seeing the Falcon, Kylo explodes in rage, screaming, "Blow that piece of junk out of the sky!" He's determined to prove that superior might conquers all.

As his forces smash through the massive door protecting the Resistance, Luke, his last and most powerful father figure, appears before it. At this, Kylo Ren goes berserk, unleashing a massive, insane level of firepower in his need to win a physical battle against ineffable spirituality. He orders, "I want every gun we have to fire on that man." They hesitate, and he insists, "Do it." The walkers overwhelmingly barrage the solitary figure. Hux looks disgusted by the excess, only for Kylo to scream "More!" Hux finally halts the barrage with an annoyed "That's enough," and finally a screamed order of the same. Eying the overgrown child who's taken charge, Hux quips, "Do you think you got him?"

Of course, Luke survives, and even ostentatiously wipes a bit of dust from his shoulder. In this moment, Kylo Ren has humiliated himself as an impulsive and incompetent military leader in front of the might of the First Order's armies. Though his grandfather inspired fear and destruction, Kylo has been revealed as an ineffectual successor. Since Kylo needs absolute control over all aspects of the galaxy and must be the ultimate ruler, he discards all his technology to go battle his uncle. When Hux, a foil to Kylo as the voice of strategy and pragmatism, tells him not to "get distracted," Kylo Force-slams him against the wall.

At last hero and villain face off. "Did you come back to say you forgive me? To save my soul?" Kylo asks. Luke demurs. They draw their lightsabers, unstable red against steady blue. There, they fight, Kylo lunging and Luke dodging. Kylo's foot scrapes the ground, producing a mark like a bloodstain. He is not only barely functioning rage, but he cannot shake off the deaths he's caused. Further, Kylo blusters threats at his uncle that his people are defeated.

Calmly, in full control, Luke quips that Kylo is completely wrong and that he is not the last Jedi. As he speaks, he appears to sense Rey saving the Resistance. Angrily, Kylo senses it too. As Luke warns, "If you strike me down in anger, I will always be with you. Just like your father." He understands Kylo's terrible guilt and knows he's adding to it. Using more brute force, Kylo triumphantly impales him only to find Luke is an illusion. Luke's physical absence suggests Kylo's blaster fire, like his hacking at a console with his lightsaber in the previous film, is directed all around him but not at a real target. Since Luke is not present for the battle, Kylo is literally only fighting himself.

Luke mocks, "See you around, Kid," and blinks out, depriving Kylo of even Vader's victory against Obi-Wan. This battle with the light side shadow has revealed his impetuous gullibility and uncontrolled rage, emphasizing Kylo's true lack of control. Since Luke's illusion distracted him, Kylo's failed military maneuver clumsily allowed the Resistance to escape in the end. His officers have witnessed all. While he maintains his position as Supreme Leader, he must suspect how much his officers are mocking him in secret. His rule is already degrading.

Redemption and Sacrifice

The opening crawl of *The Rise of Skywalker* reveals the central conflict as it explains, "The dead speak! The galaxy has heard a mysterious broadcast, a threat of revenge in the sinister voice of the late Emperor Palpatine." As it adds, "Supreme Leader Kylo Ren rages in search of the phantom Emperor, determined to destroy any threat to his power…." Clearly, having risen to the top of his hierarchy, Supreme Leader Kylo Ren doesn't seek a master but a maintaining of his precarious position.

At the same time, he envies the Emperor and his cautious control, so much more mature than his own rages. In the novelization, Kylo thinks, "The path to the dark side lay in succumbing to one's desires. But his deepest desire, the thing he wanted most, would require planning and patience. The emperor had figured out how to embrace a plan so long suffering and painstakingly careful it boggled the mind—and he did it without being tempted by the light even a little" (Carson 100–101). The raging young man sees a pathway to success from this, the ultimate dark mentor. Training with this source of evil incarnate may elevate him.

He leads his knights to Mustafar, volcanic planet of Vader's original defeat and his subsequent castle. There, they destroy the Alazmec, "cult colonists" who "voyage to Mustafar in pilgrimage" seeking Vader's powers. They have "planted a thin forest of irontrees … in a futile attempt to reinvigorate the glen that covered the land centuries earlier" (Hidalgo and Terrio 10). However, Kylo Ren, as the force of destruction, smashes everything the helpful travelers have created. No other Vader devotees are welcome—he's unwilling to share even his worship of the past.

All here is dim and red like the conflict burning within him, now focused outward. Kylo slaughters all the natives and claims their treasure, the wayfinder. Magnetically, it glows a poisonous green against the darkness. After, he stands on a wasteland of black corpses, foreshadowing the chaos he will spread through the galaxy. This image fades to his black ship soaring through a red nebula, continuing to court chaos and death.

"Adam, as well, goes to a far deeper, more interesting, compelling, and subtle place with his character," Abrams comments. "When we met Kylo, he was almost like a bit of an adolescent. He would sort of rage. He aspired to a kind of power and control, but he was out of control" (Breznican, "Reylo"). Now, he has more discipline. Even as he hopes to face the Emperor, he channels the other's skills in himself. Following the talisman to the Sith planet Exegol, he enters the giant cube there. Inside, he finds a shadowy shrine, lit in glowing ghostly blue. The Emperor's stronghold is a maze, one that forces questors to journey through its twisting passageways as they metaphorically descend into the depths of the self. "Mazes should both allow access to their centers by a sort of initiatory journey and bar it to those who are not qualified to enter" (*Dictionary of Symbols* 642). Such a quest is traditional for the young hero seeking a path through life.

Unlike Luke and Rey, Kylo never got to go on a nifty voyage of self-discovery. Instead he grew up under the crushing pressure of massive expectations. "How do you form friendships out of that?" Driver says. "How do you understand the weight of that? And if there's no one around you guiding you, or articulating things the right way … it can easily go awry." By the emotional logic that governs the Star Wars universe—and also our own—Kylo Ren is going to have to confront the past, and his fears, whatever they are, or be destroyed by them [Grossman, "Tour de Force"].

There, in the enemy's stronghold, Kylo Ren finds a resurrected Palpatine, blind, with stunted fingers. These emphasize his lack of agency, as he's connected to life-sustaining tubes like a puppet. His only ability is that of influencing others, though it's a great power: He, the mastermind of the first two trilogies, apparently has masterminded this one as well. Malevolently, Darth Sidious greets him. "At last. Snoke trained you well." Kylo threatens him, but Sidious reveals that he has been the shadowy force of evil beyond all his mentors: "My boy, I made Snoke. I have been every voice, you have ever heard, inside your head." His voice changes from Palpatine, to Snoke, to Vader, emphasizing that while evil may wear different faces, it always has the same goals. He has always been the puppet-master from the beginning. Abrams explains, "There was an absolute inevitability. For someone who says, 'Don't bring Palpatine back, it's not an original idea,' I would say, if you're looking at the story these movies tell, he's very much part of that and the big picture. All the setups that you need are in the existing movies" (Shepherd 59).

A grotesque device maintains him like a puppet, intervening even more directly than in mechanized Vader's suit. Acknowledging this, the Emperor comments, "I have died before. The dark side of the Force is a pathway to many abilities some consider to be unnatural." He reveals himself as the personification of all evil, the eternal driving force of the Sith. True, the Extended Universe gives him a backstory with a childhood and apprenticeship with his own mentor. However, from the mythic perspective, his ambitions are universal. This time, he offers Kylo "Everything. A new empire." To this end, he's built a massive fleet of Star Destroyers hidden under the Exegol ice. Each bears a planet-killing superlaser, as the Emperor multiplies his death-dealing across the galaxy. As it happens, Sidious does have a price: Kylo can have the full might of his new fleet for a simple task: "Kill the girl. End the Jedi. And become what your grandfather, Vader, could not. You will rule all the galaxies as the new emperor."

This time, as Supreme Leader of the First Order, Kylo makes his own choices and shapes his own persona. This new title is a sign of his maturity. Further, he continues to remake himself. In the previous film, Supreme Leader Snoke derided Kylo as "a child in a mask." Kylo smashed the helmet and ditched it for the rest of the movie. Now Kylo's cracked helmet has been welded together with red veins, making it appear as damaged and unstable as his flickering lightsaber. Masks may indicate possession—even as the sculptor tries to capture a spirit or behavior in this mask, it can engulf his personality. Some monster masks were a liberation and catharsis: "Instead of hiding, the mask revealed those lower tendencies which had to be driven out" (*Dictionary of Symbols* 638). This red-veined helmet is indeed Kylo's monster side, one he will need to overcome to find enlightenment.

Emphasizing his damage and insecurity, he insists his officers praise it around the conference table. This emphasizes his terrible insecurity. He may rule their hierarchy, but he knows he doesn't deserve the position. Adam Driver explains:

> Even the first time we talked about putting on his suit, the suit was appropriately uncomfortable and that seemed like a really fun thing to play with—maybe he's literally uncomfortable in his own skin. It's restrictive in a way. And then he kind of goes through a rebirth over the second movie and starts to shed that a little bit and become who he is. He's a very unformed person, which is exciting to play and to have that be represented physically in a costume piece, or a lighting choice or, in this case, a helmet. It's a coming together, he's cherry-picked things he's looked at through his history and that he's decided he wants to claim for who he is. So it's a physical representation of how that character has grown [Hibberd, "Adam Driver"].

Afterwards, using Vader's skull as a channel, Kylo watches Rey train. He's still drawn to her as his perfect companion and reflection, the one person in the galaxy he feels understands him. When she reaches the festival she's exploring, he connects with her and asks her once more to take his hand and rule at his side. As perceptive anima, she challenges him: "I see through the cracks in your mask. You're haunted. You can't stop seeing what you did to your father." The previous film established Kylo's bond with Rey, something that seemed to break the laws of the possible. It suggested a romantic connection as well as one of the spirit. However, this time she abandons him as a mass-murdering tyrant.

Kylo reaches out to her, insisting, "You can't hide, Rey. Not from me." He knows she feels the same connection. Of course, since she has chosen light as he has darkness, they represent opposite paths. At last, he finds her on the moon Kef Bir, where the Death Star fell. Its skeletal remains overshadow them, emphasizing the burden of the past. Still she refuses to partner with him. Kylo Ren and Rey battle beside the life-giving ocean, the feminine realm. They are equally matched. At last, Leia interrupts their battle to reach out to her son with all her love and strength. Across the galaxy, Leia gives him the push he needs. She loves and accepts him completely, just as Rey does, and gives her life to bring him back.

As he's distracted, Rey stabs Kylo Ren with his evil lightsaber, forcing him to feel its wickedness in what appears a fatal wound. However, she places her hands on him and heals him by transferring some of her life force. "I did want to take your hand. Ben's hand," she tells him. Thus, reconnecting with the feminine principle banishes the patriarchal energies that have possessed him and guides Ben back to his true self.

"No one can go through an experience at the edge of death without being changed in some way," warns Vogler (30). Even for ordinary humans, after a near-death experience, "colors seem sharper, family and friends are more important, and time is more precious. The nearness of death makes life more real" (164). As he revives, Ben understands that his connection to his loved ones is part of the centrality of existence. This is a moment of enlightenment for him, demonstrating that he controls his own destiny and can turn back. It's clear that his dark lord side has perished, and it is Ben who rises. Through love, the two women in his life have found his lost good side and ushered him back to the light.

Afterward, as a reward and final turning point, Han appears to him. "Hey, Kid." As Han admits, he may be only in Kylo's memory, but this encounter offers a path for Kylo to reconcile with his actions. With his memory of Han forgiving him, he's symbolically forgiving himself. Ben insists Han's son is dead, but Han denies it, affirming who Ben truly is: "No, Kylo Ren is dead. My son is alive." Han mourns Leia's loss with Ben but gives him a new mission: "What she stood for, that's not gone."

With this, Ben knows he must accept his parents' legacy and fight for their cause, ending the destruction he created. "I know what I have to do, but I don't know if I have the strength to do it." This line calls back to *Force Awakens*, while asserting that he's turning his back on the previous darkness, coming full cycle and making the wise sage's return. Han assures him he does have the strength. Ben ends their talk with a touching "Dad!" to which Han replies "I know." With this reconciliation with the father he'd tried to destroy within himself, he lets his hero side take over. Ben throws the red lightsaber into the sea, rejecting all it represents. The wreckage of the Death Star stands in the background, a shadow of the past that he's finally escaped.

He's next seen suddenly arriving at the climax of the film, helping Rey to defeat the Emperor and bring down the new empire he created. Just as Luke tells Rey it's her responsibility to face her dark creator, Ben knows the same is true for him. Ben thinks in this scene in the novelization, "Rey had healed him. He had accepted his father's forgiveness. He might even forgive himself someday. He would find the strength to make everything right, no matter what" (Carson 213).

The Knights of Ren, once his followers, beat Ben Solo, and he accepts it in penance. Facing them, Ben realizes in the novel, "The Knights of Ren had never been his. They had belonged to the Emperor all along" (Carson

218). His leadership once again has been an illusion. As the comic *The Rise of Kylo Ren* reveals, they were always just a gang of toughs, initiating him when he could prove he'd killed in a "good death" and bowing to him when he proved the toughest by killing their leader. As Snoke tells him in the comic, "The Knights of Ren do as they please, which lend them fluidity. Whatever they need to do to survive, to triumph, they will do" (Soule). They are the ones to have given Kylo Ren his black outfit and mask, his rebellious teen models for independence. However, this is all superficial power—they are followers, not leaders. This is a story of making decisions and this is something their mob mentality cannot perform.

"Do it, make the sacrifice," the Emperor gloats. However, Rey sheathes the Skywalker sword, sending it to Ben so that he draws it from his own scabbard. At last, he has inherited the legacy he abandoned for darkness. Each fights, acting as a coordinated team as they so briefly did in Snoke's throne room. Bolstered by his heroic legacy, Ben reclaims his old self and fights off the knights.

The Emperor reveals that they are a "Force Dyad," symbolic twins. With this, they echo Luke and Leia (or Jaina and Jacen from the Legends novels). The Force Dyad is a new concept that nonetheless stretches back to some of the world's oldest myths. Symbolically, twins represent duality, the contrasting halves that make a complete person. Twins represent "the twofold nature of all beings and the dualism of their physical and spiritual, diurnal and nocturnal, tendencies" (*Dictionary of Symbols* 1047). Twins, as they helped one another or quarreled between themselves, emphasized the ambivalence of every individual divided within. "When they symbolize in this way the individual's internal contradictions and the struggle which needs to be waged to overcome them, they acquire the character of sacrifice, the need for self-denial, destruction or submission, the surrender of one part of the self so that the other may come through victorious" (*Dictionary of Symbols* 1047–1048). United, Rey and Ben are whole at last. Ben has balanced the goodness of the universe with darkness, as his grandfather did, but now, he understands, his role is to bring down the Emperor and restore the galaxy to life.

Still, another death and rebirth sequence comes as the Emperor hurls him into a chasm, the place of banishment and discorporation where he himself perished. Symbolically, Ben dies in the audience's eyes even as he faces the ultimate peril. Beyond death (which he has already faced battling Rey) this is the possibility of vanishing utterly—of dying alone in the shadows from a single contemptuous blow, robbed of a hero's death or even the galaxy's notice.

This too becomes something Ben must accept in order to overcome. The hero in a heroine's journey story, he intuits that as the goddess's chosen warrior, his role is to sacrifice himself saving her. Rather than his apprentice or future wife, she is the true champion, one who, bolstered by his energies, can save the galaxy. "Epiphany is a moment of realizing you are a divine and sacred being, connected to all things" (Vogler 182). This Ben has, understanding his responsibility to his beloved. He's spent his life seeking connection, and she was the one to truly accept him.

At the moment of Rey's death, a single hand dramatically emerges from the chasm. He climbs up and cradles her. As she once did, he gives his life energy to save her—all he has. As Ben thinks triumphantly, "He had given Rey back to the galaxy. It wouldn't atone for the darkness he'd wrought but it was what he could do" (Carson 238). By sacrificing himself, he follows the path of his parents, uncle, and grandfather, even as he makes a final choice. Ironically, this is also the power Anakin so desperately sought, this time not taken from the light or dark side of the Force, rather from within through a selfless act. Here, Ben masters light and dark, life and death. As such, he's the pinnacle of wisdom, completer of the hero's journey.

Just as his murder of his father propelled him down the path to darkness, Ben's restoration of Rey puts him on the path of life. She offers him a kiss that symbolizes the sacred marriage, union of male and female in triumph and enlightenment. This is more than love—it's twinship and harmony. "The symbol of unity through the synthesis of opposites, symmetry gives expression to the reduction of the manifold to the one which is the underlying meaning of the act of creation. After a stage of expansion, the universe finds its meaning in a return to the oneness of thought" (*Dictionary of Symbols* 961). Having reached this enlightenment, however, he dies. His clothes empty, and across the galaxy, so do his mother's. The Force has welcomed them both in its embrace. This is apotheosis, godhood, even as, full of contradictions, it means a complete surrendering of selfhood and ego. With this, Ben achieves enlightenment.

Rey's Heroine's Journey

The classic heroine's journey is less publicized than the hero's, but it appears in mythology around the world, brought into modernity with stories like *The Wizard of Oz, The Chronicles of Narnia, The Hunger Games, A Wrinkle in Time,* and so forth. While some heroines dress as men and travel on a more masculine hero's journey, there is a feminine quest of spirituality and motherly salvation that belongs only to the heroine. While Padmé and Leia evoke moments of this, Rey's agency and centrality ensure that she travels the entire quest.

Many steps are the same, though others are reversed or show different priorities. First comes the ordinary world. Rey manages to survive in the ominously named Goazon Badlands between Niima Outpost and the Kelvin Ravine by Carbon Ridge and the Sinking Fields. "I've been here my whole life, scratching out a living with the lost and broken," she notes (Fry, *Rey's Survival Guide*). It's an empty place, without friends or companions.

The novel *Aftermath: Empire's End* shows the Empire's last stand on Jakku, with dozens of Star Destroyers and swarms of TIE fighters. Rey grows up in the aftermath of this war. Symbolically, her childhood is weighted by the legacy of the Jedi: their conflict with evil authoritarianism is returning. More literally, she grows up in a barren, wrecked land, without even Luke's aunt and uncle to soften its harshness. Her only mentor is Unkar Plutt, who routinely pays her the minimum for her survival. This unfeeling mentor is especially traditional for the heroine. While the hero trains with someone like Obi-Wan, many heroines only have the evil stepmother to teach them how to survive. This emphasizes the harsh indoor world of prehistory, as boys went off to war against a clear enemy, but girls had to survive within the sometimes treacherous, even murderous world within the family walls.

Like Luke, Rey grows up cut off from her spiritual heritage of the Force. Abrams notes, "George Lucas told a story about everyman, everywoman characters who were nobodies who had to step up and become somebody. The idea that there would be a new crop of nobodies in the *Star Wars* universe who didn't realize yet they would become somebody, that was a very powerful feeling" ("Director J.J. Abrams" 66). Taking the trope to extremes, she dresses androgynously, swathed in grey-beige fabric that hides not only her senses but her appearance. Dressed thus, she has lost all connection with her feminine side, and must quest to reclaim it. "When she looks at an old, wrinkly women cleaning scrap for sale, then later wistfully at a ship leaving the planet, it's clear Rey is worried she'll spend her whole life wasting away on Jakku. She wants to leave, to seek adventure, even if she doesn't fully admit it to herself," comments Sarah Moran in "*Star Wars*: How Rey Brings Balance to the Franchise."

She has a particularly painful task through the first years of her life—to survive and wait among the hostile conditions. "I don't know if Rey is really about anything in the beginning of the film except for working and feeding herself," her actress Daisy Ridley says. "Her life is pretty ... 'mundane' is the wrong word ... but it's pretty repetitive. She's literally living hand to mouth. She's solitary. She doesn't speak to people very much. She's just trying to make it work for herself" (Woerner). This suggests the heroine before her enlightenment, simply enduring endless drudgery.

Her trusty weapon is a staff—one Ridley studied bojutsu to wield correctly. Meanwhile, the wall of her AT-AT marks Rey's history here: Thousands of scratches mark how long she's been waiting. In her prequel journal, Rey describes the AT-AT, noting, "I spend most of my time inside the belly" (Fry, *Rey's Survival Guide*). This is a womb image, since the heroine continues to incubate in safety rather than venturing out into the galaxy.

She waits, as she remembers her parents once instructing. However, a call to action finally jolts her from her complacency. The innocent droid BB-8 arrives, fleeing the Empire. Touched with sympathy, Rey saves him from scavengers. She fixes his antenna as if wiping his chin, emphasizing how babylike the little droid is. His name and coy mannerisms emphasize this. Chief of Creature and Droid Effects Neal Scanlan says, "We always saw BB-8 as a naughty puppy or a very clever little child. They know how to be coy, how to be cute, how to sulk, how to pull at heartstrings to get what they want" ("BB-8" 63). The ships she fixes are additional child-substitutes, teaching her nurturing. When she meets BB-8, she discovers a surrogate child to protect and also a sense of purpose. As she protects him, his quest becomes hers.

> Her goal is to become the all-powerful mother. Thus, many heroines set out on missions to rescue their shattered families: Meg Murray of *A Wrinkle in Time* quests to save her father then her little brother. Coraline tries to save her parents, Meggie of *Inkheart* and Clary of *The Mortal Instruments,* their mothers. Tim Burton's Alice tries to rescue the Mad Hatter. Scores of young women in folklore rescue their lovers from fairies, demons, and ogres. Demeter forces herself into the realm of the dead to reclaim her daughter, while Isis scours the world for her husband's broken body. Katniss, of course, spends the series protecting Prim and her growing adoptive family, from Peeta to the children of Panem [Frankel, *Many Faces of Katniss* 113–114].

In this case, she's seeking her own family in a big picture scenario but also has an adoptive child to protect and return home. BB-8 offers additional symbolism as a talisman like the golden compass, spectacles, mirror, or potion that go to questing heroines. Roundness is a feminine symbol, and BB-8 even has subtle feminine qualities. "I'm still not sure, dare I say, whether BB-8 is male or female," Scanlan says. "BB-8 was female in our eyes. And then she became male. And that's all part of the evolution, not only visually but in the way they move, how they hold themselves" ("The Last Jedi"). As endlessly rolling spheres, echoing the lifecycle, BB-8 visually evokes a feminine talisman for the heroine.

Within minutes, the pair meet the runaway Stormtrooper Finn and find themselves scrambling off planet, First Order soldiers giving chase. When she flies for the first time in the derelict Millennium Falcon, "Rey felt Jakku trying to pull her back down," both literally and symbolically (Rucka, *Before the Awakening* 102). This is the refusal of the call, a hesitation to leave for the unknown. Nonetheless, Rey sets out to find her destiny as she launches herself skyward.

This in turn summons Han and Chewie. Within a few minutes of screen time, Rey leaves Unkar Plutt behind forever and gains three stronger male allies. "Through these companions, and her growing relationship with the Force, Rey seeks to heal the hole in her heart through the connectedness that normally comes with family" (Szostak 16). One's quest companions offer skills the heroine hasn't yet discovered in herself and evoke stronger qualities within her. This sort of team up "evokes masculine traits within her: logic, rationality, intellect. Her conscious side, aware of the world around her, grows, and she can rule and comprehend the exterior world" (Frankel, *Girl to Goddess* 22). At the most primitive level, Rey's first animus, Unkar Plutt, is a force of brute strength and cruel authoritarianism.

Traditionally, the heroine gains wiser animus figures as she continues on her quest. The next stages include initiative and planning, rule of law, and finally wisdom. Finn is a force of expediency, who saves Resistance pilot Poe Dameron not because "it's the right thing to do" as he weakly claims but because, in all honesty, he needs a pilot to fly him to safety. Likewise, Han and Chewie drag Rey into battle with two groups of gangsters seeking revenge, thanks to his own sloppy attempts to talk himself out of trouble. While Rey's new friends are self-serving and avoid the higher cause of the Resistance, they understand military maneuvers and space battles—a realm she's never mastered. She's advancing through cleverer animus figures who can deepen her understanding.

Han helps Rey grow by supporting her, even offering her a job as co-pilot. "Many remember the [original Falcon battle] scene and Han's now famous response to Luke's joy and astonishment—'Don't get cocky, kid!' But when it comes to Rey, Han is all about encouragement. This is due in part to Han having a different relationship with Rey than Luke, more mentoring than rivalry" (S. Moran). Han also emphasizes her transition to a new level as he offers her a blaster. When she insists she can handle herself, he respectfully quips, "I know. That's why I'm giving it to you." The blaster, model LPA NN-14, is compact and silver. Symbolically, this is a color of feminine mysticism and spirituality. It brings the heroine the moon magic and water magic that are her heritage (Walker 522). Leia and Maz, the story's other powerful women, share this symbolism with their own small silvery blasters.

"However, after she's proven she can outdo men in the arena of sports, warfare, or business, when she's gained external power and success, the Warrior Woman feels a spiritual lack.... Deeper than she realizes is possible, a voice is calling her to find the Dark Goddess, the savage powerful icon of femininity, and absorb her wisdom" (Frankel, *Buffy* 8). While the hero finds the spiritual guide—Galadriel or the Lady in the Lake, the heroine more often learns from the frightening death crone like Hecate, the devourer of the underworld. "This savage mentor offers the ultimate wisdom—the insight that darkness, mysticism, and even death are a woman's ultimate source of power, far different than a hero's outward force of arms" (Frankel, *Buffy* 8).

The new hero-team fly to the planet Takodana, which overwhelms Rey with its vibrant green life. There, she meets Maz Kanata, the wisewoman. Her castle, stretching high beside a fertile lake and forest, has modern sensors and high-tech gear. "Maz enjoys this contrast. To her, it is yet another manifestation of a cosmic balance" (Hidalgo, *Force Awakens* 73). Her statue overshadows the place, emphasizing female protection and identity.

A mature woman, Maz calls Chewie her "boyfriend" and understands the world far better than innocent Rey. She's lived over a thousand years, becoming fully integrated with the nature around her and boasting many feminine tools. She can feel the Force but only uses it subtly—she has no Jedi training and has never "walked that path herself, instead relying on her strong connection to the Force to keep her out of danger" (Hidalgo, *Force Awakens* 72). She's an alien, sloppy in goggles and baggy clothes and thus something of a nonconformist. This offers Rey an alternative path to study. "As a personal shadow figure, the Bag Lady symbolizes the freewheeling female survivor and bountiful female nurturer … the rejected side of the feminine that is characterized as offbeat, peculiar, crazy, or mad, and that has been scorned by our white, patriarchal society" (Leonard 171). She encourages Rey to develop the parts of herself she still hasn't explored.

Maz is also a master of perception, as she notes, "I have lived long enough to see the same eyes in different people." Her gigantic goggles emphasize her power of seeing, as she examines the galaxy from her remote castle. These goggles or glasses are a feminine perceptive tool seen in the magic spectacles and amber scope in *A Wrinkle in Time* and *The Amber Spyglass* respectively. Mirrors and crystals are common in fairytales, expanding one's insight about her surroundings. Around the world, eyes bring a maternal power of cursing as well as seeing what is hidden. "As an actor for films, your eyes are a lot of the way you communicate anyway," says her actress, Lupita Nyong'o. "So it was definitely a gift to have that be the means to her magic as a motion-capture character" (Breznican, *Star Wars*).

Maz encourages Rey to listen to the inner voice of her spiritual heritage. She adds, "The Force, it's calling to you. Just let it in." This moment offers the heroine a weighty turning point. Such a meeting teaches Rey that she is an essential part of a much larger galaxy and that she has the power to transform it. Soon, Rey stumbles into Maz's basement, representing all that is buried within. As Campbell notes:

> The unconscious sends all sorts of vapors, odd beings, terrors and deluding images up into the mind—whether in dream, broad daylight, or insanity; for the human kingdom, beneath the floor of the comparatively neat little dwelling that we call our consciousness, goes down into unexpected Aladdin caves. There not only jewels but also dangerous jinn abide: the inconvenient or resisted psychological powers that we have not thought or dared to integrate into our lives [*Hero's Journey* 8].

In the basement, she finds Luke and Anakin's lightsaber. Claiming it, she sees flashes of her heroes' past even as Yoda and Obi-Wan speak to Rey of her heritage. With this, all the mentors of the previous films invite her to claim her destiny. Even as she faces it, Maz comes to her and gives her a new mission. There in the basement, she voices all the thoughts Rey has refused to admit to herself:

> **REY:** I have to get back to Jakku.
> **MAZ:** Han told me. (takes her hands) Dear child, I see your eyes—you already know the truth. Whomever you are waiting for on Jakku, they're never coming back.
> **REY CRIES.**
> **MAZ:** But there's someone who still could.
> **REY:** Luke.
> **MAZ:** The belonging you seek is not behind you, it is ahead. I am no Jedi, but I know the force. It moves through and surrounds every living thing. Close your eyes, feel it. The light. It's always been there. It will guide you. The saber—take it.

This gift is a bit jarring within the heroine's journey, as a family sword traditionally goes to the male hero. At the same time, Rey's receiving Luke and Anakin's lightsaber establishes her as their spiritual heir. As a symbol, it offers not only a warrior status and Jedi knighthood but also the heavenly blue of spirituality and enlightenment. Maz tells Rey, echoing the language from previous films, "That lightsaber was Luke's, and his father's before him and now it calls to you!"

Battling this heritage, Rey cries, "I'm never touching that thing again, I don't want any part of this." This glimpse of the deathly unconscious has been too frightening. She runs away into a primordial forest, thick and dark, refusing the call once again. Heroines enter the forest and find a place of mysticism and mystery—the magic of the unconscious. While men learn powers there that are foreign to their lives, women discover the powers they've always possessed, only waiting to be claimed.

Rey panics as she flees, overwhelmed by a sea of flashbacks that reveal all the darkness of the past. Of course, Kylo Ren, the product of all this pain, personifies all this. He is her adversary but also her catalyst: In the forest, he knocks her unconscious, symbolically allowing her to absorb the shock of the past and progress to a new level of maturity.

He carries her off to his base, where she has no power at all … or so it appears. She will need to seek it within. He represents her inner doubts and also the dark side that will take her over if she allows it.

> The predator exists in everyone—the force that longs to devour the world, the insatiable greed that will take the entire psyche for itself. The demon lover, or killer animus, lures his victim out of life. He seduces her, shrouding her in lies, trying to convince her she's helpless. "And he will succeed unless she has the courage to bring him to consciousness.... Because the ego is afraid, it looks at the unconscious with fear and animosity, thus constellating the demon face that stares back" (Woodman 132). Facing and overcoming this predator is a necessary lesson. By facing it, we can understand its weaknesses and so deprive it of its murderous energies [Frankel, *Girl to Goddess* 82].

As the complexity of Rey's animus figures continues to grow, strength and goodness arrive in the person of the entire Resistance fleet. Leading them, General Leia Organa offers the image of a true role model. As a mother and general strong in the Force, she can make the tough choices—when to risk herself and when to risk loved ones like Han, as she sends him to get their son back. She helps Finn on his mission to rescue Rey, offering salvation from outside the self.

Rey wakens in Kylo Ren's torture chamber. The stronghold represents the masculine stronghold, a realm with which Rey is unfamiliar. It even contrasts her desert planet with a technological base within a world of ice. "Journeying here represents the heroine leaving the place of her feminine power to ascend to the prince's tower or mountain, where she faces her greatest trial far from her unconscious realm of magic. The Little Mermaid leaves the ocean and Demeter leaves her fields as both journey into the man's world—human civilization" (Frankel, *Buffy* 60). Here, Rey is cut off from her strongest supports. Further, the *Rise of Skywalker Visual Dictionary* establishes this planet as Ilum, a world formerly sacred to the Jedi where they sought their lightsaber crystals. The crystals now power the new weapon, but also allow Kylo to pervert the Jedi legacy into a tool of mass murder.

"The road of trials helps the hero figure out who she or he is by confronting a task that seems impossible at first but ultimately is one that the hero is uniquely capable of doing. By accomplishing these tasks, she or he learns something about the human condition buried deep within his or her own self" (Wright 52). Even locked on Starkiller Base, Rey glares at Kylo Ren, now armed with the higher animus power of law and military might. "You know I can do whatever I want," he taunts her. With this, he invades her mind and the private thoughts within. These include an image of a misty island where Luke Skywalker awaits her, prepared to help her deepen spiritually. This watery world, like Maz's, is an image of feminine fertility.

"The New Heroine is not entirely self-made like the future girl; however, her physical body is loaded with special talents and abilities that are part of her character but not of her own making. The future girl may have gumption and endurance, but the New Heroine uses her giftedness to overcome obstacles on her journey" (Wright 44). Rey is supernaturally talented though it still exists only as potential. She fights back, reading Kylo's mind in turn and using his training and discipline against him. "You're afraid. That you will never be as strong as Darth Vader," she realizes. In this moment, she sees the patriarchy's inherent weakness, as its rulers perpetually struggle for dominance. Kylo Ren is insecure, blustering, an emperor with no clothes.

When the heroine confronts the tyrant and refuses to give in, she discovers how easily he crumbles. She is the empowered one here.

> On the heroine's journey, the young questor comes to realize that she is mightier than the tyrant: Dorothy cowers before the "Great and Powerful Oz" when she reaches his Emerald City. But after facing the far more terrifying Wicked Witch of the West, she grows into someone strong enough to kick over the Wizard's pasteboard head and confront the fraud cowering behind it. Katniss too realizes that the Capitol's *threat* far outweighs the Capitol itself. As she declares on one of her broadcasts: "The Capitol's fragile because it depends on the districts for everything. Food, energy, even the Peacekeepers that police us. If we declare our freedom, the Capitol collapses. President Snow, thanks to you, I'm officially declaring mine today" [Frankel, *Many Faces of Katniss* 117].

Her facing Kylo gives her the necessary knowledge, born from intuition. "The Madwoman rises up inside us when we are oppressed by rigid order and control" (Leonard 16). While the catalyst comes from Kylo, she taps the deep power she never knew she possessed to strike back at him. Part of the woman's quest is to vanquish the predator, taking from it what is useful and leaving the hollow posturing. Such a triumph fills the heroine with a new energy. After this, Rey masters the "Force trick" and controls the orderly yet obedient Stormtroopers. The First Order are no match for her will.

Finn arrives to save her as Luke did Leia, only to find she's already saved herself. The pair share a brief romantic moment and embrace. He is a shapeshifting love interest just as Kylo Ren is. This represents the mystery figure's shifting moods and incomprehensible impulses. "We have all experienced relationships in which our partner is fickle, two-faced, bewilderingly changeable," Vogler explains (65). The task is to penetrate these barriers, to find and embrace the true self within. Of course, Finn's shapeshifting comes from his masquerading as a Resistance soldier and then confessing the truth. However, when Finn invades the heart of the First Order to save her, he has transformed again, this time into a true Resistance fighter and hero.

When Rey faces death, it isn't her own but Han's. He tragically falls before her, murdered by his son, and depriving her of a beloved mentor.

Like Lucy and Susan of Narnia, who witness Aslan humbled, incapacitated, and finally murdered, Rey thus discovers her father-figure's helplessness to protect her. After this, she will rely on herself.

> The classic heroine learns independence, not protection from her father-figure. Lyra of *The Golden Compass* discovers that her father is a murderer when he kills her helpless friend Roger. Meg Murray crosses time and space to rescue her blinded and confused father, and they tesseract to a friendly planet. When Meg demands that he return to rescue her brother Charles Wallace, Meg's three witch mentors appear and tell Meg her father is not powerful enough. Meg gazes sadly at him. "I wanted you to do it all for me.... I was scared, and I didn't want to have to do anything myself" (L'Engle 187). With this, she acknowledges she is the only one who can rescue Charles Wallace, so she returns to confront the monstrous IT [Frankel, *Many Faces of Katniss* 118].

The snowy forest outside awaits, offering all the spiritual power that is Rey's heritage if she's ready to claim it. A second time, she faces Kylo Ren there, but this time, she's more certain. She takes up Luke's lightsaber, battles him and wins. In fact, it flies to her hand, confirming that she has a right to inherit it. Luke's theme plays triumphantly. As Rey hears the Jedi legacy through Luke's lightsaber, calls it to her hand, and masters the Force, she discovers how the Force has chosen her over Kylo Ren to be Luke's heir and the franchise's chosen one.

Rey battles Kylo Ren, light side to dark side. The same audio as begins Luke and Vader's battle in *Jedi* emphasizes her similar mission—to end the tyrant's reign. "You need a teacher. I can show you the ways of the Force," he offers. She refuses this offer just as Luke once did Vader's. Still, as Luke found, facing this shadow helps her discover the strength within herself, even brutality and mercilessness that she will need to survive in a hostile galaxy.

In this case, Rey's inner shadow—all rage, madness, and power—is sparked by her enemy. Against him, she feels an inner challenge greater than the one he poses, particularly in the novelization: "*Kill him*, a voice inside her head said. It was amorphous, unidentifiable, raw. Pure vengeful emotion. So *easy*, she told herself. So *quick*" (Foster 253). Facing his fury allows her to channel these impulses within herself, accept them, and choose a different path. Still, these dark feelings she's now wrestling can be incorporated into the self. "By choosing to confront the Madwoman and the source of her strength, the situations of frustrations out of which she emerges, and by choosing to acknowledge, work with, and transform them, we learn to recognize and honor the Madwoman's dark feminine energies as part of a greater whole" (Leonard 283).

As a ravine splits and fire consumes the land, Rey leaves Kylo's chaotic world behind. With Chewie's help, she saves Finn and returns to the Resistance. There, Leia, the good mother embraces her.

The hero separates himself to become the new king. "For the New Heroine, it is *through those connections* with a community that she discovers who she is. The thing that ends his journey *defines* hers from the very beginning: her connections to other people, environments, and technology" (Wright 109). Rey thus does not withdraw from her friends as Luke does at the end of *Jedi* or go become a hermit. She revels in her connections with Finn, Leia, and Chewie, and goes to find another in the person of Luke. The New Resistance is her tribe now.

With Chewie and Artoo, she flies to Ahch-To, a watery world that suggests harmony with nature as well as deep contemplation. There, she climbs a hill (symbolizing enlightenment) and offers the famous Luke Skywalker his weapon. The animus in its highest stage "gives the woman spiritual firmness, an invisible inner support that compensates for her outer softness" (Von Franz, "Individuation" 194). Meeting Luke reflects this step, showing a completion of her journey through friends that can teach her her place in the universe.

Subverting the Quest

Rey, dressed in gray for the second film, is poised between dark and light. Later, she switches to a grey and dark brown version, signaling her continuing loss of innocence. She begins on the Jedi sanctuary called Ahch-To, where Luke has been hiding for decades, by approaching the mentor she'd sought through the previous film. She offers him the lightsaber that was his and his father's—the legacy of light and dark she has inherited. However, to her shock, Luke subverts the epic moment by tossing the lightsaber away. The music goes dead, anticlimactically, and she follows him, puzzled, protesting, "Master Skywalker?" She finds only a closed door.

This is one step of many that deconstruct the hero's journey: Rey has brought the epic lightsaber to the man she's dreamed of, the last Jedi Master who can complete the training she needs. She believes herself the child of destiny, perhaps descended from a great Jedi hero. Of course, the audience shares all her expectations.

Nonetheless, Luke flatly refuses to train her, leaving Rey to chase after him as he milks the sirens and catches fish—pointedly using his impressive abilities for everyday hunter-gathering. To complete her quest, the heroine must return with Campbell's Elixir of Life—the quest item meant to renew the galaxy. Luke, however, declines this role. He even refuses to mentor her. As this movie does over and over, he deconstructs her epic dreams, insisting that she's come on a pointless mission. Sarcastically, he responds, "You think what? I'm gonna walk out with a laser sword and face down the whole First Order?" He insists she leave.

Over and over she uses the phrase "We need your help," echoing Leia's original call to Luke and Obi-Wan. However, Luke remains unmoved. The refusal of the call is his, not Rey's, but the gruff, uninterested mentor is another fantasy staple, especially for heroines.

Rey reclaims the lightsaber. It's revealed that she also has Leia's token—a beacon bracelet that will let her find the fleet. After this, she hunts down the cave containing "the original Jedi texts" as Luke says. This underground cavern suggests a descent into the womb of the earth like Luke's cave scene in *Empire*. The library, hidden under the roots of a multi-branched dead tree, brims with mystic spiral designs. Books and spirals are both feminine symbols, suggesting this truly is Rey's place. The novelization adds, "The books seemed to call to her. But unlike the lightsaber on Takodana, this call didn't feel like a threat. Rather, it felt like a promise, one made long ago and now ready to be fulfilled" (Fry 91). The tree is shaped like the Jedi Temple on Coruscant, but more primitive, in a subtle bit of continuity. Luke and Rey thus revert to the Jedi's beginning in an attempt to find clarity. Luke, notably, hasn't even read the wisdom contained there. There in the womb of the earth, Luke asks, "Who are you?" the one question Rey cannot answer. This helps spur her journey towards identity as she struggles within for an answer.

Gazing about, she says, "I know this place." Presumably she's been dreaming about it as part of her Jedi legacy. She notes, "Something inside me has always been there. Now it's awake and I'm afraid." This is the stirring of adulthood—the drive to grow up. Campbell explains: "The period when one begins to realize that one isn't running the show is called adolescence, when a whole new system of requirements begins announcing itself from the body. The adolescent hasn't the slightest idea how to handle all this, and cannot but wonder what it is that's pushing him—or even more mysteriously, pushing her" (Campbell and Moyers 142).

Still, Luke refuses to train her. Aside from frustrating the heroine, this also pushes her in new directions. Luke is not Rey's only mentor, as she begins having visions of Kylo Ren. He is the devil on her shoulder, and yet, far more interested in understanding her than Luke is. At last, Rey persuades Luke, but only to a point. "Tomorrow at dawn. Three lessons. I will teach you the ways of the Jedi ... and why they need to end."

While waiting for her first lesson, Rey suddenly sees Ren and shoots him. He grips his side, but she's only shot the wall of her hut. Pushing the Jedi imagery far beyond communion, Rey and Kylo's bridging offers a raw physicality—they are literally connecting. The gaping hole (much as it dismays the Caretakers) suggests tearing down the past and also letting in the beams of enlightenment from above—opening to new possibilities. These Kylo offers as a new kind of mentor.

While her first sally against her rival was physical, his is mental. He tries a mind trick on Rey ("You will bring Luke Skywalker to me") so he can assert his dominance and destroy the last patriarch. Like Vader, he seeks to ascend to the top of the hierarchy. Rey, not being weak-minded, is completely unaffected. Symbolically, she is contained within herself unless she chooses to connect. "The conscious attention a woman has to give to her animus problem takes much time and involves a lot of suffering. But if she realizes who and what her animus is … instead of allowing herself to be possessed, her animus can turn into an invaluable inner companion who endows her with the masculine qualities of initiative, courage, objectivity, and spiritual wisdom" (Von Franz, "Individuation" 194). The fairytale reenacted here is Beauty and the Beast—the human heroine confronting the monster, a shapechanger who conceals a human face under his frightening mask, if she can only learn to see it. While she rages at him, she also feels a connection.

Rey returns to reality to find the Caretakers all annoyed with her and her lessons about to start. The compelling spiritual connection has passed. She lies to Luke, concealing her glimpse of a deeper reality. At last, Luke offers her three lessons (or rather, two, though the third appears in the novelization) not in how to be a Jedi but—to her disappointment—on why the Jedi should disappear. He has her seat herself on a cliff and asks what she knows about the Force. "It's a power that Jedi have that lets them control people and … make things float," she replies, and he must tell her that this is completely wrong.

He has her reach out (and when, continuing her clumsiness, she takes him literally, he tickles her hand with a blade of grass). As she feels the natural cycle around her—birth and death, heat and cold, light and darkness—he explains that the Force is everywhere, created by all living energy. The Force theme music swells. This is the lesson. If the Jedi and all their teachings vanish, the Force will continue. Light and darkness exist in balance without the need for maintenance.

While Luke has learned to accept evil, he still fears it in his pupils. After this, Rey senses a darkness beneath the island and goes seeking it. "It's calling me," she says, troubled. Luke is horrified as he sees her reach out curiously, making pebbles rise and the entire island shudder. He compares her strength to Kylo Ren's and tells her, voice shaking, "It offered you something you needed, and you didn't even try to stop yourself." This is an interesting observation as many fantasy stories emphasize the need to balance dark and light—the epic journey involves learning from the underworld before returning as a wise adult. Luke, it seems, does not understand such a need.

Here, Luke denies Rey this training, so she quests into the darkness for meaning. "The shadow is not necessarily always an opponent. In fact, he is exactly like any human being with whom one has to get along, sometimes by giving in, sometimes by resisting, sometimes by giving love—whatever the situation requires. The shadow becomes hostile only when he is ignored or misunderstood" (Von Franz, "Individuation" 173). This is true for the darkness on the island, which reflects the darkness within Rey—normal human emotions seeking expression.

She tells Luke, "The galaxy may need a legend. I need someone to show me my place in all this." Still, he resists her. As his second lesson soon reveals, his guilt is blocking him. Just as Obi-Wan failed in training Anakin, Luke failed in training Ben, who escaped him and burned down the temple, slaughtering the fellow students who wouldn't join him. To end this cycle of destruction, he's prepared to end the Jedi.

The third lesson was trimmed for time. The film's final editing suggests Rey leaves before she can hear it, repeating the cycle as Luke left Dagobah before completing Yoda's lessons. The novelization and cut scenes, however, include it.

This third lesson has the pair seeing boats coming to Ahch-To. When Rey inquires, Luke tells her they're bandits who have come to terrorize the Caretakers. He advises her to let them do as they wish to preserve the island's balance, so they don't escalate. Ignoring his advice, Rey runs to the village, lightsaber ignited, only to find a party, at which Chewie, the porgs, and R2-D2 are enjoying themselves. Luke tells her the third lesson is that real help comes from action, not the mystery of some old religion. Clearly, she's aware of this, as she chose to fight. Furious, Rey spits, "That old legend of Luke Skywalker that you hate so much, I believed in it. I was wrong" (Fry 152). Luke promptly feels ashamed. The lesson is something of a cruel trick and once again emphasizes Luke's flaws as teacher. This in turn pushes Rey to rely on herself instead of him. More subtly, it suggests other approaches than direct battle are needed.

As Kylo intrudes on her mind again, he encourages her to ask Luke about the true story of what happened at his temple. This moment challenges the heroine's assumptions about her world, making her dig deeper. This in turn guides her to understand her shadow side.

Ben and Luke's falling out is shown three times, in the tradition of the film *Rashomon*, which emphasizes how much a different perspective completely reframes events. Kylo shows Luke filled with a terrible killer rage, while the final version has Luke drawing his lightsaber as Kylo remembers but stopping himself. During these retellings, Rey feels her sympathies stretch and change as she considers Kylo's fate.

> "I think Rey and Kylo are almost like a dual protagonist," Johnson explains. "You identify with Rey, but also you identify with Kylo in a way that you never did with Vader. I know I do. Because if these movies are about adolescence, Kylo is that anger of

adolescence and that rejection of the parents and wanting to screw over your dad; and that's something that all of us, to some degree, can identify with. And the idea of there being a bad guy who you identify with as much as you do the protagonist in some way, that's really interesting" [Anderson].

As her shadow, Kylo is the person Rey has always longed to be—the child of mythic heroes and heir to the Force, trained by Luke and growing up in luxury. If she can save him, Rey thinks, her heroism will match Luke's in saving Vader. He's also a Bluebeard character who could devour her from within if she allows him to take over her mind and soul. With this, he offers hints of a sexual tension. In one scene, he's shirtless in his bedroom and she asks, "Have—have you got a cowl or something?" He is nearly as uncomfortable, not expecting this mental intrusion. "It's all about those Force connection scenes." Johnson added. "The keyword being intimacy.... And so it was just another way of kind of disrobing Kylo literally and figuratively a little bit more, and pushing that sense of these conversations becoming increasingly more intimate" (Anderson).

There in the privacy of their minds, Kylo as shadow tells her deep truths: "Your parents threw you away like garbage ... but you can't stop needing them. It's your greatest weakness." She denies it but knows it's true. He continues to challenge her. Choosing the future in contrast with Luke, who's tied to his regrets, Kylo tells Rey, "Let the past die. Kill it, if you have to. That's the only way to become what you are meant to be." He is trying to guide her to a higher understanding.

When seeking one's purpose, "There is only one thing that seems to work; and that is to turn directly toward the approaching darkness without prejudice and totally naively, and to try to find out what its secret aim is and what it wants" (Von Franz, "Individuation" 167). Continuing to seek the dark side, Rey lets her mind sink away and crosses over to a realm of imagination. Her mind takes her through a deep pool to a cavern of mirrors. Within it, she discovers endless reflections of herself, and a clouded central reflection. "This image reflects a little bit of the Kylo/Rey Force connections as well as the duality of light and dark, good and evil," Industrial Light & Magic art director James Clyne says (Szostak 71).

After gazing at the cloudy image of herself, Rey fulfills the audience's driving question and asks for a vision of her parents. A cloudy double figure solidifies into one. However, confusingly, it becomes a reflection of herself. Johnson explains, "In this search for identity, which is her whole thing, she finds all these various versions of 'Who am I' going off into infinity, all the possibilities of her. She comes to the end, looking for identity from somebody, looking for an answer, and it's just her" (Breznican, "Last Jedi Spoiler Talk: Rey"). This scene parallels Luke's moment in the cave. Luke faces the reflection of himself (with Yoda advising him not to bring a weapon but

Luke bringing one anyway and battling and killing himself there). Rey has no weapon and simply sees and accepts herself as Luke finally does in Vader's gaze. Just as Luke finds the bad guy is himself, Rey finds the good guy is herself—just her.

This is the test of the Innermost Cave—accepting one's flaws and strengths and with them the lesson that the conflict is internal. Luke has the potential for darkness and Rey is complete in herself and prepared for heroism. No knight will intervene and rescue her; no mentor can hold her hand through it all. Kylo is correct; her combing the past for her biological heritage is pointless. The hero is alone, but strong enough to surmount the challenges. Far less important than her birth is her future—and that, she'll create for herself.

Having passed through the cave, she's strong enough to accept her shadow and stretches out a hand to Kylo Ren. The Force theme plays. They parallel—a single tear down her cheek resembles his new scar, emphasizing how they are chosen ones of light and dark—equal and opposite. (Kylo Ren's scar also strongly resembles Anakin's from *Revenge of the Sith*.)

Luke tears them apart, the father figure trying to protect her from the dark impulses that dwell within her. Rey, however, has lost faith in him. After Luke has shared his version, Kylo Ren shares his—of a frightened teenager startled out of sleep to find his mentor-uncle planning to murder him. Rey is appalled and demands of Luke, "Did you create Kylo Ren?" Here she discovers her teacher's terrible flaws. Once again, this is a traditional turning point for the heroine—discovering her father-figure is imperfect so she will have to save the galaxy herself.

This establishes that the heroine can save herself without cowering before the patriarchy. At the same time, this increases Rey's sympathy for Luke's victim. "You failed him by thinking his choice was made. There's still conflict in him," Rey insists.

Once more paralleling young Luke, she decides to go save Kylo Ren and turn him from the dark side. During their encounters, she's sensed good in him. Of course, pity is the most wrenching test for the heroine. "For fairytale heroines, the test is often to withstand pity—if the heroine turns from the path at every cry for help, she will never reach her goal" (Frankel, *Chosen One*). Clutching Luke's lightsaber in both hands, Rey climbs into the coffinlike escape pod off the Falcon and lets herself be blasted into oblivion, all so she can save the villain so similar to herself.

Visually, this resembles Snow White in her glass coffin. Clarissa Pinkola Estés adds, "While the metaphor of sleep can denote unconsciousness, here it symbolizes creation and renewal. Sleep is the symbol of rebirth" (151). Snow White's coffin is like a crucible, transforming her from frightened child into powerful queen. Within its clear casing, the heroine is perfectly protected as she grows from a child to a woman, or in this case, from a student to a warrior. This hibernation gives her time to develop. It also resembles General Leia's near-death and rebirth cycle as she floats through empty space. Rey is questing to become her—the self-sufficient leader and matriarch. "This is every girl's dream," fairytale expert Joan Gould writes. "To fall asleep at the beginning of adolescence.... When she's ready, she'll wake as a woman, her problems resolved, and the perfect man leaning over the bed" (106). Of course, Rey emerges to find Kylo Ren, in a dark parody of romance. Beside him waits a First Order guard with a pair of handcuffs. They take her into custody, and as Rey marches beside Ren, posture and dark outfits reflecting, she tries to turn him with faith and reason, just as Luke did Vader. Of course, she fails.

Ren escorts her into Snoke's throne room—the belly of the beast. Once again, Rey is trapped in the First Order stronghold, this time Snoke's flagship, the Mega Star Destroyer *Supremacy*. Of course, Snoke resembles the Great and Powerful Oz—all tyrannical expansiveness. Within the space, however, his bathrobelike clothing and scarred face reveal fragility. "He's physically weak, so he uses theatricality.... To some extent, he's consciously creating a purposefully dramatic space, as opposed to the Emperor's throne room, which was utilitarian," Johnson says (Szostak 96). She stands in the glaring red room, with Snoke in glittering gold on his all-black throne. He labels her "Young Rey," evoking the Emperor's "Young Skywalker." With this, Snoke explains that he bridged their minds and tempted Rey with compassion, presenting a wounded, needy Kylo and softening his feelings, making him vulnerable enough that Rey would try to save him. As Snoke reveals, it was all a trap and she has fallen for it. Pity has been her downfall.

When he schemes to kill Luke and then the Resistance survivors, Rey snatches Kylo's angry red lightsaber and attacks Snoke, who smirks that she's clearly "a true Jedi." He slams her around the room, mocking her with his total control over all aspects of her body. However, as he does, Kylo ignites Rey's gentler, forgotten lightsaber that lies beside Snoke and brutally bisects him. The apprentice has become the master. Snoke is revealed as an emperor with no clothes, a pair of legs sitting impotently on his throne. "It's time to let old things die," Kylo decides. He and Rey fight Snoke's soldiers side by side, emphasizing how well they would do as partners. "Like the anima, the animus does not merely consist of negative qualities such as brutality, recklessness, empty talk, and silent, obstinate, evil ideas. He too has a very positive and valuable side; he too can build a bridge to the Self through his creative activity" (Von Franz 193).

With the Praetorian guard vanquished, Rey moves to save what remains of the fleet. Here, however, Kylo crushes her hopes. He has taken Rey's side, but only to murder the all-powerful patriarch and *take his place.*

Kylo Ren is the new dark lord, and, as the Emperor and Vader both did, he offers Rey a place at his side. In this moment, Rey could rule the galaxy, be the center of everything instead of an ignored scavenger. Fires blaze around them, marking this place as a true crucible.

Further, the shadow traditionally offers uncomfortable truths. Ren forces Rey to face the truth of who she is, who her parents were. This echoes Vader's revelation in *Empire*, with the emphasis that the young hero has always known the reality but refused to accept it. Kylo speaks gently, even kindly, as he echoes her inner doubts. When Rey admits her secret fear, that they were nobody, he continues pressing the point. They were junk traders, dead now in the Jakku desert.

Johnson was given free rein to answer this question as he wished. As he explains, "I was thinking, what's the most powerful answer to that question? Powerful meaning: what's the hardest thing that Rey could hear? That's what you're after with challenging your characters." This revelation is wrenching for the heroine. "I think back to the 'I am your father' moment with Vader and Luke, and the reason I think that lands is not because it's a surprise or a twist but because it's the hardest thing Luke and thus the audience could hear at that moment." Of course, this reverses *Empire*— Luke believes he's the child of no one significant in the universe but finding he's the son of Vader destroys him. Likewise, Rey has been hoping for parents that will bring her a great destiny, special parents seeking her for all these years, and thus is stunned to discover they were no one and will never return for her.

"The easiest thing for Rey and the audience to hear is, Oh yeah, you're so-and-so's daughter. That would be wish fulfillment and instantly hand her a place in this story on a silver platter," Johnson adds. As he concludes, "The hardest thing for her is to hear she's not going to get that easy answer. Not only that, but Kylo is going to use the fact that you don't get that answer to try and weaken you so you have to lean on him…. You're going to have to find the strength to stand on your own two feet and define yourself in this story" (Breznican, "Last Jedi Spoiler Talk: Rey"). In this moment, as in the cave scene, she receives an epiphany, that she doesn't need a parental figure or special destiny to show her her worth. What matters are her choices, so she abandons Kylo Ren and instead uses her connection to the Force to save what remains of the Resistance. Rey summons her lightsaber and rejects the offer.

She and Ren struggle for her lightsaber, finally shattering it. With this, the legacy of Anakin Skywalker and all the weight of tradition bursts. Rey must make her own choices. Still, it's noteworthy that the crystal in it goes to her, choosing her as Jedi crystals always have their owners. She steals Snoke's escape pod and, broken lightsaber in hand, meets up with Chewie.

As the First Order blasts a hole in the Resistance's last stronghold, the Falcon rushes in with Rey reunited with Chewie and R2-D2 (and the porgs!). On the planet, just as the survivors are chasing the crystalline foxes toward an escape route, Rey does the same from above.

The vulptex foxes make crystalline tinkling when they run. They're mystical guardian animals from fairytales, offering spiritual enlightenment as well as hidden aid. Like the rebels, Rey follows the fox trail, up above in the light as they're in the darkness. There, Rey finds where the last Resistance fighters are escaping. Ironically, though Luke told her the Force is so much more than lifting rocks, Rey does lift the rocks and so leads the Resistance to escape, reuniting with and saving her friends. Light fills the rebels' faces as Rey unblocks the passage in a miraculous-looking moment and rescues them all. She has accomplished the heroine's quest, having faced darkness incarnate and come to terms with who she is.

Further, in the ship's cupboard, Finn finds the Jedi books from the temple. The Force's legacy will go on, even without one of the men remaining to tutor Rey. She can choose what to take from them, but she's fulfilled her goal and gained the Jedi teachings after all.

Based on the tests that make up the Jedi Trials (now demoted in canon, but not yet replaced or contradicted by the new materials), Rey has not mastered the necessary skills. These include dexterity and centering, but most importantly a greater trauma and triumph than she's had in her battles with Ren and Snoke. Also, since Luke is the titular last Jedi of the film, presumably Rey isn't quite a Jedi yet. As with the end of the first film, she's primed for more training, from working with Leia to reading the texts to becoming a new kind of Force wielder, using her abilities in ways millennia of patriarchy hadn't envisioned.

Rey's Rise

"When only one side of the personality is nurtured, the heroine's 'secret longing also to develop the other side within her still remains, and very often a kind of unsatisfied restlessness and depression overcome her'" (Von Franz, *Fairy Tales* 94). The classic warrior woman fights with masculine weapons and has a male mentor and a male nemesis. "However, after she's proven she can outdo men in the arena of sports, warfare, or business, when she's gained external power and success, the Warrior Woman feels a spiritual lack" (Frankel, *Buffy* 9). She's mastered fighting, but to understand the mysticism that is her legacy, tied to the feminine realm of the unconscious and darkness—all Luke warned her away from in *Last Jedi*— she needs a female mentor.

Rey begins *The Rise of Skywalker* training under Leia's supervision. At last, she has found a teacher who can help her understand her connection to the Force as well as the Resistance. "And maybe that's exactly what Rey needed: training in the Force not from a formal Master, but rather someone grounded in the everyday minutiae of life and survival," Leia thinks in the novelization (Carson 8). Further, she's determined not to give up on Rey as Anakin and Ben's teachers did them. As she decides, "She would not give in to fear—neither of the darkness rising within her pupil nor of her own questionable qualifications as a teacher. Most important, she would never send Rey away" (Carson 8). This unquestioning faith supports Rey, finally giving her a teacher willing to let her find her own path. Rey in turn acknowledges Leia as her trainer, calling her "master." At last, Rey has found a real mentor, the wise mother and general.

In this scene, Rey's look is "a blend of Jedi heritage, scavenger origins, and a touch of Alderaanian nobility to illustrate Leia's influence," as the visual guide puts it (Hidalgo and Terrio 189). She dresses in white, as initiate and channel for the light side of the Force. Daisy Johnson describes her character as feeling "confident, calm, less fearful." As she adds, "It's still sort of overwhelming, but in a different way. It feels more right—less like inevitable and more like there's a focus to the journey" (Grossman, "Tour de Force"). Meanwhile, her repeated call to all the Jedi of the past, "Be with me" shows how desperately she seeks connection and certainty. It goes unanswered. Leia counsels her to be patient, but she still can't find her path.

Rey has also clearly fixed the lightsaber shattered in the prior film. She tries the training course but switches from the inherited lightsaber to her old staff, clearly clinging to her former self as she's uncertain about the Jedi destiny. Taking on Luke's bequest feels jarring, unsuited. On the course, she fails when she sees Kylo Ren and visions of menacing darkness, including of herself as a Sith, Han's death, and Vader's skull. As she fumbles through excuses, Leia tries to reassure her, but Rey is still troubled. As she silently frets, "What would the general say if she knew how Rey's frustration and anger were triggering visions of death and dark power?" (Carson 14). On so many levels, she feels unworthy. She also sloppily tumbles a tree down on BB-8, revealing that her lack of foundation is putting those close to her in danger. When she discovers the damage she's caused, she panics. With this, she refuses yet another call. She hands back Luke's lightsaber to Leia, insisting on waiting to earn it.

The Jedi texts, Rey's talisman besides the lightsaber, are written in ancient languages she doesn't know. The droids can provide direct translations, but this sacrifices much nuance. The visual dictionary explains that this means she must explore her powers to access them: "She must trust her feelings when it comes to translating less concrete, more metaphysical concepts, of which there are many" (Hidalgo and Terrio 41). Thus, to understand these traditional talismans, she must look within for the wisdom that can be passed down to others.

Rey's friends continue to tug at her with their own obligations. On his return from a flashy mission, Poe tells her, "You're the best fighter we have. We need you out there, not here." This is the opposite of Luke's struggle in *Empire,* but Rey clings to the need to understand her place in the universe and connect with the Jedi legacy before going out and fighting. When the hero holds back, refusing the call, it comes to her directly. This call arrives with Poe's intel—that more planetary destruction is coming with the Emperor's resurrection: The largest fleet the galaxy has ever known is hiding on the planet Exegol and will attack in sixteen hours. Rey realizes from Luke's notes that they need a Sith wayfinder to get there.

Even in her uncertainty, she claims the mission and sets forth. She intends to bravely go alone, but her companions, all representing part of the self, insist on supporting her. Poe offers leadership; Finn, faith; C-3PO, caution; BB-8, curiosity; and Chewie, raw emotion. The characters are united in their mission with no traitors, serious deceptions, or even romantic entanglements. Finn's interest in Rey then Rose has faded, emphasizing a unity of purpose here. Leia, her mentor, returns the lightsaber, insisting she take it as a Jedi. With a final "Rey, never be afraid of who you are," Leia embraces her and emphasizes that she believes in the younger woman and loves her. This makes all the difference.

> As wisewoman or elder of the tribe, the mentor teaches spinning, singing, or magic to prepare her pupil for her ordeal…. Nowadays, our culture offers fewer mentors as teachers are overburdened with pupils and personal contact fades into emails and statistics. The mentor offers different wisdom than the parents, but wisdom that is no less valuable. However, to learn the most difficult lessons, the heroine must face a far crueler teacher [Frankel, *Girl to Goddess* 37].

This is a villain like Snoke, who tortures the heroine to the point of breaking in order to impart lessons. With Snoke dead, Kylo inherits the mentor role and continues reaching out. On the desert planet of Pasaana at a sprawling "Festival of the Ancestors," Rey sees happy children laughing at a puppet show and celebrating their ancestry among a massive tribe, and she's reminded of all she lacks. When a child at the festival asks her family name, Rey can only respond with her uncertainty. To her startlement, this triggers a glimpse of her family. Further, the festival turns shadowed, as Kylo connects with her and gives her vital information: He will turn her to the dark side. He suddenly rips off the beaded necklace that the child had given her. It's fragile, humble, and homemade, an image of Rey's primitive innocence. Up on his ship, he uses it to track her, wielding his overbearing might. At the same time, his glimpses of her fail to reveal her location, emphasizing her wariness and his own lack of sensitivity in the Force.

After battling First Order jet troopers in a speeder chase, the team fall through shifting sands into an underground cavern. This is the journey to the subconscious once more. "These journeys into darkness represent death—only by completely surrendering to the unknown can the heroine transcend her existence and learn the wisdom and magic of mortality" (Frankel, *Girl to Goddess* 124). It's also a graveyard, where they find the Sith Ochi, whom Luke and Lando had tracked, and a dagger bearing instructions. When Rey discovers that Luke was searching for the wayfinder before his death, she insists that she will "finish what he started." The line echoes Kylo Ren's pledge to his long-dead grandfather Darth Vader in *Force Awakens* that he will finish what Vader started and destroy the Jedi. Once more, the pair are linked.

In this underground world, they face a giant vexis snake, which Rey sympathetically heals of its injuries, even as Poe itches to shoot it. This encounter is particularly significant as snakes are a feminine symbol, generally linked to prophecy and identity:

> Snakes, or serpents, as they are often called in Greek myth, are also known for their transmutational power, which is exemplified in their ability to shed their skin. This life-death-rebirth cycle is the energy of wholeness and the ability to experience anything willingly and without resistance. It is the knowledge that those things which might be poisonous, hurtful or uncomfortable may be ingested, experienced, integrated and transmuted if one is in the proper state of mind … thereby producing divine, cohesive energy [Spencer 24].

When Kylo comes for them, Rey takes down his fighter with only her lightsaber, once more stressing her superiority. However, as they tug back and forth on a transport ship, which Rey thinks has taken Chewie prisoner, Force lightning bursts from her and the ship explodes. Fleeing with her friends, she's horrified. As she tells them, she lost control, not through Kylo's fault but through her own: "That power came from me. Finn, there are things you don't know.… I had a vision of the throne of the Sith, and who was on it." It was herself, ruling beside Kylo Ren. Even as she gains enlightenment, she can feel the pull of the dark side, and it disgusts her. As occurred with BB-8, she lacks control and her power is destroying her loved ones.

Upon discovering that Chewie survived, the team board Kylo Ren's star destroyer to rescue him. Distracted from the practical by the spiritual, Rey follows the summons of Ochi's dagger and finds her way to Kylo's quarters, where Darth Vader's twisted skull stands on a pedestal. There, in his most personal sanctum, amid his evil trophies, Kylo confronts her with her memories. "Remember them, see them," he tells her as she sees the vision of herself crying and alone from her first film. They duel (even from separate places as they are) until their swords shatter Vader's helmet and its dark legacy. More of his legacy must be torn down through the film, bit by bit. With this, Kylo offers Rey her most central need—knowledge of who she really is. This, the trilogy suggests, she can only find by exploring her dark side.

As he finally explains, "You don't just have power. You have *his* power. You're his granddaughter. You're a Palpatine." With this, he offers her his vision of their shared destiny: "We'll kill him together and take the throne." Abrams enjoys the parallels between the characters. "They also are, by definition, working on opposite sides of things," he adds. "And so the dichotomy of those characters is the thing that, for me, is most fascinating" (Breznican, "Reylo"). This moment confronts Rey with the same conflict Luke had—how to be a hero when she contains such potential for darkness. In fact, this revelation staggers her, encouraging her to let her shadow side reign.

Later, Rey resolves to find the Emperor and kill him, even as Finn, the gentle helper, protests that this doesn't sound like her. As she thinks, "A new Rey was rising inside her, struggling to break free." She wonders if the new Rey she's already found, one who can use the Force, is just "a skin to be shed. A temporary person" (Carson 149). Without a guide, she considers giving up out of despair. As they continue, Rey keeps darting off on her own missions, torn between her role on the team and her mission as solo hero. Many other heroines, having confronted so much darkness, have difficulty integrating it. They're restless, even hostile. Rey's inner struggle is turning outward, pleading for support and yet fearing rejection.

Meanwhile, her friends have arcs that echo her own. Threepio valiantly sacrifices himself, or at least his memories, to aid their mission against the Sith. Poe and Finn reach out in trust to heroines much like themselves, even as they struggle with leadership. Even BB-8 becomes a mentor. The one-wheel wonder D-0 rolls in as "the perfect little sandwich that fits between R2-D2 and BB-8," says creature and droid supervisor Neal Scanlan. "When BB-8 discovers D-0, it's almost like a mother and her duckling. D-0 imprints himself on BB-8. Wherever BB-8 goes, whatever mannerisms there are, D-0 tries to mimic" (Falcone et al.). With this, BB-8 learns to love a droid that once served evil. Rey must incorporate all these lessons into her own mission against the darkest force of all.

At last, Rey finds the crashed ruins of the Death Star, protruding from the ocean like a giant dark cathedral. Rey sails out to the wreck alone, though the rough ocean is far from her realm of experience. "The ways of water were terrifying and alien to her, and she knew she'd be facing her most unpredictable enemy yet," the novelization explains (Carson 164). Inside, empty Stormtrooper armor lies scattered like corpses picked clean. This is a toxic place destroying the natural world, as the visual dictionary establishes, as "each year millions of tons of industrial toxins seep into the oceans" (Hidalgo and Terrio 168).

"As Rey climbs her way through the debris and nears her objective, she hears the presence of the dark side, and her connection to the Force once again shows her haunting images of a terrifying future" (Hidalgo and Terrio 169). In the throne room where Vader killed Sidious, she sees herself in a mirror and a Sith version appears. "Don't be afraid of who you are," Dark Rey tells her. They duel. This is the moment at which Rey must face the true shadow—not Kylo, but her own impulses. This is who she could be as Empress Palpatine, with hood, sharpened teeth, and double-bladed saber. This potential dwells within. Demetra George writes in *Mysteries of the Dark Moon: The Healing Power of the Dark Goddess*: "The Dark Goddess forces us to look at ourselves with utter, naked honesty. For many of us, this is very frightening—to see ourselves stripped of our illusions and false pretensions … when we go down into the darkness, we must cast away all that is not true about ourselves and our lives" (230). Rey must acknowledge the impulses she's been fighting—to be angry, savage, powerful. Such ugliness repels her.

However, Kylo arrives and perceives her conflict: "Look at yourself. You want to prove to my mother that you were a Jedi, but you've proven something else. The dark side is in our nature. Surrender to it." He smashes the wayfinder so she'll work with him. In the novelization, Kylo gloats over her dark side encounter. He insists that by accepting and welcoming it, she's tainted. In fact, he tells her that aware of her inner darkness as she is now, Leia will never take either of them back. He believes they're both unredeemable now. However, Rey thinks, "He was wrong. Her darkest self had told her not to be afraid of who she was. But so had Leia. Leia knew. And she had still chosen to train her" (Carson 168). Knowledge of her mentor's faith in her gives her the strength for self-acceptance.

As they battle with lightsabers beside the ocean, all suddenly goes still and quiet. "Ben," Leia says, and collapses. Rey wins the battle, impaling Kylo. She too feels this matronly mentor reaching out in love and concern. "Leia." She channels Leia, doing what the other woman wishes and also acting out of sympathy and care for the twisted young man who's fallen so far. She places a hand on his wound and heals him.

Beauty and the Beast stories invariably end with the heroine finding the beast's humanity. "The princess must eventually have children, and not beastly ones. She must have a proper society husband with a steady job, a good provider, one who can appear at the country club. In other words, when the honeymoon ends, she needs Prince Charming on her arm, and not the ferocious beast" (Frankel, *Girl to Goddess* 83). Thus, Kylo's redemption is a traditional step in Rey's story, as she turns her shapechanging love from monster to man. He hurls away his mask and lightsaber, reclaiming his identity as Ben. Leia sacrifices herself in the process, and Rey loses yet another mentor.

Afterwards, frightened by the darkness within herself, Rey flies to Ahch-To. With her white hood up, she resembles Luke—the Jedi monk who turned his back on the Resistance as well as the universe. She burns her ship and hurls the lightsaber into the fire as well, definitively wiping out her option of returning and all the gifts of the Jedi, all the legacy she'd hoped to inherit. This, she hopes, will leave her no choice but isolation. "The whole of *Star Wars* is about good and evil," Daisy Ridley says. "With every character, you see some struggle…. It's the most human thing to see someone struggle with two things within them that are pulling them both ways" (Shepherd 56). Here, she prays that she's ended the struggle.

Luke's ghost suddenly catches the saber and jokes that "a Jedi's weapon deserves more respect." Of course, this is a callback to his throwing it away in the previous film. He tells her that his own fear kept him on Ahch-To and listens to Rey's similar panic at the darkness she carries. Acting as a sympathetic mentor at last, he tells her that he and Leia knew this, but after they met her and saw how she always chose the light, they both trained her. This moment helps her see that her destiny is not based in her biology but her choices. As he adds, "Some things are stronger than blood."

To end the war and free herself from this dark past, she must confront Palpatine. For this, Luke gives her a tool—Leia's lightsaber that represents her own claiming of the Jedi legacy—inheriting the self-created feminine legacy rather than the Vader one. As mentor, Luke can support her, but he cannot take on her destiny. He tells her, "We've passed on all we know. A thousand generations live in you now. But this is your fight." She must complete the journey. "You have everything you need," he concludes, and raises his own X-Wing from the water. She has his lightsaber, but also his callsign and codes as Red Five, accepting this heritage and finishing his battle against the Emperor's planet destroyers that have appeared throughout his reign. He represents death while she resurrects the ragtag Rebellion to defy him.

Her friends go to war, gathering from throughout the galaxy to face the forces of darkness. Sith troopers wear red now, with fleet techs in black and red. All this symbolizes the darkness and violence they've embraced. All their ships are armed with weapons that can destroy inhabited worlds— their victory will mean the death of planets everywhere.

At the great battle at the end, Rey descends into the heart of the Sith planet Exegol. Many camera angles and lines echo Luke's facing the Empire in *Return of the Jedi,* of course. Within, she finds a crowd of Sith ghosts gathered in an amphitheater, in a setup darkly reminiscent of the senate chamber scenes in the prequel trilogy. This is the Sith lord's ultimate throne room, the unconscious reflection of his external power as Emperor.

Palpatine is the solution to Rey's mysterious past and the death of her parents. With this, he represents the weight of the past. He's the old guard, the ancient enemy that destroyed all four of the Skywalker parents, and the power that kept the galaxy in unchanging tyranny. All this, Rey must banish for the young generation to move forward.

The tyrant starts trying to goad Rey into striking him down in anger (as he did with Luke in *Jedi*) and tells her that once she does, the power of every Sith that has ever lived will enter her. With this, she will become the avatar of evil. "Kill me and all the Sith pass into you…. You will be empress. We will be one," the Emperor gloats. "Strike me down, take the throne." Power doesn't tempt her, but her friends' lives do. However, the new family he threatens are not just the Resistance but Ben, who arrives during his mocking words. They see each other across space. For the first time, they're allies, both committed to the light. Rey thinks, "It felt different now. The connection was … right. Good. Like coming home" (Carson 221).

She fights with Leia's lightsaber: This fulfills Leia's belief that someone else would pick it up when the time was right. At the same time, using their bond, Rey transfers Luke's to Ben, including him in the legacy and fighting beside him like twins. Their shared connection lets them function in ways never before seen in the franchise as they share a unique connection. Further, they're fighting to end galactic mass murder. "Using the Force to accomplish the impossible is a delightful metaphor (repeated through the stories) for making a conscious, aligned connection to life amidst its vicissitudes" (Galipeau 93).

The Emperor drains both young heroes, gloating about, as he puts it, "the lifeforce of your bond." In fact, it is so life-filled that it heals his wounded hands, restoring him to strength. This emphasizes their roles of champions of light and darkness. The matched heroes stagger under his attack. He hurls Ben down into the chasm, and Rey collapses. As she gazes up, his Force lightning attacks all the Resistance fleet. The entire galaxy, representing Rey's self, is being torn apart. A tear rolls down Rey's cheek as she lies in the darkest place of all, alone and defeated. This is the true initiation. Still, she has faith. "Be with me."

The Jedi of the past respond, filling her and confirming that they will always support her. Rey hears many voices that confirm her legacy while also waving to the fans. There's Yoda (Frank Oz), Anakin (Hayden Christensen), Mace Windu (Samuel L. Jackson), Qui-Gon (Liam Neeson), and both Ewan McGregor and Alec Guinness as Obi-Wan. There are also Jedi from the animated universe: Ahsoka Tano (Ashley Eckstein). Luminara

Unduli (Olivia D'Abo), Aayla Secura (Jennifer Hale), Adi Gallia (Angelique Perrin), and Kanan Jarrus (Freddie Prinze, Jr.).

Filled with their goodness and strength, Rey is prepared to fight. Palpatine declares that he is every Sith and Rey responds, "And I am every Jedi," before jettisoning his own lightning back at him. Palpatine hurls more lightning at his granddaughter, but Rey deflects it at him with both lightsabers, wielding them in concert in a symbolic unity of purpose. This shatters the Emperor and finally disintegrates him.

Rey collapses from the power she has channeled, and lies, eyes wide open, dead. This descent into true death suggests the ending of her old role. Is she prepared to be a true Jedi, wielding the Force and defending the galaxy? Even in her greatest triumph, she isn't ready for the shattering power of adulthood. Gould explains, "The princess isn't strong enough to face transformation yet. But she can't resist or avoid it either…." (105–106) Thus, the heroine sinks into a temporary "death." Her old self must perish in order for a new, stronger personality to spring forth.

A hand dramatically appears at the edge of the chasm and an injured Ben pulls himself up. He drops to his knees besides Rey and pulls her dead body into his lap. Ben represents the tiny helper like Snow White's dwarves, the heroine's agency even when she appears lost. With this, he gives his own life to restore her from death. This moment echoes the most ancient mythic patterns, in which the goddess reigned eternal, while young male god or hero died each year.

> The female deity was lover and mother combined, but did not enact the inferior role of a daughter. Her consort, by contrast, was son, lover, and husband all as one. He died periodically, sometimes because of her wrath, while she reigned eternal. As Merlin Stone notes, "The male chosen held his royal rights for a specific period of time. At the end of this time … this youth was then ritually sacrificed." This reinforced the temporary nature of the king, and the permanent rulership of the queen [Frankel, *Girl to Goddess* 250].

Thanks to Ben's act, Rey returns from her underworld journey with a new certainty about her place in the world, as the new inheritor of the Jedi legacy. She has accepted her heritage of darkness and, trusted by the Jedi, has chosen life and light. "The heroine completes her journey by mastering this knowledge, incorporating the death-energies of the underworld into herself and acknowledging their glory. Only thus can she merge with the cycle of life, growing gracefully into mother and wisewoman without fearing death" (Frankel, *Girl to Goddess* 172). Further, such a battle with the Sith and grievous injury has ascended her to the Jedi ranks. Having faced death, Rey incorporates as a mature woman who no longer fears it. Further, she has integrated Palpatine's legacy and the Jedis' wisdom. Now she is whole.

After the Resistance celebration, Rey visits the Lars homestead on

Tatooine, where she slides down a dune (nodding to her younger self) and buries the Skywalker lightsabers in the sand. She wishes to create herself as a new kind of Jedi unbound by the past.

Her new black-handled lightsaber with a yellow blade appears fashioned from her beloved staff. It casts her as a rarer type of Jedi, moving past Luke and Leia's heritage. Symbolically speaking, yellow can mean the higher thought of the sun and saffron-robed monks. Gold in alchemy represents a pinnacle and perfection. In the *Star Wars* Expanded Universe, yellow lightsabers were most often wielded by the Sentinels, who led a middle way within the Jedi Order: While Consulars with green lightsabers emphasized the power of diplomacy and the Guardians with blue fought most fiercely, Sentinels combined some of each. They also valued technical knowledge rather than solving all their problems with the Force. For Rey, who takes some traditions from the Jedi but also wants to construct some new ones, this is a logical path. More particularly, when the ancient Jedi Jaden Korr purified a red lightsaber crystal, it turned yellow. Just as Rey brought Kylo Ren back to his old self, she is seen purging the evil from the universe. In fact, in *Star Wars* dictionaries and guides, pictures of crossed red and green blades often look yellow at their juncture, suggesting a blend of light and dark.

Women caught between Jedi and Sith and abandoned by both like Asajj Ventress and Ahsoka from the animated universe have also wielded this lightsaber color. Ahsoka finally gets white lightsabers, defining her as a Force user who refuses to choose a side in the constant battle. In this tradition, the film's novelization describes Rey's as "white-gold" and adds, "the final result felt like the exact inverse of the lightsaber held by the dark Rey of her vision and she *loved* it" (Carson 246). Suggestively, Rey has chosen to be a Jedi, but one of balance—having accepted her own darkness, she will comfort people claimed by the dark side, love them and redeem them.

A local woman asks her name and, as she perceives the twin Force ghosts of Luke and Leia there, blessing her new path, Rey calls herself "Rey Skywalker." She's undergone a three-film search for identity and at last she's found her family. Choosing one's name of course indicate the path one wishes, in this case casting off the Palpatine legacy. By Rey's claiming this name through the Skywalkers' mentorship, the series abandons the insistence on lineage as the cause of greatness. As the stablehand with the broom showed at the end of *Last Jedi*, anyone can be a hero. Further, anyone can be a Skywalker.

This indeed is her origin story, the "Rise of Skywalker." With this, Rey and BB-8 gaze at the twin suns of Tatooine as they rise. Winning her battle with her evil legacy and dark potential has truly made Rey not only a Skywalker but a hero.

Conclusion

Star Wars' effect on science fiction, filmmaking, and hero's journey stories cannot be overstated. It was so beloved at its release that it went on to be a measuring stick, as well as a template, for so many other franchises and fandoms. Dean Devlin, one of the creators of *Independence Day*, explains: "To me, *Star Wars* was like the *Sgt. Pepper's Lonely Hearts Club Band* of movies. You know how people like David Bowie say that that was the album that made them see what was possible in pop music? I think *Star Wars* did the same thing for popcorn movies. It made you see what was possible." He adds that is became a personal inspiration: "*Star Wars* was the movie that made me say, 'I want to do something like that'" (Seabrook). *Phantom Menace* broke ground as well, with more CGI settings and characters than had ever been seen in one film. Scriptwriter Lawrence Kasdan adds that the original trilogy created many standards, including an action beat every ten minutes. He explains:

> *Star Wars* was a serious breakthrough, a shift in the culture, which was possible only because George was this weird character…. After you saw it, you thought, My God, anything is possible. He opened up people's minds. I mean, the amazing thing about cinema technology is that it hasn't changed since it started. It's mind-boggling. With all these changes in technology, and the computer, we're still pulling this little piece of plastic through a machine and shining light through it. Very few directors change things. Welles did things differently. But everything is different after *Star Wars* [Seabrook].

As the franchise continues, it's expanding into different mediums. The successful cartoons *Clone Wars, Forces of Destiny,* and *Rebels* are now being followed by *Resistance*. The computer games are multiplying, and two theme park lands have finally arrived with Galaxy's Edge. Disney+ launched a few weeks before *The Rise of Skywalker* with *The Mandalorian*, a show beloved for its simple frontier action. Next comes *Kenobi* and the Cassian Andor show, which, like the cartoons, will likely show an awareness that the death and rebirth cycle is one of the most beloved ways to storytell.

Of course, all the competing franchises of the decade are not only following the young white male's quest but bringing in epic heroines and minority questors of all sorts. *The Avengers* has followed Black Panther and Captain Marvel on their central epics to growth and heroism, while also exploring many heroes growing side by side. DC films follow Wonder Woman, Harley Quinn, Aquaman and Cyborg, while television's Arrowverse offers *Supergirl, Black Lightning, Batwoman*, and the *Legends of Tomorrow*. Disney offers heroines seeking enlightenment but not marriage in *Frozen, Moana,* and *Frozen II*. There are so many more: *Hunger Games, Spider-Man: Into the Spiderverse, Men in Black, Star Trek, Doctor Who*—all are diversifying film and television to explore what's really possible. In a new fourth-wave era, the spotlight is focusing on new kinds of heroes to bring new kinds of journeys to center stage. Through it all, *Star Wars* continues setting the model.

Works Cited

Primary Sources

Aaron, Jason, and John Cassaday. *Star Wars Vol. 1: Skywalker Strikes*. Marvel, 2015.

Aaron, Jason, and Stuart Immonen. *Star Wars Vol. 2: Showdown on the Smuggler's Moon*. Marvel, 2016.

Aaron, Jason, et al. *Star Wars Vol. 4: Last Flight of the Harbinger*. Marvel, 2016.

Barlow, Jeremy, and Daxiong. *Boba Fett and the Ship of Fear*. Disney Lucasfilm, 2011.

Barlow, Jeremy, and Juan Frigeri. *Darth Maul: Son of Dathomir*. Disney Luscasfilm, 2017.

Barnes, Rodney, and Paolo Villanelli. *Lando: Double or Nothing*. Marvel, 2018.

Bouzereau, Laurent, editor. *The Annotated Screenplays: Star Wars—A New Hope, the Empire Strikes Back, Return of the Jedi*. Ballantine Books, 1997.

Brooks, Terry. *Star Wars Episode One: The Phantom Menace*. Del Rey, 1999.

Bunn, Cullen, and Luke Ross. *Darth Maul*. Disney Lucasfilm, 2017.

Carson, Rae. "The Red One." *From a Certain Point of View*. Disney Lucasfilm Press, 2017, pp. 59–68.

_____. *The Rise of Skywalker: Expanded Edition*. Del Rey, 2020.

Castellucci, Cecil, and Jason Fry. *Moving Target: A Princess Leia Adventure*. Disney Lucasfilm Press, 2015.

Foster, Alan Dean. *The Force Awakens*. LucasBooks, 2015.

_____. *Splinter of the Mind's Eye*. Del Rey, 1978.

Freed, Alexander. *Rogue One: A Star Wars Story*. Del Rey, 2016.

Fry, Jason. *The Last Jedi*. Del Rey, 2018.

_____. *Rey's Survival Guide*. Reader's Digest, 2015.

_____. *Rogue One Rebel Dossier*. Disney Lucasfilm Press, 2016.

_____. *The Weapon of a Jedi: A Luke Skywalker Adventure*. Disney Lucasfilm Press, 2015.

Gillen, Kieron, and Leinil Yu. *Darth Vader: The Shu-Torun War*. Marvel, 2016.

Gillen, Kieron, and Salvador Larroca. *Darth Vader Vol. 2: Shadows and Secrets*. Marvel, 2016.

_____, and _____. *Darth Vader Vol. 4: End of Games*. Marvel, 2016.

Gillen, Kieron, Salvador Larroca, and Adi Granov. *Darth Vader Vol. 1: Vader*. Marvel, 2015.

Glut, Donald F. *The Empire Strikes Back*. the *Star Wars Trilogy*. 1980. Del Rey, 1995, pp. 193–346.

Gray, Claudia. *Bloodline*. Del Rey, 2016.

_____. *Leia, Princess of Alderaan*. Disney Lucasfilm Press, 2017.

_____. "Master and Apprentice." *From a Certain Point of View*. Disney Lucasfilm Press, 2017, pp. 81–87.

_____. *Master and Apprentice*. Del Rey, 2019.

Johnston, E.K. *Queen's Shadow*. Lucasfilm Press, 2019.

Kahn, James. *Return of the Jedi*. the *Star Wars Trilogy*. 1983. Del Rey, 1995, pp. 349–501.

Kinberg, Simon, Carrie Beck, and Dave Filoni, creators. *Star Wars: Rebels*. Lucasfilm, 2014–2018.

Lafferty, Mur. *Solo: A Star Wars Story Expanded Edition*. Del Rey, 2018.

Lucas, George. *A New Hope*. the *Star Wars Trilogy*. 1976. Del Rey, 1995, pp. 6–188.

Lucas, George, and Catherine Winder, creators. *Star Wars: The Clone Wars*. Lucasfilm, 2008–2015.

Luceno, James. *Catalyst: A Rogue One Novel*. Del Rey, 2016.

_____. *Dark Lord: The Rise of Darth Vader. Star Wars: The Dark Lord Trilogy.* Del Rey, 2005, pp. 775–1094.

_____. *Darth Plagueis.* Ballantine Books, 2012.

_____. *Labyrinth of Evil. Star Wars: The Dark Lord Trilogy.* Del Rey, 2005, pp. 5–354.

_____. *Tarkin.* Del Rey, 2014.

Moran, Daniel Keyes. "The Last One Standing: The Tale of Boba Fett." *Tales of the Bounty Hunters,* edited by Kevin J. Anderson. Bantam, 1996, pp. 277–339.

Noto, Phil. *Before the Awakening.* Disney Lucasfilm Press, 2015.

Okorafor, Nnedi. "The Baptist." *From a Certain Point of View.* Disney Lucasfilm Press, 2017, pp. 317–331.

Perry, Steve. *Shadows of the Empire.* Del Rey, 1996.

Revis, Beth. *Rebel Rising.* Disney Lucasfilm Press, 2017.

Roanhorse, Rebecca. *Resistance Reborn.* Del Rey, 2019.

Rogue One: A Star Wars Story. Directed by Gareth Edwards. Disney Studios, 2016.

Rucka, Greg. *Before the Awakening.* Disney Lucasfilm Press, 2015.

_____. *Guardians of the Whills.* Disney Lucasfilm Press, 2017.

Rucka, Greg, Marco Checchetto, and Phil Noto. *Journey to Star Wars: The Force Awakens—Shattered Empire.* Marvel, 2015.

Salvatore, R.A. *Attack of the Clones.* Del Rey, 2002.

Schmidt, Gary D. "There Is Another." *From a Certain Point of View.* Disney Lucasfilm Press, 2017, pp. 349–360.

Scott, Cavan. *Dooku: Jedi Lost.* Del Rey, 2019.

_____. "Time of Death" *From a Certain Point of View.* Disney Lucasfilm Press, 2017, pp. 333–347.

Smith, L. Neil. *The Lando Calrissian Adventures.* Del Rey, 1983.

Solo: A Star Wars Story. Directed by Ron Howard. Disney Studios, 2018.

Soule, Charles, and Giuseppe Camuncoli. *Darth Vader: Dark Lord of the Sith: Fortress Vader.* Disney Lucasfilm, 2017.

_____. *Darth Vader: Dark Lord of the Sith: Legacy's End.* Disney Lucasfilm, 2018.

_____. *Darth Vader: Dark Lord of the Sith: Imperial Machine.* Disney Lucasfilm, 2018.

Soule, Charles, and Will Sliney. *The Rise of Kylo Ren.* Marvel, 2020.

Star Wars: Episode I—The Phantom Menace. Directed by George Lucas, performances by Liam Neeson. Ewan McGregor. Jake Lloyd. Natalie Portman. Ian McDiarmid, 20th Century Fox, 1999.

Star Wars: Episode II—Attack of the Clones. Directed by George Lucas, performances by Hayden Christensen. Natalie Portman. Ewan McGregor. Ian McDiarmid. Christopher Lee. Jimmy Smits, 20th Century Fox, 2002.

Star Wars: Episode III—Revenge of the Sith. Directed by George Lucas, performances by Hayden Christensen. Natalie Portman. Ewan McGregor. Ian McDiarmid. Jimmy Smits, 20th Century Fox, 2005.

Star Wars: Episode IV—A New Hope. Directed by George Lucas, performances by Mark Hamill. Carrie Fisher. Harrison Ford. Alec Guinness. Peter Cushing, 20th Century Fox, 1977.

Star Wars: Episode V—The Empire Strikes Back. Directed by Irvin Kershner, performances by Mark Hamill. James Earl Jones. Carrie Fisher. Harrison Ford. Billy Dee Williams, 20th Century Fox, 1980.

Star Wars: Episode VI—Return of the Jedi. Directed by George Lucas, performances by Mark Hamill. Harrison Ford. Ian McDiarmid. Billy Dee Williams. Carrie Fisher, 20th Century Fox, 1983.

Star Wars: Episode VII—The Force Awakens. Directed by J.J. Abrams. Disney Studios, 2016.

Star Wars Episode VIII—The Last Jedi. Directed by Rian Johnson. Walt Disney Studios, 2018. DVD.

Star Wars: Episode IX—The Rise of Skywalker. Directed by J.J. Abrams. Disney Studios, 2019.

Stover, Matthew. *Revenge of the Sith.* Random House, 2005.

_____. *Shatterpoint.* Del Rey, 2003.

Traviss, Karen. *The Clone Wars.* Random House, 2008.

Veitch, Tom, and Cam Kennedy. *Dark Empire I.* Dark Horse, 2003.

Waid, Mark, and Terry Dodson. *Princess Leia.* Marvel, 2015.

Wallace, Daniel. *Book of Sith.* Becker & Mayer Press; 2015,.

_____. *Imperial Handbook: A Commander's Guide.* Disney Lucasfilm, 2015.

_____. *The Jedi Path.* Chronicle Books, 2015.

Wallace, Daniel, Ryder Windham, and

Jason Fry. *The Bounty Hunter Code.* Chronicle Books, 2013.
Wendig, Chuck. *Aftermath: Empire's End.* Del Rey, 2017.
Wrede, Patricia C. *Star Wars Episode I: The Phantom Menace.* Scholastic, 1999.
Zahn, Timothy. *Dark Force Rising.* Del Rey, 1992.

Secondary Sources

Abrams, J.J. "Why Leia Didn't Become a Jedi." *IGN,* 7 Dec 2015. Online video http://www.ign.com/videos/2015/12/07/star-wars-the-force-awakens-why-leia-didnt-become-a-jedi.
Alinger, Brandon. *Star Wars Costumes: The Original Trilogy.* Chronicle Books, 2014.
Anders, Lou. "Novels, Novelizations and Tie-ins, Oh My." Brin and Stover, pp. 137–144.
Anderson, Jenna. "*Star Wars: The Last Jedi* Director Says Adam Driver Wasn't Shy About Shirtless Scene." *Comicbook.com,* 24 Dec 2017. http://comicbook.com/starwars/2017/12/24/star-wars-the-last-jedi-kylo-ren-shirtless-scene-rian-johnson/
Anderton, Ethan. "Ewan McGregor, Alec Guiness and Frank Oz Are All in *Star Wars: The Force Awakens.*" *SlashFilm,* 20 Dec 2015. http://www.slashfilm.com/you-can-hear-alec-guinness-and-ewan-mcgregor-in-the-force-awakens.
Ankers, Adelle. "*Star Wars*: Carrie Fisher's Leia Organa Was Originally Going to Be the 'Last Jedi' in *The Rise of Skywalker.*" *IGN,* 7 Nov 2019 https://www.ign.com/articles/2019/11/07/star-wars-carrie-fishers-leia-organa-was-originally-going-to-be-the-last-jedi-in-the-rise-of-skywalker.
Arp, Robert. "'If Droids Could Think…': Droids as Slaves and Persons." Decker and Eberl, pp. 125–133.
Asher-Perrin, Emily. "Where Did the Name 'Millennium Falcon' Come From, Anyway?" *Tor.com,* 27 Sept 2017. https://www.tor.com/2017/09/27/where-did-the-name-millennium-falcon-come-from-anyway.
Ashworth, Jeff, ed. *Star Wars the Force Awakens: The Official Collector's Edition.* Learner Publishing Group, 2015.
"Author to Author." *Star Wars Insider 2018 Special Edition,* pp. 32–38.
Barad, Judith. "The Aspiring Jedi's Handbook of Virtue." Decker and Eberl, pp. 57–68.
Barr, Tricia. "Han Solo: A Hero's Journey." *Best of Star Wars Insider 2,* Titan Books, 2016, pp. 4–13.
_____. "Luke Skywalker: The Wizard's Journey." *Star Wars Insider* 2020 Special Edition, pp. 117–121.
"BB-8." *People Special Star Wars: The Force Awakens Edition,* Dec 2015, p. 63.
Beecroft, Simon. *Inside the Worlds of Star Wars: Attack of the Clones.* DK Publishing, 2003.
"Ben Mendelsohn." *People, 2016 Special Star Wars Edition,* p. 44. EBSCOhost.
Bennett, Tara. "Middle Man: Rian Johnson Guides the Iconic Characters Through the Second Installment of Their Journey in *Star Wars: The Last Jedi.*" *Scifi* 23, no. 6, Dec 2017, pp. 35–37.
Biggar, Trisha. *Dressing a Galaxy: The Costumes of Star Wars.* Abrams Books, 2005.
"Billie Lourd." *People Special Star Wars: The Force Awakens Edition,* Dec 2015, p. 52.
Bissell, Tom. "Pale Starship, Pale Rider: The Ambiguous Appeal of Boba Fett." Kenny, pp. 10–40.
Bodden, Valerie. *How to Analyze the Films of George Lucas.* Abdo Publishing, 2012.
Bray, Adam, Cole Horton, Michael Kogge, and Kerrie Dougherty. *Star Wars Absolutely Everything You Need to Know.* DK Publishing, 2015.
Breznican, Anthony. "Going Rogue." *Entertainment Weekly,* no. 1421, 1 July 2016, pp. 18–24. EBSCOhost.
_____. "J.J. Abrams on Kylo Ren's Shocking Act in *Star Wars: The Force Awakens.*" *Entertainment Weekly,* 21 Dec 2015. https://ew.com/article/2015/12/21/jj-abrams-kylo-ren-shocking-act-star-wars-force-awakens.
_____. "*The Last Jedi* Spoiler Talk: Did Rey Learn the Truth About Herself?" *Entertainment Weekly,* 16 Dec, 2017. http://ew.com/movies/2017/12/16/the-last-jedi-spoiler-rey-parents.
_____. "*The Last Jedi* Spoiler Talk: Mark Hamill Discusses the Secrets of Luke Skywalker's Return." *Entertainment Weekly,* 16 Dec, 2017. http://ew.com/movies/2017/12/16/the-last-jedi-spoilers-rian-johnson-mark-hamill-luke-skywalker-revelations.
_____. "*The Last Jedi* Spoiler Talk: Rey."

Entertainment Weekly, 16 Dec 2017. http://ew.com/movies/2017/12/16/the-last-jedi-spoiler-rey-parents/.

_____. "The Reylo Connection: How Rey and Kylo Ren Make Each Other Stronger." *Vanity Fair*, 3 Dec 2019. https://www.vanityfair.com/hollywood/2019/12/reylo.

_____. "*Rogue One*: Felicity Jones on the Importance of Female Heroes." *Entertainment Weekly*, 12 Aug 2016. http://ew.com/article/2016/08/12/rogue-one-felicity-jones-importance-women-rebellion.

_____. "*Star Wars: Rogue One* Director Reveals New Details on Force-sacred World Jedha." *Entertainment Weekly*, 8 Aug 2016. http://ew.com/article/2016/08/08/star-wars-rogue-one-force-sacred-world-jedha-details.

_____. "*Star Wars: The Force Awakens*: J.J. Abrams Reveals Backstory of Alien Maz Kanata." *Entertainment Weekly*, 11 Dec 2015. Http://www.ew.com/article/2015/11/12/star-wars-force-awakens-lupita-nyongo-maz-kanata.

_____. "When Light Falls. (cover Story)." *Entertainment Weekly* No. 1492, P. 22. MasterFILE Premier, EBSCOhost.

Brin, David, and Matthew Woodring Stover. *Star Wars on Trial: Science Fiction and Fantasy Writers Debate the Most Popular Science Fiction Films of All Time*. Smart Pop. 2006.

Brooks, Dan. "We Had Such a Great Time: Rian Johnson on the Path of *Star Wars the Last Jedi*." *Starwars.com*, 11 Dec 2017 http://www.starwars.com/news/we-had-such-a-great-time-rian-johnson-on-the-path-to-star-wars-the-last-jedi.

Brown, Christopher M. "'A Wretched Hive of Scum and Villainy': *Star Wars* and the Problem of Evil." Decker and Eberl, pp. 78–88.

Bruce-Mitford, Miranda. *The Illustrated Book of Signs and Symbols*. DK Publishing, 1996.

Burt, Kayti. "Toxic Masculinity Is the True Villain of *Star Wars: The Last Jedi*." *Den of Geek*, 15 Dec 2017. http://www.denofgeek.com/us/movies/star-wars/269657/toxic-masculinity-is-the-true-villain-of-star-wars-the-last-jedi.

Campbell, Joseph. *The Hero with a Thousand Faces*. Princeton University Press, 1973.

_____. *The Hero's Journey*. Harper & Row, 1990.

_____. *Pathways to Bliss: Mythology and Personal Transformation*. New World Library, 2004.

Campbell, Joseph, with Bill Moyers, *The Power of Myth*, edited by Betty Sue Flowers, Doubleday, 1988.

Chitwood, Adam. "The Mandalorian Composer Ludwig Göransson on Why Scoring Baby Yoda Was a Huge Challenge." *Collider*, 29 Nov 2019. https://collider.com/the-mandalorian-interview-ludwig-goransson.

"The Chosen One Featurette." *Revenge of the Sith*, produced by George Lucas, 20th Century Fox, 2005.

Cirlot, J.E. *A Dictionary of Symbols*. Dover Publications, 2002.

Cooper, J.C. *An Illustrated Encyclopedia of Traditional Symbols*. Thames and Hudson, 1978.

Dees, Richard H. "Moral Ambiguity in a Black-and-White Universe." Decker and Eberl, pp. 51–63.

Dictionary of Symbols. Penguin, 1994.

Eberl, Jason T. "'You Cannot Escape Your Destiny' (Or Can You?): Freedom and Predestination in the Skywalker Family." Eberl and Decker, pp. 17–27.

Eberl, Jason T., and Kevin S. Decker, editors. *The Ultimate Star Wars and Philosophy*. Wiley Blackwell, 2016.

Estés, Clarissa Pinkola. *Women Who Run with the Wolves*. Ballantine Books, 1992.

Falcone, Dana Rose, Jodi Guglielmi, Chris Tauber, and Kara Warner. "Goodbye to the Galaxy (Far Far Away)." *People*, vol. 92, no. 25, 16 Dec 2019.

"50 Greatest Reasons to Love the Prequels." *Best of Star Wars Insider 3*, Titan Books, 2016, pp. 144–155.

Foxwell, Chris. "Darth Maul: Less Is Best." *The Force.net*, 26 Aug 2000. http://www.theforce.net/rouser/essays/drizzt.asp.

Frankel, Valerie Estelle. *Buffy and the Heroine's Journey*. McFarland, 2012.

_____. *Chosen One: The Heroine's Journey of Katniss, Elsa, Tris, Bella, and Rey*. LitCrit Press, 2016.

_____. *From Girl to Goddess: The Heroine's Journey Through Myth and Legend*. McFarland, 2010.

_____. *The Many Faces of Katniss Everdeen: Exploring the Heroine of the Hunger Games*. Winged Lion Press, 2013.

———. *Star Wars Meets the Eras of Feminism: Weighing All the Galaxy's Women Great and Small*. Lexington, 2019.

Galipeau, Stephen A. *The Journey of Luke Skywalker: An Analysis of Modern Myth and Symbol*. Open Court, 2001.

George, Demetra. *Mysteries of the Dark Moon: The Healing Power of the Dark Goddess*, HarperCollins, 1992.

Gould, Joan. *Spinning Straw Into Gold*. Random House, 2005.

Grossman, Lev. "The Reboot: How J.J. Abrams Revived Star Wars Puppets, Greebles, and Yak Hair." *Time Special Edition: Star Wars 40 Years of the Force*, 2017, pp. 51–61.

Grossman, Lev, "Tour de Force." *Vanity Fair*, vol. 61, no. 7, Summer 2019. MasterFILE Complete.

Hall, Jacob. "*The Last Jedi* Doesn't Care What You Think About *Star Wars*—And That's Why It's Great." *Slash Film*, 15 Dec 2017. http://www.slashfilm.com/the-last-jedi-defense.

Hanson, Michael J., and Max S. Kay. *Star Wars: The New Myth*. Xlibris, 2001.

Hibberd, James. "Adam Driver Explains Kylo Ren's New Helmet in *Star Wars: The Rise of Skywalker*." *Entertainment Weekly.Com*, Dec. 2019. EBSCO.

Hidalgo, Pablo. *The Force Awakens Visual Dictionary*. Disney Lucasfilm Press, 2015.

———. *Lightsabers: A Guide to Weapons of the Force*. Scholastic, 2010.

———. *Rogue One: The Ultimate Visual Guide*. Disney Lucasfilm Press, 2016.

———. *Star Wars Propaganda*. Harper Design, 2016.

Hidalgo, Pablo, and Chris Terrio. *Star Wars: The Rise of Skywalker the Visual Dictionary with Exclusive Cross-Sections*. Disney Lucasfilm Press, 2019.

Hugo, Simon. "Name That Theme." *Star Wars Insider*, no. 178, Jan/Feb 2018, pp. 35–40.

"In Their Own Words." *Best of Star Wars Insider 3*, Titan Books, 2016, pp. 53–62.

Kamp, David. "Cover Story: *Star Wars: The Last Jedi*, the Definitive Preview." *Vanity Fair*, 24 May 2017. https://www.vanityfair.com/hollywood/2017/05/star-wars-the-last-jedi-cover-portfolio.

"Kathleen Kennedy; Bryan Burke." *Star Wars Insider 2018 Special Edition*, pp. 91–97.

Kenny, Glenn, editor. *A Galaxy Not So Far Away: Writers and Artists on Twenty-Five Years of Star Wars*. Henry Holt and Co., 2002.

Koch, Eric. "Star Wars as a Modern Myth." *The Force.net*, 22 Nov. 2002. http://www.theforce.net/rouser/essays/modernmyth06.asp.

Krouse, Erika. "The Chrysanthemum and the Lightsaber." Kenny, pp. 86–101.

Kushins, Josh. *The Art of Rogue One*. Abrams, 2016.

Lam, Julia. "Anakin Skywalker: The Early Years Protagonist." *The Force.net*, 10 Dec. 2002. http://www.theforce.net/rouser/essays/anakin-protagonist.asp.

"The Last Jedi." *Entertainment: Star Wars: The Ultimate Guide to the Complete Saga*, 2019.

"The Legacy of Leia." *Entertainment: Star Wars: The Ultimate Guide to the Complete Saga*, 2019.

Leonard, Linda Schierse. *Meeting the Madwoman: Empowering the Feminine Spirit*. Bantam, 1994.

"Love Featurette." *Attack of the Clones*, produced by George Lucas, 20th Century Fox, 2002.

Luceno, James. *Inside the Worlds of the Star Wars Trilogy*. DK Publishing, 2004.

———. *Star Wars: Revenge of the Sith: The Visual Dictionary*. DK Publishing, 2005.

Lussier, Germain. "The Producer of *Star Wars Rebels* on Tonight's Incredible Episode." *io9*, 18 Mar 2017. https://io9.gizmodo.com/the-producer-of-star-wars-rebels-on-tonights-incredible-1793376931.

Martine, Arkady. "*Star Wars*' Vice-Admiral Holdo and Our Expectations for Female Military Power." *Tor*, 21 Dec 2017. https://www.tor.com/2017/12/21/star-wars-vice-admiral-holdo-and-our-expectations-for-female-military-power.

Millet, Lydia. "Becoming Darth Vader." Kenny, pp. 127–139.

Minkel, J.R. "When Clones Attack: Q&A with Clone Wars Director David Filoni." *Scientific American*, 2008. https://www.scientificamerican.com/article/star-wars-clone-wars-qa-david-filoni.

Mitchell, Elvis. "Works Every Time." Kenny, pp. 77–85.

Moran, Sarah. "*Star Wars*: How Rey Brings Balance to the Franchise." *SlashFilm*, 21 Dec 2015. http://screenrant.com/star-wars-force-awakens-rey-female-characters.

Works Cited

Mullally, William. "Here's What Jon Favreau and George Lucas Have Been Talking About for *The Mandalorian*." *GQ Middle East*, 25 July 2019. https://www.gqmiddleeast.com/culture/heres-what-jon-favreau-and-george-lucas-have-been-talking-about-for-the-mandalorian.

Pallotta, Frank. "Behind the Scenes of *Rogue One* with Director Gareth Edwards." *CNN*, 24 Mar 2017. http://www.cnn.com/2017/03/24/movies/star-wars-rogue-one-gareth-edwards-interview/index.html.

Pascal, Pedro. "*The Mandalorian*: Pedro Pascal Official TV Interview—Disney Plus." *YouTube*, uploaded by ScreenSlam. 12 Nov 2019. https://www.youtube.com/watch?v=11wor2uDnkA&feature=emb_title.

Pearson, Carol, and Katherine Pope. *The Female Hero in American and British Literature*. R.R. Bowker, 1981.

Pearson, Carol S. *Awakening the Heroes Within*. HarperCollins, 1991.

Queenan, Joe. "Anakin, Get Your Gun." Kenny, pp. 113–126.

"Revival." *Clone Wars*, season five, disk two, directed by Dave Filoni, 20th Century Fox, 2004.

Reynolds, David West. *Episode II—Attack of the Clones the Visual Dictionary*. DK Publishing, 2002.

———. *Star Wars: The Visual Dictionary*. DK Publishing, 1998.

Reynolds, David West, and Jason Fry. *The Phantom Menace: The Expanded Visual Dictionary*. DK Publishing, 2012.

Rinzler, J.W. *The Making of the Empire Strikes Back*. Lucasfilm Ltd, 2010.

Robertson, Barbara. "Dark and Stormy Knight." *Computer Graphics World*, vol. 28, no. 6, June 2005, pp. 10–3. EBSCOhost.

"*Rogue One*'s Felicity Jones Says Female Action Heroes Are Now 'the Norm.'" *BBC*, 14 December 2016. http://www.bbc.com/news/entertainment-arts-38313369.

Seabrook, John. "Why Is the Force Still with Us?' *The New Yorker*, 6 Jan 1997. Https://www.newyorker.com/magazine/1997/01/06/why-is-the-force-still-with-us.

"Secrets of the Force." *Best of Star Wars Insider 3*, Titan Books, 2016, pp. 17–25.

Shepherd, Jack. "The Circle Is Complete." *Total Film*, Dec 2019, pp. 54–63.

Snyder, Jon Bradley. "Boba Fett: From Obscure Villain to Cultural Icon." *Star Wars Insider: Rogues, Scoundrels, and Bounty Hunters*. Titan Comics, 2019, pp. 28–33.

"Solo: A Star Wars Story." *Entertainment: Star Wars: The Ultimate Guide to the Complete Saga*, 2019.

Spelling, Ian. "Suiting Up." *Scifi*, Feb 2020, pp. 34–37.

Spencer, Krishanna. "Priestess Path: Under the Aegis of Athena," *The Beltane Papers*, Autumn 2002.

Star Wars: Episode III—The Return of Darth Vader. Produced by Rick McCallum, written and directed by George Lucas, 20th Century Fox, 2004.

Stephens, William O. "Stoicism in the Stars: Yoda, the Emperor, and the Force." Decker and Eberl, pp. 30–39.

"Story Featurette." *Attack of the Clones*, produced by George Lucas, 20th Century Fox, 2002.

———. *The Phantom Menace*, produced by George Lucas, 20th Century Fox, 1999.

Szostak, Phil. *The Art of Star Wars: The Last Jedi*. Harry N. Abrams, 2017.

Thompson, Avery. 'The Mandalorian's Emily Swallow Reveals The Role of The Armorer Is a Full Circle Moment For Her." *Hollywood Life*, 14 Dec 2019. https://hollywoodlife.com/2019/12/14/the-mandalorian-armorer-emily-swallow-interview.

Thorne, Will. "*The Mandalorian*: Jon Favreau and Pedro Pascal on Creating a Western on Steroids. *Variety*, 11 Nov 2019. Https://variety.com/2019/tv/features/the-mandalorian-jon-favreau-pedro-pascal-western-1203399015.

Vogler, Christopher. *The Writer's Journey*. Michael Wiese Productions, 1998.

———. "The Process of Individuation." *Man and His Symbols*, edited by Carl G. Jung. Doubleday and Co., 1964, pp. 158–229.

Von Franz, Marie Louise. *The Feminine in Fairy Tales*. Shambhala 1993.

Walker, Barbara G. *The Woman's Dictionary of Symbols and Sacred Objects*. Harper, 1988.

Wharton, Ken. "Star Wars: Fantasy, Not Science Fiction." Brin and Stover, pp. 247–256.

Wilkins, Jonathan, editor. *Star Wars, the Rise of Skywalker: The Official Collector's Edition*. Titan, 2019.

Woerner, Meredith. "The Women of *Star Wars* Speak Out About Their New Empire." *LA Times,* 4 Dec 2015. http://www.latimes.com/entertainment/herocomplex/la-ca-hc-the-women-of-star-wars-the-force-awakens-20151206-htmlstory.html.

Wright, Katherine. *The New Heroines.* ABC-CLIO, 2016.

Yamato, Jen. "*The Last Jedi*'s Laura Dern on Answering to 'Space Dern' and Getting LGBTQ Characters Into the *Star Wars* Universe." *LA Times,* 22 Dec 2017. http://www.latimes.com/entertainment/movies/la-et-mn-star-wars-the-last-jedi-laura-dern-20171222-htmlstory.html.

Index

Abrams, J.J. 151, 164, 166, 176, 177, 178, 179, 180, 187, 188, 193, 213
Aftermath 110, 150, 193
AhchTo 183, 201, 204, 215
Ahsoka 21, 22, 32, 56, 152, 216, 218
Alderaan 62, 63, 65, 85, 87, 95, 109, 147
Altar of Mortis 32
Amidala *see* Padmé
Amilyn Holdo 86, 161, 163, 169, 171–174
Anakin Skywalker 3–63, 70, 74, 79, 85, 88, 95, 96, 115–126, 129, 151, 152, 158, 178, 184, 185, 192, 197, 204, 206, 208, 216; clothes 26, 33; death 85; and Dooku 53; and love 26–28; as shadow 117; as shatterpoint 53
anima 2, 27, 61, 63, 139, 145, 170, 175, 183, 207; definition 24, 66; Holdo 169; Leia 67, 82, 84, 103; and Mando 144, 145; Millennium Falcon 103; older Leia 157; Padmé 26, 27, 35, 38, 41; Rey 168, 180, 183, 189; Rose 170, 171, 174; Shmi 28
animus 3, 47, 88, 128, 129, 132, 133, 195, 198, 203, 207; Han 88–89; Kylo 177, 180, 190, 192, 200, 202, 204, 207, 212; Luke 201
Armitage Hux 157, 179, 185, 186
The Armorer 139–143, 148
artificiality 9, 84, 115
Asajj Ventress 54, 218
asteroid cave 104
Attack of the Clones 6, 7, 17, 24, 25, 29, 30, 42, 52, 60, 72, 74

Bail Organa 42, 49, 161, 163
balance 5, 8, 12, 13, 27, 31, 50, 74, 75, 82, 106, 121, 124, 125, 152, 157, 183, 196, 203, 204, 218
Baze Malbus 133, 134, 137
BB-8 150, 165, 173, 182, 194, 210–213, 218
Beauty and the Beast 203, 214
Before the Awakening 168, 194
Belly of the Whale 2, 29, 44, 82, 99, 107, 136, 146, 173, 207
Ben Solo 4, 96, 155, 157, 184, 190; and Rey 177, 180, 190, 192, 200, 202, 204, 207, 212
Beru Lars 60
beskar 138, 139, 142; symbolism 143

Bespin 76, 89, 90, 98, 104, 106, 112, 113, 119
Biggar, Trisha 9, 26, 48, 80, 86, 115
Bloodline 92, 94, 159, 160
Bluebeard 3, 47, 205
BoKatan Kryze 149
Boba Fett 3, 78, 91, 105–107, 113
Boba Fett and the Ship of Fear 105
Bodhi Rook 135, 137
The Book of the Sith 37, 70, 76, 80, 84, 85
The Bounty Hunter's Guide 138–139
Boyega, John 170
Breha Organa 86–87
Buddhism 69–70

C3PO 16–18, 61, 62, 65, 89, 96–100, 103–107, 132, 154, 213; and Anakin 96; as god 99; and Luke 97; mind wipe 18; origin 17; and Padmé 18; and R2-D2 96–98; rebirth 98–99; *Rise of Skywalker* 100; and Sand People 97; as shadow 17
call to adventure 138, 140
Campbell, Joseph 1, 2, 39, 62, 67, 77, 82, 115, 122, 125, 140, 145, 146, 153, 171, 172, 184, 196, 201, 202
cantina 64, 102, 105, 138, 144
Canto Bight 171
Captain Phasma 142, 168, 173
Cara Dune 144–147
carbonite 2, 75, 90–94, 106, 108
caregiver 91, 141
Cassian Andor 132–133, 136–137, 219
Chewbacca 65, 78, 90, 91, 94, 98, 100, 101, 103, 108–110, 113, 150, 153, 160, 161, 165, 166, 168, 175, 181, 185, 195, 196, 200, 201, 204, 208, 209, 211, 212; on Endor 109; family 108, 110; and Han's death 110; and rebirth 109; and Rey 110; in *Rise of Skywalker* 110; in *Solo* 110; and Vader 109
Chirrut Îmwe 133, 134, 137, 155
Christensen, Hayden 26, 34, 36, 184
The Client 139, 141, 142, 143, 146
The Clone Wars 20, 21, 23, 25, 27, 29, 31–33, 35, 37, 39, 41, 43, 45, 47, 49, 51, 53–57, 85, 123, 128–130, 138, 149, 152, 219

229

Index

Cold War 1
comics 19, 21, 40, 71, 78, 87, 95, 117, 123, 132, 178, 191
Coruscant 10, 11, 38, 42, 48, 51, 71, 123, 150, 202
Count Dooku 13, 21, 23, 30, 31, 33, 34, 36, 42, 44, 45, 48, 52, 53, 54, 57; in *Clone Wars* 54; as shadow 52
Crait 157, 163, 164, 173, 175, 185

D-0 213
Dagobah 56, 72–75, 79, 93, 98, 125, 204
Daniels, Anthony 96, 97, 100
Dark Force Rising 95–96
Dark Lord 109
Darksaber 149
Darth Maul 8, 14–22, 51, 52, 54; *Clone Wars* 54; and ObiWan 20, 22; and shadow 19, 21; as shadow 14, 21
Darth Maul: Son of Dathomir 21
Darth Plagueis 19, 20, 23, 35, 36, 51, 83
Darth Vader 3, 4, 15, 16, 20, 26, 31, 33, 35–41, 47–51, 60, 63–66, 68, 71, 75–86, 88, 90, 91, 93–95, 102, 103, 106, 109, 112–126, 135, 136, 152, 158, 177–189, 199, 200, 203–208, 210, 212, 214, 215; castle 41; comics 40, 117; costume 114; death 121; and Emperor 37, 117–119, 121; funeral 122; and Luke 118–121; maskless 119; rebirth 39; redemption 122; and shadow 117, 119
Death Star 10, 55, 63, 65–70, 78, 82, 83, 88, 91–93, 97, 98, 103, 109, 113, 117, 123, 124, 127, 132, 136, 137, 178, 189, 190, 213; symbolism 65–66
Death Troopers 127–128
Dern, Laura 169, 170, 173
descending symbolism 30
desert 5, 7, 10, 22, 59, 61, 67, 123, 126, 166, 198, 208, 211
disguise 9, 10, 12, 38, 42, 45, 52, 66, 91, 107, 169, 173
dismemberment 77, 99
divine child 141, 147
D.J. 172–173
Driver, Adam 178, 182, 187–189
droids as killers 7, 13; as slaves 17–18
Duchess Satine Kryze 20, 123

Edwards, Gareth 129, 130, 133, 134
Ehrenreich, Alden 101
Emperor Palpatine 3, 5, 11, 20, 23–25, 32–40, 42, 45–55, 57, 75, 78, 79, 82–86, 100, 109, 116–121, 125, 131, 136, 152, 165, 167, 177, 187, 188, 190, 191, 207, 208, 211, 213–218; backstory 52; costume 83; in *Rise of Skywalker* 57, 167, 187
The Empire Strikes Back 1, 10, 40, 46, 64–75, 86–90, 95, 98, 103–105, 108, 109, 111–119, 124, 125, 127–136, 153, 155, 160, 178, 202, 208, 211
End of Games 117

Endor 81–85, 93, 95, 99, 107–109
Ewoks 73, 81, 82, 93, 99, 109
Exegol 165, 175, 187, 188, 211, 215
expanded universe 5, 19, 105, 130

fairytales 1, 9, 10, 41, 43, 44, 47, 59, 73, 78, 92, 98, 128, 140, 162, 196, 203, 206, 207, 209
faith 6, 12, 21, 50, 55, 56, 65, 69, 70, 77, 78, 84, 113, 122, 125, 133, 134, 137, 140, 144, 166, 172, 176, 206, 207, 210, 211, 214, 216
fatal flaw 27
Favreau, Jon 138, 140
feminine 2, 9, 14, 24, 26, 27, 63, 67, 70, 78, 82, 83, 90–93, 127, 142, 145, 175, 181, 189–196, 198, 200, 209, 212, 215
Filoni, Dave 20–22, 32, 138, 145
Finn 110, 150, 161, 163, 165, 167–177, 194, 195, 198–201, 209, 211–213; lightsaber battle 169; love triangle 174, 175, 211
fire imagery 9, 33, 39, 49, 50, 85, 114, 200, 208, 215
First Order 114, 150, 153, 157, 160, 161, 164, 167–177, 183–188, 194, 199, 201, 207, 209, 212
Fisher, Carrie 85, 86, 164
Flash Gordon 1
The Force Awakens 100, 110, 150, 177, 178, 196
Force ghosts 4, 16, 85, 95, 125, 156, 157, 218
Ford, Harrison 1, 102
forest 10, 13, 27, 59, 61, 72, 73, 82, 93, 94, 187, 196, 197, 200; symbolism 81, 93
forgiveness 22, 95, 166, 174, 186, 190
Fortress Vader 40
foxes 164, 174, 209
From a Certain Point of View 98

Galen Erso 127–129, 137
garbage monster 67–68
General Grievous 21, 49
Geonosis 29, 30, 44, 45, 53
goggles 196
gold bikini 80, 91, 92
Göransson, Ludwig 141
Grand Moff Tarkin 3, 66, 85, 86, 116, 128, 135, 136
gray Jedi 13
greed 16, 35, 44, 80, 91, 92, 102, 118, 198
Greedo 102, 105
Greef Karga 138, 139, 141, 143, 144, 146, 147, 149
Guardians of the Whills 133
Gungan village 13
Gungans 7, 11, 13

hair 8, 9, 11, 32, 45, 46, 48, 82, 88, 92, 135, 163, 169
Han Solo 3, 4, 12, 32, 60, 65–67, 70–72, 75, 78, 80, 84, 88–114, 117, 119, 139, 150, 151, 153, 157, 160, 161, 166, 168–170, 180, 183, 190, 195–199, 210; and Ben 150, 151, 166, 180, 190; and Boba Fett 105–106; command team 92; *Force Awakens* 150; and growth 102, 103,

104, 107; and Jabba 102, 107; and Lando 111; rebirth 106; in *Rise of Skywalker* 151; romance 89–92, 106; and Vader 106, 117
Han Solo novel trilogy 100, 108
hand 12, 13, 20, 28, 29, 31, 39, 55, 76–79, 82, 84, 85, 94, 98, 119, 120, 152, 153, 184, 189–193, 200, 203, 206, 214, 217
helmet 51, 114, 115, 138, 141–143, 145, 147, 148, 179, 188, 189, 212; *see also* mask
herald 103, 138
heroine's journey 2, 3, 9–11, 43–48, 88, 90–92, 127–129, 133–137, 152, 160–164, 172, 175, 191–209, 211, 214, 217
Hidalgo, Pablo 17
Holiday Special 110
Howard, Ron 101

idealized 28, 35, 46
IG-11 140, 141, 146–148
Ilum 25, 198
Imperial Handbook 66, 72
individuation 63, 128
initiation 1, 8, 31, 34, 39, 43, 69, 77, 82, 102
Innermost Cave 10, 206
Isaac, Oscar 161, 171, 172, 176

Jabba the Hutt 65, 80, 90–94, 99, 102, 105, 106, 107, 139
Jabba's palace 65, 80, 90, 92, 99
Jaina and Jacen 161, 191
Jakku 167, 193, 194, 197, 208
Jannah 175–177
Jar Jar Binks 14
Jedha 133, 135
Jedi Council 6, 12, 13, 19, 23, 24, 26, 30, 34, 37, 48, 50, 51, 54, 56, 151, 152; callousness 152; costume 50, 83
Jedi handbook 16, 23, 49, 77, 120
Jedi Trials 77, 209
Johnson, Rian 154–156, 160, 170, 181, 183, 185, 204, 205, 207, 208, 210
Jyn Erso 3, 4, 127–137

K-2SO 131, 132, 137
Kasdan, Lawrence 73, 178, 219
Kashyyyk 55, 109, 110
Kennedy, Kathleen 182
Kershner, Irwin 69, 74, 98, 104–106, 109
kiss 34, 88, 89, 104, 175, 192
Knights of Ren 179, 190, 191
Krennic 3, 127, 128, 129, 136
Kuiil 140, 142, 144, 146, 147
Kylo Ren 4, 151, 152, 153, 155–158, 162, 166, 167, 169, 174, 175, 177–190, 197–203, 206–208, 210, 212, 218; evolution 178; and Rey 177, 180, 190, 192, 200, 202, 204, 207, 212; *see also* Ben Solo

L3-37 112
Labyrinth of Evil 25, 32, 36, 51, 52, 54, 55

Lando Calrissian 3, 78, 89, 90, 100, 101, 104, 106, 107, 111–114, 119, 166, 176, 177, 212; collaborator 112; costume 112; daughter 114; and Death Star 113; and Han 113; in *Return of the Jedi* 113; in *Rise of Skywalker* 114; and shadow 111; in *Solo* 112
The Lando Calrissian Adventures 111
The Last Jedi 85, 100, 151, 152, 158, 169–176, 194, 205, 208, 209, 218
Lee, Christopher 30
Legacy's End 40
Leia Organa 4, 16, 46, 48, 50, 57, 59–63, 66, 67, 70, 78, 81, 82, 85–108, 113, 114, 123, 137, 150, 151–169, 172, 173, 174, 178, 180, 182, 189–195, 199, 201, 202, 207, 209–211, 214, 215, 218; and Ben 161, 162, 166, 182, 189; costume 90, 94; death 166; disguise 91; and Force 94, 165; Force ghost 218; general 198; and Han 89–92, 106; leader 67, 88; lightsaber 167, 215–216; name meaning 85, 86; and Padmé 89; parentage 93, 94, 95, 159, 161; and Poe 160, 161, 166, 169; rebirth 163; and Rey 165; and Sana 95; sequels 160–165; trauma 87; and Vader 88
Leia, Princess of Alderaan 85, 86, 152, 163
library 155, 156, 202, 210
lifecycle 3, 16, 25, 81, 93, 194
lightning 37, 41, 53–55, 84, 121, 156, 157, 212, 216, 217; symbolism 84
lightsaber, colors 25, 218; Kylo's 178, 190, 207; Leia's 167, 215–216; loss of worthiness 39; Luke's 78–79; Sith 178; Skywalker 62, 153, 166, 168, 181, 191, 197, 200, 201, 210, 215, 216, 218; symbolism 33, 62; yellow 218
Lucas, George 1, 2, 6, 9, 23, 25–27, 31, 34–36, 43, 54, 59–63, 66, 68, 69, 72–77, 79, 85, 97, 102, 108, 109, 121, 122, 130, 140, 185, 193
Luke Skywalker 2, 3, 4, 10, 12, 16, 32, 33, 36, 50, 57, 59–108, 113–126, 149–161, 164–167, 174, 180–190, 193, 195, 197, 198, 199–218; and Ben 155, 157, 158, 179, 184, 186, 204, 206; costume 59, 79; death 157; and Force 78, 154, 157; Force ghost 215, 218; and Han 102; Jedi 77, 79; *Last Jedi* 151, 153; and R2-D2 154; and Rey 154–156; and Vader 15, 71, 76, 77, 82, 119, 120; and Yoda 156
Lyra Erso 128, 129, 137, 200

Mace Windu 32, 37, 48, 52, 53, 216
masculine 3, 129, 132, 181, 192, 195, 198, 203; weapons 129, 132
mask 189, 203, 215; Anakin 47; Armorer 142; Emperor 37; Kylo 179, 180, 181, 182, 188, 191; Leia 91; Mando 138, 141, 145; Maul 19; Padmé 9, 11, 45; persona 182; Phasma 173; symbolism 115, 148, 189; Vader 85, 114, 115, 120, 122; Zorii 175
Master and Apprentice 12
Mayhew, Peter 108, 110
Maz Kanata 150, 160, 166–168, 195–198
McCoy, Jon 136

Mendelsohn, Ben 127, 136
Millennium Falcon 65, 66, 68, 100, 104, 107, 111, 114, 150, 154, 177, 181, 185, 194, 195, 206, 209
mirrors 196, 205
Moff Gideon 146, 147, 149
Mollo, John, 60, 114
Mon Mothma 42, 72, 90, 92, 130, 131, 136, 137
monster 29, 30, 39, 47, 67–68, 71, 91, 92, 100, 104, 115, 142, 161, 162, 184, 189, 203, 215
Moving Target 90
mudhorn 142, 143, 148
Mustafar 38, 40, 46, 49, 187

Naboo 7, 8, 9, 13, 14, 19, 25, 26, 29, 38, 42, 45, 48, 51
Nazis 64, 85, 112, 114–116, 179
Neeson, Liam 50
A New Hope 11, 16, 59, 71, 86, 87, 95, 96, 102, 117, 123, 126, 137, 150, 154, 163, 169
Nyong'o, Lupita 196

Obi-Wan Kenobi 4, 8, 11–81, 85, 93, 110, 116–126, 137, 150–153, 158, 161, 164, 186, 193, 197, 202, 204, 216; and Anakin 25; and comics 123; death 116, 124; hermit 61; and Luke 123, 124; and Maul 15–16; mentor 61; and Vader 15, 39, 49, 68, 116, 119, 124
Old Republic 8, 16, 169
ordeal 68
Order 66, 49
Orphan{een}63
Owen Lars 28, 60, 62–64, 98, 123

Padmé 5–11, 16–18, 23–47, 52, 117, 123, 165, 192; costume 27, 42–43; disguise 8–11, funeral 48; as lotus 26, 41; spirit guardian 48; and Tatooine 10
Pasaana 114, 211
Pascal, Pedro 138, 145
persona 9, 37, 47, 89, 122, 167, 182, 188
The Phantom Menace 3–21, 51, 155, 219
Poe Dameron 100, 160, 161, 163, 165–177, 195, 211–213; and Leia 172, 176
porgs 204, 209
Portman, Natalie 28, 42, 43, 44, 48
pregnancy 34, 38, 45
prince's castle 10, 44, 91, 198, 207
prophecy 5, 12–14, 36, 50, 52, 121, 212

Qi'ra 100–101
Queen Amidala *see* Padmé
Queen's Shadow 9, 42
Qui Gon Jinn 5–8, 11–16, 19, 25, 50–51, 56–57, 70, 123–126, 152, 216; spirit 56–57

R2-D2 16–18, 56, 61, 62, 65, 66, 73, 82, 84, 85, 96–100, 154, 166, 201, 209; first appearance 16; hero's journey 16–17, 97–99, and shadow 18, 98

radio play 87
Rancor 80, 92
Rebel Rising 130
Rebels 22, 40, 129–132, 136, 138, 145, 149, 219
rebirth 18, 26, 31, 39, 47, 49, 67, 68, 72, 77, 91, 98, 104, 106, 114, 121, 137, 189, 190, 191, 206, 207, 212, 219
redemption 4, 35, 86, 122, 124, 135, 151, 167
Resistance Reborn 174
retcon 16
Return of the Jedi 79, 94, 110, 117, 121, 157, 178, 215
revenge 19, 21, 22, 29, 32, 33, 64, 109, 113, 135, 137, 146, 187, 195
Revenge of the Sith 3, 16, 18, 21, 32, 33, 36, 37, 40, 45, 48–57, 109, 116, 118, 125, 152, 155, 206
reward ceremony 8, 11, 70, 88, 98
Rey 3, 4, 71, 100, 110, 150–218; death 217; and Emperor 216, 217; and Han 195, 199; and Kylo 177, 180, 190, 192, 200, 202, 204, 207, 212; and Leia 200, 209, 210, 214; and Luke 201; parentage 205, 208, 216; Sith 214
Rey's Survival Guide 193, 194
Ridley, Daisy 193, 215
The Rise of Kylo Ren 178, 179, 191
The Rise of Skywalker 57, 100, 114, 151, 159, 165, 175, 186, 198, 209, 218, 219
Rogue One 127–136, 151
Rogue One: Catalyst 127–128
romance: heroine's journey 3; Leia 89, 104, 106; Padmé 27, 42, 45; sequel love triangle 174, 175, 211
Rose Tico 170–175
Ruler 111–112
Russell, Keri 175

Sabé 9, 42
sacred marriage 184, 192
sacrifice 97, 100, 116, 137, 162, 169, 174, 191, 192
Samurai 51, 140
Sand People 29, 33, 36, 61, 62, 121
Sarlacc 92, 99, 107
Savage Oppress 20
Saw Gerrera 129–131, 135
Scanlan, Neal 194
Scarif 136, 137, 159
shadow 2, 3, 11, 14, 30, 32, 33, 35, 38, 40, 43, 51–56, 91, 95, 105–109, 116–118, 127, 140, 144–146, 158, 172–175, 177, 178, 180, 186, 189, 196, 200, 203–206, 208, 213; Amidala 9; Ben and Rey 183; dark Rey 214; D.J. 172; Dooku and Padmé 44; Emperor 4; Evaan and Leia 87; Han and Luke 65, 80; heroine's journey 3; IG-11 141, 148, 149; Kylo 200, 205; Paz Vizla 142, 144; Rey and Kylo 181; Sabé 9, 42; Sith 32, 51; Toro Calican 146; Vader 3, 4; Vader's 40
Shadows of the Empire 78, 90, 120
Shatterpoint 53
Shearmur, Allison 127, 132

Index

Shmi Skywalker 5–8, 17, 23, 28
Showdown on the Smuggler's Moon 123
silver symbolism 143, 195
slippery slope 36
snake 212
Snoke 3, 155, 178–185, 188, 191, 207–209, 211
Snow White 92, 163, 206, 217
solar symbolism 60
Solo 20, 22, 100, 104, 110, 111
souljourney 117
soulmate 102
Splinter of the Mind's Eye 87
Star Wars see movies by title
Starkiller Base 150, 160, 161, 198
Stormtroopers symbolism 65
Suotamo, Joonas 110
Supremacy 173, 207

Takodana 196, 202
Tales of the Bounty Hunters 105
Tatooine 6, 7, 10, 12, 14, 28, 30, 42, 59, 70, 71, 80, 123, 126, 146, 159, 167, 218
technology 14, 17, 29, 39, 48, 49, 53, 65, 72, 81, 93, 115, 117, 118, 149, 171, 186, 219
temptation 24, 27, 36, 38, 44, 56, 60, 75, 76, 77, 80, 83, 145, 149, 180, 188
Thrawn 95
threshold 2, 6, 7, 13, 24, 61, 64, 71, 122, 144, 163
throne 11, 33, 51, 80–85, 91, 121, 149, 184, 185, 191, 207, 212–214, 216
Tobias Beckett 100–101
torture 75, 94, 99, 121
Trade Federation 10–16, 38, 45, 52
Tran, Kelly Marie 170
The Truce at Bakura 95
twin symbolism 191, 216
tyrant 2, 3, 49, 55, 81, 116–119, 127, 149, 181, 189, 199, 200, 216

unconscious realm 2, 10, 12, 24, 31, 34, 48, 63, 64, 69, 71, 82, 86, 123, 142, 143, 197, 198, 209, 216

underworld 1, 33, 71, 79, 80, 106, 130, 141, 196, 217
Unkar Plutt 193, 195
Utapau 48

Vader see Darth Vader
Vietnam War 1
virgin birth 5
Vogler, Christopher 60, 64, 65, 66, 68, 69, 84, 102, 107, 122, 123, 138, 140, 144, 190, 192, 199
Von Franz, Marie Louise 24, 27, 35, 117, 129, 201, 203, 204, 205, 207, 209

wampa 71
water imagery 7, 13, 26, 43, 46, 48, 49, 67, 189, 196, 201, 213
Watto 7, 14, 28
wayfinder 187, 211, 212, 214
Weathers, Carl 139
wedding 16, 27, 31, 45
Wedge Antilles 113, 177
Western 1, 102, 144
Whills 16, 133, 134, 151
Whitaker, Forest 129, 135
white dress symbolism 70, 86, 210
Whitta, Gary 130
Williams, Billy Dee 112–114
Williams, John 121
Wookies 55, 73, 109

Yavin 69, 88, 131, 133, 136
Yoda 2–4, 12, 13, 16, 25, 26, 30–32, 35, 39, 49, 50, 53–57, 60, 72–79, 81, 85, 93, 118, 120, 122, 124–126, 137, 152, 153, 155, 156, 157, 163, 165, 197, 204, 205, 216; in *Clone Wars* 56; death 81; and Dooku 54; and Emperor 49, 55, 56; journey 54; *Last Jedi* 156; name meaning 72; and shadow 56; swamp 125; training 74; and weakness 57
Yoda's cave 75, 91, 125

Zorii Bliss 175, 177

www.ingramcontent.com/pod-product-compliance
Ingram Content Group UK Ltd.
Pitfield, Milton Keynes, MK11 3LW, UK
UKHW041945140426
5217IPUK00014B/669